D0907296

Sebastiano Serlio

THE FIVE BOOKS
OF ARCHITECTURE

An Unabridged Reprint of the English Edition of 1611

DOVER PUBLICATIONS, INC., NEW YORK

Copyright © 1982 by Dover Publications, Inc.
All rights reserved under Pan American and International Copyright Conventions.

Published in Canada by General Publishing Company, Ltd., 30 Lesmill Road, Don Mills, Toronto, Ontario.
Published in the United Kingdom by Constable and Company, Ltd., 10 Orange Street, London WC2H 7EG.

This Dover edition, first published in 1982, is an unabridged republication of the work as described in the Bibliographical Note. This edition is reproduced at 95 percent of the size of the original.

Manufactured in the United States of America
Dover Publications, Inc., 180 Varick Street, New York, N.Y. 10014

Library of Congress Cataloging in Publication Data

Serlio, Sebastiano, 1475–1554.
　The five books of architecture.

　Translation of: Tutte l'opere d'architettura.
　Translated from Italian into Dutch, from Dutch into English.
　Originally published: The first [-fift] booke of architecture. London: Printed for R. Peake, 1611.
　1. Architecture — Early works to 1800.
　I. Title.
NA2517.S513　　1982　　720　　82-4580
ISBN 0-486-24349-4　　　　　　AACR2

Bibliographical Note

O ne of the earliest books on architecture written in a vernacular language (rather than Latin) and incorporating extensive illustrations, the *Architettura* of Sebastiano Serlio (1475–1554) exercised great influence during the Renaissance. The work did not originally appear in its present order: Book IV was first published in Venice in 1537; Book III in Venice in 1540; Books I and II in Paris in 1545; and Book V in Paris in 1547. The five books were first published together in 1584 in Venice, under the title *Tutte l'opere d'architettura et prospettiva.* The work was quickly translated into many languages. In 1606 *Den eerstē vijfsten boeck van architecturē Sebastiani Serlij* was published in Amsterdam in a translation by Pieter Coecke van Aelst, the master of Pieter Brueghel the Elder, who had probably met Serlio in the 1520s. This Dutch translation was in turn translated into English for the edition published in 1611, printed by Simon Stafford for Robert Peake, a printseller and Serjeant Painter to James I. The blocks for the illustrations had previously been used for the editions printed in Antwerp (1553) and Basel (1608). The 1611 English edition is reproduced here unabridged at 95 percent of original size.

The first Booke
of Architecture, made
by Sebastian Serly, entreating of Geometrie.

Translated out of Italian into
Dutch, and out of Dutch
into English.

LONDON
Printed for Robert Peake,
and are to be sold at his shop neere
Holborne conduit, next to the
Sunne Tauerne.
ANNO DOM. 1611.

TO THE HIGH AND
MIGHTIE PRINCE,

HENRY,

Prince of VVales.

S I R,

O vaine ambition of mine owne Defire, much leffe prefumption of my none Defert, incited me to prefent this Volume to your Princely view; but rather, the gracious Countenance, which (euen from your Childehood) you haue euer daigned to all good endeauours, invited Mee alfo (after fo many others) to offer at the high-Altar of your Highneffe fauour, this new-Naturalized VVorke of a learned Stranger: Not with pretence of Profit to your Highneffe (who want not more exquifite Tutors in all excellent Sciences) but, vnder the Patronage of your powerfull Name, to benefite the Publicke; and conuay vnto my Countrymen (efpecially Architects and Artificers of all forts) thefe Neceffary, Certaine, and moft ready Helps of *Geometrie :* The ignorance and want whereof, in times paft (in moft parts of this Kingdome) hath left vs many lame VVorkes, with fhame of many VVorkemen; which, for the future, the Knowledge and vfe of thefe Inftructions fhall happily preuent, if the euent but anfwere (in any meafure) to that Hope of mine, which alone both induced this Defire and produced this Defigne: VVherein I muft confeffe my part but fmall, fauing my great aduenture in the Charge, and my great Good-will to doe Good. All which, together with my beft Seruices, I humbly proftrate at your Princely feete, as befeemes

Your Highneffe

moft humble Seruant

Robert Peake.

To the Louers of Architecture.

*Vr learned Author* Sebaſtian Serly, *hauing great foreſight to ſhew and explaine the common rules of Architecture, did firſt publiſh his* Fourth Booke, *entreating of Architecture, and after his* Third Booke, *declaring excellent Antiquities. Fearing that if hee had begunne with* Geometrie *and* Perſpectiue, *common workmen would haue thought (that the two former although ſmall) had not beene ſo needefull to ſtudie and practiſe as the other: Which friendly Reader, conſidered, hindered mee long either from Tranſlating or Publiſhing the two former, being perſwaded by ſundry friends and workemen, to haue deſiſted my purpoſe, both from tranſlating or publiſhing. The which J had ſurely effected, if I had beene ouer-ruled by their requeſts and perſwaſions; alleadging ſtrong reaſons, that the common Workemen of our time little regarded or eſteemed to Worke with right Simmetrie: the which is confuſed and erronious, in the iudgement of the Learned Architect, if they will follow the Order of Antiquities hereafter enſuing. Wherefore leaſt my good meaning, together with my Labour in Tranſlating and Publiſhing, ſhould not be regarded and eſteemed (as worthie) conſidering it not onely tendeth to the great profit of the Architect or Workeman, but alſo generally to all other Artificers of our Nation: I aduiſe all generally, not to deceiue themſelues, nor to be ſelfe-conceited in their owne workes, but well vnderſtand this my labour (tending to common good) and be perſwaded that who ſo ſhall follow theſe rules hereafter ſet downe, ſhall not onely haue his Worke well eſteemed of the common people, but alſo generally commended and applauded of all workemen, and men of iudgement.* Vale.

❧ The first Booke of Architecture,

made by Sebastian Serly, entreating of Geometrie.

¶ The first Chapter.

OW needfull and necessary the most secret Art of Geometrie is for euery Artificer and workeman, as those that for a long time haue studied and wrought without the same can sufficiently witnesse, who since that time haue attained vnto any knowledge of the said Arte, doe not onely laugh and smile at their owne former simplicities, but in trueth may very well acknowledge that all whatsoeuer had bene formerly done by them, was not worth the looking on.

Seeing then the learning of Architecture comprehendeth in it many notable Artes, it is necessary that the Architector or workeman, should first, or at the least (if he cannot attaine vnto any more) know so much thereof, as that hee may vnderstand the principles of Geometrie, that he may not be accompted amongst the number of stonespoilers, who beare the name of workmen, and scarce know how to make an answere what a Point, Line, Plaine, or Body is, and much lesse can tell what harmonie or correspondencie meaneth, but following after their owne minde, or other blinde conductors that haue vsed to worke without rule or reason, they make bad worke, which is the cause of much vncut or vneuen workemanship, which is found in many places.

Therfore seeing that Geometrie is the first degree of all good Art, to the end I may shew the Architector so much thereof, as that he may thereby be able with good skill, to giue some reason of his worke. Touching the speculations of Euclides and other Authors, that haue written of Geometrie, I will leaue them, and onely take some flowers out of their Garden, that therewith by the shortest way that I can, I may entreat of diuers cutting through of Lines, with some demonstrations, meaning so plainely and openly to set downe and declare the same, both in writing and in figures, that euery man may both conceiue and vnderstand them, aduertizing the Reader not to proceed to know the second figure, before he hath well vnderstood and found out the first, and so still proceeding, hee shall at last attaine vnto his desire.

ξ * *ξ
*

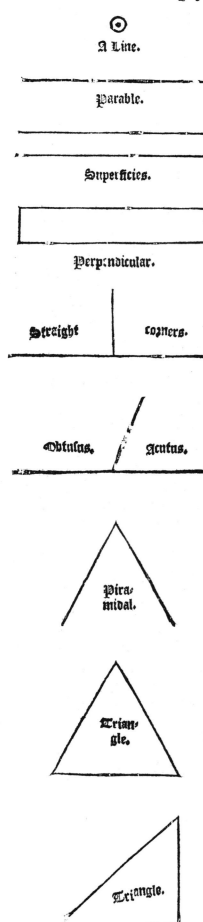

A Poynt.

A Line.

Parable.

Superficies.

Perpendicular.

Straight   cozners.

Obtulus.   Acutus.

Pira-
midal.

Trian-
gle.

Triangle.

FIRST, you must vnderstand that a poynt is a pzicke made with a Pen oz Compasse, which can not bee deuided into any parts, because it conteineth neither length noz bzedth in it.

A Line is a right consecutiue imagination in length, beginning at a poynt, and endeth also at a point, but it hath no bzedth.

When two Lines are set oz placed of a little wydenesse one from the other, those two lines, accozding to the Latine phzase, are called Parable, and by some men they are named Equidistances.

When those two Equidistances afozesayd are at each end closed together by another Line, it is then called a Superficies: and in like sozt all spaces in what manner soeuer they are closed, and shut vp, are called Superficies oz plainnes.

When there is a straight vpzight Line placed in the middle of a crosse straight line, then it is called a Perpendicular oz Catheta Line: and the ends of the crosse oz straight Line on both sides of the Perpendicular, are called Straight cozners.

When a leaning oz straight Line is placed vpon a straight Line without Compasse oz equalitie, as much as the same Line bendeth, so much shall the cozner of the straight Line be narrower below, and the other so much bzoader then a right oz euen cozner: and the straight cozner in Latine is called Acutus, which signifieth sharpe, and the wider cozner Obtulus, which signifieth dull.

A cozner oz point called Piramidal, and also Acutus in Latine is, when two euen long straight lines meet oz ioyne together at the vpper end, as the figure right against this declareth.

And when such a figure is closed together at the foote thereof, with a long straight line, it is then called a Triangle, because it hath thzee sharpe cozners.

When a Triangle with two euen straight lines, is closed together with a longer line then these two are, it shall haue such a fozme as here you see.

But

But a Triangle which is made of three vnlike lines, it shall also haue three vnlike corners.

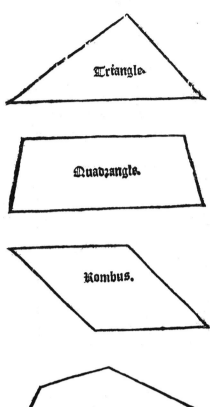

Triangle.

When two long and two direct downe right lines are ioyned together at the foure corners, it is called Quadrangle with euen sides or corners, but when the foure lines are all of vnlike or contrary lengths, then it is a Quadrangle of vneuen sides, as this figure sheweth.

Quadrangle.

You must note that although all foure cornerd figures may be called Quadrangles: neuertheles, for that the direct foure cornerd figures are called Quadratus: for difference from them, I will name all figures which are like vnto a table, (that is longer then broad) Quadrangles.

When foure euen long straight lines are ioyned together at the corners, they are called Quadratus, which are foure cornerd: when you make the two corners thereof sharpe, and the other two corners somewhat blunter, then it is called a Rombus.

Rombus.

Although you may turne and make all the figures aforesaid right foure square: Yet the workeman may finde other figures with diuers corners. The which (as I will hereafter shew) hee may make foure square.

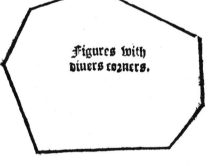

Figures with diuers corners.

When a man with his Compasse draweth a bowe, and after that draweth an other bow right against it, that is called a Superfitie of crooked Lines, with two like corners: and then draweth a straight Line from the one corner to the other, and from one poynt or center where the Compasse stood to the other, another straight Line. Thereby you shall finde the right foure parts thereof.

Superficitie of a crooked Line.

But if a man drawe a whole round Line with his Compasse, that is called a full Circle, or round Superficities, and the poynt in the middle is called the Centre. The vtmost line is called Circumferentie: and if you draw a straight line through the Center, it is called a Diameter: because it deuideth the Circle in two euen parts.

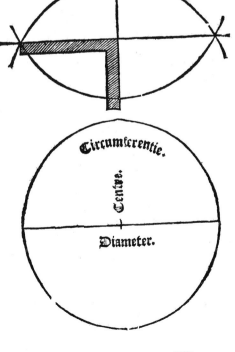

Circumferentie.

Centre.

Diameter.

The halfe Circle.

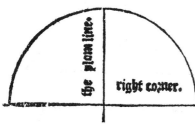

the plom line.

right corner.

VVhen the halfe Circumference is cut through the Center of the Diameter, then it is called halfe a Circle: and if you make a straight line vpright in the halfe Circle, then that line maketh two euen quarters of a Circle, and deuideth the Diameter also into two halfe Diameters.

perfect foure square.

VVhen a man draweth foure euen long lines, and ioyneth them together, they make a perfect cornerd Quadratus: then if you draw a straight line from the one corner to the other, it is called Diagonus: because it deuideth the foure corners into two euen parts.

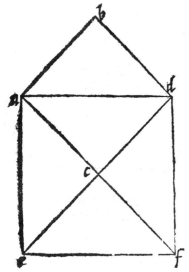

Now when a workeman hath seene a forme of some of the most necessary Superficies, hee must proceed further, and learne to augment or diminish the same, and to turne them into other formes: but yet in such sort, that they may haue euen parts in them.

AND first, if out of the length of the Diagonus aforesayd, by the adding of three other euen long lines, hee maketh another foure square: that foure square shal be once as great againe as the first, which is to bee vnderstood in this sort: That ye foure square of A. B. C. D. by the Diagonus is deuided into two Triangles, and the greater foure square A. D. F. E. containeth foure such Triangles: but for that the two first foure squares hang one within the other, therefore for the better shewing thereof, they are here once againe set downe seuerally: whereby you may see that the Quadrate G. (as I said before) containeth two Triangles, and the Quadrate H. containeth foure such Triangles, so that the proofe thereof is clearely to be seene.

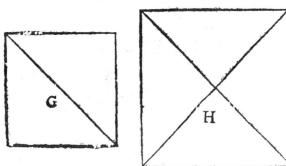

G

H

If within a foure square you make a Circle which toucheth the foure sides of the said foure square, and without the said foure square an other Circle which toucheth the corners marked A.B. C.D. Then the outmost Circle must bee once as great againe as the intermost: and then if about the greatest Circle you make another foure square as C. D. E. F. then the two foure squares must in like sort be once as great againe as the other. The proofe whereof standeth hereby marked with the letters K.L. for clearer vnderstanding of the same.

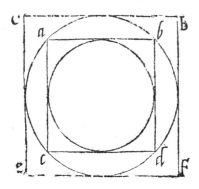

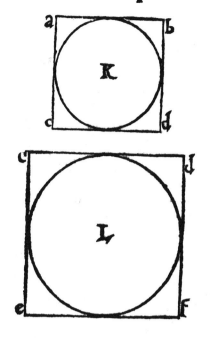

BY this also, the proiecture or the foote of the Bases of the Thulcane Columnes or Pillars, and also the bredth of the fundation of them vnderneath by Uertruuius declared, is set foorth.

THE workeman must yet proceed further, and learne to know how to change a Triangle into a Quadrangle, and also at last bring it to a right Quadrate, to the which I will set downe diuers formes. First, take a Triangle with euen corners, as A. B. C. and deuide the Base (which is the name of all lower lines) B. C. in two euen parts, and there place the letter E. Then from the point E. to A. drawe a line, which will deuide the Triangle into two euen parts. Then if you take that part which is marked A. E. C. and ioyne it to the other part, marked A. E. B. it will make a Quadrangle, as A. D. B. E. made of a Triangle.

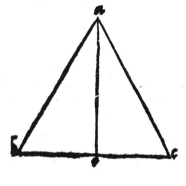
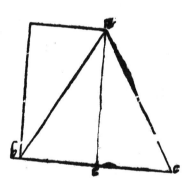

YOu may also change this Triangle in other manner, deuiding the lines A. B. and A. C. each in two like parts as F. and G. Then drawe a line through D. E. as long as the Base B. C. Then shut vp the two Equidistances, corner wise: and then the Quadrangle B. C. D. E. containeth so much in it as the Triangle A. B. C. and the proofe thereof is, that the two Triangles B. C. F. and G. E. C. containe so much in them, as the two other Triangles A. F. H. and A. I. G.

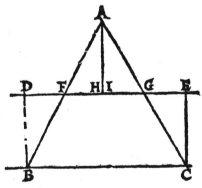

A Triangle with euen points, may be deuided thrice into two equall parts, deuiding each side in two parts, as in the figure P. Q. R. it is seene through the three lines, which on either side make two great Triangles.

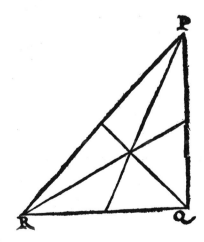

　　c　　　　　　　　　The

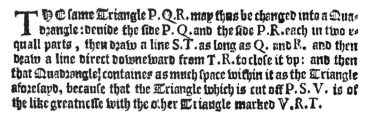

THe same Triangle P.Q.R. may thus be changed into a Quadrangle: deuide the side P.Q. and the side P.R. each in two equall parts, then draw a line S.T. as long as Q. and R. and then draw a line direct downeward from T.R. to close it vp: and then that Quadrangle containeth as much space within it as the Triangle aforesayd, because that the Triangle which is cut off P.S.V. is of the like greatnesse with the other Triangle marked V.R.T.

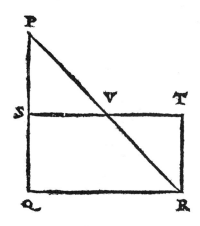

AND although there is a Triangle of vnequall sides, yet a man may make it a Quadrangle, in such sort as I sayd before of the right Triangle: for although the two Triangles that are cut off, and those two that are added vnto it, are not of one greatnesse, yet the Triangles A.F.I. and B.D.F. are one as great as the other, and againe, the Triangles A.G.K. & G.C.E. are also of one greatnes: so that those that are cut off, and those that are added thereunto, are of one quantitie. By these alterations aforesayd, a man may easily measure how many féte, elles or roodes fouresquare, are contained in a three cornerd Superficies.

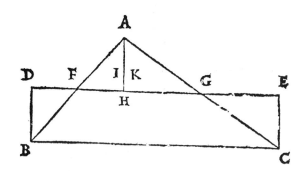

BUT it falleth out, that a Triangle (which is thrée cornerd) superficie or plaine, must be parted crossewise in two equal parts: then out of one of the sides that you will cut through, you must make a right foure square, as from the side A.B. and draw therin two Diagonus from corner to corner, which will shew you the Center C. and draw one Circle through that three cornerd part which you will deuide, and so you shall find the two points, where you shall drawe your deuiding line. He that desireth any proofe hereof, may take each piece and alter it into a Quadrangle, and after into a Quadrate, as heereafter shall be shewed, and he shall find it true.

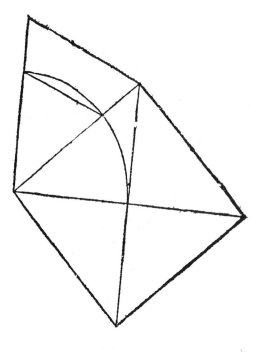

AN Architector must also vndergoe other burthens, for that hee must know how to deuide a piece of ground, that no man may be hindred thereby. As for example, if there were a piece of ground that lay thrée cornerd wise, with vnequall parts, hauing on the one side thereof a Well, but not in the middle: and this ground, or thrée cornerd piece of Land is to bee deuided into two equal parts, in such sort that each of them may haue the vse of the Well: it must bee done in this manner. I make a Triangle marked A.B.C. and the Well is marked with G. Now deuide the line B.C. with a darke line in the two equall parts as the letter D. sheweth, and then drawing a line from D. to A. then the Triangle is deuided into two equal parts: but both of them can not yet come to the Well: then drawe another line from the Well G. to A. and from the poynt D. you must set an Equidistancie against G.A. marked with E. & drawing from G. which is the Well: the blacke line to the letter E. it will deuide the ground in two euen seuerall parts, and each of them shall haue the Well at the end of his ground, for that part A.B.G.E. containeth in it iust as many féte or rods, as that part which is marked G.E.C.

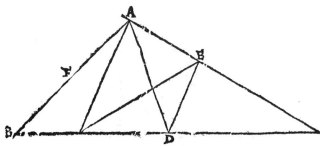

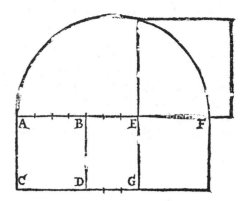

I Shewed before, how a man should make a four square Superficies once as great again as it is, but it may fall out, that a man is to make it but halfe as great again, or more or lesse, as he thinketh good, or as occasion serueth, which the Architector is also to learne of necessitie. Which to shew, I set downe a right foure square thing marked A. B. C. D. which I will haue three quarters greater: the same three quarters I set by the side thereof, so that the same with the Quadrate together make a Quadrangle A. E. C. G. To bring this Quadrangle into a right Quadrate, you must lengthen the line A. E. yet a quarter longer, or from the side of the Quadrangle E. G. and place F. there: then vpon the line A. F. make halfe a Circle: which line wil shew you the one side of the Quadrate which you seeke for: which Quadrate being made, will containe as much in it, as the Quadrangle already made. And in this maner you may change all Quadrangles which are long foure cornerd pieces of worke, into a iust and true Quadrate.

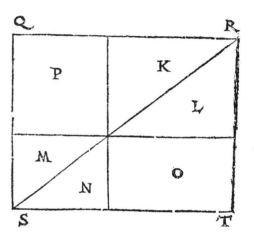

NOw to prooue that, which I sayd before, you must ioyne the Quadrangle with the Quadrate together, in one foure square superficie as Q. R. S. T. and from the corner R. to the corner S. draw a Diagonus, and it is certaine that that Diagonus will make two euen parts. Now Euclides saith, that when a man taketh any euen parts from euen parts, the rest of the parts also remaine alike: then take the Triangle K. L. and the Triangle M. N. which are both alike: the right foure cornerd superficie P. is of the same greatnesse, that the longer superficie O is.

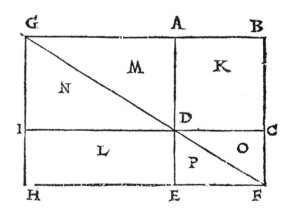

AGaine, you may easily change a Quadrate into a Quadrangle, as long or as narrow as you desire to haue it, doing thus: Make your Quadrate A. B. C. D. and lengthen your line A. B. and the line B. C. Which done, then set the length of the Quadrangle, which you desire to haue vpon the line A. G. Then from the poynt G. draw a line along by the corner of the Quadrate D. to the line C. F. and there you find the shortest line of the Quadrangle: and so to the contrarie, you shall by the least side of the Quadrangle finde the longest also, as you may also prooue by the foresayd Figure for when you take away the Triangles M. N. and O. P. which are both alike, then the two parts which are K. L. are also alike.

An

Of Geometrie

An Architector may by chance haue a piece of worke of diuers vnequall sides come to his hands, which he is to put into a Quadranguler or Quadrate forme, to know what it containeth, and specially when it belongeth to more then one man, whether it bee Land or any other thing. For although the Architector or Surueyor of Land could not skill of Arithmaticke or Ciphering: yet this rule cannot faile him, nor any other man that desireth to find out the deceite of a Taylor. Thus, I say then, let it bee what forme soeuer it will, I set downe this hereafter following. First then, seeke the greatest Quadrate or Quadrangle, that you can take out of it: that done, seeke yet another Quadrate or Quadrangle, as big as you can take out of it, out of the rest of the said worke: and if you can after that make more Quadrates or Quadrangles out of it, I meane all with right corners, take them out also: but if you can find no more in it, then make Triangles also as big as you can, of which Triangles (as you are taught before) you may make Quadrangles, and let euery piece seuerally be marked with Carecters, as in the figure following may be seene.

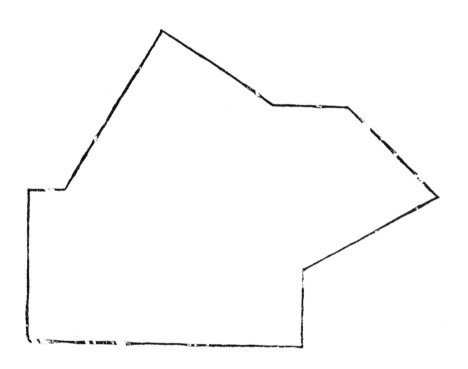

Let by example your many cornerd figures first bee marked with the great Quadrangle with these letters A. B. C. D. and then with a lesse Quadrangle, as E. F. G. H. the rest are all Tryangles. Now set the greatest Quadrangle L. in a place by it selfe, and then the other marked with M. which set vpon it, that the two corners or sides may be alike: which done, lengthen the line E. F. and the line E. G. and where they stay or touch vnder the great Quadrangle L. there set an I. from this I. a Diagonall line, being drawen through the corners B. H. the same line shall be drawen to the point: that, by the shutting of the Carecters B. M. L. D. will shew you another Quadrangle, of the like quantitie that the Quadrangle M. is: so that the whole Quadrangle D. C. L. M. containeth the two aforesayd Quadrangles. Touching the Triangles, when you haue changed the same (according to your former instruction) into Quadrangles, as you may see by the Triangle N. so may you put that Quadrangle also in the greatest Quadrangles (for lesse trouble.) The great Quadrangle A. L. M. C. is once againe placed aboue with the small Quadrangle O. P. Q. R. set vpon it, and the Diagonall line is placed behind the greater (which is L. M. T. S. both marked with N. so that the Quadrangle A. C. S. T. containeth three Quadrangles L. M. N. and as many more as there are: you may in this sort bring them all in one Quadrangle: if there falleth out any crooked lines, the skilfull Architector or workeman may almost bring them into a square, and those Quadrangles, if need be, may also be reduced into perfect foure squares, as aforesayd.

THE Architector muſt haue a well proportioned Cornice, which if he would make greater, keeping the ſame proportion, hee may doe it as he is formerly taught, as in this Figure following is ſhewed by the ſhort line marked A.B. and the longer line marked A.C.

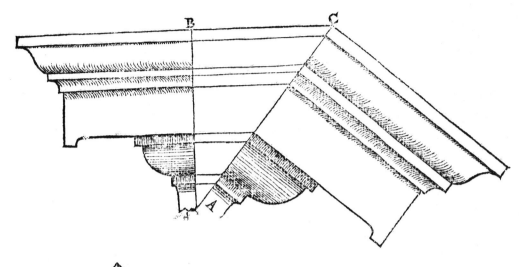

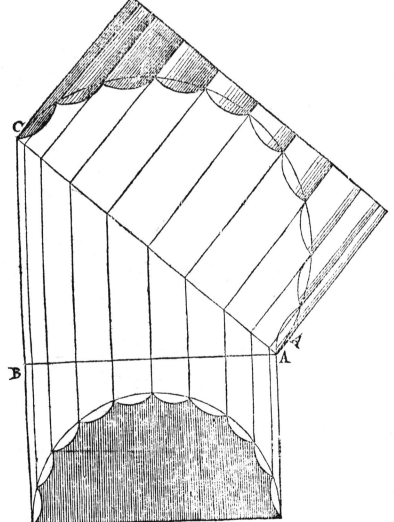

AN Architector or workman, muſt likewiſe learne to augment & make greater a holowed coluine, which hee may alſo doe by the two lines aforeſayde, and although the Columne ſhould be a Dorica (yet it is to bee vnderſtood of all kinds of Columnes. This rule wil alſo ſerue (not only for the three figures ſet downe) but alſo for as many, as if I ſhould ſhewe them, it would containe a whole booke of them alone, and therefore this ſhall ſuffice at this time for the workeman.

The

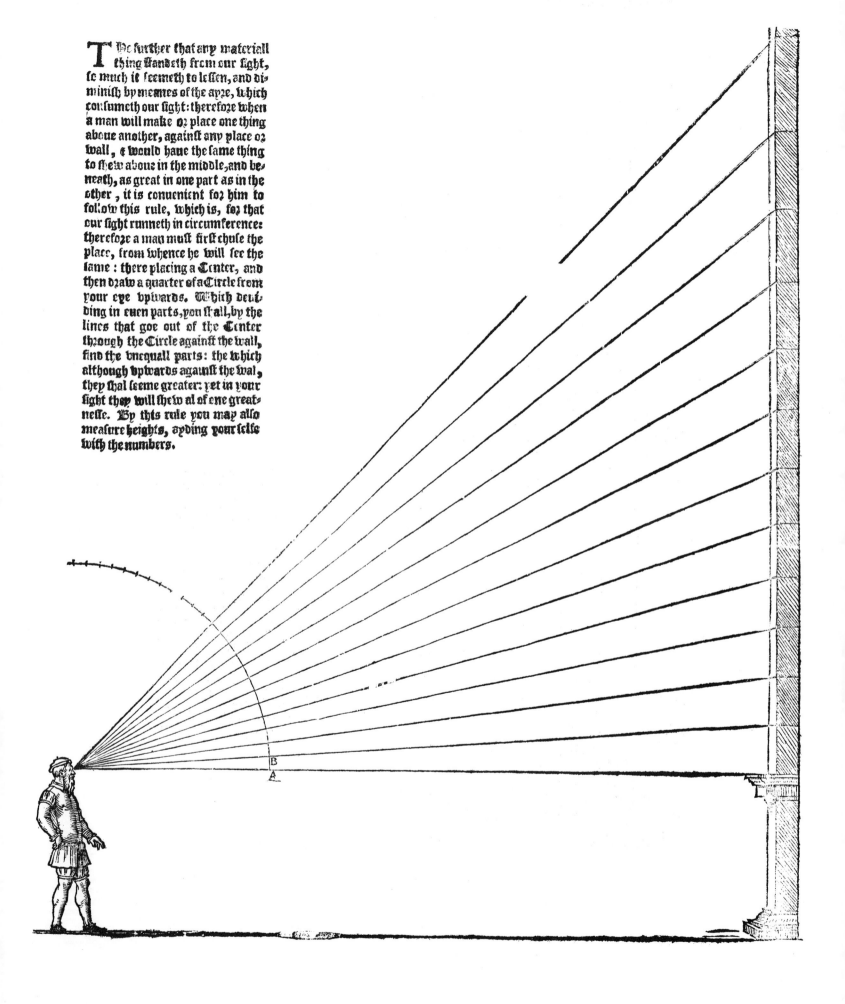

The further that any materiall thing standeth from our sight, so much it seemeth to lessen, and diminish by meanes of the ayre, which consumeth our sight: therefore when a man will make or place one thing aboue another, against any place or wall, & would haue the same thing to shew aboue in the middle, and beneath, as great in one part as in the other, it is conuenient for him to follow this rule, which is, for that our sight runneth in circumference: therefore a man must first chuse the place, from whence he will see the same: there placing a Center, and then draw a quarter of a Circle from your eye vpwards. Which deuiding in euen parts, you shall, by the lines that goe out of the Center through the Circle against the wall, find the vnequall parts: the which although vpwards against the wal, they shal seeme greater: yet in your sight they will shew al of one greatnesse. By this rule you may also measure heights, ayding your selfe with the numbers.

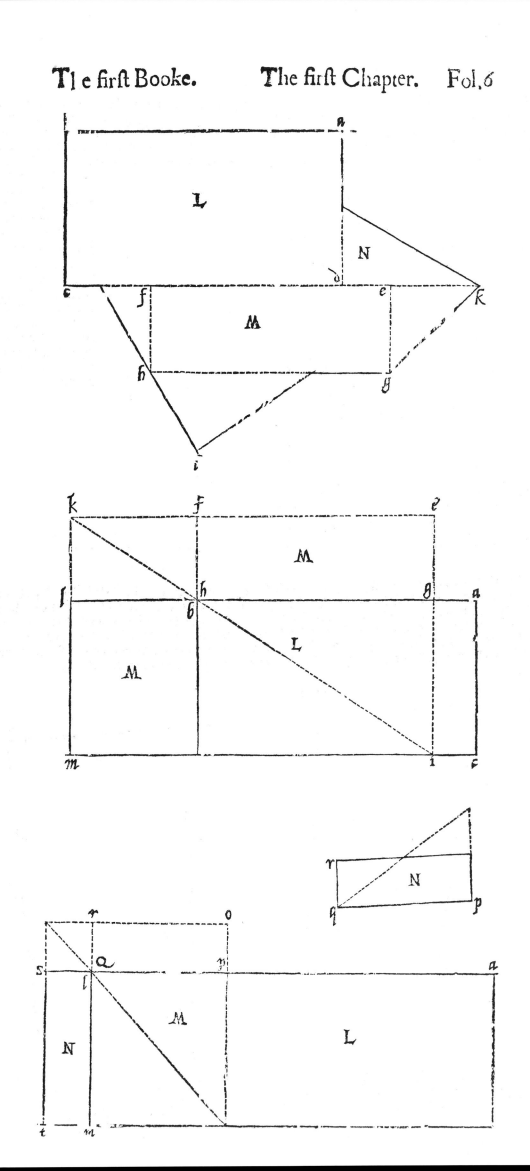

VVHen a man hath a line or other things of vnequall parts, and there is also another longer line, or some other thing, which a man would also deuide into vnequall parts, according to the proportion of the shorter line, then let the shortest line be A. B. and the greatest line A. C. now tis necessary that from the vppermost poynt A. you should make a corner as A. B. and A. A. Then take your longer line, and set it with the end C. vpon B. and let the other end rest at the hanging line A. A. then from euery poynt of the vppermost line A. B. let a hanging line fall vpon the line A. C. so that they may be equidistant with the line A. A. ¶ where y said lines cut through each other, there is the right deuision proportioned, according to the smaller. This rule that not only serue the Architector for many things, as I will partly shewe: but will also serue many Artificers to reduce their small workes into greater.

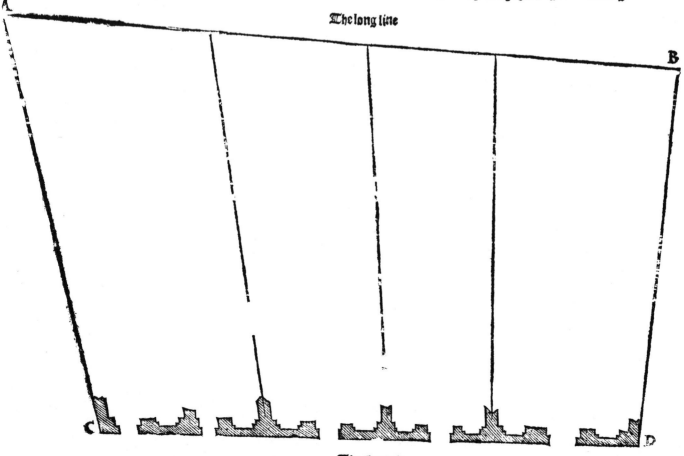

For example of the figure aforesaid, I suppose, Houses or pieces of Land to be of diuers widenesse, which should be narrower before then behinde. Which Houses, by fire or warre are so decayed, that in the forepart betweene C. D. there were but some signes of diuision to bee seene of the houses, and behind the houses betweene A. and B. no signes at all to be seene. Now as the misfortune was past, and that euery man desired to haue his part of his inheritance, then the Architector, as an vmpire, according to the rule aforesaid, should deuide the longest line according to the proportion of the shortest, to giue euery man his owne; as you may see by this Figure following.

The long line

The short line.

Any men are of opinion, that ſtraight lines, in what maner ſoeuer they are cloſed, contayne as many ſpaces one way as another, (that is to ſay) if a man had a cord of forty foote long, and ſhould lay it diuerſly in a round, long, three cornerd, foure ſquare, or fiue cornerd forme: but the ſuperficies are not of one ſelfe ſame ſpace, which may be ſéene by theſe foure ſquare figures following; for the firſt line holdeth on either ſide ten, which is forty: and the ſpace contaynes ten times ten, which is an hundred. The other line vpon the two longeſt ſides contaynes fiftéene ſpaces, and on the ſhorteſt ſides fiue, making forty alſo: but fiue times fiftéene make but ſeuentie and fiue.

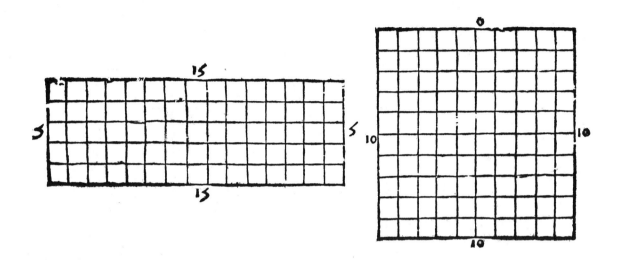

If the Quadrate ſtretcheth further out, ſo that the two longer ſides were eyghtéene a péece, then the ſhorteſt ſides muſt each haue two to haue forty vpon the line, but the ſpace ſhould contayne but ſixe and thirty. And hereby you ſée what a perfect forme may doe agaynſt an vnperfect. And this rule the workeman ſhall vſe, that he may not be deceiued when he will change one forme into another.

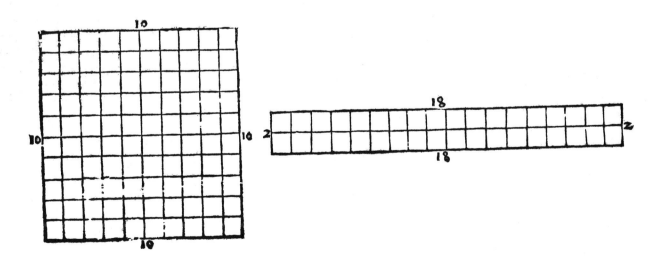

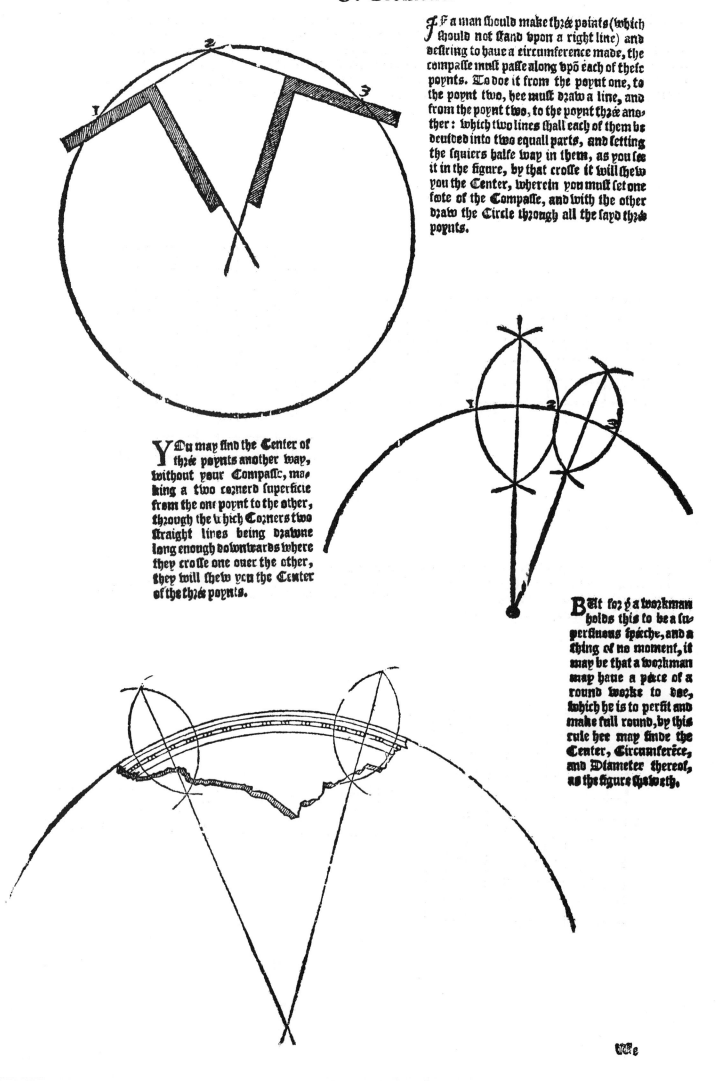

Jf a man ſhould make thꝛée paints (which ſhould not ſtand vpon a right line) and deſiring to haue a circumference made, the compaſſe muſt paſſe along vpõ each of theſe poynts. To doe it from the poynt one, to the poynt two, hée muſt dꝛaw a line, and from the poynt two, to the poynt thꝛée another: which two lines ſhall each of them be deuided into two equall parts, and ſetting the ſquiers halfe way in them, as you ſee it in the figure, by that croſſe it will ſhew you the Center, wherein you muſt ſet one fote of the Compaſſe, and with the other dꝛaw the Circle thꝛough all the ſayd thꝛée poynts.

YOu may find the Center of thꝛée poynts another way, without your Compaſſe, making a two coꝛnerd ſuperficie from the one poynt to the other, through the which Coꝛners two ſtraight lines being dꝛawne long enough downwards where they croſſe one ouer the other, they will ſhew you the Center of the thꝛée poynts.

BUt foꝛ ɣ a woꝛkman holds this to be a ſuperfluous ſpéche, and a thing of no moment, it may be that a woꝛkman may haue a péce of a round woꝛke to bſe, which he is to perfit and make full round, by this rule hée may finde the Center, Circumferéce, and Diameter thereof, as the figure ſheweth.

WE finð in Antiquities, and
alſo in moderne woꝛks, many Pillars oꝛ Columnes, which
beneath in the ioynts at the Baſes
are bꝛoken aſunder, which is, becauſe their Baſes were not well
made accoꝛding to their coꝛners:
oꝛ elſe, becauſe they are not rightly placed: ſo that they haue moꝛe
weights vpon them on the one
ſide, then on the other, whereby
the Cantons breake, which the
woꝛkeman by knowledge of the
lines, and helpe of Geometry, may
pꝛeuent in this maner: That is.
Yee muſt make the Pillar round
vnderneath, and his Baſe hollow
inward: ſo that when you place
the Pillar by the Lead, it may
pꝛeſently ſettle it ſelfe without a-
ny hurt. To finde this roundnes,
you muſt ſet the one poynt of the
Compaſſe vpon the higheſt part of
the Pillar that is vnder the A.
and the other poynt thereof vpon
B. and then dꝛawe, oꝛ winde it a-
bout to C. and that ſhall bee the
roundneſſe, making the hollowing
of the Baſe, accoꝛding to the ſame
meaſure: you may doe the like
with the Capitall, as you ſee in
the Pillar by it.

F a workeman will make a Bridge, Bowe, or any other round Arched piece of worke, which is wyder then a halfe Circle, although Masons practise this with their lines, whereby they make such kinde of workes, which shew will to mens sight, yet if the workeman will follow the right Theoricke and reason thereof, hee must obserue the order heretofore shewed. When he hath the wydenesse of the height, then he must make halfe a Circle out of the middle : after that, vpon the same Centre, hee must make another lesser Circle, which must be no greater then he will make the height of the Bow or Arche: then he must deuide the greatest Circle in equal parts, which must al be drawen with lines to the Centre: then you must heng out other Perpendiculars vpon your Lead: and where the lines that go to the Centre cut through the lesser Circle, from thence you must draw the crosse lines toward the Perpendicular, and where they close together, there the Bowe or Arche which is made, shall be closed: as by the points or prickes hereunder is shewed.

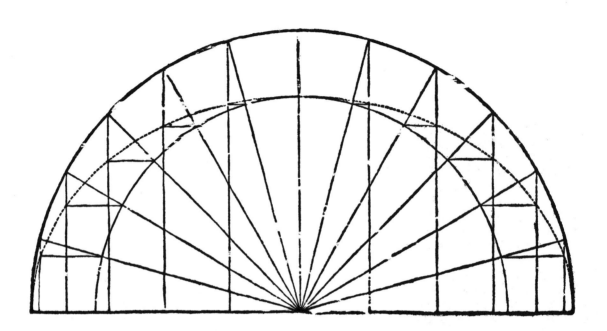

BUT if you desire to make the Bow or Arche lower, then you must follow the rule aforesayd, and make the innermust Circle so much lesse, which is to bee vnderstood, that the more parts that you make of the greater Circle, so much the easier you shall draw the crooked lines which you would haue: from this rule there are many others obserued, as hereafter you shall see.

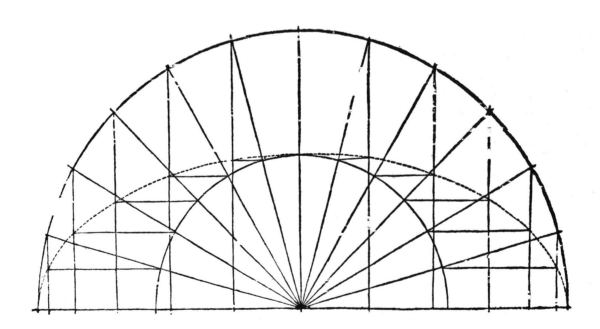

Calling the former rule to minde, I deuiſed the manner how to forme and fashion diuers kindes of veſſels by the ſame, and I thinke it not amiſſe to ſet downe ſome of them: This onely is to bee marked, that as wide as you will make the veſſels within, ſo great you muſt make the innermoſt Circle. The reſt, the ſkilfull workeman may marke by the figures, that is, how the lines are drawne to the Center, and the Parables, and out of the ſmall Circle. The Perpendiculars hanging, the veſſels are formed: the foote and the necke may be made as the workeman will.

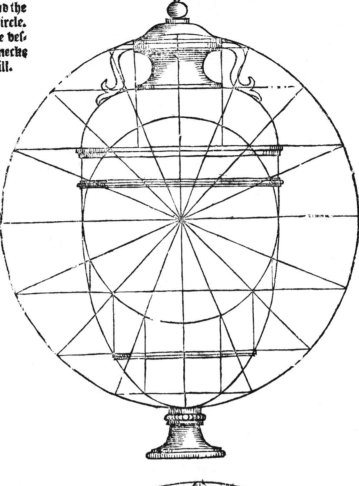

BUT if you will make the body of the veſſell thicker, then you muſt make the halfe Circle ſo much the greater, and make the belly hanging downe vnder it, to touch the great Circle, by the falling of the Perpendiculars vpō the croſſe line, as by theſe Figures 3. 4. 5. it is ſhewed: whereby a man by this meanes may make diuers veſſels, differing from mine. The necks and couers of theſe veſſels are within the ſmall Circles: the other members and Ornaments are alwayes to bee made, according to the will of the ingenious workman.

IT is an excellent thing for a man to study or practise to do any thing with the Compasse, whereby in time men may find out that which they neuer imagined : as this night it happened vnto me, for that seeking to find a nèrer rule, to make ẙ forme of an Egge, then Albertus Durens hath set downe: I found this way to make an Anticke vessell, placing the foote beneath at the foot of an Egge, and the necke with the handles aboue vpon the thickest part of the Egge. But first, you must frame the Egge in this manner: Make a straight crosse of two lines, and deuide your crosse line in ten equall parts: that is, on each side fiue.

Then, set the Compasse vpon the
Center A. and with the other foote
thereof, draw in two parts, that is,
to C. making halfe a Circle vpwards. That done, set one foote of
the Compasse vpon ẙ poynt marked
B. and with the other draw in the vttermost poynt C. drawing a péece of
a Circle down-wards toward ẙ Perpendicular, and doing the like on the
other side, you must make a point below. Then take the halfe of the halfe
Circle aboue that two parts, and
place it at the vndermost point of the
Perpendicular vpwards aboue O.
where the Centre to close the Egge,
shal stand: the rest vnder shalbe for ẙ
foote: the necke, without doubt, may
be made two parts high, and the rest
according to the workemans pleasure, or according to the figure herevnder set downe.

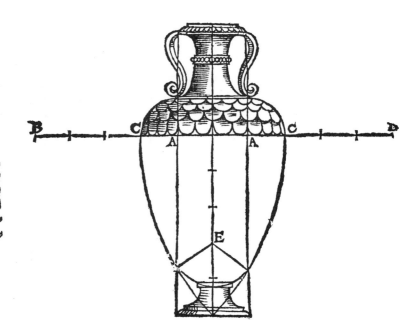

YOu may also make another forme of a Cap or vessell, after the rule aforesayd. But from the poynt A. (which doeth shew to the bredth of the foote, and the widenesse of the mouth) you must make your Circle vpwards, from C. vnto the two Perpendiculars, where the body shall be closed vp. The necke standing aboue it, shall be two parts high: but the rest of the workemanship shall be made according to the will and deuice of the workeman.

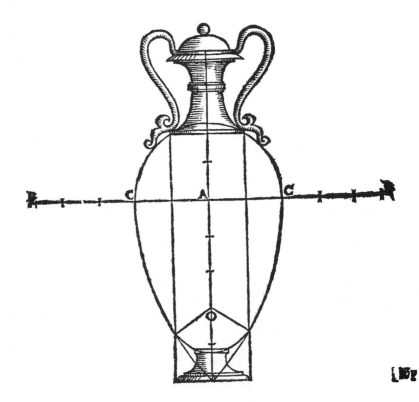

BY this meanes you may make other different kindes of Cups oꝛ veſſels: but theſe that follow, you muſt make in this ſoꝛt: you muſt deuide your croſſe line in twelue parts thꝛough the poynt A. making two Perpendiculars to ſhew the foote and the necke: then ſetting one foote of the Compaſſe vpon B. and the other foote vpon I. dꝛawing a piece of a Circle downe-wards, towards the Perpendicular: and the like being done on the other ſide to the Figure of 2. then place your Compaſſe vpon the poynt C. and touching the ſides 3. and 4. then the bottom of the veſſell will be cloſed vp: then place the Compaſſe vpon the poynt betweene I. and A. and it will bee the roundneſſe of the veſſell aboue: the other foure parts ſerue foꝛ the necke of the veſſell, with the reſt of the woꝛke.

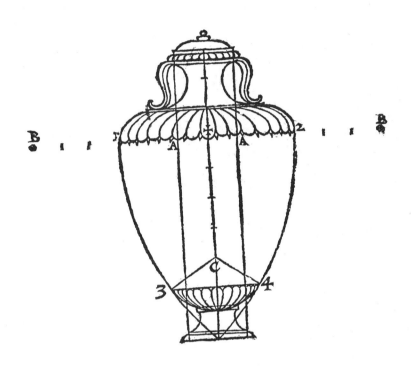

A Man may make a veſſell onely vp a Circuler foꝛme, making therein a Circuler croſſe, and deuiding euery line in-to ſixe parts: the halfe circle ſhall be the belly of the veſſell, and a ſixt part vpward foꝛ a Freſe, that there may bee moꝛe place to beautifie it: an other part ſhall be the height of the necke, and another part the couer: and foꝛ the foote, although it be but a halfe part high, it may well goe a ſixt part without the round: and although I haue ſet downe but ſixe maner of cups oꝛ veſſels, yet according to the rule afoꝛeſayd, a man may make an infinite number of veſſels, and a man may alter them by their Oꝛnaments, whereof I ſay nothing, that you may ſee the line the better.

Of Geometrie

A Man may make Ouale formes in diuers fashions, but I will onely set downe foure. To make this first figure, you must set two perfect Triangles one about the other, like a Rombus, and at the ioyning of them together, you must draw the lines through to 1.2 3.4 and the corners A.B.C.D. shall be the foure Centers, then set one foote of the Compasse vpon B. and the other vpon I. and draw a line from thence to the figure 2. After that, from the

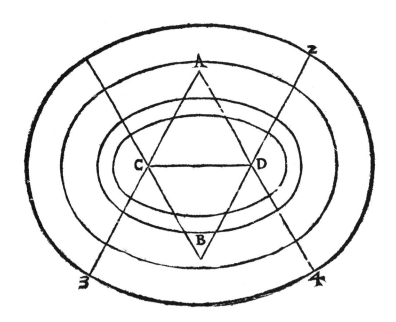

poynt A. and 3. to 4. you must also draw a line: which being done, set the one ende of the Compasse in the poynt C. and then draw a piece of a Circle from 1. to 3. and againe, the Compasse being in the Center D. draw a piece of a Circle from 2. to 4. and then the forme is made. You must also vnderstand, that the néerer that the figures come to their Centers, so much the longer they are: and to the contrary the further that they are from their Centers, the rounder they are: yet they are no perfect Circles, because they haue more then one Center.

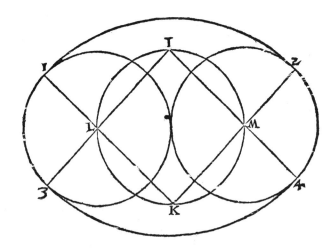

FOR the making of the second Ouale, you must first make thrée Circles, as you sée here drawing, where ye foure straight lines stand: the foure Centers shalbe I.K.L.M. Then placing one point of the Compasse in K. you must drawe a line with the other point from the figure of 1. to 2. Againe, without altering the Compasse, you shal set the one foote of the Compasse in I. and so drawe a piece of a Circle from the figure 3. to the figure 4. and that maketh the Compasse of the Circle. This Figure is very like the forme of an Egge.

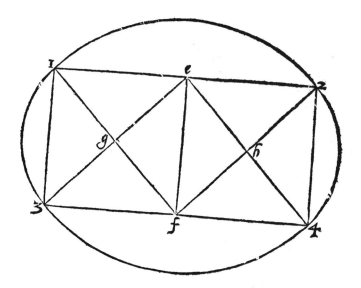

THE third forme is made by two foure cornerd squares, drawing Diagonen lines in them, which shal shew the two Centers G. H. and the other two the corners E. & F. Then draw a piece of a Circle frō F. to the figure I. and so to 2. Do the like from E. to 3. and 4. which done, from the points G. and H. make the true sides from 1. to 3. and from 2. to 4. and so shut vp the Ouale.

IF you will make this fourth Ovale, then make two Circles that may cut through each others Center, & the o'her two Centers for the closing of the Circle be N.O. after that, whether you draw the right lines or not from the poynts O.N. you shall shut up the sides from 1 and 2. and from 3. to 4.

And although our Authour sayth, there are foure formes of Ovales: yet this laſt figure is of the same forme as the first, onely this is easier to make.

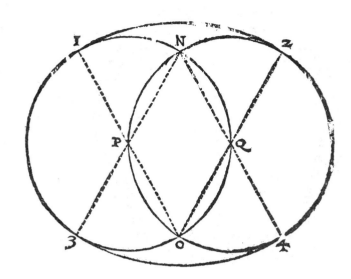

TOuching the Circles, there are many figures which are round, and yet some haue 5.6.7.8.9 and 10. corners, &c. But at this time, I will speake onely of these three principally because they are moſt common.

THis Octogonus, or eight points, is drawen out of a right foure corner'd square, drawing the Diagonus which will shewe you the Center: then set one foote of your Compas vpon the corners of the Quadrate, and leading the other foote through the Center, directing your Circle toward the side of the Quadrate, there your right poynts shall ſtand to make it eyght corners: and although a man might only doe it by the Circle, making a croſſe therein, and deuiding each quarter in two, yet it will not be ſo well, and therefore this is a ſurer and more perfect way.

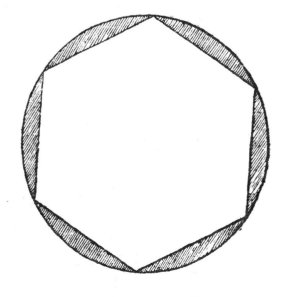

THE Hexagonus, that is, the ſixt corner'd Circle, is eaſieſt made in a Circle: for when the Circle is made, you may deuide the Circumference in ſixe parts equally, without ſtirring the Compaſſe, and drawing the line from one poynt to another, the ſixe corners are made.

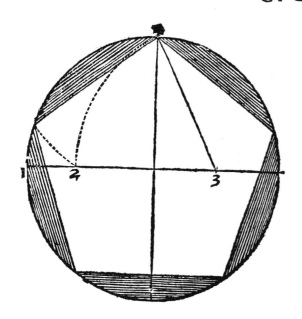

ꓐ Ꮩ Ꭲ the Pentagonus that is fiue cornerd, is not so caſily to be made as the others are, becauſe it is of an vneuen number of corners, notwithſtanding you may make it in this manner : when the Circle is made, then make a ſtraight croſſe therin: then deuide the one halfe of the croſſe line in two parts, which is marked with the figure 3. then place the one foote of the Compaſſe vpon 3 and with the other, placing it vnder the croſſe, drawe downe-ward to the croſſe line marked 2. from thence alſo from vnder the croſſe, you ſhall finde the length of euery ſide of the Pentagonus. In this figure alſo you ſhall finde the Decagonus, that is, ten corners: for, from the Center to the figure 2. that ſhall be one ſide thereof, you may alſo make a ſirtéene cornerd figure out of this wideneſſe 1. 2. and place a Particular line vpon the poynt 3. And Albertus Durens ſaith, that the ſame alſo will ſerue to make a ſeuen cornerd figure.

Ꭲ His figure will ſerue ſuch men as are to part a Circumference into vnequall parts, how many ſoeuer they be: but not to bring the Reader into confuſedneſſe, with making of many formes, I will onely ſet downe this deuided into nine corners, which ſhall ſerue for an example of all the reſt, which is thus: Take the quarter of the Circle, and deuide it into nine parts, and foure of theſe parts will bee the ninth part of the whole Circumference: you muſt alſo vnderſtand the ſame ſo, if you deuide a Quadrate into eleuen, twelue, or thirtéene parts, &c. for that alwayes foure of theſe parts bee the iuſt wydeneſſe of your parts required.

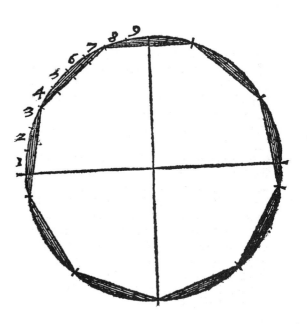

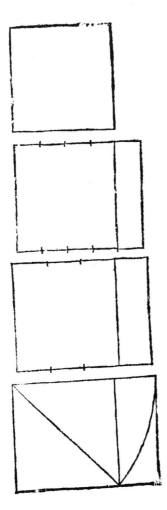

Ꭲ Here are many Quadrangle proportions, but I will here ſet down but ſeuen of the principalleſt of them, which ſhal beſt ſerue for the vſe of the workeman.

Ꞙ Irſt, this forme is called a right foure cornerd Quadrate.

Ꭲ He ſecond forme or figure in Latine, is called Sexquiquarta, that is, which is made of a foure cornerd Quadrate, and an eyght part thereof ioyned vnto it.

Ꭲ He third figure in Latine, is called a Sexquitertia, that is, made of a foure ſquared Quadrate, and a third part therof ioyned vnto it.

Ꭲ He fourth, is called Diagonea, of the line Diagonus: which line deuideth the foure ſquare Quadrate croſſe through the middle, which Diagonall line being toucht from vnder to the end thereof vpwards with the Compaſſe, and ſo drawen, will ſhew you the length of the Diagonall Quadrangle: but from this proportion there can bee no rule in number well ſet downe. Ꭲhe

THE sixt figure is called a Serquialtera, that is, a foure square, and halfe of one of the foure squares added vnto it.

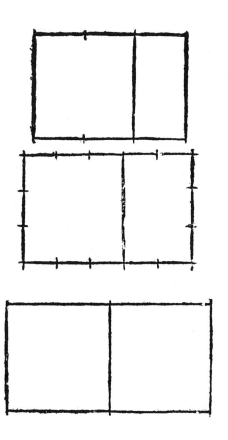

The sirt is called Superbitienstercias, that is, a foure square, and two third parts of one of the foure squares added thereunto.

THE seuenth and last figure, is called Dupla, that is, double: for it is made of two foure square formes ioyned together: and we finde not in any Antiquities, any forme that passeth the two foure squares, vnlesse it bee in Galleries, Entries and other to walke in: and some gates, doores, and windowes haue stood in their heights: but such as are wise will not passe such lengths in Chambers or Halles.

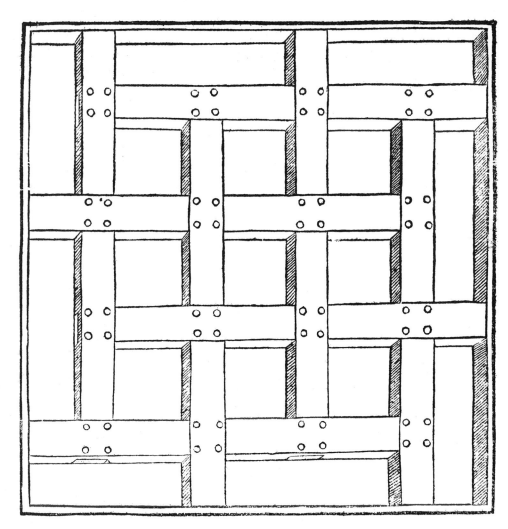

Many accidents like vnto this, may fall into the workmans hand, which is, that a man should lay a sieling of a house in a place which is fiftéene foote long, and as many foote broad, & the rafters should be but fouretéene foote long, and no more wood to be had: then in such case, the binding thereof must be made in such sort as you sée it here set downe, that the rafters may serue, and this will also bee strong enough.

T may alſo fall out, that a man ſhould finde a Table of ten foote long, and three foote broade: with this Table a man would make a doore of ſeuen foote high, and foure foote wyde. Now to doe it, a man would ſaw the Table long wiſe in two parts, and ſetting them one vnder another, and ſo they would be but ſixe foote high, and it ſhould bee ſeuen: and againe, if they would cut it three foote ſhorter, and ſo make it foure foote broade, then the one ſide ſhall be too much pieced. Therefore he muſt doe it in this ſort: Take the Table of ten foote long, and three foot broad, & marke it with A. B. C. D. then ſawe it Diagonall wiſe, that is, from the corner C. to B. with two equall parts, then draw the one piece thereof three foote backwards towards the corner B. then the line A. F. ſhall be foure foote broad, and ſo ſhall the line E. D. alſo hold foure foote broad: by this meanes you ſhall haue your doore A. E. F. D. ſeuen foote long, and foure foote broade, and you ſhall yet haue the three cornerd pieces marked E. B. G. and C. F. and C. left for ſome other vſe.

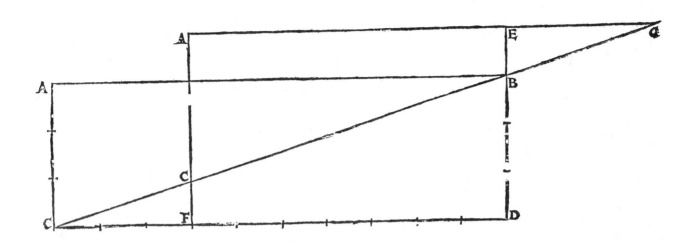

IT happeneth many times, that a workman hath an eye or round window to make in a Church, as in ancient times they vſed to make them, and he doubted of the greatneſſe thereof. which if he will make after the rules of Geometry, hee muſt firſt meaſure the bredth of the place where he will ſet it, and therein he muſt make a halfe Circle: which halfe Circle being incloſed in a Quadrangle, then he ſhall finde the Center by the Diagonall lines: then he muſt draw two lines more, which ſhall reach from the two lowermoſt corners aboue the Center, and touch the iuſt halfe of the Circle aboue: and where the ſayd lines cut through the Diagonall lines there you muſt make two Perpendicular lines, which Perpendicular lines ſhall ſhew the wideneſſe of the deſired window: the liſt about it, may bee made the ſixt part of the Diameter, being round in bredth.

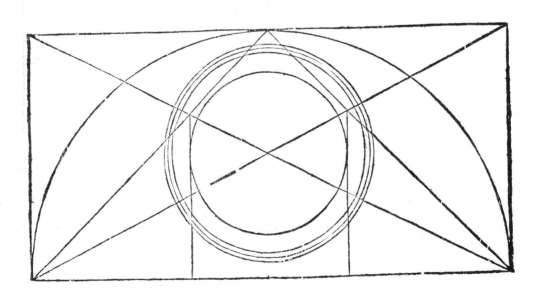

IF a workeman will make a Gate oꝛ a Dooꝛe in a Temple oꝛ a Church, which is to be pꝛopoꝛtioned accoꝛding to the place, then he muſt take the wideneſſe within the Church, oꝛ elſe the bꝛedth of the wall without: if the Church bee ſmall, and haue Pilaſters oꝛ Pillars within it: then he may take the wideneſſe betwéene them, ⁊ ſet the ſame bꝛedth in a foure ſquare, that is, as high as bꝛoad, in which foure ſquare, the Diagonall lines, and the other two croſſe cutting lines will not onely ſhew you the widenes of the dooꝛe, but alſo the places and poynts of the oꝛnaments of the ſame Dooꝛe, as you ſée here in this Figure. And although it ſhould fall out, that you haue thꝛée dooꝛes to make in a Church, and to that ende cut thꝛée holes, yet you may obſerue this pꝛopoꝛtion foꝛ the ſmalleſt of them. And although (gentle Reader) the croſſe cutting thoꝛow oꝛ deuiding is innumerable, yet foꝛ this time, leſt I ſhould be tw tedious, I here end my Geometry.

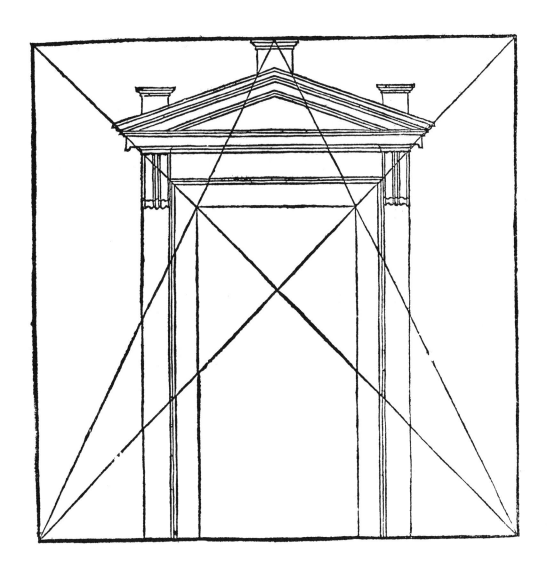

Here endeth the firſt Booke of Architecture, treating of Geometry, tranſlated out of Italian into Dutch: And now out of Dutch, into Engliſh, foꝛ the benefit of our Engliſh Nation, at the charges of Robert Peake. 1611.

D

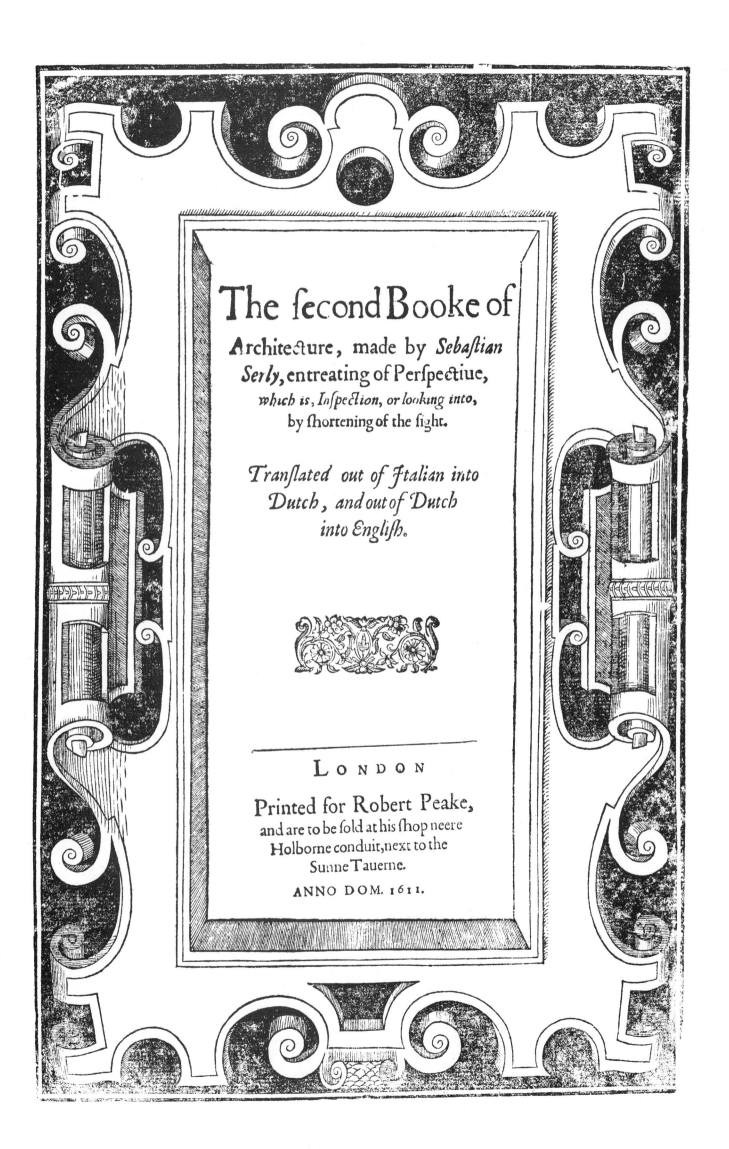

The second Booke of
Architecture, made by *Sebaſtian
Serly*, entreating of Perſpectiue,
which is, Inſpection, or looking into,
by ſhortening of the ſight.

Tranſlated out of Italian into
Dutch, and out of Dutch
into Engliſh.

LONDON

Printed for Robert Peake,
and are to be ſold at his ſhop neere
Holborne conduit, next to the
Sunne Tauerne.

ANNO DOM. 1611.

The second Booke.

A Treatise of Perspectiues, touching the Superficies.

The second Chapter.

Lthough the subtill and ingenious Arte of Perspectiue is very difficult and troublesome to set downe in writing, and specially the body, or modell of things, which are drawn out of the ground : for it is an Arte which cannot be so well expressed by figures or writings, as by an vndershewing, which is done seuerally : Notwithstanding , seeing that in my first Booke I haue spoken of Geometry, without the which Perspectiue Arte is nothing : I will labour in the briefest manner that I can in this my second Booke, to shewe the workeman so much thereof, that hee shall bee able to aide and helpe himselfe therewith.

In this worke I will not trouble my selfe to dispute Philosophically what Perspectiue is, or from whence it hath the originall : for learned *Euclides* writeth darkely of the speculation thereof.

But to proceede to the matter, touching that the workeman shall haue cause to vse, you must vnderstand, that Perspectiue is that, which *Vitruuius* calleth Scenographie, that is, the vpright part and sides of any building or of any Superficies or bodies.

This Perspectiue then, consisteth principally in three lines : The first line is the Base below, from whence all things haue their beginning. The second line is that, which goeth or reacheth to the point, which some call sight, others, the horison : But the horison is the right name thereof, for the horison is in euery place wheresoeuer sight endeth. The third line, is the line of the distances, which ought alwayes to stand so high as the horison is farre or neere, according to the situation, as when time serueth, I will declare.

This Horison is to be vnderstood to stand at the corners of our sight, as if the workeman would shew a piece of worke against a flat wall, taking his beginning from the ground, where the feete of the beholders should stand. In such case it is requisite, that the Horison should bee as high as our eye, and the distance to see or behold that worke, shall be set or placed in the fittest place thereabouts, as if it were in a Hall, or a Chamber, then the distance shall be taken at the entry thereof : but if it bee within, or at the end of a Gallery or Court, then the distance shall be set at the entry of the same place , and if it bee in a Streete against a wall or an house, then you must set your distance on the other side, right ouer against it. But if in such a case the streete is very narrow, then it were good to imagine a broad distance, lest the shortening fall out to be ouertedious or vnpleasant vnto you : for the longer or the wyder the distance is , the worke will shew so much the better and pleasanter.

But if you will begin a piece of worke of fiue or sixe foote high from the ground whereon you stand, then it is requisite that the Horison should stand euen with your eyes (as I sayd before) but if a man should see no ground of the worke, whereon the vppermost part doeth stand (and a man would worke very high) it would not be correspondent with the eyes : In such a case a man must take vpon him to place the Horison somewhat higher, by the aduice of some skilfull workman, which maketh histories or other things vpon Houses, thirtie or fortie foote high aboue a mans sight, which is vnfittingly. But cunning workmen fall into no such errors ; for where they haue made any thing aboue our sight, there you could see no ground of the same worke, for that the notable Perspectiue Art hath bridled them : and therefore (as I sayd before) Perspectiue Art is very necessary for a workeman : And no Perspectiue workeman can make any worke without Architecture, nor the Architecture without Perspectiue.

To proue this, it appeareth by the Architectures in our dayes, wherein good Architecture hath begun to appeare and shew it selfe : For, was not *Bramant* an excellent Architector, and was he not first a Painter, and had great skill in Perspectiue Art , before he applyed himselfe to the Art of Architecture ? and *Raphael Durbin,* was not he a most cunning Paynter, and an excellent Perspectiue Artist, before he became an Architector ? And *Balthazar Perruzzie* of *Sienna*, was also a Paynter, and so well seene in Perspectiue Art, that he seeking to place certaine Pillars and other Antike works perspectiuely, tooke such a pleasure in the proportions and measures thereof, that he also became an Architector: wherein he so much excelled, that his like was almost not to be found. Was not learned *Ieronimus Genga* also an excellent Paynter, and most cunning in Perspectiue Arte, as the faire works, which he made for the pleasure of his Lord *Francisco Maria,* Duke of *Vrbin,* can testifie; vnder whom he became a most excellent Architector ? *Iulius Romanus,* a scholler of *Raphael Durbin ;* who, by Perspectiue Arte and Paynting, became an excellent Architector, witnesseth the same. Then to come to my purpose; I say , that a man must be diligent and vigilant in this Arte, wherein I will begin with small things , and then proceed to greater ; vntill I haue shewed you the full Arte and manner thereof, as I desire.

To the ende that men by ſmall matters may attaine to greater, therefore I will begin to ſhew how to ſhorten a foure cornerd thing, from whence all the reſt ſhall bee deriued. Then the Baſe of this foure ſquare thing, ſhall be A.G. and the height of the Horiſon (as I ſayd before) ſhall bee imagined according to the ſight, and that ſhall be P. whereunto all the lines doe runne, as the lines of the ſides A.P. and G.P. then at the one ende of the Quadrante you muſt ſet a Perpendicular line, which is G.H. which done, then draw the Baſe A.G.K. long inough, and then out of the Horiſon draw a Paralell or an Equidiſtant line from the Baſe, as far as you will that the eye or ſight ſhall ſtand from that which you will looke on ; for how much the more you will haue the foure ſquare thing to ſeeme ſhorter, ſo much further you muſt goe with your ſight I. from H. to behold the foure ſquare thing. And then, taking H. I. for the diſtance from the point I. to the corner A. draw a line, and where the line cutteth through the Perpendicular line H.G. that is on B. there the termination of the ſhortening of the foure ſquare thing ſhall bee, as you may ſée in the figure following. But if you will make more foure ſquares one aboue the other, vpon the ſame Horiſon or poynt : then you muſt draw another line from the ſhortening poynt of the foure ſquare or Quadrant, to the letter I. and where it cutteth through the Perpendicular line aforeſaid, that is at C. there the ſecond Quadrant ſhalbe cut off, and in like ſort you muſt draw another line to the poynt of the diſtance : and where it toucheth the Lead, or Perpendicular line that is on D. you ſhall make the third Quadrante, the ſame may be done with E. and ſo you muſt goe, vntill you come iuſt vnder the Horiſon.

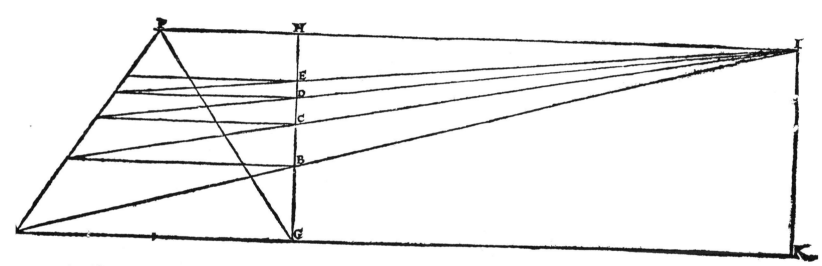

The rule aforeſaid is the perfecteſt, and you may proue it by the line G, H, which is called the line of the Quadrants : but becauſe it is cumbred with a greater number of lines, and ſo more tedious : therefore the rule enſuing ſhall be ſhorter, and eaſilyer to be done then the other : for when the Baſe A.G. is drawne, and the two ſide lines make a Triangle A.P.G. then you muſt draw the Paralels of the Baſe & of the Horiſon long inough ; and as farre as you will ſtand from the worke to ſée it, ſo farre you muſt ſet the Perpendiculars I.K. from the poynt G. then you muſt draw a line from the poynt I. to the poynt A. and where it cutteth through the line G.P. there ſhall be the termination of the firſt ſhortened Quadrant : and if you will place more Quadrants vpwards from that Quadrant, you muſt doe as I ſayd before : and although there are other wayes to ſhorten a Quadrant, yet will I follow this order, as being the ſhorteſt and eaſieſt to be ſet downe in writing.

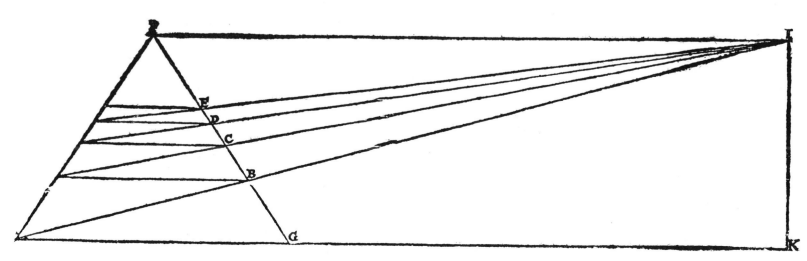

Of Perspectiue

A Man must also vse himselfe vnto diuers distances and grounds, and therefore you must make the ground following, which is of three Quadrantes high, in this manner. First, you must draw the line A . B. as long as the breadth of the worke shall be : which line or Base, must bee deuided into so many equall parts as are needfull, which being all drawne to the Horison or point, then you must place the distances as farre as you desire, according to the rule aforesayd; for here is no places set it in, although it is a length and a halfe from the Base, as you see it marked with 1½. Which Base, because it is of foure parts, therefore the first Quadrant containeth sixteene small Quadrantes, which are found by the line B. D. for where that line cutteth through the foure lines, which goe to the poynt; there you must draw the Paralel ouer, that thereby the sixtene Quadrantes may be formed: But if you will set other Quadrantes vpon it, then (as aforesayd) you must draw another line to the distance D. and where that cutteth through the other lines that reach to the poynt, that shall bee the termination of the second Quadrant, containing in it also foure times foure Quadrantes: The like must bee vnderstood of the third Quadrant, (and more besides if need bee.) But you must also vnderstand, that the lines marked D. runne all the distances, as it is taught before.

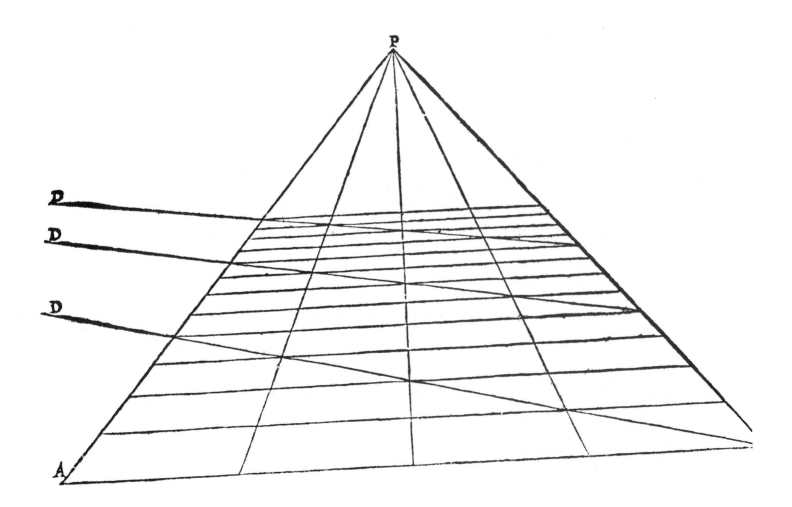

If you will make a pauement with great Quadrantes to be cut or Compassed with fascien, fasen or lists, as you will terme them, then vpon A. B. you must deuide the fasen or Quadrantes, and draw them all to the Horizon; then you must imagine the distances as you are taught before: and the line D.B. being drawne from the poynt B. to the point of the distances; then by cutting through of the Horisentall lines, it will shew the terminations of the Quadrants, Fasen, or Borders. To draw the Paralels, then if you will make the like Quadrantes somewhat higher, then you must draw another line to the distances: and where it toucheth the Horisentall or Radiall lines, there also you must draw the Paralels through; so you must also doe with the third, and the poynt of the distances of these figures stand as farre from A. as the line or Base A. B. is long: If you will make diuers formes in these Quadrants, as Rotes, Crosses, fixe poynts, or eyght poynts, I will shew the manner of them particularly, because I will bee as briefe heere in as I may.

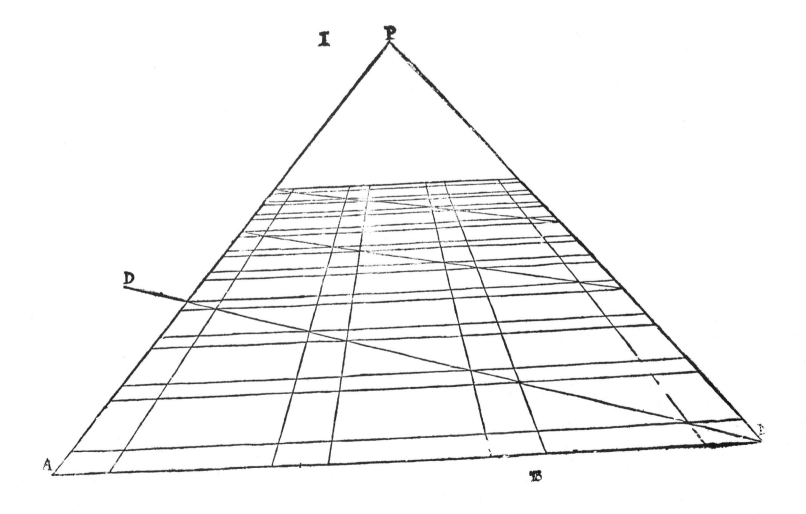

This figure is a Quadrant, containing in it a Rote or an other Quadrant, which with the poynts thereof toucheth the sides of the vttermost Quadrant; whereby it is but halfe so great as the vttermost Quadrant, as I haue taught you in the first Boke of Geometrie, and the maner to make this, is thus. First, you must make a Quadrant (as you are taught before) with his distances; and in this Quadrant you must draw two Diagonall lines, and also the right crosse lines, whereby you may easily finde the Rote, as you see it in the figure directly against this. In this sort you may make the Rotes in the other Quadrantes before set downe, that is, to draw Diagonall and crosse lines in them without seeking other distances.

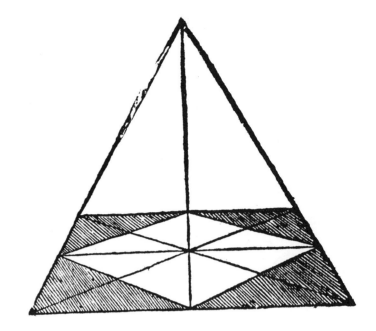

In this figure there is a crosse shewed (to make it) you must deuide the lowest line or Bole of the Quadrant in fiue parts; of the which fiue parts, one parte is the bredth of the crosse: which bredth being drawen to the points, the Diagonall lines will shew you the Paralel lines of the crosse, to vse where nede is.

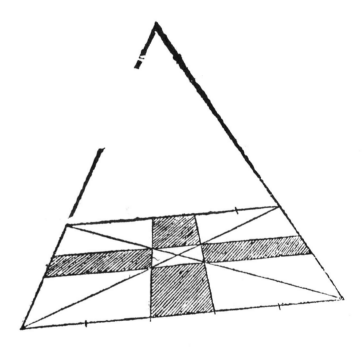

The eyght poynted figure you may see in Perfpectiue workes in diuers formes, which formes are all difficult inough: but that I may seke the easiest way so nere as I can in this my wri∣ting: Therefore I haue set downe the manner there∣of hereunto annexed, which is very easily; and that is thus. The Quadrant being made in shortening, you must deuide the Bafe into ten equall parts, and on either side you shall leaue three parts, and in the middle foure parts, then the two lines being drawen to the Horifon, you shall finde the terminations of the Paralel lines, by the Diagonall lines, whereby you may clofe vp the eyght corners, as you may see it in the Figure.

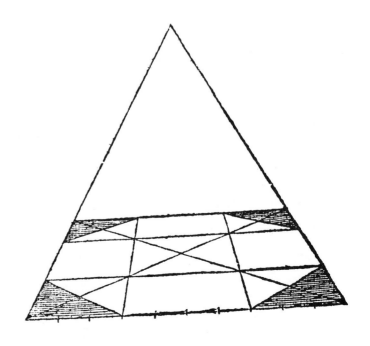

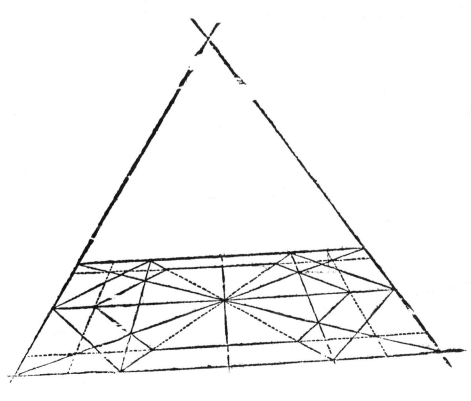

THE shortest way to place this sixe cornerd Quadrant, in Perspectiue workes, is thus; When the Quadrant according to the rule aforesaid, is placed in shortening, then you must make foure equall parts of the Bases, whereof two shall be in the middle, and on each side you must leaue one, and then draw the lines vpwards to the Horison or poynts: then you must draw the Diagonall lines, and in the middle where they meet together, you must draw a Paralel line cleane through, by the which you shall finde all the points to make this sixe cornerd Figure.

NOw I haue shewed how you shall make simple or plaine Perspectiue workes of foure corners, of sixe corners, and eyght square corners: Now I will shew, how you shall make them double, that is, that euery simple figure shal haue his band. When you haue made a plaine Superficies of sixe poynts, according to the rule aforesayd; then as much as you will haue the band or fase to be in bredth, that you must draw vpon the Base, and draw that also vp to the Horison: and where the Diagonall lines cut through it, there you must draw Paralel lines both vnder and aboue: and then draw two Diagonal lines more, out of the foure innermost points or corners of the sixe cornerd Superficies; and so you shall finde your terminations to shut or close vp your smallest sixe poynts or cornerd Superficies. Which second Diagonal, Paralel, and Horisontall lines are all drawen with prickes, for a difference from the first lines; that you may know them one from another.

THE like must bee done with the eyght cornerd Superficies or Perspectiue work, for when the same is made within a fouresquare, making the Compas of what bredth you will, according to the rule aforesayd: then out of euery poynt or corner of the eyght square, a small line being drawen to the Center, you shall finde the termination to shut vp the innermost eyght square; and then, when from poynt to poynt the lines are drawen, then one square or Compasse is full made. This eyght squa e forme may bee changed into a round, touching the middle on eyther side, or else without, ouer the poynts or corners; a good workeman may easily draw a Circuler shortening round line with his hand.

Of Perspectiue

Lthough I haue said before that a man may make a round Circle about an ryght square, yet for more securitie you may by this way attaine to a more perfection therein; for that the more points or sides the Circuler forme hath, the round Compasse or Circle will be the fuller. But to make this Figure, it is necessary to make halfe a Circle vnder the Bases, and to deuide the Circumference into as many parts as you will, so that they be euen; in this forme the halfe Circle is deuided into eyght parts, so that the whole Circle must bee sixteene parts: which being done, you must set Perpendicular lines in all the parts of the Circumference, as farre as to the Bases of the shortened Quadrant, these parts being eleuated to the Horison, and two Diagonall lines drawen in the Quadrante, they by cutting through the Horisontall or Radiall lines, will shew you the Paralel lines. Then if you will draw a little Diagonall line, beginning at the middle poynt of the Base, from the one side vnto the other, and so from the one poynt vnto the other vpwards going ouer the points: then the formes will be closed, as you see them heere; whereby it will be easie for you to draw a round forme with your hand, for it is vnpossible to bee done with the Compasse to make it short'n well. This figure you must be expert in, and you must also vnderstand it well, and so you must those that I haue before set downe, before you proceed further: for they will serue you for many pieces of worke hereafter ensuing, as you shall both see and finde to be true.

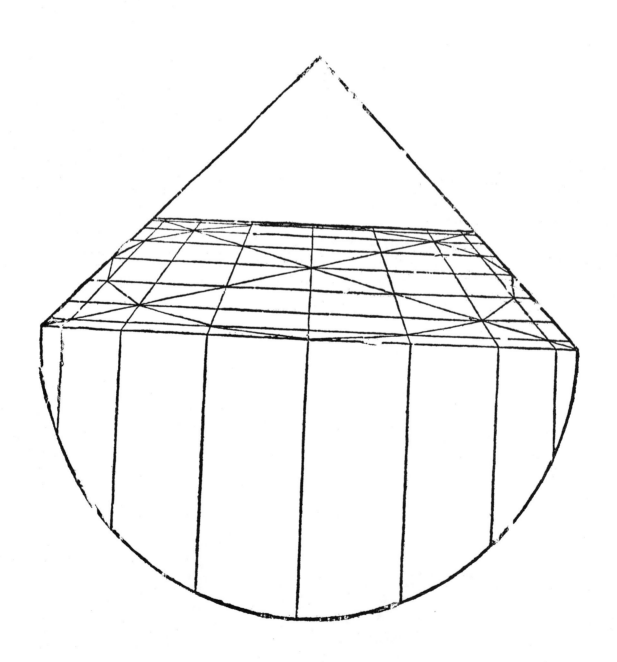

WHen you vnderstand the Figure aforesayd perfectly, then you must proceed further, and shut the round Circle also with an edge or border, according to the bredth that you will haue; you must also make the vttermost halfe Circle, and the aforesayd parts of the great Circle drawen towards the Center, will come into the smale Circle: the which parts of the small Circle being also set downe in Perpendicular lines with prickes not to darken the other lines, and those likewise that are drawen to the Horison. Then by cutting through of the Diagonall lines, you shall finde the Paralel lines.   To make the innermost shortening a round or Circle, according to the first example set downe, as you may see; the first round with perfect lines, and the second with prickes, as you see in this Figure.

But, friendly Reader, you must not be weary to bee long in learning this Figure, or in making it often times; vntill you can doe it perfectly and vnderstand it well: for I am sure and certaine, that it will bee very hard vnto many men, yet without this, you cannot doe much; and he that can doe it well, shall easily vnderstand and make all the things hereafter ensuing.

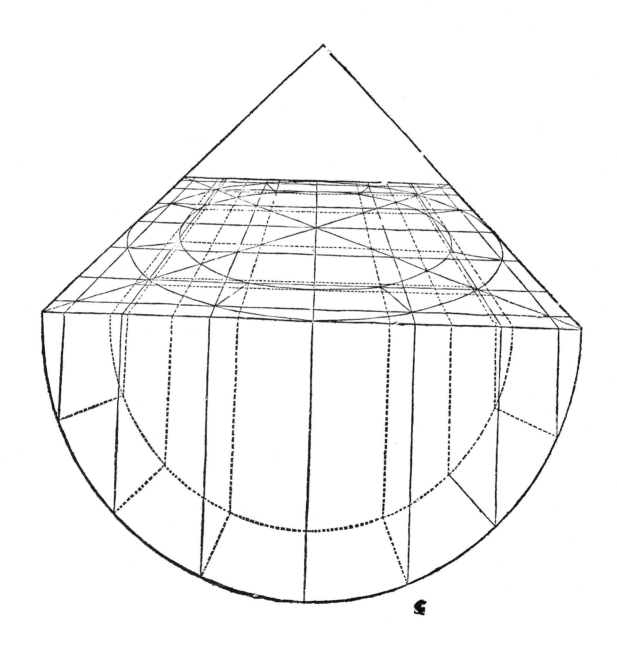

Of Perspectiue

IT falleth out many times that a workeman will shew a House both without and within, which to doe, he must place the ground in Perspectiue forme, that he may the surer and better draw that vp which hee will haue seene, and to lerne the rest on the ground: if then you will place a foundation in Perspectiue manner, to make it well, you must first set it on a flat forme, that out of that you may draw it into a Perspectiue forme.

To doe this, I haue set downe a kinde of open Building, that a man may the easelier conceiue it for a beginning, for when a man can doe this well, he may after that place many other and harder things in Perspectiue forme. I need not to take any great paines to write or show how this shortening should bee done, because it is so easily and so openly placed in a figure that a man may presently conceaue it: for that leading all the lines that goe from the corners and outsides of the flat ground to the Base, which you will make in the shortening; and the same being drawne vp to the Horison, together with the imagination of the distances: then you may shut or close vp the shortening foure square. When you must draw the Diagonall lines therein, through drawing the Paralel lines, presently you shall find the way how to forme the Columnes and pilasters, so that it is vnpossible to faile therein; and especially for those that doe well conceaue and vnderstand that, which I haue set downe before.

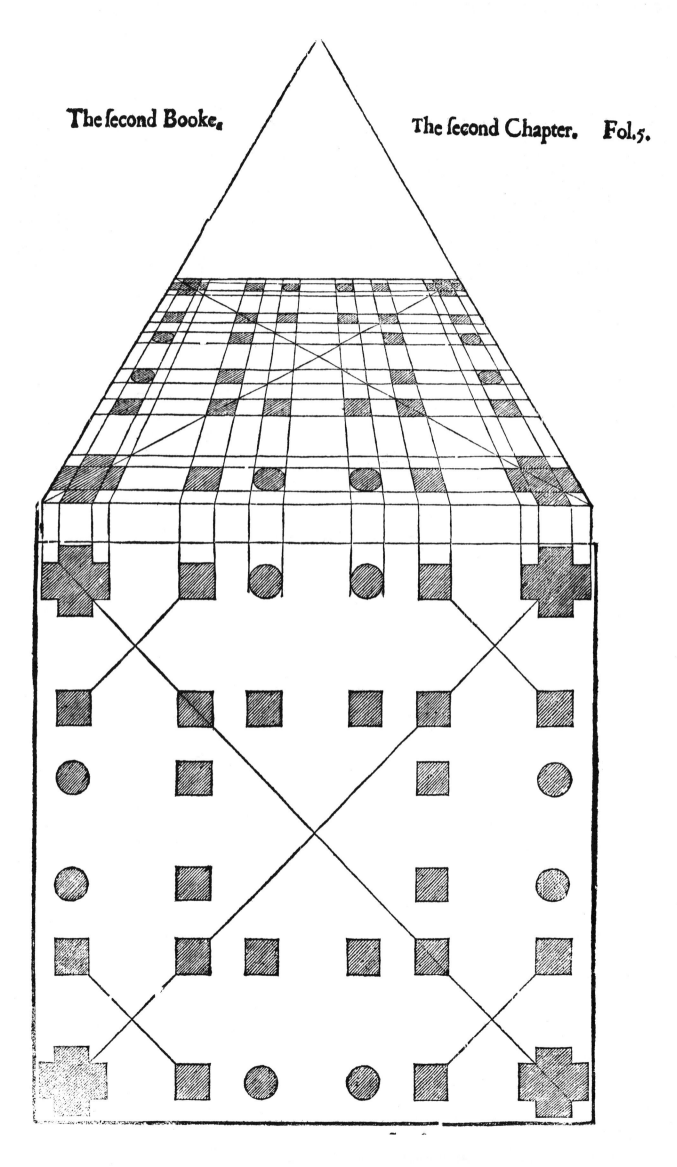

Of Perspectiue

This Figure following is somewhat harder then that before, but when you goe from the smalest to the greatest, you conceaue things the easier, and specially he that will learne this Arte ; he must not leaue nor refuse to exercise any of the Figures before set downe, but must vse all the diligence he can to be perfect in them all , and hee must also take a pleasure to doe them all, otherwise he that will omit now one, and then another, because he can hardly vnderstand or conceaue them (although I labour and striue at all times in setting downe these rules to shew all difficulties) shall little profit himselfe in this Arte. The manner how to place this ground in Perspectiue forme, is easily conceaued, without any other demonstration : for you must follow the manner or opperation of the figure before set downe, with this aduertisement ; that the two Diagonal lines euermore direct the worke, together with the Horisentall lines : and although a man may shew many formes of grounds that are to bee placed in shortening , yet these two shall suffice for this time, because I haue other things to entreat off : for a skilfull workeman, by the helpe of these, may forme others for his purpose, and such as he shall haue occasion to vse. And if he will erect any péece of worke for a show, he must necessarily first measure the Ortographie with the same measure that he measureth the ground withal, and then place it in a shortening manner, as when time serueth, shall be shewed.

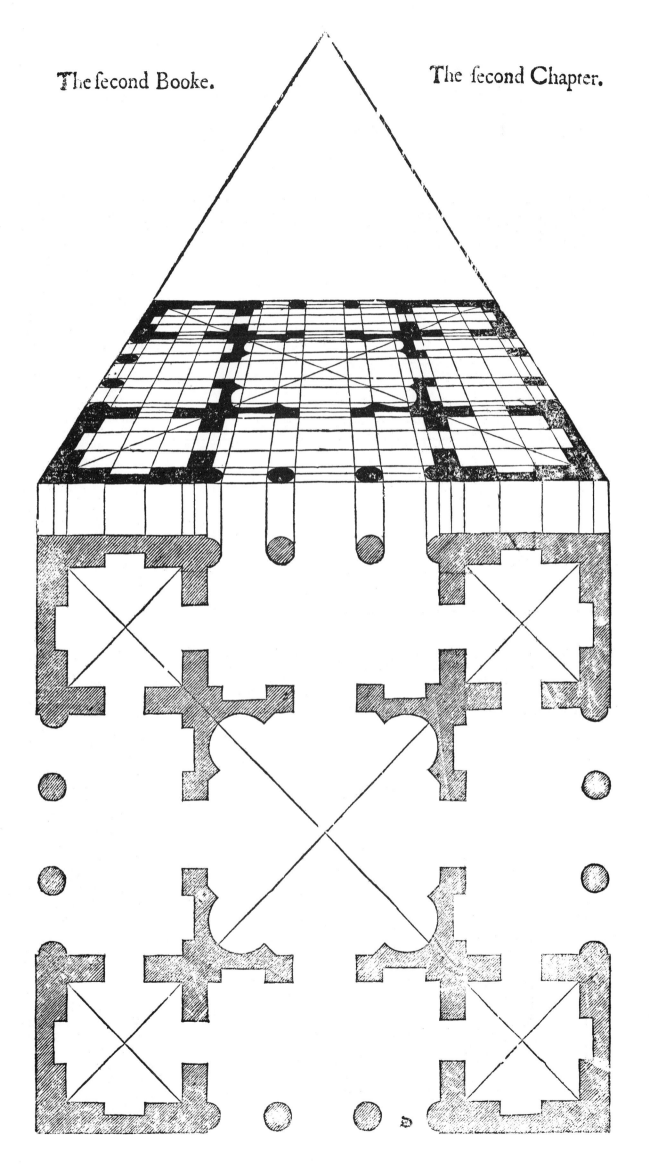

Of Perſpeĉtiue vvorkes, touching
Bodies or Maſſiue things.

The third Chapter.

Ouching the grounds and other Superficies of diuers formes, I thinke I haue sufficiently spoken. Now I will speake of Bodies which are drawne vp out of the ground : and first, you know that I haue taught before, how you should frame an eyght square forme plainely in it selfe ; and then, I haue shewed how you should compaſſe this Figure about, with a border or edge : but if a workeman will shew an eyght square Figure in Perſpectiue

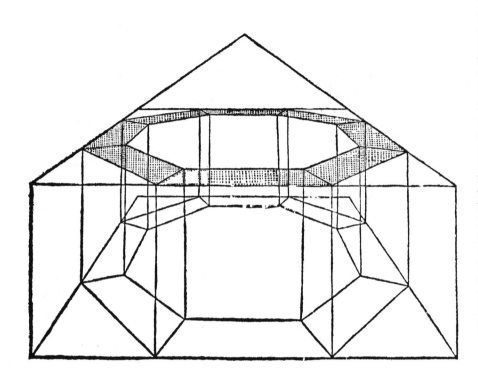

wiſe, as a Well; then he muſt firſt make the ground, as he is taught before, as high as hee will, that the ſayd Well ſhall ſtand eleuated aboue the ground or foote thereof: there hee muſt make the ſame forme once againe, drawing it to the ſame Horiſon; then from all the vppermoſt corners or points to the loweſt; you muſt drawe Perpendicular lines as well from the innermoſt figures, as from the vttermoſt, wherby the through cutting eyght ſquare bodies will be formed, as you may ſe in the Figure hereunto annexed.

I Haue ſpoken before of the open frame of a Well with eyght points or corners, which is neceſſary to be learned, how to make it, before you make the ſolide body thereof, as this figure ſheweth, which is the ſame that is before ſhewed, both forme and meaſure, but all the lines which cannot outwardly be ſéne, are hidden ; and there is as much difference betwéene an open body and a ſolide, as there is betwéne the modell of a mans body, that is nothing but bones without fleſh and ſkinne: and a liuing body of a man couered ouer with fleſh (although it is hidden vnder it.)

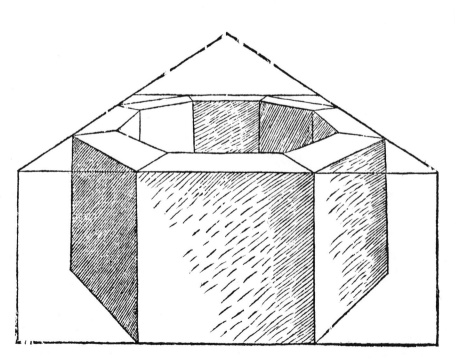

And as thoſe Paynters are much perfecter that haue ſéene, and perfectly beheld right Anatomies, then others that onely content themſelues with the outward bare ſhew of the Superficies, ſo it is with Perſpectiue workes ; for they that wel vnderſtand and perfectly beare in minde the hidden lines, they ſhall better vnderſtand the Arte then others, that content themſelues only with the ſhew of outward Superficies. It is very true that when a man hath ſufficiently experimented, practiſed and beareth in his mind theſe inward hidden lines, then helping himſelf with the principall, hee may make many perfect things, without vſing all this labour.

For these three figures following, euery one is drawne out of the fouresquare, in such manner as I haue taught before; and they goe all three to one Horison or poynt as they should do, or as need requireth; by the which figures any man may helpe himselfe in many things, as I haue further declared: and he that is perfect in these, may make all kinde of round formes, and without knowing of these, hee can doe little in round formes. For out of these figures you may draw a round Solide or Piramidall Building with Pillars, or without Pillars; and also a round winding paire of Stayers: for this Figure will shew you how to make the Stayers round, with other things more, and yet not without your owne industry: for the things that by these may be made are wonderfull and infinite, so that you waxe not weary, and spare no paynes till you are perfect in them, because that the bowing or Arches of gates and other things will seeme hard vnto you, as I will hereafter shew you; notwithstanding that they take their beginning altogether from these.

But if any man that desireth to learne this Arte, will at the first vnderstand these figures, as some bluntly will take vpon him to doe it. I beleeue certainely, he will bee put to an non plus, and deceaue himselfe; but if by learning all the former things, he proceedeth vnto these as well in Geometrie as in Perspectiue Arte: Then, I say, he is of a very grosse vnderstanding, if he cannot vnderstand or conceaue these figures, or the figures that hereafter follow.

These three figures, to speake trueth, are but Superficies; neuerthelesse, if you draw Perpendicular lines from all the terminations, as well within as without: then you shall haue a through cutting or open body, and the innermost lines couered, then they will be a Massy body: And wonder not, gentle Reader, nor let it be strange vnto you, though I doe sometimes make a long discourse of some things, for (as I sayd before) they are not only learned by many words and great paines, but it is also necessary that they were shewed vnto some men playnely by drawing them before them, that they may the better conceaue them.

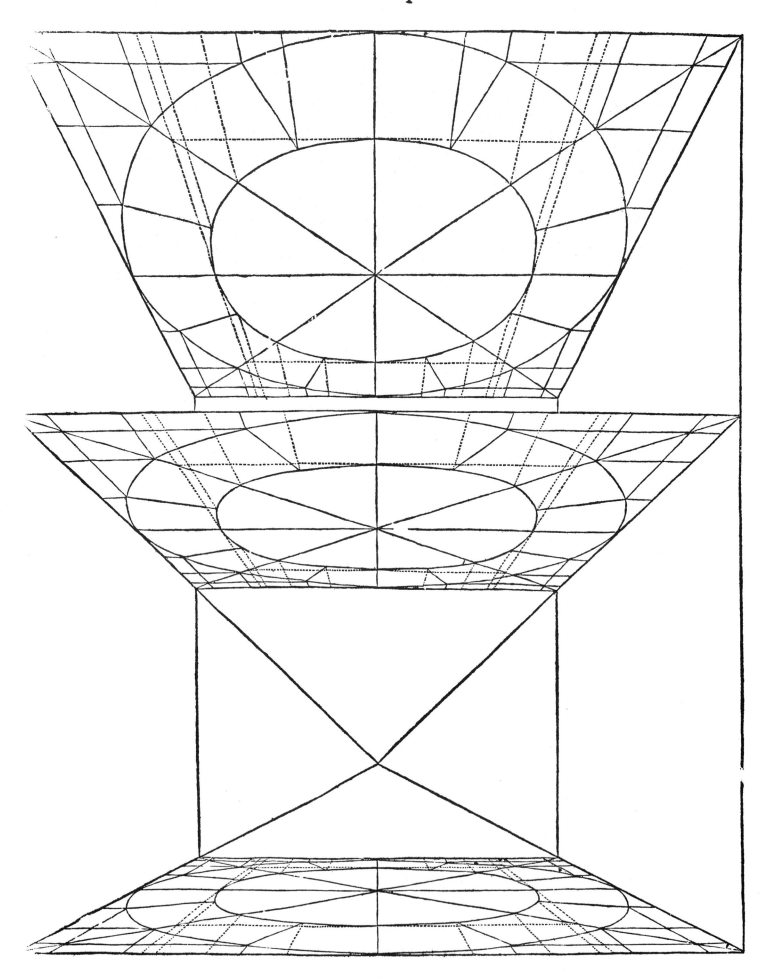

THE moſt part of great Riuers oz wa-
ter-falles that fall downe from high
Hils oz Mountains, by meanes of tem-
peſts with great fozce and power, when
they enter into a Valley, then ſometimes they
run out of their Channel, and ſo much groũd
as they then vſurpe vpon on the ene ſide, ſo
much they loſe againe on the other ſide; and ſo
doeth Perſpectiue wozke in cozncred things;
foz that as much as a man loſeth of the poynt
oz cozner whereon he looketh, ſo much greater the other point oz cozner ſheweth that
ſtandeth out, which is ſhewed in the Figures
hereunto anexed.

The Reader muſt then marke that the
ſquare in the middle ſigniſieth the thickeneſſe
of a foureſquare Columne oz Pillar, and the
bozder that is without and goeth about it,
ſigniſieth the thickneſſe oz bearing out of the
Baſes and the Capital. The Figure vnder
this platfozme is the Baſe, and the vppermoſt
Figure is the Capitall; the manner how to
ſhozten them I will ſhew you: Pou muſt
make the Pillar flat befoze without thicknes,
and vpon it you ſhall fozme the Baſes and
Capital, making the Pzoiecture oz bearing
out thereof on either ſide alike, but you muſt
dzaw them lightly as the pzickes herein ſet
downe doe ſhew you: then dzaw the ſide of
the Pillar which you will haue ſene towards
the Hoziſon; and hauing found how thicke
the decreaſing oz ſhoztening ſide muſt bee, by
the rules that are ſhewed in the firſt part of
Perſpectiue wozk, ſo you ſhal haue the ſhoztening ground of the Pillar, wherein you muſt
lightly dzawe the two Diagonall lines long
inough through, and from the Baſes below,
which is ſene in the ſhoztening; you muſt
dzaw a line towards the Hoziſon, which you
ſhall alſo let goe downe oz ſincke ſo farre, till
it reacheth beneath the Diagonall lines, and
there ſhall be the terminations of the ſhoztening Baſes: and thus you ſæ that the Per-
ſpectiuenes taketh ſomewhat off from them,
that is, the ſpace betwæne the poynts and the
full blacke line; then from the terminations
to the other vttermoſt poynt of the Baſes,
you muſt dzawe a Paralel line vnder the
ground of the Pillars, ſo long that it may
touch the Diagonal lines, and there you ſhall
finde that which is taken of from the Baſes
on the one ſide, and giuen to them on the o-
ther ſide, and the Pzoiecture of the Baſes
ſheweth, that the one poynt is dzowne inwards, and the other commeth further out,
then the vppermoſt line of the Baſes being
alſo to the Hoziſon: then vpon the ſhoztening
ſide by a line you finde the third parte of the
Baſes below, and that which is here ſpoken
of the Baſes, you muſt vnderſtand the ſame
alſo of the Capitals.

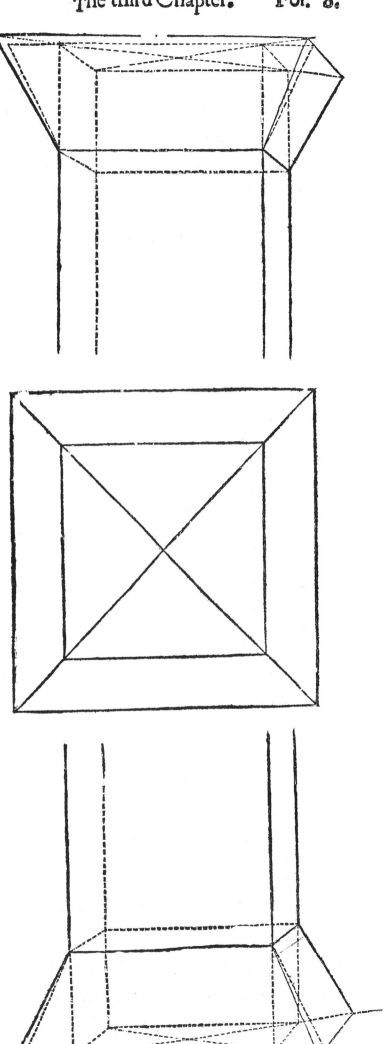

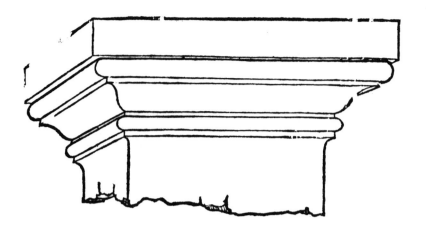

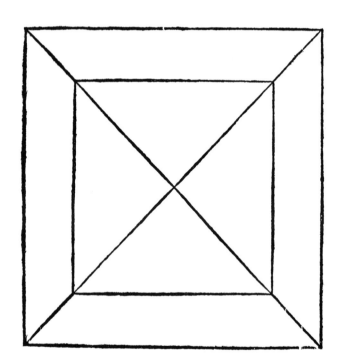

THE other three Figures are the same which are shewed before; the first were hollow, but these are perfect and solide with all their members, and although that in the Figures before I haue not shewed how you should forme and frame these members, which in trueth would be a very confused and troublesome thing to set downe in writing, therefore I haue only shewed the first terminations, that a man may keepe them well in his memory, and in these present Figures I haue shewed how they show in a mans sight, that you may see the effect that they worke: but from henceforward because (as I said before) it is a troublesome thing, I will make another forme of them with all their members by darke lines: and then (according to my abilitie) I will set downe the manner how to finde the terminations of the members one after another, for all of them grow a little one ouer, or more then the other.

But you must consider that these Bases and Capitals on the one side giue inward, and on the other side beareth out, which you must well remember, that you may first bee well instructed herein touching that which you will make. For it is true that the Theoricke consisteth in the vnderstanding; but experience is gotten by practise and right vse or handling: Therefore the most notable Paynter Leonardus Vinci, was neuer pleased nor satisfied with any thing that he made, bringing but litle worke to perfection, saying, the cause thereof was that his hand could not effect the vnderstanding of his mind: And for my part, if I should do as he did, I should not, neither would I suffer any of my workes to come forth: for (to say the truth) whatsoeuer I make or wryte, it pleaseth me not: but (as I sayd in the beginning of my worke) that I had rather exercise in worke that small talent, which it hath pleased God to bestow vpon me, then suffer it to lye and rot vnder the earth without any fruit; and although I shall not please thereby such as are curious, to set downe the ground and perfection of al things, yet at least I shall helpe yong beginners that know little or nothing thereof, which hath alwayes beene my intent.

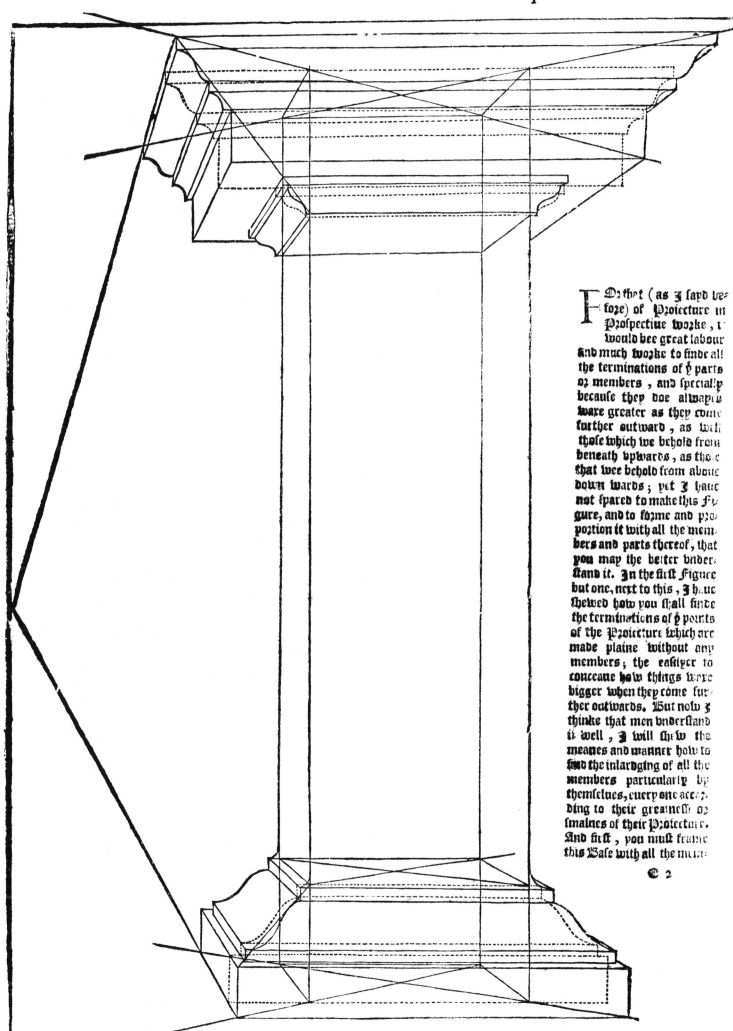

FD² that (as I sayd be-
foze) of Proiecture in
Prospectiue wozke, it
would bee great labour
and much wozke to finde all
the terminations of ý parts
oz members, and specially
becauſe they doe alwayes
ware greater as they come
further outward, as well
thoſe which we behold from
beneath vpwards, as thoſe
that wee behold from aboue
down wards; yet I haue
not ſpared to make this Figure, and to fozme and propoztion it with all the members and parts thereof, that
you may the better vnder-
ſtand it. In the firſt Figure
but one, next to this, I haue
ſhewed how you ſhall finde
the terminations of ý points
of the Proiecture which are
made plaine without any
members; the eaſiyer to
conceaue how things were
bigger when they come further outwards. But now I
thinke that men vnderſtand
it well, I will ſhew the
meanes and manner how to
find the inlarging of all the
members particularly by
themſelues, euery one accozding to their greatneſ oz
ſmalnes of their Proiecture.
And firſt, you muſt frame
this Baſe with all the mem-

       C 2

here, and with the right Proiecture thereof, to bee without any flattering before, yet you must draw it lightly with a piece of Lead, or some other thing, as it is shewed vnto you here with pricks; then in the ground or foot of the Pillar you must draw the two Diagonall lines long inough out, and thereby (as I sayd before) you shall find the diminishing and the increasing of the particuler parts of the creſts of the ſaid Baſe, whereas the vndermoſt line or foote of the creſts of the Baſe, beare much more broader and longer then thoſe that are marked with the prickes; then at each corner of the Creaſt of the Baſe you muſt draw an vpright line almoſt as high as the firſt creaſt of the Baſe (although I haue done it) but vpon the vttermoſt poynt not to comber the worke within: then you muſt draw the vppermoſt corners of the firſt Creaſt with prickes alſo, toward the Horiſon, which towarewards will touch againſt the two vpright lines; and there ſhall be the terminations to cloſe or ſhut vp the ſecond great Creaſt with a full blacke line: then draw another blacke line from the innermoſt poynt of the Creaſt vpwards to the Horiſon, and there the ſhortening Creaſt ſhall be cloſed.

And as this Creaſt or Plinthus is cloſed and drawen on all ſides with blacke lines, ſo you muſt doe with all the other lines of the Baſe, for when from the vppermoſt corner of the firſt marked Baſe you draw a helding line to the innermoſt corner of the greateſt Creaſt with the blacke lines, by it you ſhall lightly find the terminations of all the parts or members, drawing the corners of the firſt Baſe towards the Horiſon. And when you haue formed all the innermoſt corners of the Baſes, by the Horiſentall line you may eaſily doe the ſecond, and by the Paralel lines the vttermoſt of all; although by the lines of the diſtances, you may bring the ſaid corners ſomewhat neerer as you may ſee by the Diagonall lines. But at this time I will not ſpeake of that difficult or hard worke, for he that hath any vnderſtanding herein, may here with helpe himſelfe.

That which is here ſayd of the Baſes, you muſt alſo vnderſtand of the Cornices, onely that euery thing is contrary; and where you ſet Perpendicular lines below, which cut through the Horiſentall or Radiall lines, ſo you muſt alſo fall aboue the Lead lines or Catheten vpon the Horiſentall lines, as you may better ſee it and learne it in the Figure, then it can be expreſſed by words: and you muſt not be afraid or abaſhed, although at firſt you cannot conceaue it, for that by practiſing you ſhall in time finde it; for it is not ſayd that a man ſhall or can learne all things at once in one day: by this Cornice you may make all Cornices, bee they higher or lower, harder or eaſier, alwayes drawing euery member and part towards the Horiſon as it ſhould be done.

ALthough there are diuers manners & wayes to place Columnes one behind the other, ſtanding vpon one ground in Perſpectiue wiſe, thereby to make Portals, Galleries and other things, yet this hereunto annexed is the eaſieſt. Firſt, you muſt make a Pauement with a quantitie of foure cornerd Quadrants, as it is alſo ſhewed in the beginning of this Booke; which may be of ſuch breath, as you will: Say that theſe foure ſquare ſtones are two foote broad, which ſhall be the thickeneſſe of a Pillar: betweene the two firſt Pillars beneath in the breath, there ſhall be eyght ſquare ſtones, and the height of the Pillars made of what quantitie you will; and they being raiſed toward the Horiſon, then you muſt draw two ſeuerall lines ouer both the Pillars, and then out of the middle of the firſt line you muſt make two halfe Circles aboue vpon the flat ſide before, and deuide them in as many parts as you will; which parts ſhall be drawne to the Center of the halfe Circle, ſtanding in the vppermoſt line: then out of the middle of the two ſeuerall lines you muſt draw the leſſe halfe Circle, and all terminations of the flat Arch being drawne to the Horiſon, then the firſt Arch or Gate is made: the other two Pillars vpwards drawne to the Horiſon, then the firſt Arch or Gate is made: the other two Pillars vpwards ſhall alſo ſtand eyght Quadrants diſtant from the firſt Pillars, which will make a foure cornered place on all ſides: containing 64. ſquare ſtones: and you muſt doe with this gate as you did with the firſt, onely (when they are all of one wydeneſſe as theſe are) you need not deuide the Arches againe, for the Horiſentall lines of the ſtones of the firſt Arch will ſhew you the terminations of all the other Arches, and alſo how long the Gallery muſt be, and how many Arches it muſt containe. I haue placed no Arches here in the ſides, becauſe I would not cumber you too much at this time; but I will ſpeake thereof hereafter perticularly.

The two Dores on each ſide are both partly couered with the Pillars, but the wydeneſſe of them is of foure Quadrantes, beſides that from the corner of the dores to the Pillars on each ſide there is two Quadrantes, as you ſee the halfe thereof; and the other halfe you muſt ſuppoſe to bee behind the Pillars. The beames aboue the Arches which beare vp the Chamber aboue, you may well gueſſe, although I write not particularly thereof: I haue not likewiſe ſet the Baſes nor the Capitals vpon theſe Pillars, becauſe they ſhould not darken them too much; but in another place I will alſo entreat thereof.

Heſe two Bowes or Arches are onely made to know how to ioyne their Baſes and Capitals to them, whereof in two ſeuerall places I haue ſpoken before, and ſhewed how they riſe on the one ſide, and fall or decreaſe in ſight on the other ſide; that a man may the better learne how to doe them : for in trueth, if a man could ſhew it vnto you in effect, you would the eaſyer vnderſtand it ; but to ſet it downe in writing or Figures as I doe, that men heereafter might know and learne them : it is requiſite to entreat of them more at large, and that you may the better diſcerne and perceiue the poynts of the thin lines from the other poynts or corners of the blacke lines ; therefore here I haue placed the poynt of the diſtances and the Horiſon downeward ; and haue placed the Pillars in other manner vpon this ground without Quadrant ſtones : In this manner ſet the bredth of the two firſt Pillars vpon the Baſe of ſuch thickeneſſe as you will, and draw them inwards, towards the Horiſon, then you muſt imagine the diſtances, as I haue already taught you : and theſe diſtances are ſet on both ſides, and on eyther point of the diſtances you muſt draw a line both toward the right and left poynt or corner of each Pillar.

Theſe Diagonall lines will not onely ſhew you the thickeneſſe of the firſt or formoſt Pillars when they ſhorten, but alſo the thickeneſſe of the two other Pillars which ſtand inward, which are all marked with prickes (and as I haue likewiſe ſaid before) that which is here ſayd of the Baſes of the Pillars, the ſame alſo muſt be vnderſtood vpward of the Capitals : touching the thickeneſſe of the bowes or Arches vnderneath, I haue ſhewed in the Figure before, how you muſt place the Center in the middle of the foure croſſe point lines, to draw the halfe Circumference : The foure ſquare or Quadrant aboue, is as great as that below on the ground ; I need not ſhew how you ſhall make it, for you ſee it plaine enough in the Figure.

This Figure is like the former, onely that the members of the Bases and Capitals are added thereunto ; thereby to make it more perfect vnto you, and to shew you how a thing will stand when it is full made and finished , although I haue shewed it before ; neuerthelesse, when a man is perfect herein, then he may by practise helpe himselfe well inough without all this labour, vsing discretion and bearing in memorie that, which he hath imprinted in his mind : For in trueth, by this meanes (I meane the ground) a man may by practise make many things ; which if they be made with discretion, and by a workeman, will alwayes beautifie the worke, as these bowes or Arches do, which vnder are deuided with Quadrantes as you may see them.   There are, as you know, first two Centers to forme the Arche vnderneath ; now a wise workeman must not alwayes seeke for the perfection of the edge of these Quadrants ; but for example, Say that the Arche vnderneath is deuided into eyght parts, whereof sire shall be for the Quadrant, and two parts for the edge or border that runneth about it : now you must deuide the space betweene the one Center and the other, also in eyght parts, but they must shorten or lessen a little, that is, the neather part against the vpper ; & then the compasse being set somewhat lower, and made narrower : then you must draw the vppermost border, and then the compasse being set a little below the neathermost Center ; you must in like sort drawe the other edge or border : after, you must square or deuide the Quadrants, leauing the space betweene both, once so broad againe as the other, which must be drawen vp towards the Horison ; and as much as you will make the Quadrant sinke : you must also draw out of the last Center with the Compasse.   And in this manner a man may make diuers formes and compartements (but as I haue said) you must make them all with iudgement, and therefore it is very conuenient that a man should be well instructed therein ; for that vsing onely the principall terminations, you must make the rest by practise : But I am of opinion, that some rigorous Perspectiue men will take hold of these my words, (to whom I answere) that if they meane I haue failed or done amisse, let them proue what difference there is betweene saying and doing.

The manner how to make a croſſe roofe of a Gallery or Houſe in Perſpectiue worke, is alwayes very troubleſome to ſhew it vnto any man; and therefore alſo, it is muchmore troubleſome to declare it in writing for men
hereafter to vnderſtand it. Neuertheleſſe, becauſe it is very neceſſary to be knowne, I will doe the beſt I can
to ſhew it.

First, you muſt chuſe the breadth and height of the greateſt Arch or Bow that you deſire to make, and then by the diſtances you muſt make a perfect ſhortening Quadrant, and alſo a leſſe Bow or Arch. The greateſt Arch before ſhalbe
deuided into eyght equall parts, and theſe parts muſt be drawne towards the Horiſon to the ſmale Arch, which being
done, then you muſt ſet thoſe parts of the greateſt Arche below vpon the Baſe; and with the helpe of the Horiſontall
and Diagonall lines, you may make a ſhortening Circle within the Quadrant, as in the other places before you haue
bene taught. The terminations hereof ſhall be 1.2.3.4.5. which ſhall be ſet vpwards beſide the great Arche, as you
ſee it there alſo marked with 1.2.3.4.5 Without this round below I haue drawne the Paralels with prickes to the
wall, and where they end, there you muſt ſet all your Perpendicular lines vpright, which are come out of the Paralel
lines of this Circle.

Then you muſt draw the terminations aforeſayd, which are placed aboue, along by the Perpendicular lines with
lines to the Horiſon; and where the ſayd Horiſontall lines cut through the Perpendicular lines, which are drawne vp
from below; there you muſt make halfe a ſhortening Circle: and that which is marked on this ſide with Ciphers, muſt
alſo be vnderſtood to ſtand on the other, as you ſee it in the Figure.

Theſe two halfe ſhortning Circles being made, then you muſt draw a right blacke line aboue out of each of the
middles, which are marked 5. and where that cutteth through the middlemoſt line, which goeth from the greateſt
Arch to the Horiſon, there ſhalbe the terminations & alſo the middle of the croſſe worke; and then out of all the terminations of the two halfe Circles, you muſt draw croſſe lines on the ſides, and where euery one of them following an Horiſ-
ſentall, toucheth the Arch marked with 2.3.4. there the terminations ſhal ſtand to forme the halfe Circles in the croſſe,
through the which a man with a ſtedfaſt hand from termination to termination ſhall make a ſhortening halfe rounde
croſſe with prickes, as both on the right and left hand you may plainely ſee in the Figure. In this manner the worke
ſhould goe, although it ſtood ſomewhat out at the ſides; but it is better firſt to print it well in your memory, before you
ſeeke another forme where the Horiſon ſtandeth on the one ſide, that then you may the eaſilyer make that which is
ſeene on that ſide.

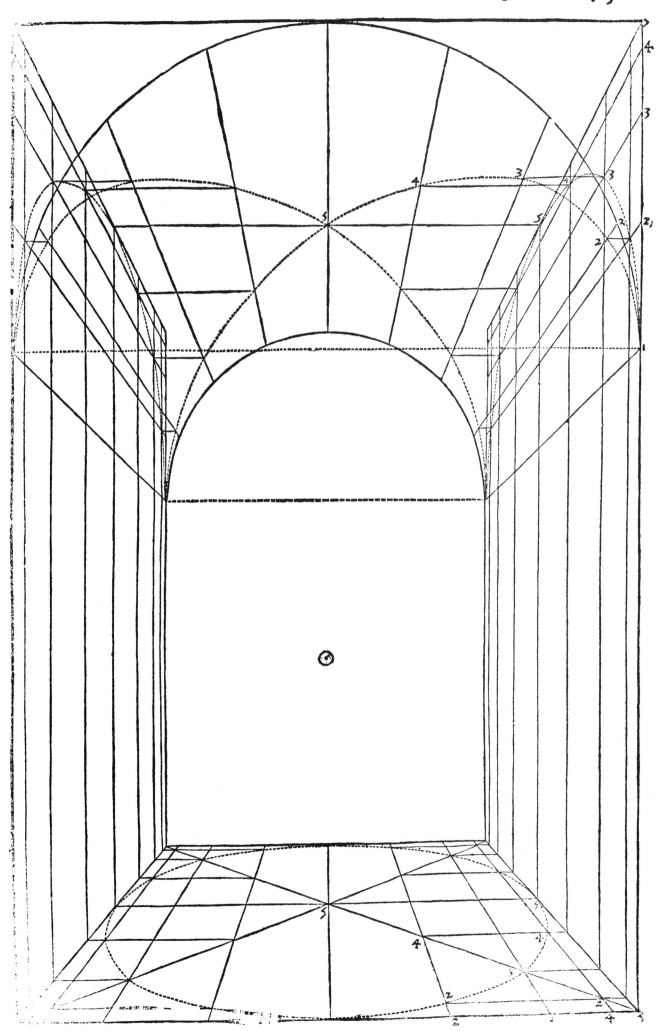

Auing shewed in crossewozke on both sides, how you should place the Arches on the sides in shoztening manner and dzawne them vp out of the ground, although that they be single: now will I shew you a holle to Arche, and the maner how to shozten it: But befoze I pzoceed thereunto (foz it is very combersome and difficult) first I wil shew you the Pilaisters that should carrie the sayd Arches: which Pilaisters stand so plainely in the Figure that I shall not need to take much paines to wzyte of them. In this Figure I haue not made the first Arch, that I might not darken the sight of the Arches on the sides, which Arches on the sides, I haue also but marked how they shall stand, and are alwayes dzawne out of the fouresquare Quadzant, as you see by the ozder of the foure square Quadzant, but the hindermost Arch which standeth not in the way, I haue dzawne fully, and placed it also in his foure square.

Aboue in the top oz roofe, I haue made the round fozme, whereof you may make a Kettel oz Tribunall; and you may also make it thus, when it is somewhat soncke. Touching the foure Pilaisters, they (as I haue taught befoze) are found by the Diagonall lines comming from the poynt of the distances, and also that each Pilaister is thzee coznerd: standing like a thzee coznerd hooke, and on each end (the Arch resteth whereof there shall be foure) two Arches befoze, and two on the sides, so that the roofe will be right foure square, wherein you may make crosse wozke oz other manner of Roofe wozke. And if you will make other kindes of wozks by the same; you must alwayes follow this rule: Item, where you can not well vnderstand my wzitíng, you must helpe your selfe with the figures, which figure also standeth open, so that with a little labour; a man may easily conceaue it altogether, although there were nothing spoken of it.

NOw you ſée, what way you muſt follow to place Arches on the ſides in ſhoꝛtening manner: And firſt, you muſt thinke vpon the third foꝛmer manner Superficies, wherein I haue ſufficiently ſhewed you the manner how to frame a round body; but in this Figure I wi'l ſhew it moꝛe perfectly. Wherefoꝛe a man muſt imagine that the round Body lying below in his foureſquare is made, and ſhall ſerue foꝛ the two Bowes on the ſides. This Body then being made (as I haue ſhewed befoꝛe) and as you ſée it better now, you muſt firſt ſet it, where the Arches begin aboue the Hoꝛiſon. And the ſame Perpendicular lines which ſtand coꝛner wiſe from the middle of the foure coꝛnerd body, muſt be ſet like Paralel lines on the right & left ſides vpwards from the two Arches, there (at it is afoꝛeſaid) to direct the Hoꝛiſentall lines, as you may ſée it plainely in the Figure. But you muſt vnderſtand, that the two croſſes below in this Body, are the two Centers to dꝛaw the ſtones of the Arches both aboue and below, they alſo ſignifie the Centers of the Bowes vpon the Hoꝛiſentall lines within the Arches.

You muſt alſo vnderſtand, that the blacke lines doe foꝛme the Circumference without, and the pꝛickes oꝛ thin lines betoken the foꝛme within; which is couered in the Arches: ſo that the Arches do ſhew thꝛough to be made of pieces, of the which pieces a man may learne to make diuers Compartements vnderneath in the Arch. Now when a man can make this Arch well, then hee ſhall not néede ſtill to take all this labour, but by two pꝛincipall lines helping himſelfe with pꝛicks, he may frame the Arch; and ſpecially, becauſe that the Arch which ſhould come befoꝛe, coucreth oꝛ hideth a great part of the Arches on both ſides: which Arch I haue not made here, that I might not darken oꝛ ſhadow the other ſhoꝛtening Arch. Neither néed I wꝛyte any thing of the Circumferences aboue in the top oꝛ Roofe, (noꝛ the eyght coꝛners within) foꝛ that in the next Figure you ſhall ſée them; neither will I ſpeake any thing of the Circumferences in the ground, foꝛ they are made (as I haue taught you heretofoꝛe of all others) and of the round body below (of the which there ha'h béene moꝛe ſayd) a man may make many other things which are not here to be ſpoken of.

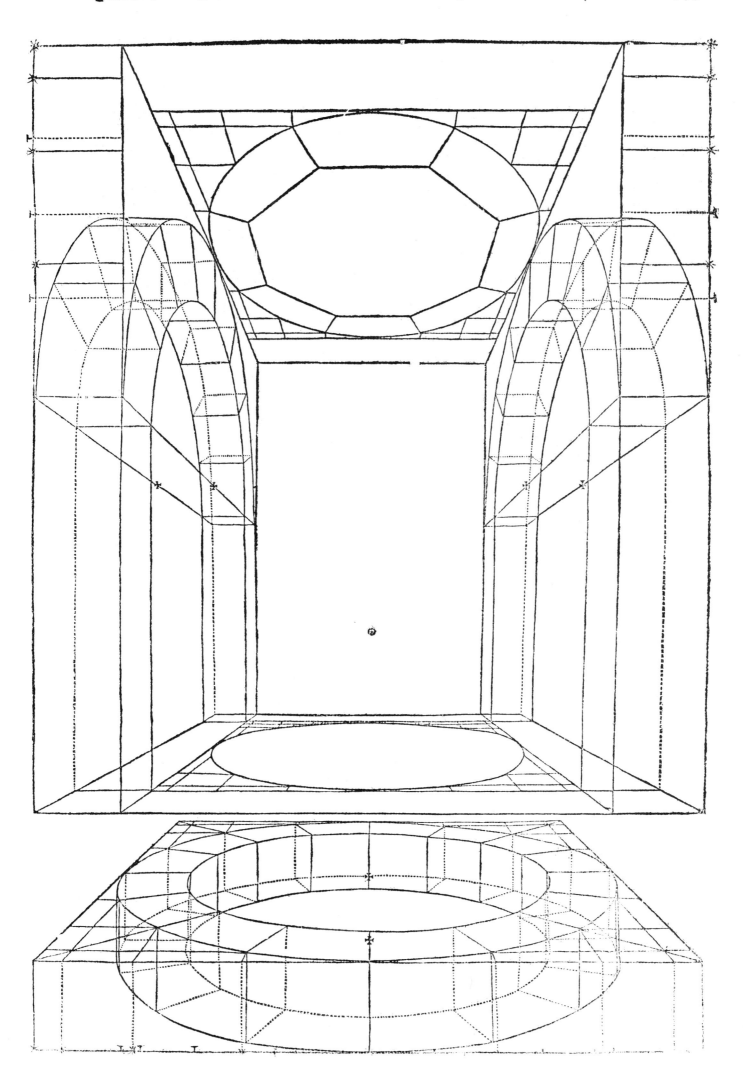

Of Perſpectiue

To place Pillars with their Arches vpon grounds or platformes, I thinke there is ſufficient ſpoken before; and what ſoeuer I haue ſpoken of foure ſquare Pillars, is alſo to bee vnderſtood of round Columnes, for that a man muſt take all round things, out of foure ſquare things as well the Spira of the Baſe, as the round of the Capital.

He that can make all the Figures aforeſayd perfectly, and particularly this laſt body, ſhall helpe himſelfe well, and not onely to doe the like things, but alſo to do many more. If I ſhould in this ſmall Treatiſe ſhew all that I could ſet downe, it would make a moſt great Volumne; and peraduenture I ſhould want time to ſet foorth the reſt of my Booke, which I haue already promiſed: for there are many things that belong to Building, which need not to bee ſet downe in Perſpectiue worke.

Let vs now begin to rayſe the Building here ſet downe out of the ground, which before, and at the one ſide is ſeene, as I promiſed before to ſhew you.

The ſhorteſt and ſureſt way is, to make a ground with many Quadrants; and imagine that it is mete with the Foot, with the Elle, or other meaſure: But let vs now take euery Quadrant for two foot, and as before there are foure Quadrants from one Pillar to the other; and the Pillar alſo containeth a Quadran, there ſhall alſo be foure Quadrants vpward in the length from one Pillar to the other, as you may ſee it altogether in the Figure.

The Pillars then being ſet of ſuch height as you deſire, then the Arches vpon them muſt be made; and the manner how to make them, you may expreſly ſee in the Figure. And although you cannot ſee the Arches that are behind them, yet I haue made them here that you may ſee their terminations: they are in ſome places drawne with full blacke lines, and in ſome places with prickes.

Aboue the Arches you muſt make the Architraue, Friſe and Cornice; the Proiecture whereof, you muſt make as I haue ſayd and taught heretofore, that is, how they make their corners againſt the two Diagonall lines, and by the like rule you ſhall alſo make the vppermoſt Cornice, as you may ſee in the vppermoſt part, where the ſmall Quadrant with the Diagonall lines ſtand. The doores that ſtand vnder in the Gallery, are each of them two Quadrants broad, and foure Quadrants high: below in the ground there are certaine tokens which ſhew like Nayles, which ſignifie the wydeneſſe of the windowes aboue the Cornice: which windowes if they ſtood whole there, then they would be twice as high as they are broad. The other Nayles vpwards betweene the ſhortening Pillars, are alſo the breath of the ſhortening Pillars, which (as I ſayd before) are all foure Quadrants high, but they are partly couered with the Cornices. The part of the Arch which ſtandeth at the ende, is ſeparated from this Gallery, as the ground alſo ſheweth it.

I haue here made no Baſes nor Capitals, that the other things might not bee confounded: but you muſt vnderſtand that they muſt be placed in the worke, as is ſufficiently before ſhewed. And by this rule you may draw diuers Buildings out of the ground, as in the Figure following ſhall be ſhewed in diuers formes. The Centers of the Arches you ſee them marked, ſtanding all vpon one Horiſentall line.

NOw I haue ſhewed the manner how to make a Gallery with Arches and Pillars, with other things thereunto belonging; now by an eaſier way I will ſhew ſome forme of Houſes that are to be built out of the ground. You muſt make a ground or foote worke with Quadrants reaching long inough vpwards, which Quadrants muſt each of them be reckoned at two foote ſquare.

And firſt, at the entry of the Houſe there ſhall be a doore of fiue foote broad, for that it containeth two Quadrants and a halfe in the ſhortening : and the hight thereof ſhall be of ten foote, becauſe it is fiue Quadrants high : Her Pilaiſters or Antipagmentum ſhall bee a foote broad, becauſe they containe a halfe ſhortening Quadrant; the Friſe ſhall alſo containe as much : and the Cornice ſhall containe ſo much leſſe, as the vnder part thereof bearing ouer containeth, and ſhall be made according to the rule aforeſhewed. Touching the part ietting ouer the doore, the Mogdiliones or Mutiles, ſhal ſtand right aboue the Pilaiſters or Antipagmentum of the doore. And that litle doore vpon the ietting, ſhall ſtand right in the middle aboue the loweſt doore, and ſhall be two foote broad. In the other corner of this firſt Houſe, there ſhall be another doore, the wideneſſe thereof ſhall be fire foote; you may make it round or ſquare aboue as you wil. But why doe I ſpend my time to ſet downe all theſe meaſures, which you may ſo plainely ſee in the Figure ; onely it is neceſſary to warne ſuch as are ſtudious herein, that what worke ſoeuer a man rayſeth out of the ground, conſiſteth in three principall things, that is, in length, breoth and height. The length is of certaine Houſes or Rowmes, containing a certaine number of feet. The breoth conſiſteth of Windowes, Doores, Gates, Shoppes, and ſuch like things. The height conſiſteth of Portes, Windowes, Iettings, Cornices, Columnes, Rooffes, and ſuch like things. But there is yet another, that is of the thickeneſſe of the Walles, Pillars, Columnes and Pilaiſters : The length is taken from the ſhortening Quadrants, and from thence alſo you take the breoth. But the height is taken out of the breoth in the Quadrants, which breoth muſt be taken from the Quadran or halfe Quadran, which toucheth it on the hithermoſt ſide as it ſtandeth : as alſo from the hithermoſt doore, which is ten foote high, there you muſt take the meaſure from the Quadrans, which come to the Paralels on the nethermoſt corner or poynt of the doore ; for if there you take fiue Quadrans in breoth, it ſhall be height within the Antipagementum. And that which I haue ſayd of theſe doores, you muſt alſo vnderſtand of all the other things : The thickeneſſe of the Wall is two foote, for you ſee it containeth a Quadrant. The bearing ouer of the ſecond Houſe is of fire foote, meaſured vpon the ground : the like alſo the bearing ouer or ietting of the firſt Houſe containeth. To conclude all things, as I haue ſaid, riſing out of the ground on all ſides, I haue ſet no Cornices, nor any other ornaments in this Figure, that you may the eaſier vnderſtand it ; but a man of ripe iudgement and vnderſtanding knowing the terminations, can by his owne inuention helpe himſelfe to make faire Buildings. And for that I may not ſpend too much time herein, I will make others to giue you more light therein.

Of Perspectiue

THE Stayres, degrées or goings vp, are very necessary in Buildings, and therefore I will shew diuers kinds thereof, and first I will begin with the easiest. According to common custome a Stayre or step is about halfe a foote high, and about a foote broad vpon the step ; then let the square stones of this ground be a foote square, therewith we will make a paire of staires of fiue foote high, and thrée foote broad : at the foote of the ground wee will take the measure of the bredth, which both on the right and left sides shall be set in Perpendicular lines on the Corners of the Stayres, which shall be deuided into ten, as the lines A. B. shew you. Then all the parts of A. B. shall be raised to the Horison, and then you shall take nine Quadrantes vpwards in length : and where as two lines are set vp cutting through the Horisentall lines of A. B. there the corners D. C. of the vppermost steps shalbe, containing a foure square of thrée Quadrants on each side. From the hithermost points of the same vpper steps, you shal draw two helding lines to the lowest steps ; against the which the Horisentall and the Perpendicular lines of the Quadran shall come together and shut vp the Stayres.

These Stayres are shortened on the one side, and the other is plaine or profil, and containeth a step lesse in the height, which maketh foure foote and a halfe ; it is also thrée foote broat, as it is marked vnder it on the ground. By this rule you may make Stayres or degrées as high as you will, and make some resting places in the way: alwayes taking the measure from the foote of the ground, as well of the shortening, as of those that are vpright.

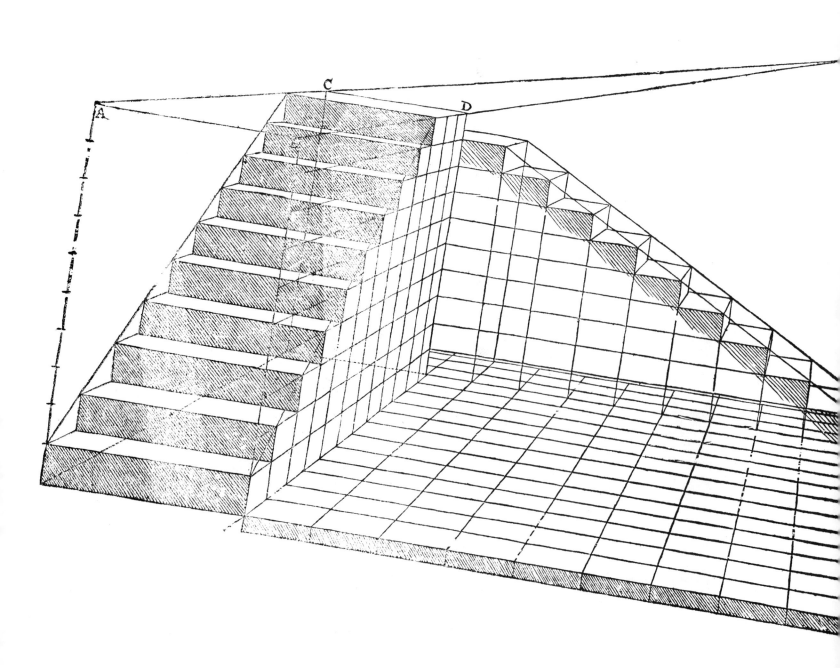

THE going vp being plaine or profil maketh a great show, and yet are very easie to set in all places, I meane in the turning, and may serue for many things, specially in Buildings, where a man going vp softly and with ease, giueth the beholders a kind of pleasure to view them, principally in common places, for that there is a going vp on eyther side, so that vpon the one side men may goe vp, and on the other side they may goe downe; and although there are only but two goings vp, yet by this a man by his own inuention may deuise others. How these Stayres are made, and with what reason, you may by the Figure perceaue them, although I should say nothing thereof: for as it is sayd before, the Quadrants are of a foote broad, and the steps halfe a foot high, and so the bredth of the step is one foot. The bredth of the Stayres is fiue foote, both the first and second: The resting gate contayneth in widenesse three foote, and is sixe foote high; which although it seemeth to be shut, and a small doore opening in it: yet it may be made whole open and otherwise closed. The two sides aboue the three steps are fiue foote broad, although here it is but one foote, because of the narrownesse of the Paper. The Perpendicular lines on the sides, signifie leaning places, and they should serue well also to the steps, but lest they should comber the worke, I haue left them out.

K

Of Perſpectiue

A Mongſt other things which ſhow well in Perſpectiue worke, I finde that goings vp or ſteps are very ſeemely, and the oftner that they turne, the better they ſhew ; therefore I haue made theſe two goings vp turning, which ſtand in profil, yet you ſee the ground and the ſteps. This firſt going vp is ſixe foote high and three foote broad, as you may ſee it marked in the ground with pricks : the reſting place betweene the firſt and ſecond going vp, is two foure ſquares long, which is neceſſary, becauſe of the turning. At the end thereof you firſt a Portale, the dore thereof is two foote wyde, the Antipagmentum is halfe a foote on eyther ſide, ſo that the place is three foote full. The Perpendicular lines on the right ſide of the plaine, ſignifie certaine leanings, which may bee made of Iron, Wood, or Stone ; the like may be made along the Stayres both vpward and downeward, ſetting a Baluſter vpon euery Stayre : The height of this raile or leaning, ſhall be two foote and an halfe ; for ſo it is eaſie to lay a mans hand vpon. How theſe Stayres are made vpwards out of the ground, although it may well be ſeene by the Figure without declaring it : yet I will ſay ſome thing thereof, to eaſe them that are ſhort of memory. The reſting gate or round dore vnder the plainneſſe betweene the ſecond and the third going vp, is no deeper then to the wall : Aboue the ſame dore there ſtandeth another going vp, of foure ſteps, which to make, I haue ſufficiently ſhewed ; otherwiſe a man ſhould continue the ground at the reſting dore, to draw them vp from it.

Touching the feuerall kinds of Stayres, I am affured that they may partly be vnderftood without defcribing them in wryting, and fpecially the middlemoft which goeth vp on both fides; and fo fhall the vppermoft alfo, becaufe it is rayfed vp from the ground as well as the other, and is fire foot broad, as you may fee and tell it on the ground vpon the plaine ftones.　The two Arches vnder the two goings vp are each a foot in thickeneffe, whereby a going downe is foure feote within, and is alfo drawne out of the ground as the reft are.　The other goings vp, which you fee through the Arches; you may fufficiently perceiue by them how they are made: and fo it is with the two paire of Stayres on the left hand, for from the firft fteps at the refting doore, you may eafily fee how they are rayfed vpout of the ground, and aboue at the end of them they haue a piece of plaine ground to come to the other Stayres, which alfo is drawne vp out of the pauement as the reft are, that is, each ftep halfe a foote high, and a foote broad.　But it is hard to meafure in fo small things, but it fuffifeth that hereby you may fee the manner thereof: and when you make them great you fhall find that they will come well inough to paffe.　Vnder the Stayres laft named, there ftandeth alfo a round doore which is fiue foot wyde: vpon this ground, and on thefe Stayres a cunning Paynter might place diuers Figures in feuerall formes, eyther ftanding or fitting vpon the Stayres; and lying vpon the ground in fhortening manner, and that in this wife: You may place the Figures where you will with foete, and then take fire feete or fquares whereon they ftand, and that fhal be their height, for that it is the height of a common or ordinary man: this you muft obferue both before and behind, and in euery place.　If the Figure be vpon a ftep, then take the meafure of that ftep whereon it ftandeth, and make it twelue fteps high, which fhall be fire foote: And is the Figure lying, doe the like; but if it lieth in fhortening manner vpon the ground, then you muft take the length by the fhortening Quadrant.

I Haue shewed many kinds of goings vp, but there are other kinds, and he that is not well instructed in the former will hardly vnderstand these two which I haue here set downe. The first shall be winding Stayres in foure square, and he that can make these foure square Stayres, may well make the round Stayres, for it is all one thing, specially if he vseth the rule before set downe of the round bodies.

The Figure P. is the ground of this winding Stayre, but it is much lesse then the vppermost to get ground. This foure square ground in shortening you must make halfe a foote high, which shalbe for the first step. Then before at either end, you must make a Perpendicular line vpright, and in it make as many halfe feete as you desire to make the Stayres high; you must also place the like Perpendicular lines betwéene the middle, & the corners : then you must draw the terminations both on the right and the left sides vpwards to the Horison, which must cut through the Perpendicular lines, which are drawne out of the terminations of the steps; and of the same height that the two cornerd Perpendicular lines are : and of the same measure you must make the other two Perpendicular lines betwéene the corners and the middle. Then in the middlemost termination of the ground you must place an other Perpendicular line, and deuide it also in halfe féet, as the other Perpendicular line on the side is : So out of this Perpendicular line of the Centers against the néerest Perpendicular line beneath on the left hand, you must frame the first step with two lines : The second step you shal also frame and shut vp out of the Perpendicular line of the Centers in the corner following. Then from that poynt or corner you must draw a line to the Horison, which against the second Perpendicular line will make the termination of the third step, which shall also bee shut aboue, according to the aforesaid rule : from that poynt or corner of the step you must also make an Horisental line, which will touch the termination of the fourth step; which being closed, then you must raise that corner also to the Horison, and that will shew you the termination of the fift step. And when that step is also closed with lines : then you must draw the poynt towards the Horison, which line will shew you the terminations of the sixt step against the hindermost Perpendicular line : and that being also closed vp with lines, then out of the same corner you must draw a Pararel line to the termination of the seuenth step, and not towards the Horison, because it is another side of the foure square. Thus you must worke round about from step to step, alwayes following this rule by the which you cannot faile.

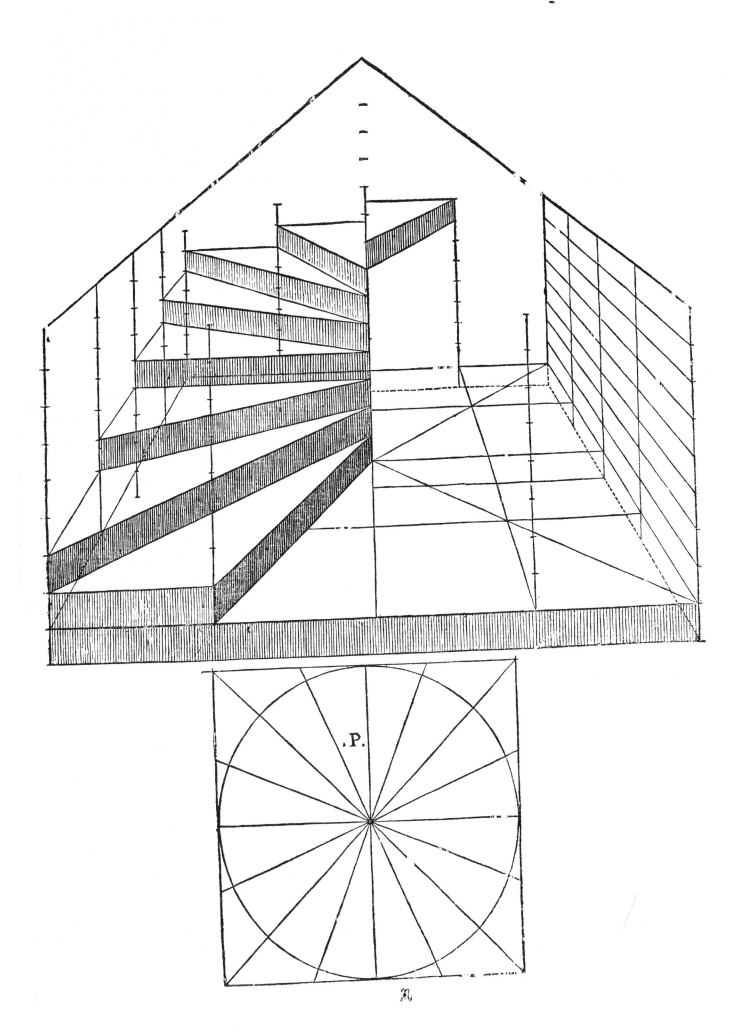

Of Perspectiue

That I may not forget to set down all kinds of Stayres, and specially such as often times fall out to be made; therefore I haue made these Stayres, whereon a man may goe vp on all sides, whereof the ground standeth aboue on the right hand, but yet very small. These Stayres must thus bee made. First, you must make a foure square shortening body of halfe a foot high, vpon this you must draw two Diagonall lines, and from the corner inwards there shall be a foote broad left on eyther side, and the terminations thereof drawne to the Horison, and so from the Diagonall lines you shall see the corners of the second step. Now I need not set downe vnto you how you shall finde the lessening corner of the second step, the which is round about shut vp with Paralel and Horisentall lines: then vpon the second plaine you must draw two Diagonall lines, which doing as I sayd before) will shew you the third step; which also being closed vp with lines, you shall also find the fourth and fifth, with the like rules: This Piramides is fantastically framed vpon them to fill vp the place. Also I need not set down to what vses these Stayres may serue, for th t the halfe of them is commonly found in diuers pieces of worke, as the gates of Pallaces, Churches, and other dwelling Houses, and the ascending vp to Altars: By this way also you may make round Stayres, and also Stayres of sixe or eyght corners, as by their formes I haue shewed.

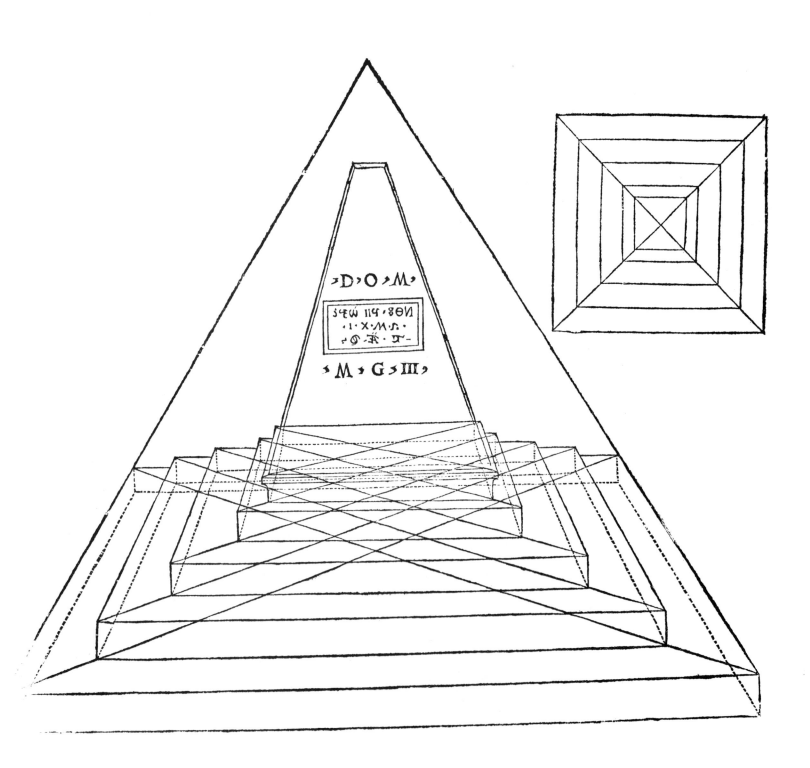

I Haue promised the studious Reader by this my labour to shew as much touching Perspectiue worke, as I can; that hee might shew his conceit touching Houses or Buildings in Perspectiue wise, meaning to set downe some simple manners thereof, as if he should forme a single or double ground, thereupon to rayse a body, and therewith means to make an end. But falling from one worke to another, I am entred into a Laborinth; which peraduenture is too farre aboue my reach: which commeth to passe by meanes of some men that haue entreated me thereunto. And therefore, as I thought at this time to make an end of my second Booke, I begin to handle a harder matter, which rule is onely called an outward foure square: neuerthelesse, it is aswell drawne by the Horison as by the distances, as you may see in the Figure following; which sheweth a right shortening foure square, containing in it another foure square, the which also may bee formed by the distances without Horison: some men place the sides of the foure square vpon the Base, once so wyde againe as before. And as you see two like sides of the foure square ouer the corner, so are the distances alike marked D. And as much more as you will haue this foure square to shorten, so much you must draw the distances from the Horison; and as much as you will that the edges of the foure square shall be broad, so many bredths must you draw vpon the Base, betweene A. C. twice drawne. All the terminations of this foure square standing aboue the corners goe all to the distances, and none to the Horison, but onely the foure square that is set therein.

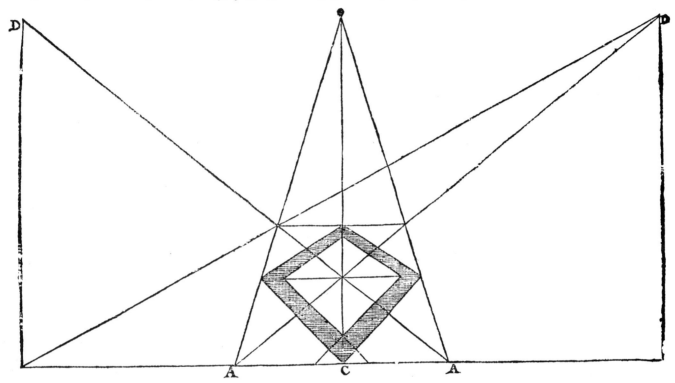

Now I haue shewed, how you should shorten a Superficies, ouerpoynt or outward foure square: here I will shew how to imbosse or beare out the body thereof with the same Horison and distances also, which body within is hollow, and you may heaue it vp as high as you: but I haue purposely left it somewhat low, that you might see the ground thereof. And by this Figure you may conceaue to how many things this may serue; and also how you may increase or diminish it, according to skil and iudgement. This shall suffice for these foure square models or hollow things: but I will shew how you shall make them w Crests or Cornices

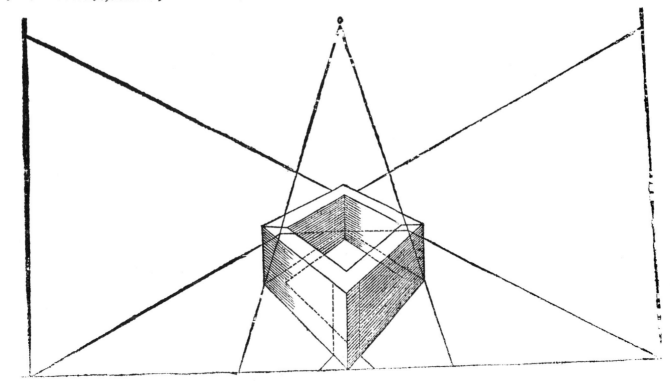

This Figure is also formed by the aforesayd Horison, and the like distances as the other before, onely that they stand a little neerer: Now to creast this body both aboue & beneath, you must imagine the greatnes of the creast, and draw the same greatnesse both aboue and beneath the body; then giue the Creasts aboue their due Proiecture, and from those poynts you must let Perpendicular lines fall to the poynts or corners below, whereby you shal haue the Proiectiues of the Base and top thereof, which must be drawne towards the Distances, and not towards the Horison. Now you see how the Cornices stand without the foure square body: but this is only for Cornices that are made without members, not to comber you with the shadowing of them, for I will speake of them hereafter particulerly.

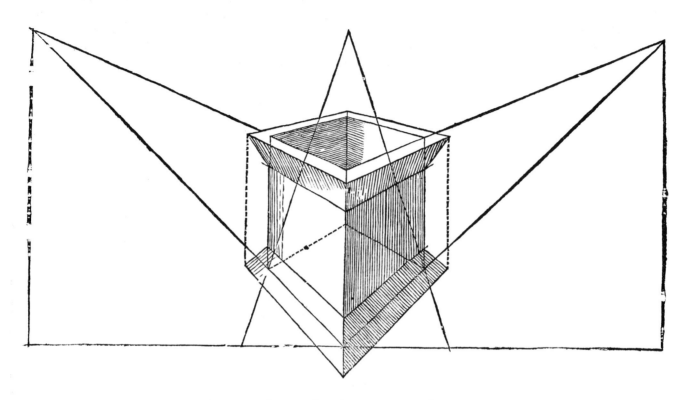

I spake before of Cornices without members, which might serue this hollow Quadran, and how you shall make the terminations thereof. Now in this Figure I show you the sayd Cornices with their members, which you may also make in other maner as it pleaseth the workeman, that is, to make them bigger or lesser, as I haue spoken of other Cornices, alwayes vsing good discretion and iudgement to chuse and make such members therein, as may show well in mens sight. There are some Cornices which reach so farre ouer, that men can not see the members thereof vnder them; therefore in that case the members are so to be made, that they may be seemely and pleasant in mens sight.

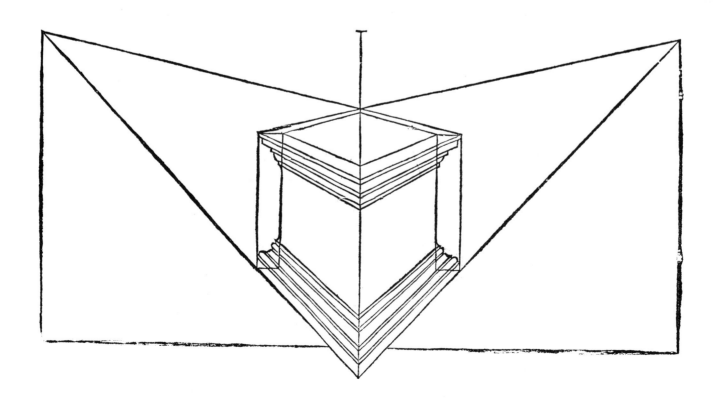

The foure Figures aforesayd haue their distances equally broad from the Horizon, that is, as much on the one side as the other; but the Figure following is of another maner, so that the Horizontal lines serue both for distances. To vnderstand it, begin thus: First, the Base A. B. is deuided in foure equall parts, as C. D. E. the lines C. D. are drawne on the right hand towards the Horizon, and the lines A. C. are drawne towards the Horizon on the left side, which forme a perfect shape, namely, a square, and this figure you see more on the one side, then on the other. The foure points or corners of these foure square things, are F. G. H. C. If you deuide these foure square things in two parts, then you must deuide the Base D. E. in two parts, and the termination thereof being drawne to the right side, there you shall finde the halfe of your foure square marked with two Stars. But if you will lengthen it an other halfe foure square, then draw a termination E. to the right Horizon, the lines at I. K. the other halfe foure square, so that these Superficies shall be of two perfect foure corners: And this will serue the ingenious workeman for many things, which I will not here set downe for breuitie sake.

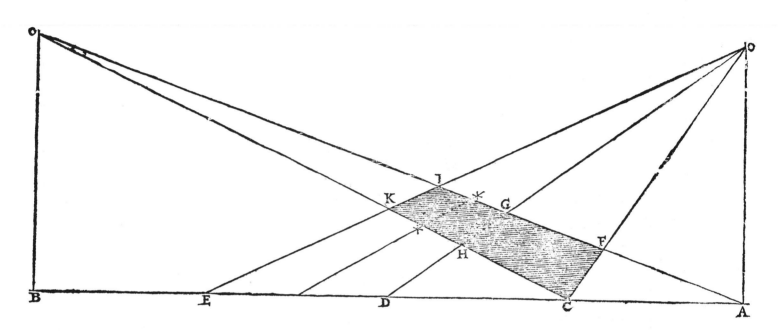

This body hereafter following is raysed vp out of the former Figure before set downe, and is made with the same Horizon; which body containeth two Quadrants in length, & one Quadrant in height, for the line C. D. is set in Perpendicular maner vpon the nethermost corner, wheron the other Superficies are set: thus then this body is of two foure squares, I meane two foure squares in length, and one foure square broad and high. And this body (as I said before) shall serue for many things: But if you will haue more cubits in the length, then deuide rather the Base in so many parts more, and you shall alwayes finde the trueth hereof. And if you will make a border or crease about this body, then you must follow this rule aforesayd.

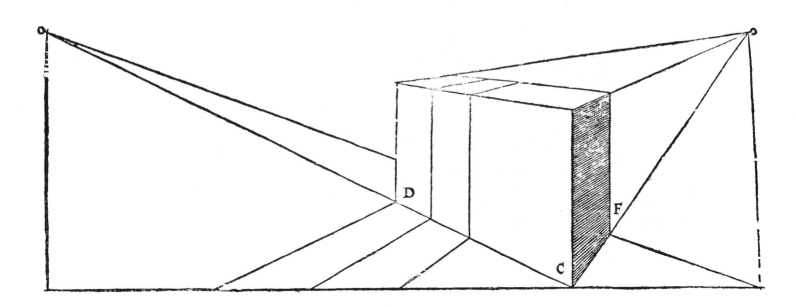

Of Perſpectiue

BUT wil you make diuers things vpon one ground, then it is conuenient that firſt you make a pauement, as you ſee it here ſet downe, and thereupon frame what you thinke good vpon the Quadrans, and the leſſe the Quadrans are, and the moze in number, you may the eaſier frame things vpon them. The croſſe made vpon this ground is onely to ſhow you the way and entry thereunto; but foz ſuch a forme, you may make a forme of a Chriſtian Church as they are now built. The other forme by it, ſheweth a piece of a foundation of a Houſe, but all theſe things you may make in a greater forme, and ſet them forth as you will; ſometime placing the Hozifentall lines in ſuch manner that you may ſee moze of the out ſides, but yet the Hozifons muſt ſtand all of one height.

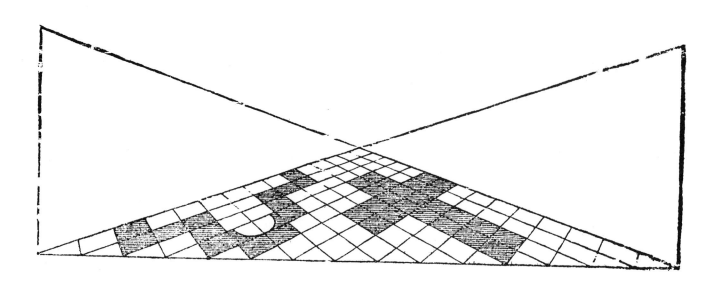

OUT of this Superficiall Figure aforeſayd, I haue rayſed theſe bodies, to ſhew how the Hozifons of them dt ſtand in the wozke as well aboue as below, as you ſhall finde by experience, and in trueth theſe wozkes which you ſee ouer the poynts oz cozners, contain a Booke alone by themſelues: but (as I ſayd befoze) my meaning was to ſhow but thzee oz foure Figures of them, yet I will ſhow ten of them; intending to leaue the Student ſome wozke, whereof I am well aſſured: Foz that he hath moze eyes, and moze patience then my ſelfe, hee ſhall finde many things which I wzite not of, noz yet ſet downe.

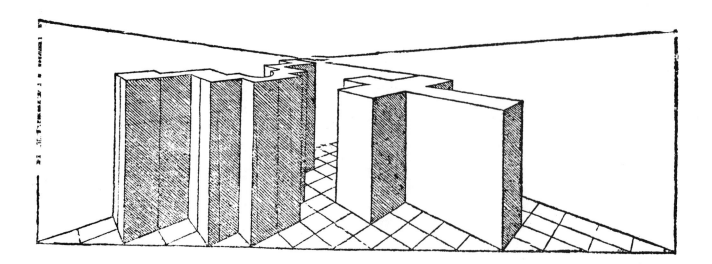

Vpon this Pauement (as I fayd) you may forme or frame what you will, but in this Pauement here ensuing, you see a columne lying, being eight square, which is thre Quadrans in thickenesse, and foureteene in length. This eyght square columne may be made out of a columne of foure square, as before in an other place is shewed: which foure square you may see drawne herein with prickes, and the terminations of the eyght square with blacke lines. But because that this eyght square columne is too much seene on the sides, the readier to make it out of the foure square : I haue therefore made an other piece by it, the which, because it draweth narer to this Horison, is seene more before, then the other, although not so long; for it is but halfe so long as the other, as you may see & tell it in the ground or foot thereof. And if it were so that this eyght square Figure reached narer to the Horison, it would then be better seene, yet it would not be wholly seene before, because it standeth without the foure square and corner.

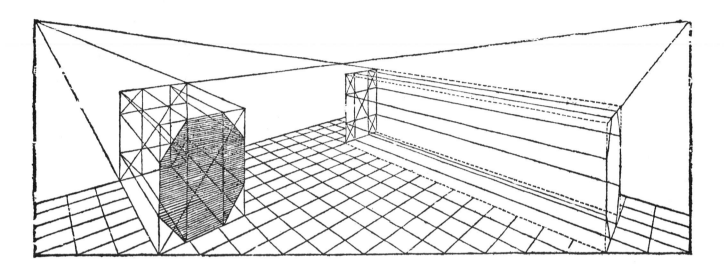

These Columnes are the same which are before set downe, but the other swell hollow, and these massie, whereby an expert workeman may finde out many things exercising this way, although there are other meanes to be vsed, as Albert Durer hath shewed, to looke through holes with a thread: There is also another way, which is drawne out of flat formes which is the surest way, but very troublesome and hard to describe in writing; wherefore I haue chosen this as the easiest way to be shewed. And if I had not vndertaken to show other things of more importance, I would haue drawne diuers bodies and houses after this manner. But for that I meane to entreat of Scenes, and the preparing of places for to show Comedies and Tragedies, which is now vsed in this age, and specially in Italy, therefore I will make an end of these foure cornerd things, leauing it to another (as I sayd before) to set foorth more thereof.

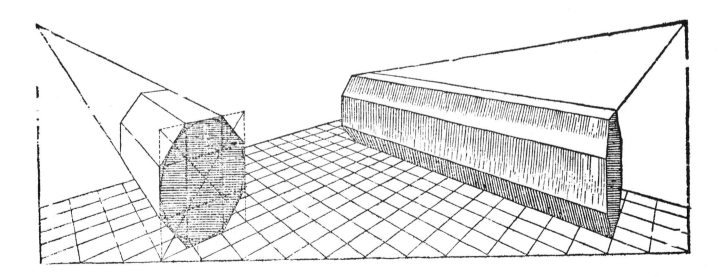

Of Perspectiue

BEcaufe I meane hereafter to entreat of Theaters, and Scenes belonging vnto them, as we vfe them in thefe dayes. In the which Scenes it will bee very hard for a man to fhew how, & where a man fhould place the Horifon herein, becaufe it is an other thing then the rule before declared: Therfore I thought it good firft to make this profil, that the ground by the profill may both together be the better vnderftood; yet it were conuenient firft to ftudie the ground, and if it fo falleth out that a man cannot attaine to all within the ground, then hee muft proceede to the profill to bee the better inftructed therein.   Firft therefore, I will begin with the Scaffold before, which as the eyes fhal ftand eleuated from the earth, and fhalbe flat, made by the water compaffe, marked with C. And the Scaffold from B. to A. fhall ftand heaued vp vnder the fame A. a ninth part of the length thereof, and that ftanding vp behind the feate marked with an M. aboue it, is the wall of the Hall or other place, againft which, or where this Scene fhall be made.   That which ftandeth a little diftant from the Wall perpendilar wife, is marked P. fhal be the backe or vpholding behind of the Scene, that a man may go betweene it and the other wall. The termination O. is the Horifon.   The lines with prickes comming croffe vpon the water compaffe from L. to O. where it toucheth the backe P. there you fhall placethe Horifon onely to ferue for the fayd backe.   And comming forwards to L. this line fhall alwayes be the Horifon, for all the Ortograpie of the Houfes which fhall ftand forwards or outwards: But the Scenographies or fhortening fides of the Houfes, they muft haue their Horifons ftanding further to O. And it is reafon, which in effect haue two fides (as thef muft be built that men may fee out of them on both fides) fhould happen two Horifon lines, this is touching the profill of the Scene. But the place which is called Procenie is that which is marked with P. and the part marked with E. is called Orcheftra, which is rayfed halfe a foote from the earth, where you fee F. marked, are the places for Noblemen and Knights to fit on. And the firft feate or ftep, marked G. are for the Noblewomen and Ladyes to fit on: and going vp higher, there muft the meaner fort of Nobles fit. The broader place, marked H. is a way, and fo is the place marked E. Betweene H. and E. muft fit Gentlemen of quality. And from L. vpwards meaner Gentlemen fhall fit.   But the great fpace, marked K. fhall be for common Officers and other people: which place may be greater or leffe, according to the length of the Hall, or any other place. And the Theator, with the Scene or Scaffold, which I made in Vincente, was almoft in this fort: and from the one corner of the Theater to the other, was eyght and twenty foote; for it was made in a place where I had roome inough, but the Scene or Scaffold was not fo broad, becaufe it was placed in a lodge. The frame of the feates was all made in one, as you may fee in this Figure. And becaufe the Theator ftood in an open place which had no wall, whereunto it might be made faft, therefore in the circumference I haue made it fticking out, for the more ftrength and faftneffe thereof.

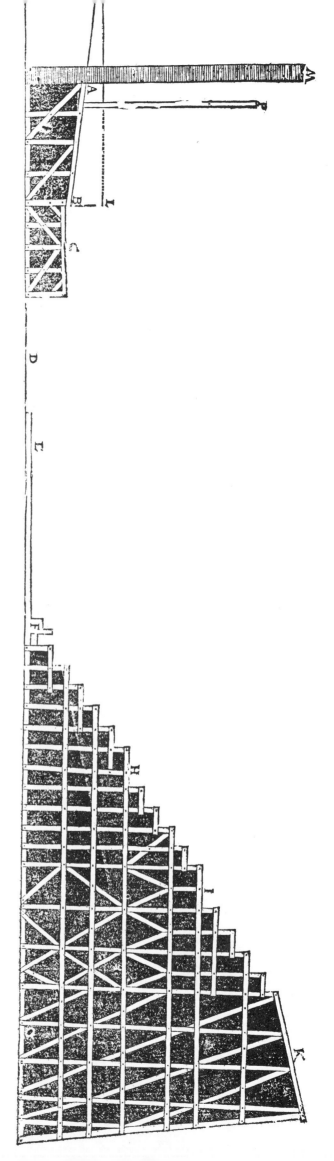

A Treatise of Scenes, or places to play in.

Mong all the things that may bee made by mens hands, thereby to yéeld admiration, pleasure to sight, and to content the fantasies of men; I thinke it is placing of a Scene, as it is shewed to your sight, where a man in a small place may sée built by Carpenters or Masons, skilfull in Perspectiue worke, great Palaces, large Temples, and diuers Houses, both neere and farre off; broad places filled with Houses, long stréets crost with other wayes: tryumphant Arches, high Pillars or Columnes, Piramides, Obeliscens, and a thousand fayre things and buildings, adorned with innumerable lights, great, middle sort, and small, as you may sée it placed in the Figure, which are so cunningly set out, that they shew foorth and represent a number of the brightest stones; as Diamonds, Rubins, Saphirs, Smaragdes, Iacinthes, and such like. There you may sée the bright shining Moone ascending onely with her hornes, and already risen vp, before the spectators are ware of, or once saw it ascend. In some other Scenes you may sée the rising of the Sunne with his course about the world: and at the ending of the Comedie, you may see it goe downe most artificially, where at many beholders haue bene abasht. And when occasion serueth, you shall by Arte sée a God descending downe from Heauen; you also sée some Comets and Stars shoot in the skyes: then you sée diuers personages come vpon the Stage, richly adorned with diuers strange formes and manners of Apparell both to daunce Moriscoes and play Musicke. Sometimes you sée strange beasts, wherein are men and children, leaping, running, & Tumbling, as those kind of beasts vse to doe, not without admiration of the beholders: which things, as occasion serueth, are so pleasant to mens eyes, that a man could not sée fairer made with mens hands. But for that we are entred into another maner of Perspectiue worke, therefore I will speake more at large thereof. This Perspectiue worke whereof I will speake, although it be contrary to those rules which are shewed before, because these aforesayd are imagined to be vpon a flat wall: and this other rule because it is materiall and vnbossed or raysed outward, therefore it is reason we obserue another rule therein, according to common custome. First, you must make a Scaffold, which must bee as high as a mans eye will reach, looking directly forward for the first part thereof which is marked C. But the other part behind it, whereon the Houses stand, you must rayse vp behind against the wall at least a ninth part thereof, that is, you must deuide the playne Stage or Scaffold in nine parts; and then you must make the Scaffold higher by a ninth part behind: then before at B. which must be very euen & strong, because of the Morisco dancers. This hanging downward of the Scaffold, I haue found by experience to be very pleasing, for in Vincenza which is as sumptuous and rich a Towne as any in all Italy; there I made a Theater and a Stage of wood, then the which, I thinke, there was neuer a greater made in our time, in regard of the wonderfull sights that there were seene, as of Wagons, Elephants and other Moriscoes. There I ordained, that before the hanging Scene there should be a Scaffold made by water compasse, which Scaffold was 12. foot broad, and 60. foot long, according to the place wherein it stood; which I found to be very pleasing and fit for shew. This first Scaffold, because it was right, therefore the pauement therof must not obey the Horison, but the Quadrants, whereof on euery side were foure square, from whence at the beginning of the rising Scaffold B. all the Quadrans went to the outtermost Horison O. which with their due distances do shorten very well. And for that some men haue placed the Horison of this Sciographie against the wall right aboue the Scaffold, whereby it séemeth the Houses runne all in one; therefore I determined to place the Horison before the dore, which pleased me so well, that I vsed the same kind of order in all these kind of workes: and so I counsell those that take pleasure in such Arts, to vse and esteeme this way for the best, as I will shew in this Figure following, and haue also declared in the profill of the Theater and Scene.

And because the preparation for Comedies are done in thrée sorts, that is, Comical, Tragicall and Satiricall; I will first entreat of the Comicall, whereof the Houses must be made as if they were for common or ordinarie people, which for the most part must be made vnder roofes in a Hall, which at the end thereof hath a chamber for the pleasure or ease of ẏ personages: and there it is that the ground of the Scaffold is made (as I said and shewed before) in the profil. Therefore C. is the first part being the flat Scaffold; and suppose that each Quadran containeth two foote on eyther side, so shal they vpon the hanging Scaffold before on the Base be also two foot broad, which is marked B. And (as I sayd before) my meaning is not to place the Horison hereof against the backe behind in the Scaffold, but as farre as it is from the beginning of the pauement B. to the wall, so farre I would also that men shall passe behind through the wall, and so shall all the houses and other things show better in the shortening: and when by conuenient distances you haue drawne all the Quadrans towards the Horison, & shortened them, then you must shorten the houses right with the foure square stones; which houses are the great lines marked vpon the ground, aswell for those that stand vpright, as those that shorten. All such houses I alwayes made of spars, or rafter or laths, couered with linnin cloth; making dores and windowes, both before and in the shortening, as occasion fell out. I haue also made some things of halfe planks of wood, which were great helpe to the Paynters to set out things at life. All the spaces fró the backe to the wall marked A. shall be for the personages, to the which end the hindermost backe in the middle shall stand at the least two foot from the wall, that the personages may goe from the one side to the other, and not be séene. Then you must rayse a termination at the beginning of the pauement B. which shall be the poynt L. and from thence to the Horison there shalbe a line drawne, as it is marked in the profil with prickes, which shall be of like height; and where that toucheth the hindermost backe of the Scene or Scaffold, there the Horison of that backe shall stand: and that Horison shall serue onely for that backe. But if you stretch a corde or any other thing to the termination L. then you may fasten a thread to it, to thrust backward or forward, to vse it out of the stedfast Horison, & all the Ortographie of the houses before. But the Horison which goeth through the wall, shall serue for all the shortening sides of the houses: and for that men should breake the wall, if they would vse all this Horison in grosse, which may not bee done, therefore I haue alwayes made a small modell of wood and Paper iust of the same bignes, and by the same modell set it downe in grosse, from piece to piece. But this way will fall out hard for some men to vnderstand, neuerthelesse, it will be necessary to worke by models and experiments, and by studie a man shall find the way: and for that a man can hardly finde any Halls how great soeuer, wherein he can place a Theater without imperfection and impediment; therefore to follow Antiquities, according to my power and abilitie, I haue made all such parts of these Theaters, as may stand in a Hall. Therefore the part marked D. shall be the post scene, and the circular place marked E. shall bee the Orchestra: round about this Orchestra shall be the places for the noblest personages to sit, marked F. The first steps marked G. for the noblest women to sit vpon. The place H. is a way, so is the part marked I. In the middle betwéene these degrées are steps the easier to goe vp. The places marked K. must bee made so great backward as the Hall will afford, which is made somewhat stooping, that the people may see one ouer the others head.

M

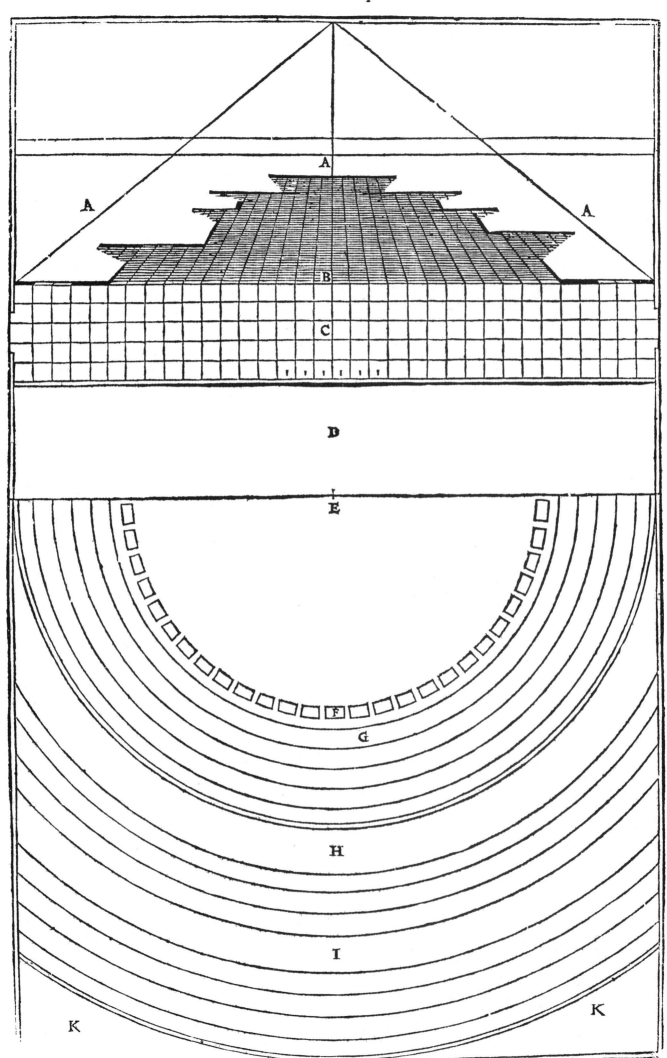

Touching the difpofiton of Theaters and other Scenes, concerning the grounds thereof, I haue fpoken fufficiently; now I will fpeake of the Scene in Perfpectiue worke: and for that Scenes are made of three forts, that is, Comicall, to play Comedies on, Tragicall, for Tragedies, and Satiricall for Satirs. This firft fhall be Comicall, whereas the houfes muft be flight for Citizens, but fpecially there muft not want a brawthell or bawdy houfe, and a great Inne, and a Church; fuch things are of neceffitie to be therein. How to rayfe thefe houfes from the ground is fufficiently exprefled, and how you fhall place the Horifon: neuerthelefle, that you may be the better inftructed (touching the former of thefe houfes) I haue here fet downe a Figure, for fatiffaction of thofe that take pleafure therein; but becaufe this Figure is fo fmall, therein I could not obferue all the meafures, but refer them to inuention, that thereby you may chufe or make houfes which fhew well, as an open Gallery, or lodge through the which you may fee an other houfe. The hangings ouer or fhooting out, fhow well in fhortening worke, and fome Cornices cut out at the ends; accompanied with fome others that are painted, fhow well in worke: fo doe the houfes which haue great bearing out, like lodgings or Chambers for men, and efpecially aboue all things, you muft fet the fmaleft houfes before, that you may fee other houfes ouer or aboue them, as you fee it here aboue the bawdy houfe: for if you place the greateft before, and the reft behind ftill leffen, then the place of the Scene would not be fo well filled, and although thefe things vpon the one fide be made all vpon one floore: Neuerthelefle, for that you place great part of the lights in the middle, hanging ouer the Scene or Scaffold, therefore it would ftand better if the floore in the midft were taken away, and all the roundels and Quadrans which you fee in the Buildings, they are artificiall lights cutting through, of diuers colors; which to make, I will fhew the manner in the laft of this Booke. The windowes which ftand before, were good to be made of Glaffe or Paper, with light behind them. But if I fhould here write all that I know to ferue for this worke, it would be ouerlong to rehearfe; therefore I referre that to the wit and difcretion of thofe that exercife and practife themfelues herein.

Of Perſpectiue

Houſes for Tragedies, muſt bee made for great perſonages, for that actions of loue, ſtrange aduentures, and cruell murthers, (as you reade in ancient and moderne Tragedies) happen alwayes in the houſes of great Lords, Dukes, Princes, and Kings. Therefore in ſuch caſes you muſt make none but ſtately houſes, as you ſee it here in this Figure; wherein (for that it is ſo ſmal)
I could make no Princely Pallaces: but it is ſufficient for the workeman to ſee the manner thereof, whereby he may helpe himſelfe as time and place ſerueth: and (as I ſayde in the Comicall) hee muſt alwayes ſtudy to pleaſe the eyes of the beholders, and forget not himſelfe ſo much as to ſet a ſmall building in ſtead of a great, for the reaſons aforeſayd. And for that I haue made all my Scenes of laths, couered with linnen, yet ſometime it is neceſſary to make ſome things riſing or boſſing out; which are to bee made of wood, like the houſes on the left ſide, whereof the Pillars, although they ſhorten, ſtand all vpon one Baſe, with ſome ſtayres, all couered ouer with cloth, the Cornices bearing out, which you muſt obſerue to the middle part : But to giue place to the Galleries, you muſt ſet the other ſhortening Cloth ſomewhat backwards, and make a cornice aboue it, as you ſee : and that which I ſpeake of theſe Buildings, you muſt vnderſtand of all the reſt, but in the Buildings which ſtand far backward the Painting worke, muſt ſupplie the place by ſhadowes without any bearing out : touching the artificiall lights, I haue ſpoken thereof in the Comicall works. All that you make aboue the Roofe ſticking out, as Chimneyes, Towers, Piramides, Obliſces, and other ſuch like things or Images ; you muſt make them all of thin bords, cut out round, and well coloured : But if you make any flat Buildings, they muſt ſtand ſomewhat farre inward, that you may not ſee them on the ſides. In theſe Scenes, although ſome haue painted perſonages therein like ſupporters, as in a Gallery, or doore, as a Dog, Cat, or any other beaſts : I am not of that opinion, for that ſtandeth to long without ſtirring or moouing ; but if you make ſuch a thing to lie ſleeping, that I hold withall. You may alſo make Images, Hiſtories, or Fables of Marble, or other matter againſt a wall ; but to repreſent the life, they ought to ſtirre. In the latter end of this Booke I will ſhew you how to make them.

The Satiricall Scenes are to represent Satirs, wherein you must place all those things that bee rude and rusticall, as in ancient Satirs they were made plaine without any respect, whereby men might vnderstand, that such things were referred to Rusticall people, which set all things out rudely and plainely: for which cause Vitruuius speaking of Scenes, saith, they should be made with Trees, Rootes, Herbs, Hils and Flowres, and with some countrey houses, as you see them here set downe. And for that in our dayes these things were made in Winter, when there were but fewe greene Trees, Herbs and Flowres to be found; then you must make these things of Silke, which will be more commendable then the naturall things themselues: and as in other Scenes for Comedies or Tragedies, the houses or other artificiall things are painted, so you must make Trees, Hearbs, and other things in these; & the more such things cost, the more they are esteemed, for they are things which stately and great persons doe, which are enemies to nigardlinesse. This haue I seene in some Scenes made by Ieronimo Genga, for the pleasure and delight of his lord and patron Francisco Maria, Duke of Vrbin: wherein I saw so great liberalitie vsed by the Prince, and so good a conceit in the workeman, and so good Art and proportion in things therein represented, as euer I saw in all my life before. Oh good Lord, what magnificence was there to be seene, for the great number of Trees and Fruits, with sundry Herbes and Flowres, all made of fine Silke of diuers collors. The water courses being adorned with Frogs, Snailes, Tortuses, Toads, Adders, Snakes, and other beasts: Rootes of Corrale, mother of Pearle, and other shels layd and thrust through betwene the stones, with so many seuerall and faire things, that if I should declare them all, I should not haue time inough. I speake not of Satirs, Nimphes, Mermaids, diuers monsters, and other strange beastes, made so cunningly, that they seemed in shew as if they went and stirred, according to their manner. And if I were not desirous to be briefe, I would speake of the costly apparel of some Shepheards made of cloth of gold, and of Silke, cunningly mingled with Imbrothery: I would also speake of some Fishermen, which were no lesse richly apparelled then the others, hauing Nets and Angling-rods, all gilt: I should speake of some Countrey mayds and Nimphes carelesly apparelled without pride, but I leaue all these things to the discretion and consideration of the iudicious workeman, which shall make all such things as their pattrons serue them, which they must worke after their owne deuises, and neuer take care what it shall cost.

Of Artificiall lights of the Scenes.

I Promised in the Treatise of Scenes to set downe the manner how to make these lights shining through, of diuers collours, & first I will speake of a sure collour which is like to a Zaphir, and yet somewhat fayrer. Take a piece of Salamoniacke, and put it into a Barbers Bason, or such like thing, and put water into it : then bruse and crush the Salamoniacke softly therein, till it be all molten, alwayes putting more water vnto it, as you desire to haue it light or sad collour; which done, if you will haue it fayre and cleare, then straine it through a fine cloth into an other vessell, and then it will be a cleare Celestiall blew, whereof you may make diuers kinds of blew with water. Will you make an Emerauld collour, then put some Saffron as you will haue it pale or high coloured; for heere it is not necessary to prescribe you any weight or measure, for that experience will teach you how to doe it. If you will make a Rubbie collour, if you bee in a place where you may haue red Wine, then you need not vse any other thing; but to make it pall with water, as need requireth: but if you can get no wine, then take Brazill beaten to powder, & put it into a Kettell of water with Allum, let it seethe, and skum it well; then strayne it, and vse it with water and Vinneger. If you will counterfeit a Ballayes, you must make it of red and white Wine mingled together ; but white Wine alone will showe like a Topas or a Crisolite : The Conduit or common water being strayned, will be like a Diamond, and to doe this well, you must vpon a glasse ground frame certaine points or tablets, and fill them with water. The manner to set these shining collours in their places, is thus, Behind the painted house wherein these painted collours shall stand, you must set a thin board, cut out in the same manner that these lights shall be placed, whether it be round or square, cornerd or ouale, like an Egge ; and behind the same board there shall be another stronger board layd flat behind them, for the bottels and other manner of glasses for th these waters to stand in, must be placed against the holes, as it shall necessarily fall out, but they must be set fast, lest they fall with leaping and dancing of the Moriscoes. And behind the glasses you must set great Lampes, that the light may also be stedfast : and if the bottels or other vessels of glasse on the side where the light stands were flat, or rather hollow, it would showe the clearer, and the collours most excellent and fayre ; the like must be done with the holes on the shortening side : But if you need a great light to show more then the rest, then set a torch behind, and behind the torch a bright Bason; the brightnes whereof will shew like the beames of the Sunne. You may also make glasse of all collours and formes, some foure square, some with crosses, & any other forme with their light behind them. Now all the lights seruing for the collours, shal not be y̌ same which must light the Scene, for you must haue a great number of torches before the Scene. You may also place certaine candlestickes aboue the Scene with great candles therein, and aboue the candlesticks you may place some vessels with water, wherein you may put a piece of Camphir, which burning, will show a very good light, and smell well. Sometime it may chance that you must make some thing or other which should seeme to burne, which you must wet throughly with excellent good Aquauite, and setting it on fire with a candle it will burne all ouer : and although I could speake more of these fires, yet this shal suffice for this time; & I will speake of some things that are pleasing to the beholders. The while that the Scene is emptie of personages, then the workman must haue certaine Figures or formes ready of such greatnes as the place where they must stand, will affoord them to be, which must be made of paste board, cut out round and paynted, signifiing such things as you will, which Figures must leane against a rule or lath of wood crosse ouer the Scene where any gate, dore, or way is made, and there some one or other behind the dore must make the Figures passe along, sometime in forme of Musitions with instruments, and some like singers; and behind the Scene some must play on, vpon certaine instruments and sing also: sometime you must make a number of foote men and horsemen going about with Trumpets, Phifes and Drummes, at which time you must play with Drumbes, Trumpets and Phifes, &c. very softly behind, which will keepe the peoples eyes occupied, and content them well. If it be requisite to make a Planet or any other thing to passe along in the Ayre, it must bee framed and cut out of paste-board; then in the hindermost and backe part of the houses of the Scene, there must be a piece of wire drawne aboue in the roofe of the house and made fast with certain rings behind to the paste-board painted with a Planet or any other thing that shal be drawne softly by a man with a blacke thred from one end to the other, but it must be farre from mens sight, that neither of the thredes may bee seene. Sometime you shall haue occasion to shew thunder and lightning as the play requireth; then you must make thunder in this manner: commonly all Scenes are made at the end of a great Hall, whereas vsually there is a Chamber aboue it, wherein you must roule a great Bullet of a Cannon or of some other great Ordinance, and then counterfeit Thunder. Lightning must be made in this maner, there must be a man placed behind the Scene or scaffold in a high place with a bore in his hand, the couer whereof must be full with holes, and in the middle of that place there shall be a burning candle placed, the bore must be filled with powder of vernis or sulphire, and casting his hand with the bore vpwards the powder flying in the candle, will shew as if it were lightning. But touching the beames of the lightning, you must draw a piece of wyre ouer the Scene, which must hang downewards, whereon you must put a squib couered ouer with pure gold or shining lattin which you will: and while the Bullet is rouling, you must shoote of some piece of Ordinance, and with the same giuing fire to the squibs, it will worke the effect which is desired. It would be ouerlong if I should speake of all things which are to be vsed in these affaires, therefore I will leaue speaking or Perspectiue things.

FINIS.

Here endeth the second Booke of Architecture, entreating of Perspectiue Arte; translated out of
Italian in's Dutch, and out of Dutch into English, at the charges of Robert Peake,
for the benefit of the English Nation ; and are to be sold at his house neere
Holborne Conduit, vnder the Sunne Tauerne. 1611.

The third Booke,

Intreating of all kind of excellent Antiquities, of buildings of Houſes, Temples, Amphitheaters, Palaces, Thermes, Obeliſces, Bridges, Arches triumphant, &c. ſet downe in Figures, with their grounds and meaſures : as alſo the places where they ſtand, and who made them.

ROMA QVANTA FVIT IPSA RVINA DOCET

To the Reader.

Lthough diuers Authors write many strange things touching Architecture, as the Egyptians, the people of Asia and Grecia, with diuers other nations, and haue left them for our example, so that reading them, we may sufficiently satisfie our eares, and fill them with the greatnesse thereof, that is, touching the length, bredth and depth, that certaine places haue contained; yet we can not satisfie our eyes, nor the desire we haue to see such incredible works, vnlesse it had beene our hap to haue the contemplation thereof, for that the reliques of such works are almost, or for the most part vtterly defaced; or vnlesse we might haue seene them drawne in proportion vnto our eyes, as in this Booke we may not onely read, what the Romanes at the last, after other nations had built, but also the same Authors haue set downe vnto vs in Figure (as you may see them here) piece by piece, not only how many rods, ells, feet & palmes, but also the minutes thereof, and what compas they contained, all perfectly described. And although it was no part of my intent, to translate this Booke of Antiquities of Rome into our mother tongue, regarding the barrennesse of our language; or peraduenture such as studie or fauour the same, are all too few to defray my charges therein: yet I haue not refrained to doe it, being thereunto compelled by the great works of the forification of the City of Andwerp, and other great places; and for this cause specially, that euery man that wondreth at the greatnes thereof, which was made with most great cost & charges, may hereby see and consider, yea how much greater, & needles charges (to be compared vnto this) the Romanes (not speaking of other nation) haue in time past bestowed, in making of Obelisces, Piramides, Thermes, Theaters, Amphitheaters, tryumphant Arches, and many more such like things, which serued only for pleasure & tryumph: whereby it is to be presumed, that they would haue made the fortifications of such Cities or Townes, made for the safety of the Land, far better then they now are. Now it is to be noted, that all, whatsoeuer the Romanes haue made, doth not wholly agree with Vitruuius rules, so that many which haue counterfeyted these, and such like peeces of worke, haue thereby beene abused and deceiued: for some would hardly beleeue, that in those dayes (as well as at this time) all maner of workemen were one better then another, which many, vnawares and vnskilfully do many things, which good Antiquities would willingly not suffer, hereof they shall find good instructions in this Booke (and they may learne, if they will read it) how to discerne good from bad; whereunto the former printed fourth Booke is specially made: for in it the whole quantity of the measures is contayned, as in the Epistle of the sayd Booke it is promised. So in this third Booke, you shall not onely find, first the Ichnographia, and then after the Orthographyes, with part of the Sciographies of the most famous Antiquityes of Rome, Italy, and some of other places, but also of the most excellent buyldings in our dayes, specially those that are made by Bramant. So that the Reader being well instructed in the aforesayd fourth Booke, where all the Orders are well set foorth and declared, he may of himselfe iudge what is well or ill made, that at one time a man may, without any further labour, make a good and incorrigible peece of worke.

The

The third Booke of Antiquitie.

The fourth Chapter.

Mong all the ancient building to bee feene in Rome, I am of opinion, that the Pantheon (for one piece of worke alone) is the fayreft, wholeft, and beft to be vnderftood; and is fo much the more wonderfull then the reft, becaufe it hath fo many members, which are all fo correfpondent one to the other, that whofoeuer beholdeth it, taketh great pleafure therein, which proceedeth from this, that the excellent workeman, which inuented it, chofe the perfiteft forme, that is, the round forme, whereby it is vfually called, Our Lady of the Round : for within, it is as high as it is broad. And it may be, that the fayd workeman, confidering, that all things proceeding orderly, haue a principall and onely head, whereon the nether parts depend, was of opinion, that this piece of worke fhould haue onely but one light, and that, in the higheft part thereof, that it might fpread abroad in all places alike, as in effect you fee it doth : for befides other things which haue their perfect light, there are fixe Chappels, which (for that they ftand within the thickneffe of the wall) fhould be darke, yet they haue their due light, by the meanes of fome drawing windowes, aboue in the top of the fayd Chappels, which giue them fecond light, taken from the vppermoft hole, fo that there is not any fmall thing in them, but it receiueth a part of the light, (and this is not made without great iudgement :) for this Temple, in old time, being dedicated to all the gods, by which meanes there ftood many Images in it, (which the diuers Tabernacles, Seates, and fmall windowes fhew) it was neceffary that euery one had his due light. Wherefore fuch as take pleafure to make Images, and other imboffed or grauen worke, muft confider, that fuch a Cabinet fhould haue his light from aboue, that euery one, ftanding in his place, neede not looke for light to fee, but that they may bee feene altogether at one time. But to come to my firft fpeach : For that the Pantheon feemeth vnto me to be the perfecteft peece of worke that euer I faw, therefore I thought it good to fet it firft in the beginning of this Booke, and for a principall head of all other peeces of worke. The founder of this Temple (as *Plinie* writeth in more then one place) was *Marcus Agrippa*, to accomplifh *Auguftus Cæfars* laft will, who being intercepted by death, could not finifh it : and fo it was built about foureteene yeeres after the byrth of our Lord, which is about 5203. yeeres from the beginning of the world.

In this Temple (as *Pliny* writeth) the Capitals were of Copper; and hee writeth alfo, that *Diogenes*, the Image-maker of Athens, made the excellent Caracters in the Pillars, and that the Images placed aboue the Frontefpicium were much commended, although by the highneffe of the place they could not be fo well difcerned. This Temple was confumed with lightening, and burnt, about the 12. yeere of the raigne of the Emperour *Traian*, which was about 113. yeeres after the byrth of Chrift, and in the 5311. yeere of the creation of the world : and *Lucius Septimus Seuerus*, and *Marcus Aurelius Antonius*, repayred it agayne, with all the Ornaments thereto belonging, as it appeareth in the Architraue of the fayd frame : which Ornaments, you muft prefume, were all new made, otherwife the Caracters of *Diogenes* would ftill haue bene feene there. But in truth, the workman that made it, was very iudicious and conftant; for that he proportioned the members thereof very iudicioufly to the body, and would not fuppreffe the worke with many cuttings : but as I will fhew, when time ferueth, how to place and deuide them excellent well. Alfo, in all the worke, hee hath obferued the worke of Corinth, and would mixe no other with it : and withall, the meafures of all the members are as well obferued as euer I faw or meafured in any other peece of worke, whereby we may call this Temple an example of workemanfhip. But leauing this matter (for that it giueth the workeman little, or no inftruction to the purpofe) I will proceede to the particular meafures : and that I may goe forward orderly in thefe Antiquities, the firft Figure fhall be the Ichnography. The fecond, the Orthography. The third, the Sciography.

This

Of Antiquitie

This Figure following is the Ichnography, that is, the ground of the Temple aforesayd, which is measured by the ancient, or old Romish Palmes placed along by the side hereof. And first, speaking of the Portall, whereof the Columnes are 6. Palmes & 29. minutes thicke. The Intercolumnes (which are the spaces from one Columne to another) are 8. Palmes and 9. minutes : the breadth of the Portall is 40. Palmes: the breadth of the flat Pillars of the Portall, is like the Diameter of the Columnes : the breadth of the Seates betweene the Pillars, is 10. Palmes : and the Pilasters on the sides are 2. Palmes : the widenesse of the Gates is 26. Palmes and a halfe : the widenesse of the whole Temple (that is, of the Floore within, from one wall to another) is 194. Palmes : and iust so much is the height from the Floore to the vndermost stone of the window aboue. The sayd round hole is 36. Palmes and a halfe broad : each of the sixe Chappels that are made within the thicknesse of the wall, are 26. Palmes, and 30. minutes; and goe halfe as deepe into the wall as the thicknesse of the foure square Pillars on each side. But the principall Chappell is thirtie Palmes broad, and also is an halfe Circle, besides the Pillars aforesayd. The thicknesse of the Columnes of all the Chappels, is 5. Palmes, 3. minutes lesse : the fouresquare corner Pillars also of the sayd Chappels, contayning as much. The Columnes of the Tabernacle betweene the Chappels are two Palmes thicke : the thicknesse of the wall that goeth round about the whole body of the Temple, is 31. Palmes. And although that the Chappels make the walles hollow, yet betweene them there are hollow places made within the walles, which some say, were left for places to receiue wind, because of earthquakes. But I am of opinion, that they were left so vnfilled, to spare stuffe, because they are made circlewise, and are strong inough. The going vp, which you see here on the left side, was also on the right side, to go vp the Portall : men also went from thence round about the Temple, ouer the Chappels, through a secret way, which is yet there: through the which also, they went without on the steps, to clime vp into the highest parts of the buildings, with many goings vp which are round about it. It is thought, that this foundation was all one masse or lumpe, and without, many places hollow, so that some neighbours marking it, and seeking to build, haue found such a foundation when they digged.

This is the old Romish Palme, which is deuided into twelue fingers, and each finger
is deuided into foure parts, which are called Minutes, by the which
measure this present Figure, with all the parts following,
was measured.

The ground of the Pantheon called Rotonde.

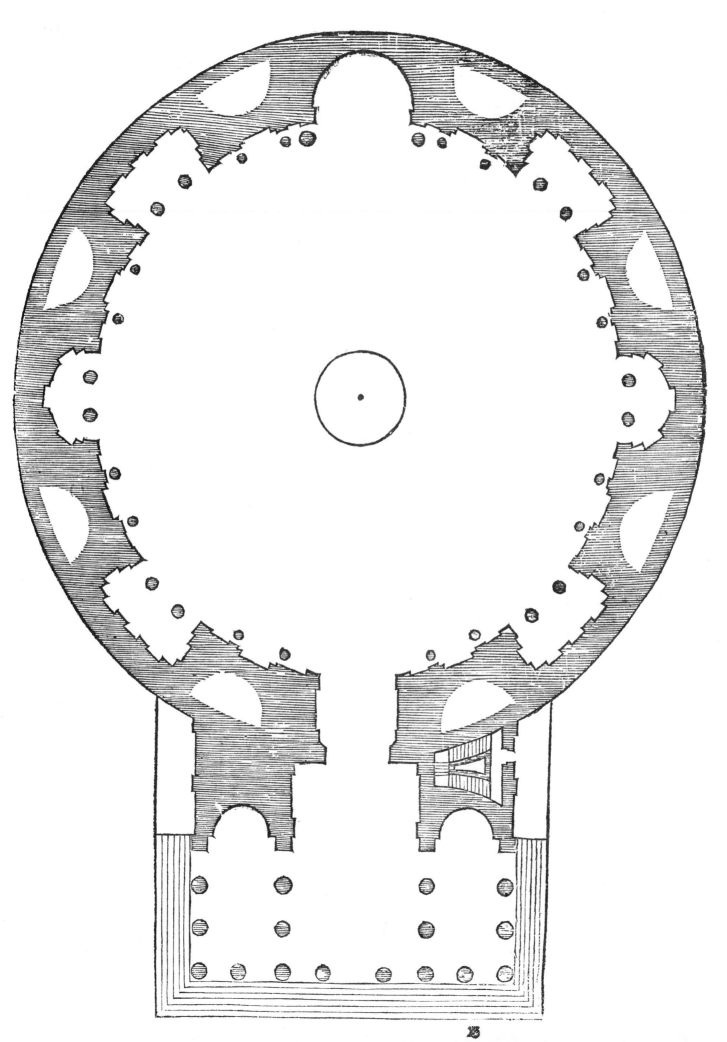

Of Antiquitie

The forme of the Pantheon without.

THE Figure hereunder, sheweth the whole forme of the Pantheon right before, and although at this time men go downe into it by certaine steps; yet as it was made at the first it was seuen steps aboue the ground. It is no wonder that such and so old a piece of worke is yet whole and standing still, for that the foundation was not sparingly made; for it is thought that it was once as broad againe vnder as it is aboue, as it had beene found by the neighbour workemen: but let vs proceed to the particular measure thereof from the earth vpwards. I sayd before, that the Diameter of the Columens of the Portal is sixe Palmes & nine and twenty minutes, but the height is foure and fiftie Palmes and nine and twentie minutes, without the Bases and Capitals: the Bases are three Palmes and nineteene minutes high, and the Capitals seuen Palmes and seuen and thirtie minutes high; the height of the Architraue is fiue Palmes, the Freese is fiue Palmes and thirteene minutes high; the Cornice is foure Palmes and nine minutes high, aboue from the top or Scina of the Cornice, to the poynt of the Geuell, are foure and thirtie Palmes, and nine and thirtie minutes. The Timpanum, that is, the flat part of the Geuell, is thought to haue bene adorned with siluer images, although it is not set downe in writing; but considering the great power of such Emperors, I am perswaded that it was so, for if the Goathes, Wandals, or other nations (which spoyled Rome more then once) had beene desirous or couetous of Copper, they might haue taken it from the Architraues and other Ornaments in Portals in great abundance: but let it be as it will, there are Figures and tokens seene, which shew that there were Figures and tokens of Mettall standing thereon.

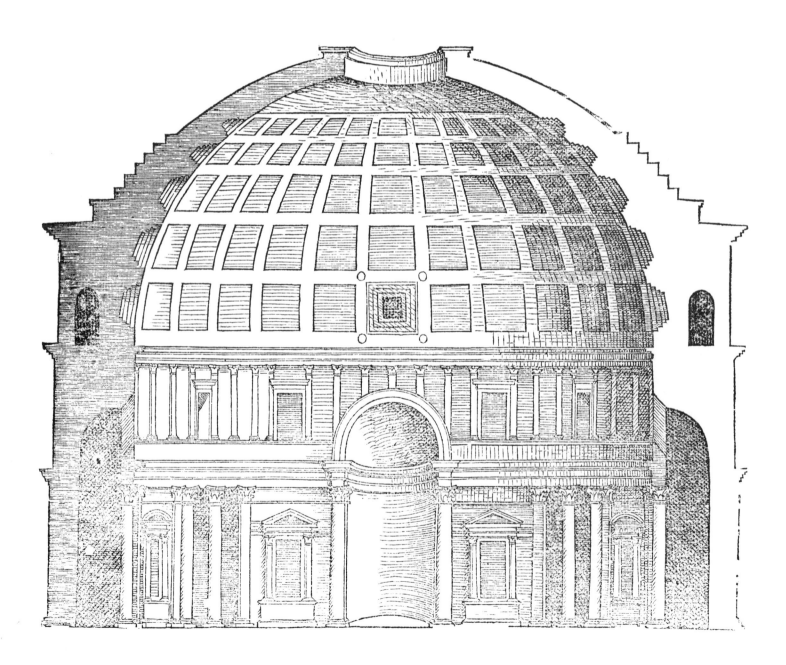

The inner part of the Temple or Pantheon.

This Figure following sheweth the Pantheon within, which forme (as I said) is taken from Sphera, because it is so wide from one wall vnto the other, as it is high from the Pauement to the open place vpon the top thereof; which widenesse and height are both a hundred ninetie and foure Palmes vpwards, from the Pauement to the highest; and from the Cornice to the highest part of the roofe is also the same measure, that is, each the halfe of one hundred ninetie and foure Palmes. The Quadrants in the roofe are all like that in the middle; and it is thought that they were also beautified ouer with Siluer plate by certaine remnants thereof yet remayning to be seene : for if they had beene of Copper, they would yet be seene there, or else those ouer the Portals would also haue beene taken away.

Let no man wonder that in these things (requiring Perspectiue Arte) that there is no Pauement or other shortening seene, but I make it onely out of the ground to shew the measure of the height thereof, that you might not misse it by shortening : But in the Booke of Perspectiue Arte these things are shewed in their right shortening manner (and that in diuers wayes) that is to say, in Superficies and many bodies, and diuers sorts of houses, seruing thereunto: I will not now set downe the measure of Cornices downewards, for hereafter I will shew the Figures piece by piece, and thereof set downe a seuerall measure.

The Chappell in the middle, although here it sheweth well with the other worke, yet many men are of opinion that it is not ancient, because the Arch thereof wanteth the flue palars, which is a thing neuer vsed by good Antiquities; but it is thought that it was made greater in the Christians time, as the Christians Temples alwayes haue one principall Altar which is greater then the rest.

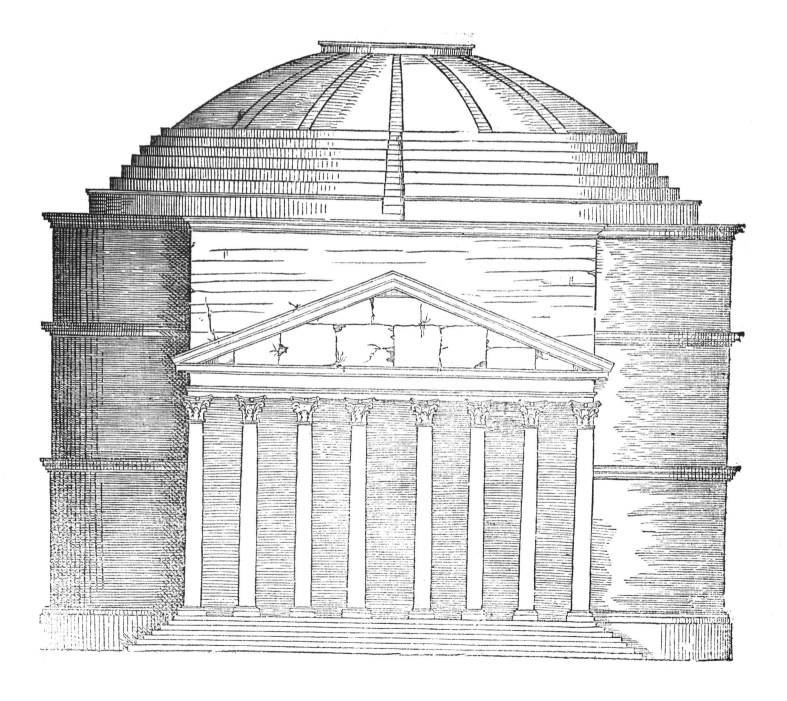

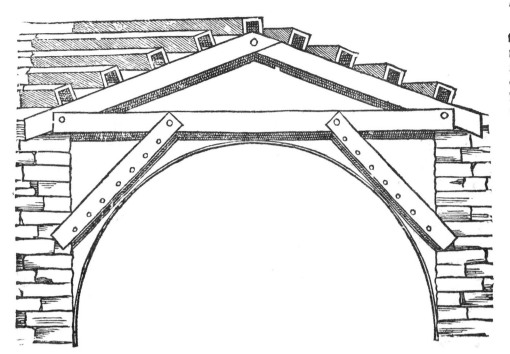

This Ornament is yet ſtanding aboue the Portall of the Pantheon, which is made in this manner, all of Copper plates, the halfe Circle is not there; but there was a crooked Superficies finely made of Copper: and many men are of opinion that the beautifying thereof was of Siluer, for the reaſons aforeſaid: but wherof it was, it is not well knowne; but it is true, it was excellent faire worke, conſidering that which is yet to bee ſéne.

This Figure here vnder ſet downe, ſhoweth the manner of the Portall within, the which both on the ſides and before is well ſet out with Marble, and alſo without, although by continuance of time is much defaced. The foure Pillars are caneled with ſuch a number of Canels, as you ſee it here vnder ſet downe; and becauſe this round Columne is thinner aboue then the Diameter, where the edge or border of the Architrabe is as thicke as the Columne: If a man would make the Architrabe equall with the foure cornerd Pillars, which leſſen not aboue, then the edge would haue had no Perpendicular, for it would haue wanted as much as the leſſening of the round Columnes. Thus the ſkilfull workeman hath placed the Architrabe ſo much right aboue the the foure Pillars, becauſe ſuch things ſhow well. Touching the dores, they are twenty Palmes, and two minutes wide, and fortie Palmes and foure minutes high. Of the other ſeuerall meaſures I will hereafter ſpeake at large.

The Gate and Face within the Portall.

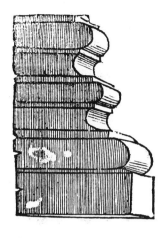

This Base is one of thofe which ſtandeth faſt to the flat Pillars, in the ſecond order, which for that they ſtand farre from mens ſight, haue one Aſtragelus for two, not to ſhorten the worke.

The proportion of this Doore is already ſet down touching breadth and height, but the Pilaiſters thereof is the eyght part of the breadth of the wideneſſe of the light: and although Vitruuius maketh ŷ Pilaiſter of Dorica and Ionica about the ſixe part, yet this is not vnſæmely, becauſe it is Corinthe; for the Corinthian Columnes are more ſightly then others, yet it ſæmeth to be ſo much thicker then the ſides are of a good dæepeneſſe, ſo that a mans ſight beholding them all at one time, it ſæmeth not to be ſo ſmall as in effect it is; the Pilaiſters on the ſides and the Superficies or Architraue vpon them is ſaid to be all of one piece, and I for my part haue ſæne no diuiſion or parting therein: the particular meaſures ſtand here on the ſides.

The Cornice, Fréeſe, and Architraue ſtands aboue the Doore of the Pantheon, touching the meaſure thereof, the Architraue or Superficie is the eight part of the light; the Fréeſe, becauſe it is vncut, is a third part leſſe then the Superficies, the Cornice is as high as the Superficie; the other members are proportioned according to the greatneſſe, whereby a man may finde the reſt with the Compaſſe.

C

TO shew all the parts of this most excellent and beautifull piece of worke it is convenient to turne it on every side, and therefore having shewed the outside thereof maiestically as it standeth, with all the things which you see before: now will J shew the lodge, the Portall and the entring into the Temple, side wayes as it standeth. Touching the measure, the thicknesse, and the height of the Columnes and the Pillars, it is before set downe, and therefore needelesse to be rehearsed, it sufficeth onely to see the disposition of the things within, which, although they be smal, they are drawne and proportioned in their measure according to the greatnesse. The small Pillars at the going into the Temple are foure square, in manner of Pillaisters, the measure thereof J will hereafter set downe, for they are also at the Corners of the Chappels within round about the Temple, and as much as the space of these three inter Columnes holds, so farre reacheth the Copper roofe, whereof J spake before.

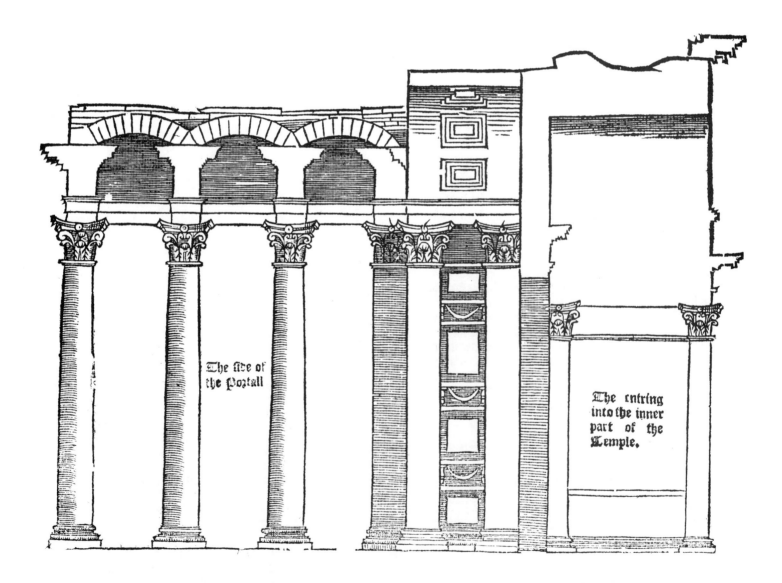

The side of the Portall

The entring into the inner part of the Temple.

I Will not take vpon me to write of euery feuerall cutting or hollowing of the Columnes whereof there are many in the Pantheon, but onely of the Columnes before the great Chappell, becaufe they are very fayze and excellent worke, I will fhew fomething, to the which end the Figures marked with A. and B. fhew the outward worke of the grauing of the Columnes of the great Chappell, that is, in the flat and in the vprightneffe and ftanding vp: touching the forme and the fafhion it is fufficiently fhewed in thefe two Figures; and thus will I fhew you the meafures thereof. The Canaels are foure and twenty in number, euery Canall being nine minutes and a halfe broad, the Thozns with the two Quadrats oz lifts are both together foure minutes and a halfe, for the Thozus is three minutes, and then there refteth a minute and a halfe, which deuided into two parts, euery Quadrate on eyther fide is three quarters of a minute. This hollowing pleafeth the beholders paffing well, and fuch worke is vpon the Bafilica de foro tranfitorio, for the beautifying of a Gate, as it is fhewed in the fourth Booke. The Bafe marked with C. is the Bafe of the fayd Columnes of the great Chappell in the Pantheon, whereof the height is two Palmes and eleuen minutes and a halfe, which is in this manner diuided. The Plinthus vnder is nineteene minutes high, the vndermoft Thozus is feuenteene minutes, and the Quadrate aboue it is three minutes and a halfe: The firft Scotie oz Trochile is eight minutes and a third part, the Quadrate vnder the Aftragal is halfe a minute, fo is the other aboue the Aftragall, the two Aftragals are fixe minutes and a halfe, and fo each Aftragall is three minutes and a quarter. The fecond Scotie oz Trochile aboue the Aftragals is fixe minutes, the Supercilie (fo named by Vitruuius) oz the Quadrate vnder the fecond Thozus is one minute: That Thozus is feuen minutes and two third parts high, the Cincte, that is the band of the Columne aboue the Thozus, although the Bafe be not one, is three minutes; the Proiecture of this Bafe is three and twenty minutes proportioned in manner as it is here vnder fhewed.

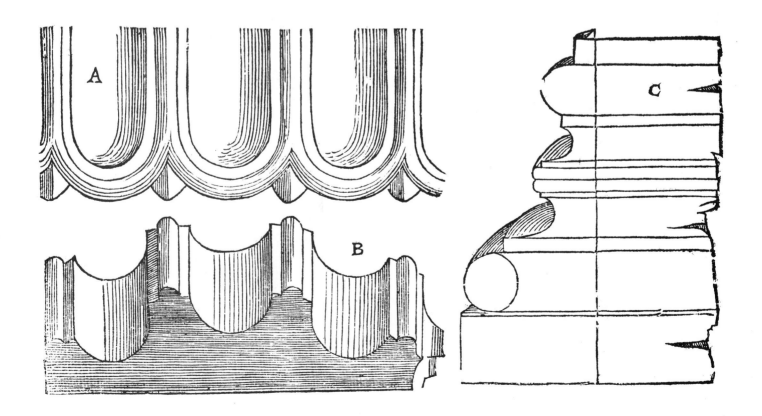

This Figure following representeth a part of the Pantheon within, that is, from the Pauement till you come vp to the second Cornice, which beareth vp the Tribune or the round roofe; and also aboue the Cornice you see the beginning of the foure square hollowing of the said Tribune: This Figure also in the nether part sheweth the widenesse of one of the sire Chappels, whereof two are in forme of the halfe Circles, and the other foure in forme of a Quadrangle; yet in show they seeme all to be of one forme: each of these Chappels haue two round Columnes, and the corners haue their feure square Pillars, as you may see in the ground of the Pantheon aforesaid, and in this Figure following. And although it be not set in Perspectiue manner, whereby a man might see whether it were a rounde or foure square Chappell, that is omitted because of the measure thereof; notwithstanding this is made for a foure square, which you may see by the forme of the blind windowes which are within the Chappell, for the other should runne more about. The thickenesse of these Columnes is fiue Palmes three minutes lesse, the height of the Bases is two Palmes and one and twenty minutes, the height of the Columnes without the Capitals is fourtie Palmes, the height of the Capitals is fiue Palmes and thirtie minutes; and so the whole Columne with the Bases and Capitals: is fourtie and eight Palmes high. The height of the Architraue, Freese and Cornice, are altogether thirteene Palmes and a halfe, and this height in all is deuided into ten parts, whereof three parts are for the Architraue; the other three are for the Sophero or the Freese, and the other foure parts are for the Cornice: Touching the rest of the other members, I set downe no measures, because this is proportionably declared touching the principallest of them that stand on the side thereof marked with P. And in trueth, a man in this Cornice may perceiue the iudicious skill of the workeman, who therein touching the mutiles, would not cut any deutiles therein, thereby not to fall into that common errour, wherein so many ancient workemen haue fallen, and at this day more moderne workemen. The errour I meane is this, that all the corners wherein mutiles stand, and vnder haue ventiles cut in them are vicious, and by Vitruuius are reiected in the second Chapter in his fourth Booke: and although that in this Cornice the forme of denticles are, notwithstanding, because it is vncut, it is not to be condemned in this respect. Aboue this Cornice there is a Podium, or a manner of bearing out, whereof the height is seuen palmes and sire minutes, which commeth not farre out, for the Pillars stand not farre out from the Wall: the height whereof, together with the Architraue, Freese and Cornice, is fourtie Palmes and sire and thirtie minutes, which height being deuided into fiue parts, the one part shall be for the Architraue. Freese and Cornice, the which Architraue, Freese and Cornice proportioned according to the greatnesse, stands marked with the letter M. In this Cornice, and also in the Architraue, the members are so well deuided, part cut, and part vncut, that it darkeneth not the forme thereof, but rather the more, because vncut members are mixed with the cut members, and so you see a wonderfull grace in them: the window aboue the Chappell is to giue light to the same Chappell, which light, although it be not principall, neuerthelesse, because it is radially drawne vp from the vppermost open place, it giueth the Chappell the dewe light: betweene the Pillars, and also aboue the windowes, there are many fine stones intermixed, and the Freese of the first Cornice is fine profill stone.

This Figure sheweth one of the Tabernacles which stand betwéene the Chappels, and the Pillars on the sides repzesent the foure square coznerd Pillars of the Chapples, here againe you may sée the notable iudgement of this wozkeman, who séeking to ioyne the Architraue, Frée se and Coznice close to the wall, and marking that the foure square Pillars standing on the sides, were not so farre distant from the Wall, that a man might make the whole Pzoiecture of the Coznices therein: therefoze hée made the Scine theron, and the rest of the other members hée turned into a Fascie, wherby the wozk was moze séemely and accompanied with ozder. The two blinde windowes are thoght to haue béene placed foz idols. The fote of the Tabernacle is 9. Palms and 11. minutes high, the thicknes of the Columnes are two Palmes, the height sixtéene Palmes without Bases oz Capitals, the Bases are one Palme high, the height of the Capitals are two Palmes e a halfe; the Architraue is a Palme, y Frée se also is as much, which is also of fine pzofil, but the height of the Coznice is a Palme e a halfe, the frontispice is 5. Palms high, y architraue aboue y two greatest Pillars, is a Palme and thzée quarters, the othermeasures shal hereafter be shewed; e of these Tabernacles there are thzée with sharpe genels, and thzée with round genels, that is the fourth part of a Circle.

These foure Figures thereunto annexed, are members of the Tabernacles in great; as the letters A. B. C. D. shewe them. Touching their measures in height, it is shewed before, and for the rest it is sufficient for the workeman that all things from member to member are set out in great, and proportionably with great diligence brought into this forme, although it may bee that such as study Vitruuius will thinke this Cornice to bee to high for the proportion of the Architraue and Freese; and I for my part would not make it so high, but to see the same in a place that hath great distances, and which standeth not very high, it sheweth to bee in good proportion. The Capitall is farre from Vitruuius order of writing, for it is higher without the Abacus, then Vitruuius maketh it with the Abacus: notwithstanding, according to common opinion, they are the fayrest Capitals that are in Rome, (and not onely the Capitals of the Tabernacles) but they also of the Chappels are of the like forme, and those of the Portall also in such sort, that I iudge (as I sayd at the beginning) that I haue not found a building of greater obseruation of order then this: but if I should wryte all that are in it, both within and without, I should peraduenture be ouer tedious, therefore I will make an end of this wonderful Building, and speake of other Antiquities.

This Temple of Bacchus is very ancient, and also whole inough, and also for worke, fayzenesse of stones, Plaister, both in the Pavement and in walles, also in the Tribunes oz round roofes in the middle, and in the roofe of the round walke, made altogether after the order of Composita: the whole Diameter within from Wall to Wall, is 100. Palmes long, whereof the middlemost body set about with Pillars, containeth 50. Palmes: in the intercolumnes I find great difference to liken ŷ one to the other, because that the middlemost intercolumnes oz spaces betwene the Columnes where pen come in, and out of the Poztall are 9. Palmes and 30. minutes; and the other right over against them are but 9. Palmes and 9. minutes: those that are over against the greatest Chappel are 8. Palmes and 31. minutes, and the other foure Columnes resting bolt 7. Palmes 8. minutes, and some 7. Palmes 12. minutes. The widenesse of the entry within and of the foure cozners Chappell over against it, follow the intercolumnes, and so doeth the widenesse of the two great places oz round Chappels their intercolumnes. The other places oz Chappels are 7. Palmes and 5. minutes broad. The measure of the Poztall before, may be taken by the measure of the Temple, which Poztall is round Roofed: without before the Poztall, there was a walking place made in forme of an Egge, which was 588 Palmes long, and in the middle it was 140. Palmes broad; and as it appeareth by the decayed monuments, it was full of Pillars, as it may be sene in the Figure.

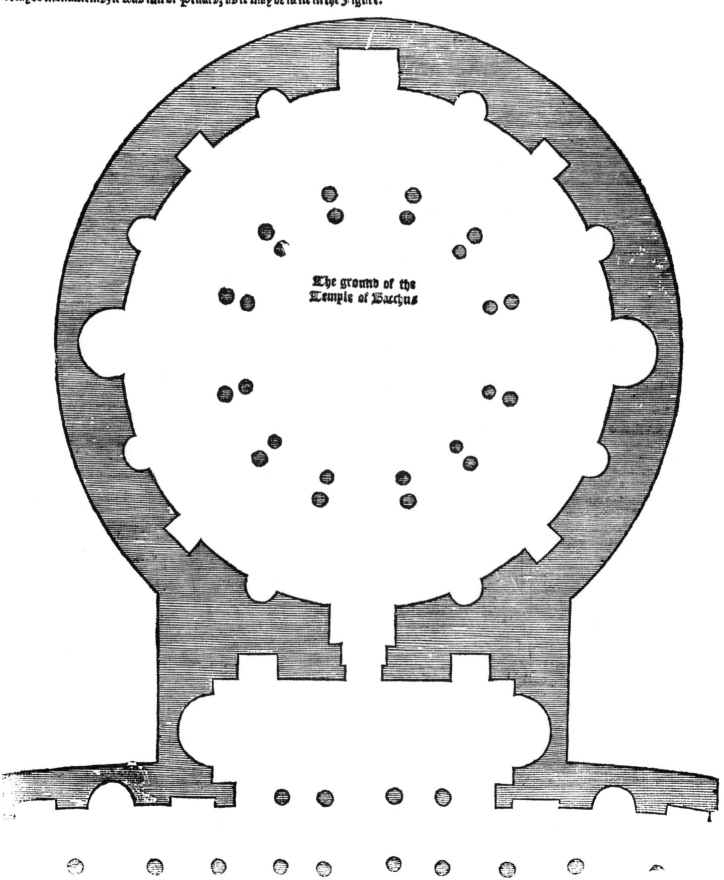

The ground of the
Temple of Bacchus

Here before I shewed the ground of the Temple with the measure thereof, now in this Figure I will shew the Ortographie thereof within, for without it is wholy defaced; the height from the Pavement to the vppermoſt part of the roofe is 86. Palmes, the thickneſſe of the Columnes is two Palmes and 14. minutes; the height of them is 22. Palmes and 11. minutes. The height of the Baſe is one Palme and 7. minutes. The height of the Capitall is 2. Palmes and a quarter. The height of the Architraue is one Palme and a quarter, so much also the Freſe holdeth. But the height of the Cornices are two Palmes and a halfe. The particular members, as of the Baſes, Cornices and Capitals, you ſee here vnder proportioned, according to their greatneſſe, and marked in their ſeuerall places. This Temple ſtandeth without Rome, and is dedicated to S. Anne.

Of Antiquitie

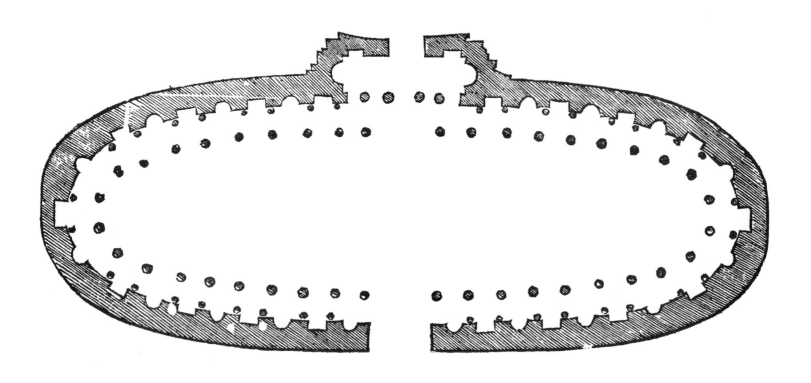

The Ichnographie hereunder placed is the aforesayd walking place before the Temple of Bacchus, with a ledge round about it, as you may perceive by some very ruinous places thereof, and all about betwéene each intercolumne there was a place or seat beautified with small Pillars, where it is thought a certaine Idoll stood, (and as it is sayd) this walking place was made Ouale wise, yet very long as of 588 Palmes and 140. Palmes broad.

The Temple of Bacchus (as I sayd) is full of many Ornaments, and of diuers Compartements, whereof I haue shewed some part, but not all.   The thrée inuentions hereunder placed are in the same Temple, some of faire stone: and the other of Pilaister.

THis Temple of peace the Emperor Vespatian caused to bee made by the Market in Rome , which Temple is commended of Plinie, for it was much beautified with grauen worke and Pilaister of Stucco ; and besides these Ornaments of the said Temple, after the death of Nero, Vespatian caused all the Images both of Copper and Marble to bee placed therein, which King Nero had gathered together out of diuers places, which were no small number. Vespatian also placed in it both his owne and his childrens Images made of a new kind of Marble brought out of Ethiopia, called Bassalto, being of an Iron collour, a kind of stuffe much commended in those times. In the said Temple and the principall Chappell thereof, there stood an Image of white Marble very great, made of many pieces; of which reliques there are many pieces yet to bee seene in Campidoglio; and among other pieces there is a foote, whereof the naple of the great Toe is so great that I sate easily vpō it, wherby a man may guesse the greatnesse of the Image, and it was made by an excellent workeman.

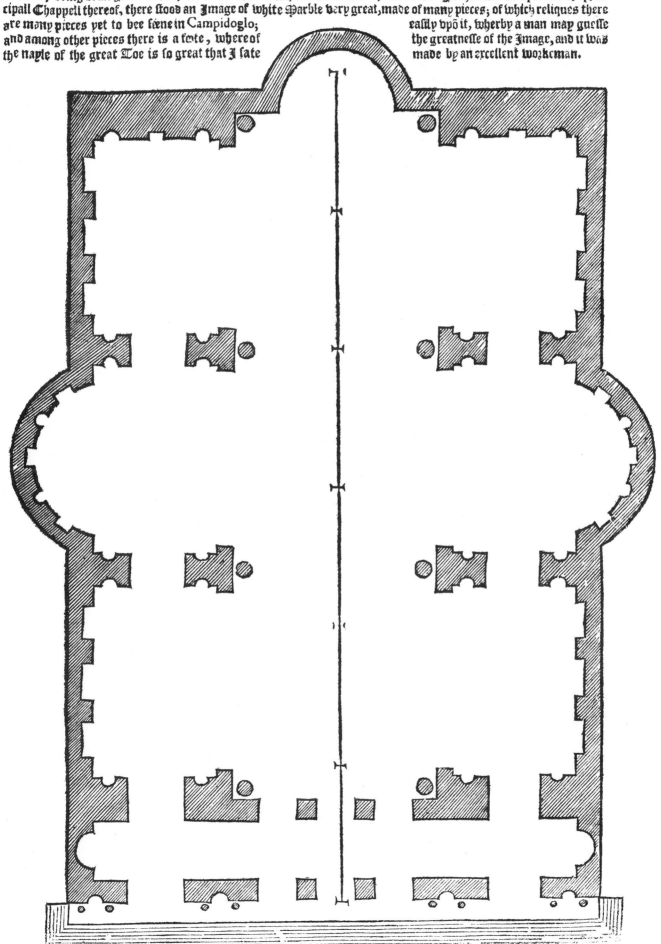

Of Antiquitie

This Temple is meafured with Elles, and the Elle is deuided into 12. parts, called ounces, the meafure which ftandeth in the middle of the ground of the Temple is halfe an Elle: Firft, the length of the lodges about is 122. Elles, the bredth is 15. Elles, the wideneffe of the places before in the lodgis contain 10. Elles, the thickeneffe of the Pillars at the entrie is fiue Elles, and betwæne the one Pillar and the other is 10. Elles, the goings in on both fides, both of the Portall and of the Temple are 16. Elles wide, the length of the whole Temple is about 170. Elles, the bredth containeth 125. Elles; the principall place in the middle of the Temple is 35. Elles. The fides of the Pilafters againft the which the round Columnes ftand are 9 Elles and a halfe, and the thickeneffe of thefe Columnes are 4. Elles, 4. ounces and a halfe, and they are canelert, euery one hauing 24. Canels: the caue or hollowing of each Canell is 5. ounces broad, and the lift thereof one ounce and a halfe; the bredth of the principall Chappell is about 32. Elles, and is halfe a Circle. Thofe on the fides marked A.B. are 37. Elles broad, and goe 16. Elles into the Wall, which is leffe then halfe a Circle: the thickeneffe of the Wall round about the Temple is 12. Elles, although in many places, becaufe of the Bowes, it is much thinner. The Circumferences of the Chappels are 6. Elles thicke, betwæne the one Pilafter and the other, it is 45. Elles; you may conceaue the quantitie of the meafure of many places and windowes with other particular things, by the meafures aforefayd, for the Figure is proportioned. Touching the Ortographie, which is the Figure hereafter following, becaufe the ground is all couered ouer with the ruines thereof; I could not meafure it from the ground to the top, but as much as I conceiued by that part of the ground, and alfo of the ruines which are there to be féene; I make this piece ftanding vpright. I am not certaine whether the Columnes haue this pedeftall vnder them or not, becaufe that men cannot fée the foot of the Columnes. And although that Plini much commendeth this Building, yet there are many vnhandfome things in it, fpecially the Cornices about the Columnes, which are not accompanied with any thing, but ftand bare and naked alone.

This Building is called Templum pietatis , it is made altogether of a kind of rough stone, which is there called Tiburtium, after the Riuer of Tiber; but for that the stone is spongie and ful of holes, it was couered all ouer with a kind of Plaister called Stucco, it is very ruinous, for therein you see no proportion of windowes: neuerthelesse, I haue placed them in the ground where I thought them fittest to stand. This Building is measured with an other Elle, which is deuided into 60. minutes; & the line through the middle of the ground of the Temple is the third part of the said Elle: First, the Columes are an Elle & 18. minutes thicke; the intercolumnes 3. Elles and 14. minutes, the bredth of the gates is 4. Elles and 14. minutes and a halfe, the thicknes of the wall is one Elle and 20. minutes , the length of y̆ Temple is 18. Elles and 20. minutes, the bredth of the Temple is 8. Ells and 30. minutes : the Gallery round about the Temple was flat roofed with foure square pearches : but how the broad place before the Temple was roofed I cannot conceaue, because it is so ruinous. The columnes of this Temple haue no Bases nor any Cinthie, or Proiecture, but stand bare vpon their ground, & well made of Tiburtium, and couered ouer with Stucco. This Temple had the frontespice both behind and before.

Of Antiquitie

The height of the Columnes with the Capitall is 3. minutes lesse then 10. Elles, the thicknesse below (as I sayd before) is 1. Elle and 18. minutes; and the thicknes aboue is 1. Elle and 15. minutes. The height of the Capital is 47. minutes, but the bozel & the cinctie of the Columnes are also reckoned with it; the height of the Architraue is 36. minutes, the height of the Fréses is 1. Elle & 65. minutes. The Cornice is 1. Elle & 8. minutes high, & from thence vpwards, the Timpanum is two Ells and two minutes high. The other particular members marked with ÿ caracters are in greater forme, and accordingly proportioned.

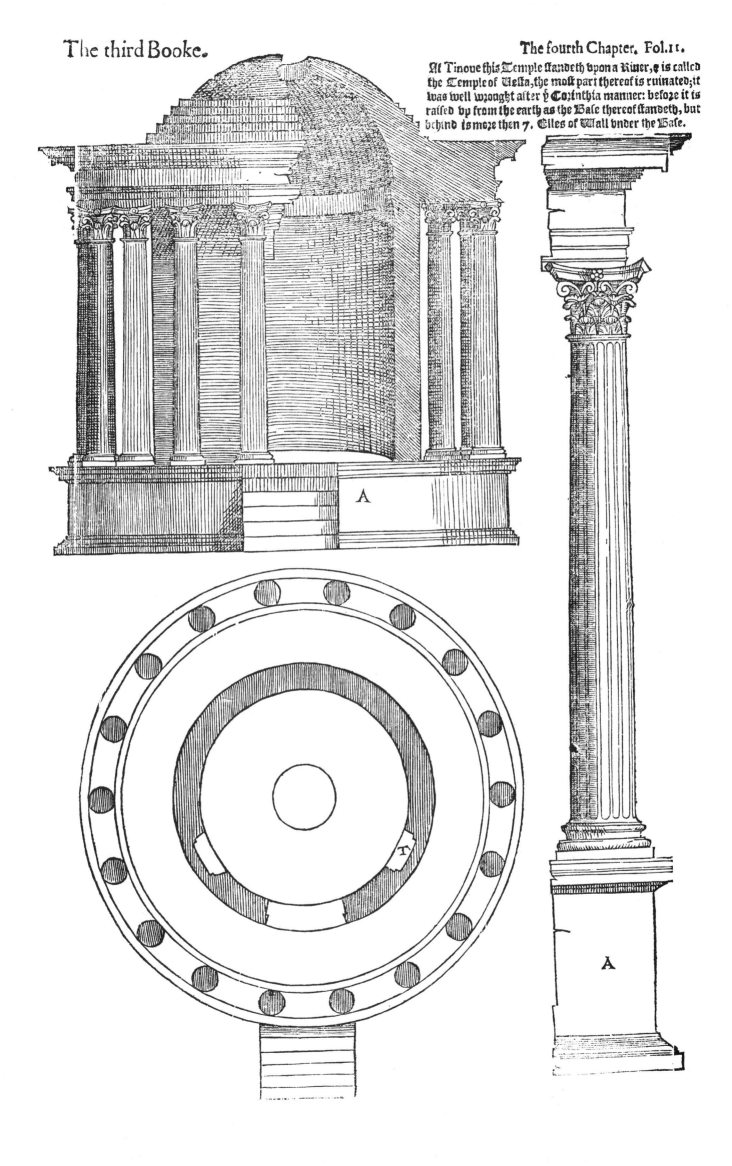

This laſt Temple is meaſured with the laſt Elle of 60. minutes, and firſt, the Columnes are one Elle and 17. minutes thicke, the intercolumnes 2 Elles and 34. minutes; betwéene the Columnes and the Wall is 2. Elles and a halfe, the thickeneſſe of the Wall is an Ell and 13. minutes, the Pauement of the Temple within is 12. Elles and a halfe: the Pedeſtall marked A. with the Columnes and their ornaments ſerue for the whole order of the Temple. The height of the Baſe of the Pedeſtall is 45. minutes, and the fielde of the Pedeſtall is 2. Elles and 48. minutes. The Cornice is 37. minutes and a halfe high, the height of the Baſe of the Columnes is 38. minutes and a halfe; the Trenke of the Columnes is 10 Elles high: the Capitall is an Elle and 24. minutes high. The Architraue, Fréeſe and Cornice all together are about two Elles and a halfe high. The Doore marked with S. Y. is 9. Elles in height, the bredth of the light vnder is 4. Elles 4. minutes, but the wideneſs aboue is 3. Elles 54. minutes, the which is leſſened aboue, according to Vitruuius doctrine. The Antepagmentum is 52. minutes and a halfe broad, but the Supercilie (becauſe of the leſſening) is but 51. minutes; the Fréeſe is 30. minutes high, and the Cornice 24. The Window marked with T. X. is one Elle 46. minutes and a halfe broad, the height containeth 5. Elles 3. minutes, and is leſſened aboue, as the Doore is. The Antepagmentum is 31. minutes and a halfe broad, and the Cornices containeth as much, but the other particular members, are in greater forme marked with the ſame letters ſet by them, and well proportioned: This Window is wrought both within and without.

This is the third part of the common Elles of 60. minutes, wherewith the Temple aforeſayd, and this alſo is meaſured.

W Ithout Rome this ruinous Temple standeth, and for the most part is made of Bricke; you see none of these ornaments therein which I haue here placed in Figure; but as it may be conceiued by the ground thereof, and also considering the proportioned height, it was made of that fashion as the pieces marked A. B. standing by the ground doe shew. Thus we haue the measure of the Ichnographie of the ground of the Temple, by the which measure a man may conceaue the worke of the Orthographie: This Ichnographie or platforme, is measured by the olde Romane Palme : and first, the doore of the Temple is 24. Palmes wide, the Diameter of this Temple is 69, Palmes and a halfe : the two places on the sides are as wide as the Doore; the Doore of the lesser Temple is also of the same bredth, so are the foure Chappels also where men goe in, of the same widenesse, but backward they are wider, because the walles of the side runne to the Center of the Temple, and those foure Chappels (as it may be conceaued) receiue their lights from the sides : the Diameter of the small Temple is 63. Palmes long; the little Chappels, both they that are hollowed out, and those that are eleuated, are 15. Palmes bread: but of those two eleuated or raysed Chappels, I cannot tell how they ended aboue, for there standeth not so much vpright as a man may conceaue any thing thereof certainely, but onely a beginning aboue the earth; and (as I haue said) although a man cannot see in what maner this Building stood aboue the ground , yet according to my conceipt, I haue made this Orthographie.   And therefore on the one side marked B. representeth a piece of the great Temple, and the other marked with A. sheweth a part of the lesser Temple.

The old Roman Palme of 12. fingers, and 48. minutes.

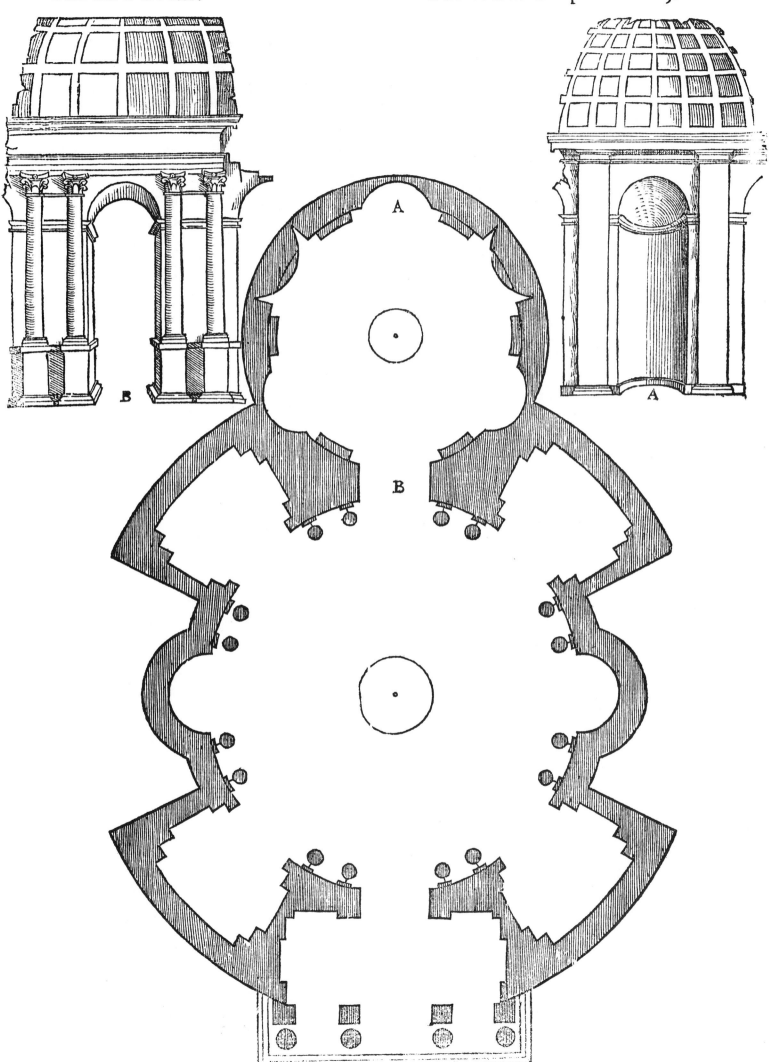

Of Antiquitie

This Temple placed vnder this is without Rome, and is very much ruinated, and for the most part is made of Bricke, it is not very great, it cannot also be discerned, that it had any light in it but at the doores, and from the windowes aboue the Cornices. And all the rest of the holes were placed for Idols or such like things; the measure of this Temple was lost by the way, but yet I remember well that the Temple was a full Quadrant and a halfe, as well on the ground as aboue, therefore I let downe no other measure, but a skilfull workeman may helpe himselfe therewith by inuention.

This small Tempel is of no great compas, and all made of Bricke; it is measured by the olde Romane Palme, the length of the lodge or Gallery is 40. Palms, the breadth therof is 16. Palmes, the Doore is 10. Palms, the places in the walles within, are all of one widenes, that is, 14. Palmes; the space between them is 6. Palmes, the rest may bee guessed by sight; for I guess the height from the Pauement to the Architraue to be 40. Palmes, and the Architraue, Freese and Cornice to bee 9. Palmes; and touching the rest, I made account that if I allowed a Palme vpright for the round roofe, then the whole Tempel should be about 70. Palmes.

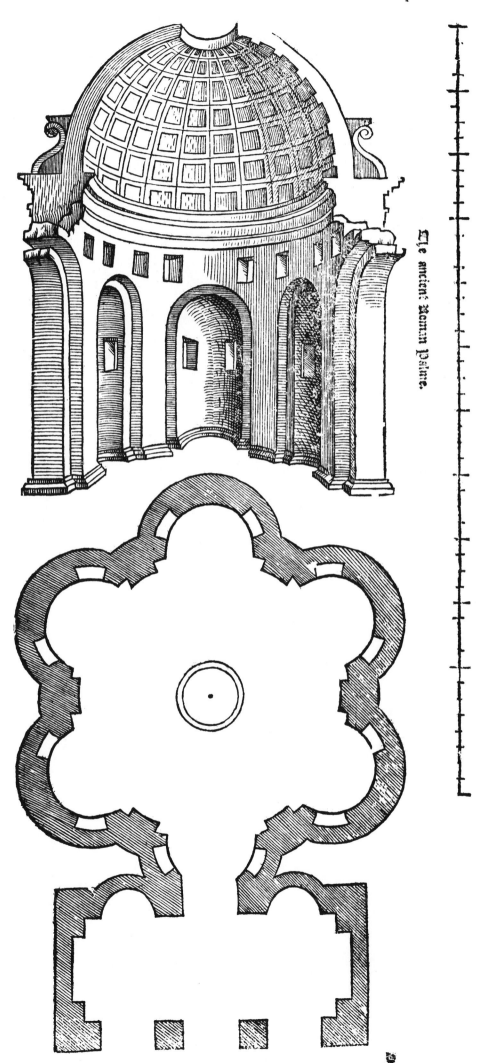

The ancient Roman Palme.

This Temple is without Rome, made part of Marble, and the rest of Brick, it is much decayed, it is thought that it was a Sepulchre, and on all sides it is right foure square; frō the one Wall to the other is 30. Palmes broad, the thicknesse of the walles is 2. Palms and a halfe, the widenesse of the Chappel is ten Palmes, the Dore is fiue Palmes broad, the height of the Pillars with Bases and Capitals is 22. Palms and a halfe; the thickenesse of the Pillars is not much aboue two Palmes: The Architraue, Freese & Cornice are 4 Palmes high, from the Cornice to the height of the roofe is 11. Palmes: the height of the Bowes of the Chappel is 20. Palmes.

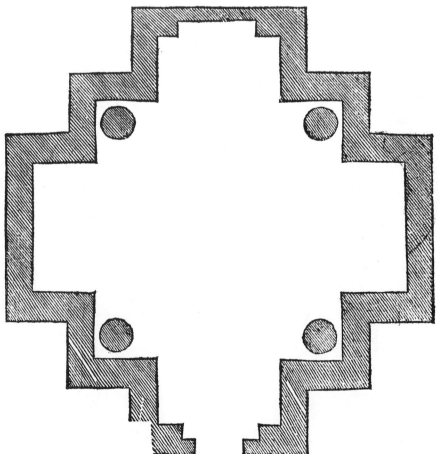

Ｔﾋis Temple hereunder set downe is A Tiuoli by the Riuer, much decayed, which had the frontispice before and behind the Columnes, on the sides are more then halfe without the wall; the widenesse of the Temple from the one wall to the other, is 11. Elles measure by the same measure that Templum pacatis is measured withall, the length of the Temple is 8 Elles, the thicknesse of the wall is one Elle and 11. minutes, the thicknes of the Columnes of the Portall is an Ell and a third part, the height of them with Bases and Capitals is about 12. Elles, the height of the Architraue, Frese and Cornice is three Elles, the Frontispice from aboue the Cornice to the height is 3. Elles, the height of the basement is 3. Elles and a halfe. In the Fascie before, there is no show of a Doore, nor of any places in the Walles, by reason of the ruinousnesse thereof, but I haue drawne it out thus, to make the more show, because I iudge it had bene so; neither can you see any windowes in the wales nor sides, nor yet behind, although I haue placed them here in the ground, where I thought best. The measure of the members both of the Basement and the Cornices aboue, I will not name particularly, for they are proportioned according to Antiquitie, whereof you may see some parts.

The third part of the Ell aforesayd.

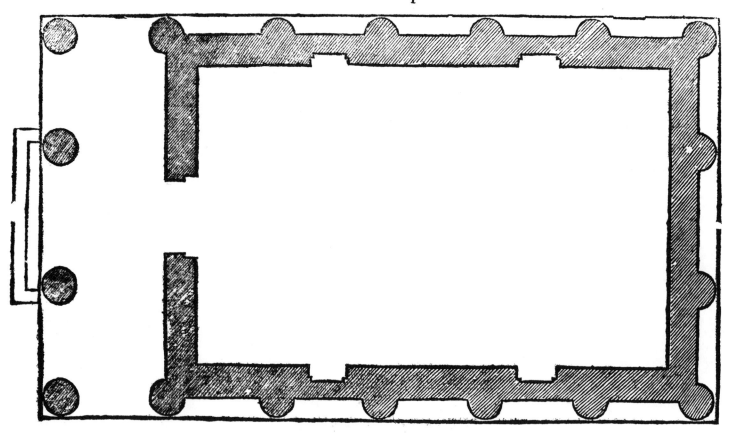

ALthough at the beginning of this Booke, I said I would speake onely of Antiquities, yet I will not omit withall to entreat of some moderne things made in our time, and specially, because our age hath flourished with so many good wits for invention of Architecture.   There was in the time of Pope Iulio the second, a workeman called Bramante of Casteldurante in the Dukedome of Vrbin, who was a man of so great understanding in Architecture, that it might be sayd (by meanes of the ayde and performents which the Pope gaue him) that hee raysed vp good Architecture againe, which from ancient time till then had báne hidden and kept secret: which Bramant in his time layd the foundation or beginning of the wonderfull worke of S. Peters Temple in Rome, but being preuented by death, did not onely leaue it vnfinished, but the modell thereof also was left vnperfect, wherein diuers ingenious workemen sought to busie themselues both to perfect and finish it; and amongst many others Raphael Durbin, Paynter, a man also very skilfull in Architecture, following Bramants steps, made perfect this draught, the which in my opinion is one of the fayrest draughts that are to be found, out of the which the ingenious workeman may helpe himselfe in many things. I will not set downe all the measures of this Tempel (because that it is well proportioned) and a man may by part of the measure find out the rest.   This Tempel is measured with the old Romane Palme, and the broadest walkes therein is 92. Palmes broade, those of the sides are but halfe as much: by these two measures you may guesse the rest.

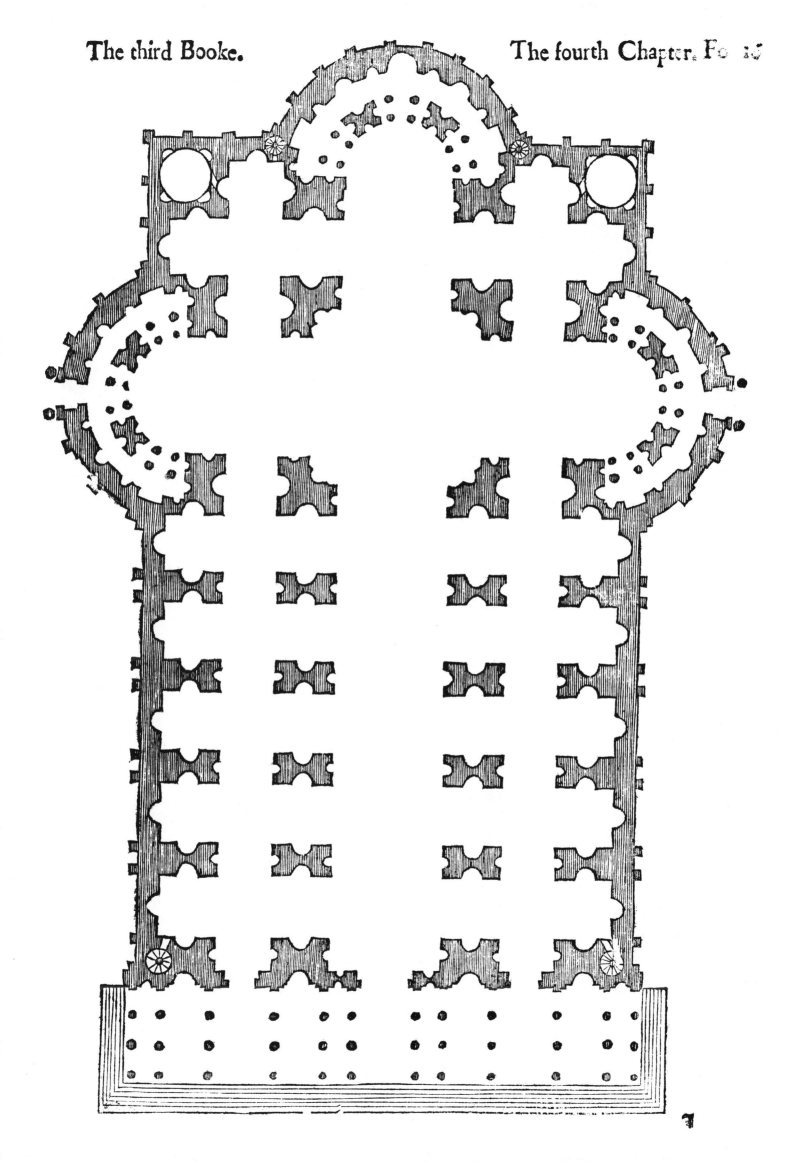

Of Antiquitie

In the time of Iulius the second, there was in Rome one Balthazar Petrucio of Sienne, not onely an excellent Paynter, but also very skilfull in Architecture, who following the doctrine of Bramant, made a modell in forme hereunder set downe: whose meaning was, that the Temple should haue foure gates to go into it, and that the high Altar should stand in the middle thereof: at the foure Corners he made foure Sacristes, vpon the top whereof men might place the Clocketowers for an ornament thereunto; and the first part or Facie thereof looked into the Citie. This Temple is measured with the olde Romane Palme, and first, it is in the middle from one Pilaster to another 204. Palmes, the Diameter of the Circle in the middle is 184. Palmes long. The Diameter of the foure small Circles is 65. Palmes. The Sacristes are 100. Palmes wide. The foure Pilasters in the middle make foure Bowes or Arches which beare vp the Lanthorne, and these foure Bowes or Arches are all full made, which are in height 220. Palmes, and aboue these Arches a Tribune excellently set foorth with Columnes, with a round Roofe vpon it, which Bramant ordayned before hee died, whereof the ground is here set downe.

The Figure hereunder set down, is the ground of the Tribune that should haue gone aboue ouer the foure Bowes or Arches (as I sayd before) whereby a man may perceiue, that Bramant in such case was bolder to draw a piece of worke, then circumspect therein; because so great and massie a piece of worke should haue an excellent foundation to stand very fast, and not to be made vpon foure Bowes or Arches of such an height. And for confirmation of my speech, the foure Pilasters, and also the Arches without any other waight vpon them, are already settled and suncke, yea, and rent in some places : Neuerthelesse, because the inuention is fayre and costly, and a thing to giue good instruction to a workeman : I thought it good to place it here in a modell: but not to be tedious in setting downe the measures, I will shew some of the principallest; the rest you may finde with the small Palme which standeth here within the ground, which length containeth 50. Palms: the thicknesse of the first Columne without, is 5. Palmes, the thicknesse of the second Columne within, is 4. Palmes, and the thicknesse of the third Columne is 3. Palmes and three quarters. The widenesse of the Tribune within, is 188. Palmes, the Diameter of the small Lanthorne within the middle, is 36. Palmes; the rest you may guesse by the small Palme.

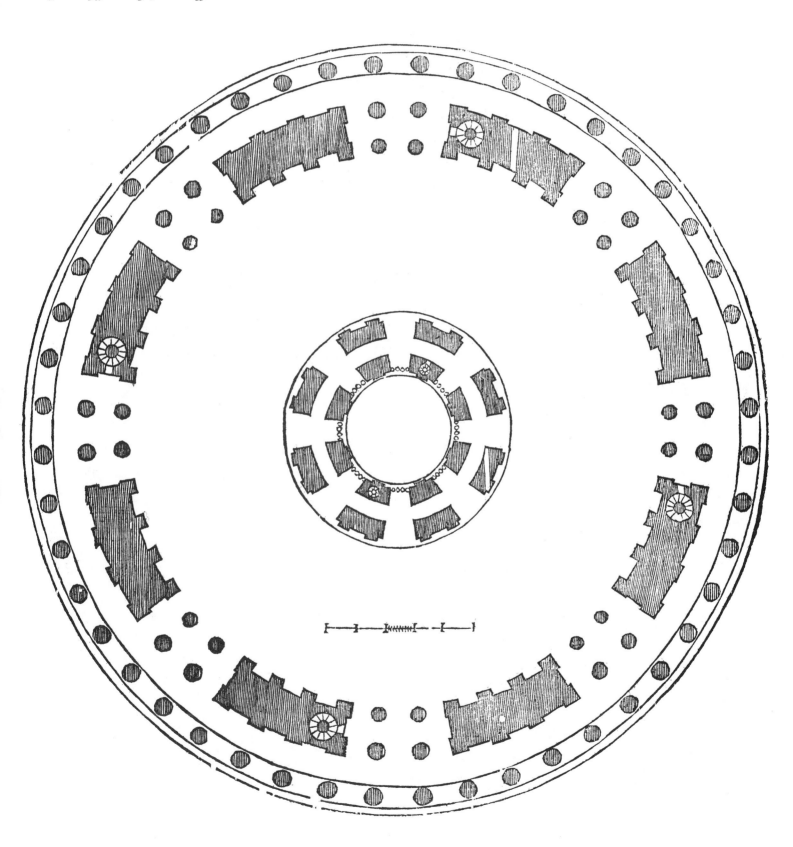

This is the Orthographie both within and without, drawne out of the Ichnographie afore set downe, whereby you may conceaue the great maffe & waight which should haue ftood vpon the foure Arches; which waight may giue any wife workeman matter to confider, that it had bene fitter to fet it vpon the ground, and not in the ayre vpon fuch a height; and therefore I counfell all workemen rather to be doubtfull then to rafh: for if hee bee doubtfull, he will make his worke furer, and not defpife another mans counfell;

which doing, hee fhall feldome faile; but if hee be rafh and ftout, hee will not take any other mens aduife, but will trufft only to his own inuention, wherby oftentimes his worke doeth him more fhame then honeftie: therefore I conclude, that ftoutnes proceedeth from prefumption, and prefumption from fmall vnderftanding; and I fay, that doubtfulneffe or bafhfulneffe is a vertue, making a man to thinke hee knoweth little, although his vnderftáding be great: the meafure of this worke is to be found by the aforefayd fmall Palme.

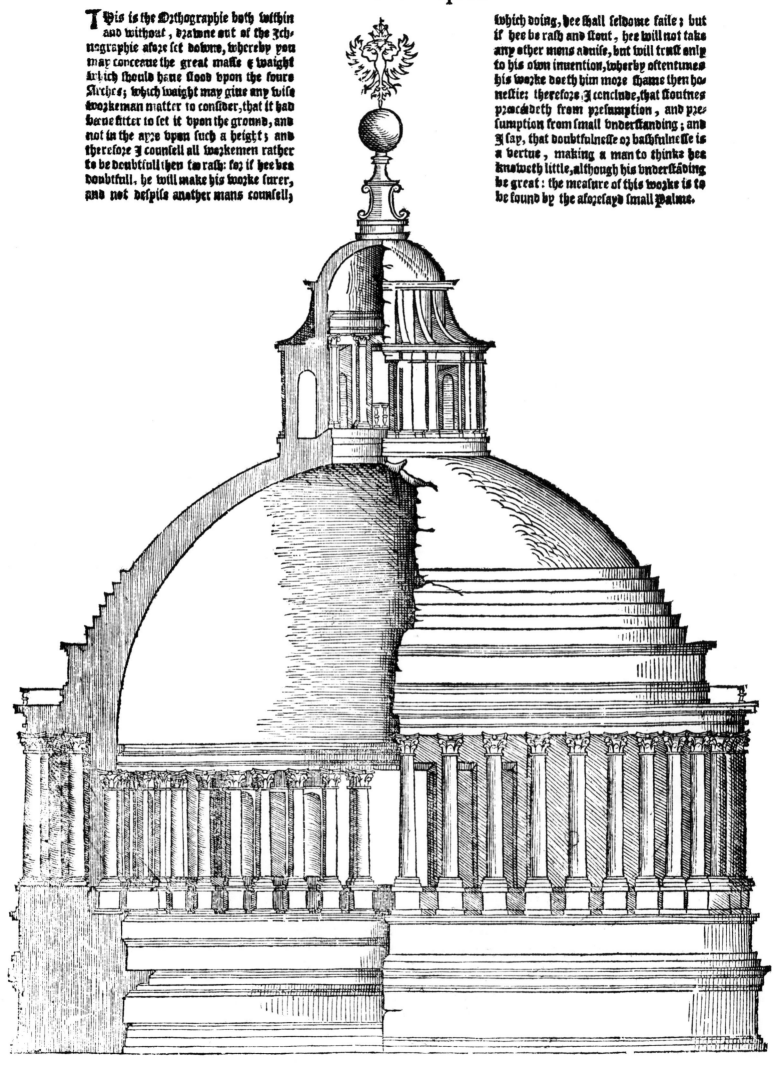

This ground set vnder this, is also an inuention of Bramant, though it was neuer made, which agreed with the old worke: that part which is marked with B. is S. Peters Church in Montorio without Rome; and that part marked with A. is an old Cloyster, but that part in the middle, Bramant ordayned, thereby to helpe himselfe with the old worke: the place marked C. signifieth a Gallery with foure Chappels in the corners. The place B. standeth vnder the apre: the part marked E. is a litle Temple, which the said Bramant made: the measures wherof shalbe shewed in much greater forme in the leafe ensuing. I haue said nothing touching the measure of the ground, but I haue set this here onely for the inuention.

B

C

D

E

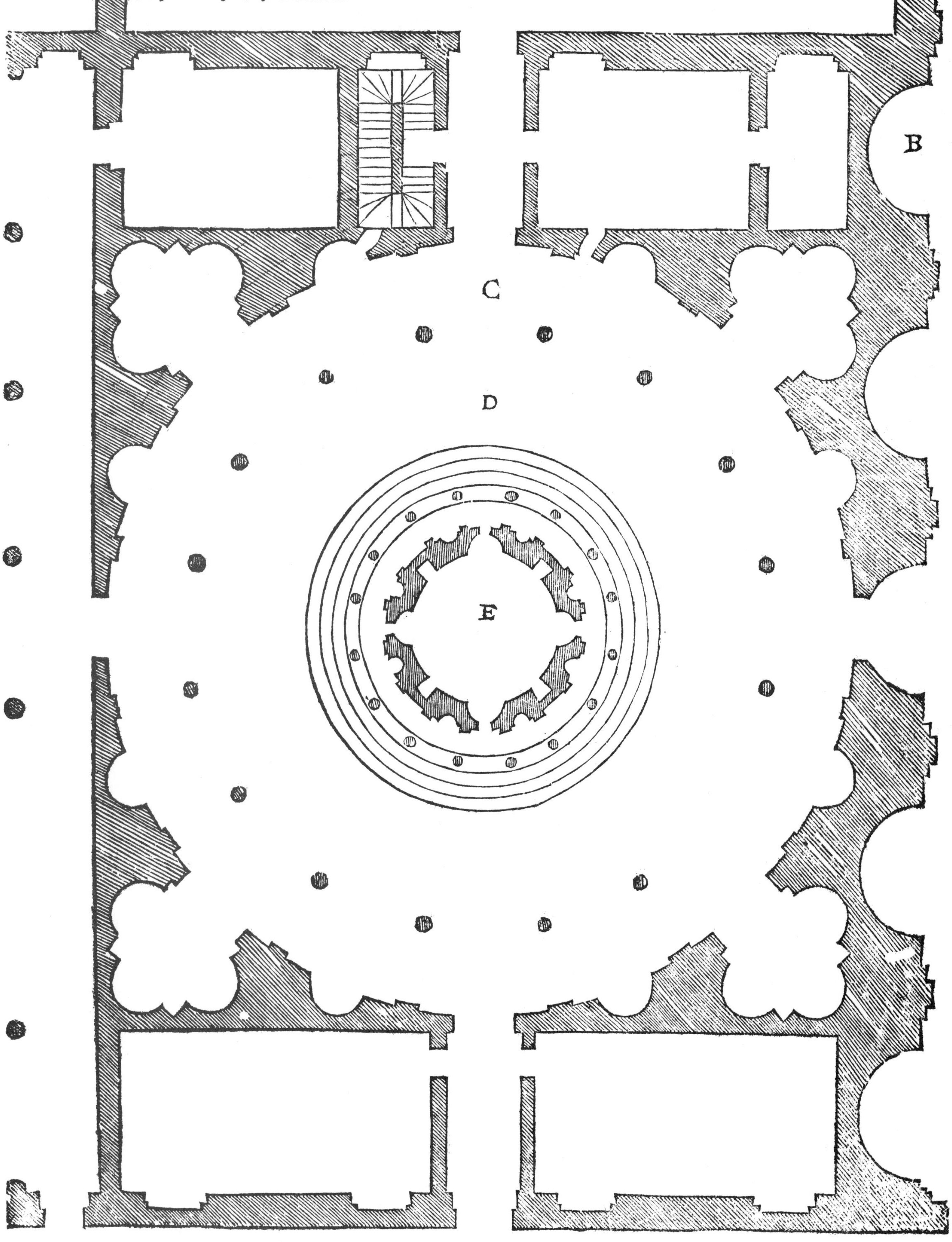

IN the laſt ſide I promiſed to ſhew Bramants Temple in greater forme, which is not very great, but was onely made in remembrance of S. Peter the Apoſtle, for it is ſaid that hee was crucified in that place: the ſayd Temple is to bee meaſured by the old Romane foote, which foote is ſixteene fingers; and every finger is foure minutes: wherof alſo you ſhall finde the meaſure by the Romane Palme, augmenting the ſaid foure fingers. The Diameter of this Temple is of five and twenty foote, and two and twenty minutes. The wideneſſe of the walke round about the Temple is ſeven foote, the thickneſſe of the Columnes are one foote and 25. minutes. The wideneſſe of the Doore is three foote and a halfe: The Quadrants with the rounbels within, which goe round about the Temple, ſhew the Lacunary of the Temple above the Columnes: the thickneſſe of the wall is five foote; the reſt of the other meaſures you may conceave by the firſt.

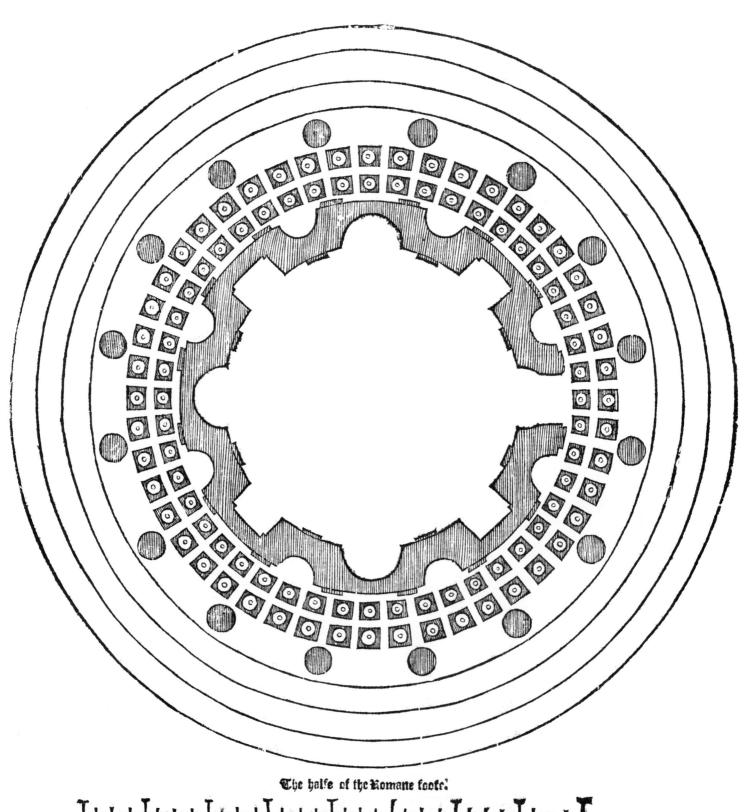

The halfe of the Romane foote.

This is the said Temple standing vp , which sheweth the one halfe without, and the other halfe within, and is made altogether after the Dozica, as you see by the Figure.   I will not speake of the patticular measures: for by the ground you may conceaue this which stands vpright, for that this (though it be small) is set downe by the measures thereof, and from the great reduced into the small.

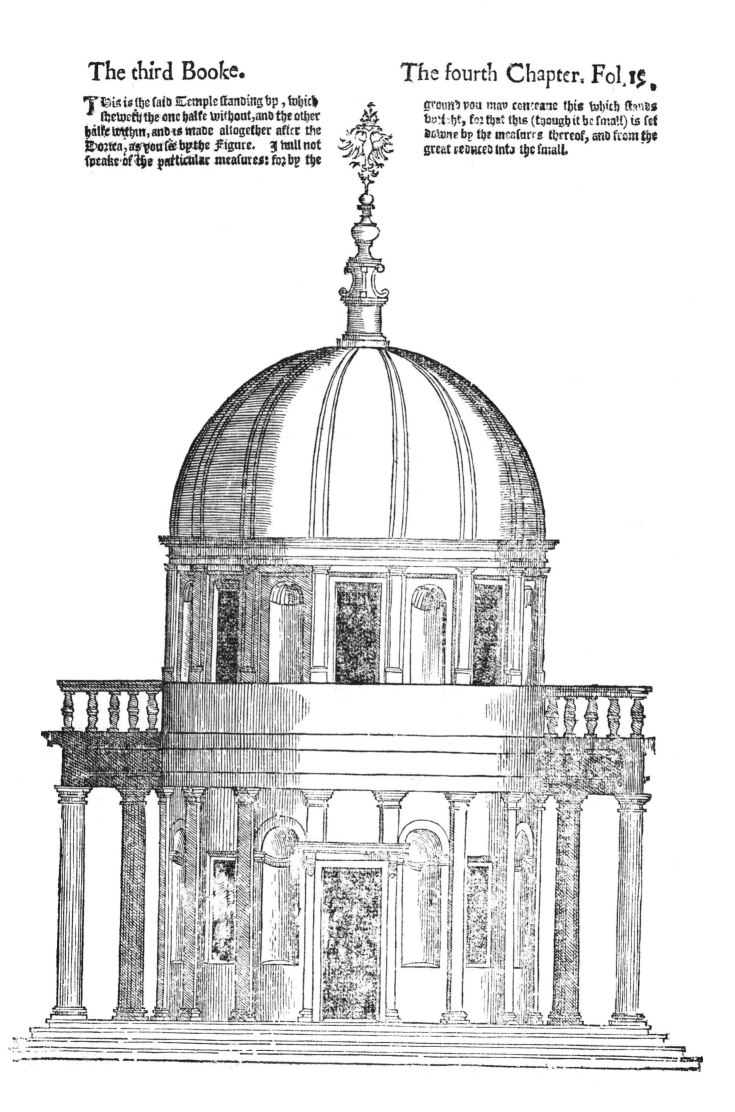

Now I haue shewed the outside of S. Peters Temple, in this I will shew the innermost part, which is made with such proportion, that the workesman by the widenesse of the ground, may finde all the measures: and although that this Temple sheweth to high for the bredth, for that it is thought and shewed to be as high as it is broad: Notwithstanding, by the opennesse of the windowes, and the Kichens or Chappels that are in it, the height thereof is not amisse, and especially by meanes of the double Cornices, which goe round about, and couer much of the height together with the Proiecture, the Temple sheweth much more as it is.

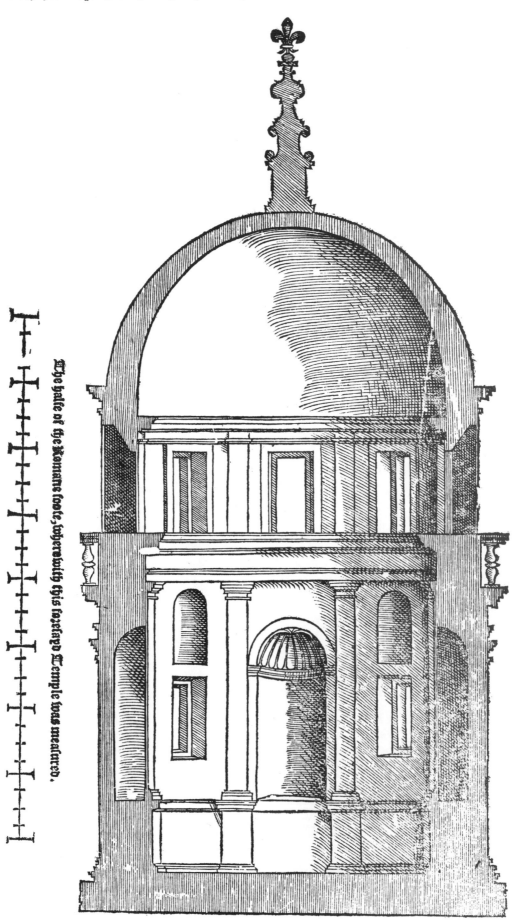

The halfe of the Romane foote, wherewith this foresayd Temple was measured.

This Building is without Rome, at S. Sebastians, and is all fallen downe to the ground, especially the walks about, but the Building in the middle (because it is very sure worke) is yet whole, and is made of Bricke: you see no ornaments in it at all, & it is darke, because it hath no light but at the Doore; and about the foure hollow places in the wall, some small Windowes. The ground of this worke is measured with the old Romish Palme, and the lengths with the breadths are measured with roodes, and every roode is ten Palmes. First, the walke or Gallery marked A. is 49. roodes and 3. Palmes, the other two longer, are 56. roodes and 3. Palmes: the breadth of the walkes is 32. Palmes: the thicknesse of the corner Pillars, with all their members, is 12. Palmes: by the which measures you may conceaue the rest. Touching the Building in the middle, the place B. is vncouered, and is in length 7. roodes and 6. Palmes: the breadth is 3. roodes and 4. Palmes: the part marked C. is couered, and containeth 4. roodes in foure square. The foure Pilasters are ten Palmes thicke: the thicknesse of the wall round about the round Building, is 24. Palmes: the place marked E. is rooft: and that part in the middle is a masse, which beareth the roofe; in the middle whereof, there is an opening: and this masse is beautified with many hollow seates in it, which stand right, and accompany those that stand in the wall: touching the heights (because of the brokennesse) I measured it not; and especially, because there was no beautifulnesse of Building.

This Theater Augustus made in the name of Marcellus his Nephew, and therefore it was called Marcellus Theater, it standeth within Rome, you may at this day see part of it standing vpright, that is part of the Galleries without: it is onely of two rules, that is, Dorica and Ionica, a worke, in truth, that is much commended, although the Doricall Columnes haue no Bases, nor any Cincte or Proiecture vnder them, but stand plainely without any thing vnder, vpon the flat ground of the Gallery. Touching the ground of this Theater, men could not well conceaue it: but not long since, the great Patrician of Rome, going to make a house, the scituation whereof was to be set vpon part of the Theater (this house was made by one Balthasar of Sienna, an excellent workman) and as he caused the foundation to be digged, there were found many reliques of diuers Cornices of this Theater, and a great part of the same Theater was discouered, whereby Balthasar conceyted the whole forme thereof, and measured it with great circumspection, placing it in the forme following: my selfe being at that time in Rome, saw many of the Cornices, and found friendship to measure them, and in truth, there I found as excellent formes as euer I saw in any old Ruins, and most in the Capitals of Dorica, and also in the imposts of the Arches, which, me thinks, agree well with the doctrine of Vitruuius. Likewise the Freese, Trigliphen, and Methopen, agree well inough: but the Dorica Cornice, although it be very full of members, and well wrought, yet I found it to differ much from Vitruuius instructions: for being licencious inough of members, was of such a height, that the two third parts of such height should haue beene inough to the Architraue and the Freese. But I am of opinion therefore, (by the licence of these, or other Antiquities) that a workeman in these dayes should not erre, (which error, I meane, is to doe contrary to Vitruuius precepts) nor to bee peremptory that hee will make a Cornice, or other thing iust of the same proportion as hee hath sene and measured, and then set it in worke; because it is not sufficient for him to say, I may doe it: for ancient workemen haue done it, without consideration whether it be proportioned according to the rest of the building. Besides, although an old workeman was so bold, yet we must therefore not bee so, (but as reason teacheth vs) wee should obserue Vitruuius rules as our guide, and most certayne and infallible directions: for that from that time of great Antiquity, till now, there is no man found to haue written better, nor more learnedly of Architecture then he: and as in euery Arte there is one more learned then another, to whom such authority is giuen, that his words are fully, e without doubt belaeued. Who then will deny (if he be not ignorant) that Vitruuius, for Architecture, is worthy of the highest degree? and that his writings (where no other notable reason or cause is to moue vs) ought for the worthinesse thereof to be inuiolably obserued, and to bee better credited, then any workes of the Romanes? which Romanes, although they learned the vpright maner of building of the Grecians, neuerthelesse, afterward when they became Rulers ouer the Grecians, it may be that some of them thereby became licencious: but certaynely, if a man might see the wonderfull works which the Grecians then did make, (which are now almost all spoyled and cast downe in time of warre) hee would assuredly iudge the Grecians worke to surpasse that of the Latines farre.

Therefore all those workemen that shall condemne Vitruuius writing, e specially in such cases as are clearely vnderstood, as in the order of Dorica, whereof I spake, should erre much in the Art of Architecture, to gainesay such an Author, as for so many yeeres hath beene, and yet is approoued by wise men, learned. Now hauing made this digression, which was necessary for the good of those that would not haue considered so much, turning againe to the purpose, I say, that this ground was measured by the old Romane foote; and first, the place in the middle, marked A. which is called Orchestra, is in the Diameter 194. foot, and is halfe a Circle from one corner to the other: of the stages or seates, marked H. it is 417. foote: the place marked B. called Proscenium, is very spacious; and where C. standeth, is the Gallery, which they call Porticus of the Scene, in the middle whereof stood the Pulpit: that part marked with D. was a Portall, with Stayres on both sides, which went vp to the places marked E. called Hospitalia: the two Galleries on the sides marked G. they vsed to walke in: Of which things men can see no more aboue the ground, for that they are couered with other houses. Touching the seuerall measures, as well of the Scene as of the Theatre, and of the degrees, I will say no more: for that in the Amphitheatre called Coliseo, I will declare it more at large, whereby a man may conceaue how this stood: but that part without, which went about the Theatre, I will shew in the second Figure, which was measured (before this) with a common Ell, which is deuided into twelue parts, which parts are called ounces: and euery ounce hath fiue minutes; of which Ell, this is a third part.

The third part of the Ell.

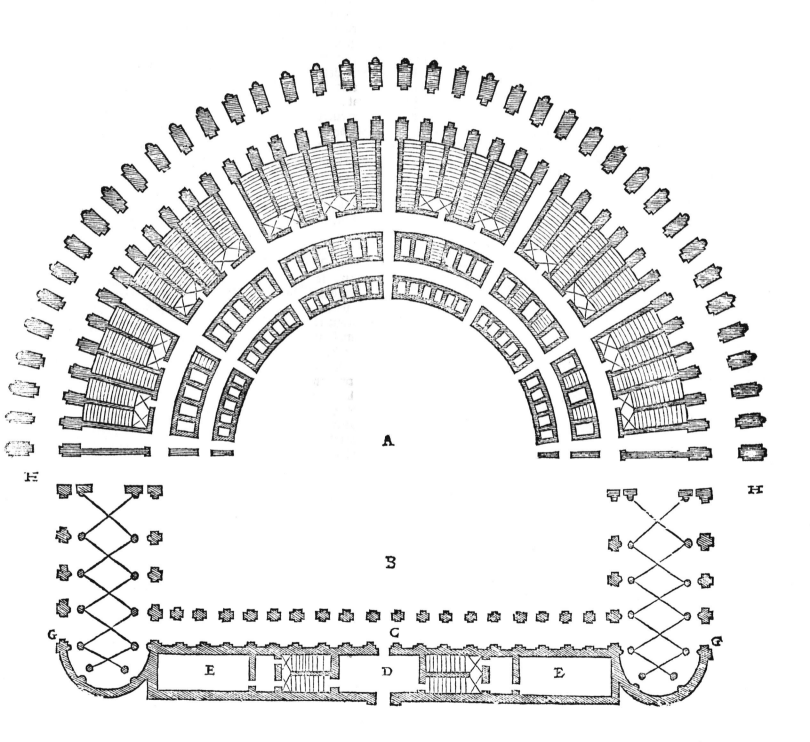

This Figure following representeth that part without, of the foresayd Theater, and is measured with the Ell aforesayd: and first, the thickenesse of the Columnes beneath in the nether part of the first order, is an Ell and 43. minutes in Diameter: and the thicknesse of the Diameter aboue vnder the Capitall, is an Ell and 16. minutes: the height of the Capitall, is halfe the thicknesse of the Columnes beneath, the which Capitall is more perfecter marked in the fourth Booke, in the order of Dorica, in Folio E. 3. And the same Capitall is marked with B. Likewise also the impost, whereon the Arch resteth, is as high also as the Capitall, and standeth also in the same leafe E. 3. The Pilasters, beside the Columnes, are 19. minutes: the wideneſſe of one Arch, is 7. Elles and 9. minutes: and the height is eleuen Elles and sixteene minutes; the height of the Architraue, is 49. minutes: the height of the Freese is one Ell and eyght minutes. The height of the whole Cornice, is an Ell, and fourtie minutes: the wideneſſe of the second Arch of the second order, is as wide as that below; but the height is ten Elles and fourtie and eyght minutes: the height of the Pedestall vnder the Columnes of this second order, is an Ell and fourtie and eyght minutes: the thicknesse of the Columnes, is an Ell and twenty & foure minutes: the height of the said Columnes without Bases or Capitals, is 11. Elles, 27. minutes: the height of the Bases is 44. minutes: the height of the Capitall, that is within the Volutes, from the list of the Columnes, to aboue the Capital, is 36. minutes: but the Volute hangs ouer the Astragall or Bozell 20. minutes and a halfe, which in all, from beneath the Volutes, to aboue the Abacus, is 47. minutes and a halfe: the breadth of the Abacus of the sayd Capitall is one Ell and a halfe: but the breadth of the Volutes is two elles: the height of the Architraue is 59. minutes: the height of the Freese is 58. minutes: the height of the Cornice is an Ell, & 48. minutes: which Cornice, in truth, is halfe so much more as it should be (if we will credit Vitruuius precepts.) But I pray you, gentle Reader, esteeme me not presumptuous, neither yet account me for a corrector of the workes of Antiquitie, from whence men learne so much: for my meaning is onely, willingly to let you vnderstand and know that which is well made from that which is ill made: and that I will not doe after my owne conceite, as if you were taught by me, but by the authority of Vitruuius: and also of good Antiquities, which are those which best agree with the doctrine of that Author. The Base of this second order, and the Pedestall vnder it, the Impost of the Arches, and withall, the Architraue, Freese and Cornice, you shall altogether find in the fourth Booke of the order of Ionica in Folio K. the second, and are all marked with T. Likewise you shall find the Capitall in the same fourth booke, behind in the leafe I. the 4. marked with M.

The third part of the foresayd Ell, of 60. minutes.

IN Dalmatia there is an ancient town called Pola, lying by the Sea side, wherin you may sée a great part of a Theatre, in the making wherof, the expert workeman did helpe himselfe with the hill whereon it standeth, vsing the hill for part of the degrées or steps to goe vp, and in the playne below, he made the Orchestra, Scene, and other buildings belonging to such a piece of worke. And in trueth, the ruines and the pieces which are yet at this day found, doe shew that it was a most beautifull and sumptuous piece of worke of stone and workemanship; besides this, there you may sée a great number of Columnes, some standing alone, others with Pilasters, and some Corners with foure square Pillars, and some halfe round, all bound together, and well wrought, after the Corinthia; for the whole work, both without and within, was made after the Corinthia manner. This Building was measured with a moderne or usuall foote: which foote is deuided into twelue parts, named ounces, whereof the one halfe hereafter followeth. The Figure hereafter following, sheweth the Ichnographie, and also the Profill of the Theatre, whereof this is the measure: the widenesse of the Orchestra which is halfe a Circle, is in Diameter about 130. foote; the degrees or steps round about, with the two wayes or strates, are of 70 foot: the way marked T comes euen with the plaine of the Pulpit of the Scene to the fouretéenth step. The widenesse of the Porticus round about the Theatre, is 15. foote, and the sides of the Pillars inward, is of 17. foot & a halfe; but the fore-rancke of the Pillars round about the Gallery, together with the Columnes, holdeth about fiue foot in bredth, and from the one Pilaster to the other, it is about 10. foot wide: and this is touching the ground of this Theater. The two greatest Quadrans marked O. are the Hospitalia, from the which places men went into the entry or passing through, marked T. which comes vp to the street, halfe way to the steps, as you may perceiue by the Profill marked T. and vnder the going through, is part of the going in. The Hospitalia is fiue and fourtie foote, the bredth of the Scene, is 21. foot, the bredth of the Porticus or Gallery before, is 27 foote, and the length is like the house; the Building which standeth aboue the ground of the Theatre, signifieth the Profill, which is cut through the sides of the Theatre. The Arch marked with A. signifieth the going in, the second Arch C. and B. are vnder the steps, the Cornice besides marked with D. is the impost of the Arches: there néeded no going vp to this Theatre, for the hill aforesayd eased the workeman therein, and men might also goe vp to the Theatre from the Scene, because it was ioyned to the sayd Theatre: but the Theatre of Marcellus is seperated from the Scene, and therfore the goings vp were necessarie.

This is the halfe foote of measure, whereby this Theatre was measured with all the ornaments.

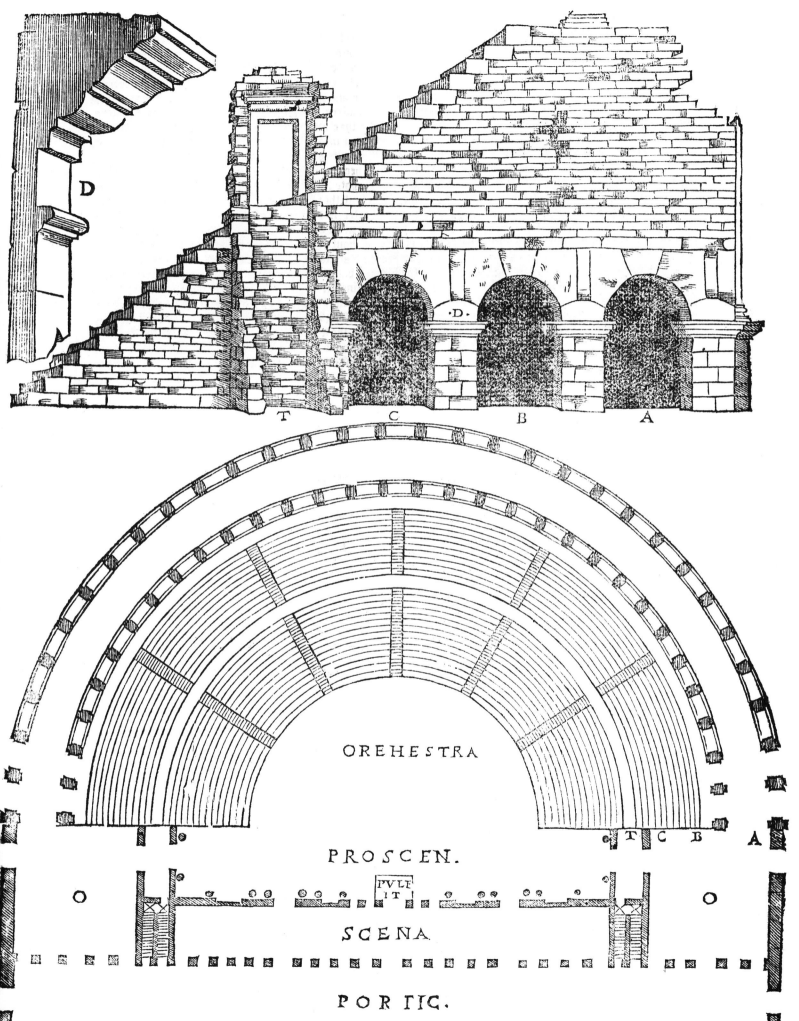

OREHESTRA

PROSCEN.

PVLE IT

SCENA

PORTIC.

This Theater (as I haue sayd) was very rich of ornaments, all of stone, and made of Corinthia worke, very well and richly wrought, and by as much as is seene by the ruines which lie scattering about the Scene, was very beautifull of Columnes vpon Columnes, both double and single, and also in the innermost and outtermost parts, with diuers ornaments of Doores and Windowes. The innermost part of the Building is much ruinated: and touching the measures, I can say little; but of the outtermost parts, I will say somewhat of their measures. The first, a rusticall or clounish order, wherein there is no Columnes, is eleuated from the earth, together with the whole Cornice, marked E. about 16. foote: the height of the first Pedestall, is fiue foote, the height of the Columnes with the Bases and Capitals, is 22. foot; the thickenesse of the Pillars, with the Columnes, is 5. foote: the thicknesse of the Columnes alone, is two foote and a halfe: the widenesse of the Arches, is about ten foote: and their height twenty foote: the height of the Architraue, Freese and Cornice, is about fiue foote; the second Pedestall marked X. is of foure foote and a halfe: the height of those Columnes are about sirteene foot, the Architraue, Freese and Cornice, is foure fot high. I set not downe the measures of the particular members, but in the Figure you may conceaue them; for they are iust of the same proportion: I set not downe the measure of the Scene, nor of the other parts within: onely I haue here set foorth a part of the Porticus of the Scene, which is marked P. And also the Cornice, Freese and Architraue marked F. was in the highest thereof: the Capitals marked S. stode within, with some halfe round Columnes, rayled out of some Pilasters, things that were very well wrought: all which things (as I sayd before) are so sumptuous, both for stone and workemanship, as they may well be compared with those of Rome: the Cornice, Freese and Architraue, marked A. was in the highest part of the Theatre: the Cornice marked B. is the impost of the second Arch: the Architraue, Freese and Cornice, marked C. is the Cornice aboue the first Arch, the Cornice marked D. is the impost of the Arch: the Cornice marked with E. goeth aboue the rusticall basement round about the Building: this line hereunder is halfe a foote, of the whole foote wherewith this Building was measured. And wonder not, gentle Reader, that I set not downe all the measures more precisely; for these things of Pola, were measured by one that had more vnderstanding in casting, then in measuring.

The halfe foote, whereby this is measured.

AT Ferenten, an old Towne lying by Veterben, there is yet to bee ſeene the forme of a Theatre, much decayed, being of no great workemanſhip, and leſſe ornaments, for any thing a man may perceaue by the ſame ; for there are no pieces to be ſeene whereby a man may concept any matter of importance. But you may yet ſee in the Porticus going from the Theatre, there were foure ſquare Pillars, alſo the Stayres thereof were very ſimple and playne: and becauſe it is ſo much decayed, you can hardly diſcerne how they ſtood. The Scene of this Theatre is much different from others, as you may ſee in the ground thereof: neither is there ſo much ſtanding aboue ground, that a man may perceaue how the Scene and the Pulpit thereof ſtood. This ground was meaſured by the ancient foote, and firſt, ſpeaking of the Orcheſtra A. which is halfe a Circle, the Diameter thereof is 141. foot and a halfe long. The body of the Theatre, that is, from the Orcheſtra, to the outtermoſt of the Corner Pillars of the Porticus, is 35. foot : the Pillars of the corner on eyther ſide, is 5. foote broad : the entry of the Porticus on the ſide of the Scene, is 8. foote : the vault vnder the Stayres, is 22. foote : the thickeneſſe of the Wall about the Orcheſtra, is 3. foote and a halfe : the Hoſpitalia, marked X. is in length 40. foot and a halfe; and in bredth 30. foote : the wideneſſe of the Porticus about the Theatre, is 11. foote : the Pillars are thicke and broad, 3. foote and 3. quarters : the wideneſſe of the Arch, is 9. foote : the iuſt bredth of the Orcheſtra marked B. is 20. foote : the place of the Pulpit C. is in length 40. foote and a halfe ; but the bredth is 12. foote : the going through, is 9. foote. The place marked D. ſhould be the Porticus behind the Scene: yet there is no ſhew of any Columnes ; but it ſhewth that there was a wall ſtanding by the water ſide. The bredth of this place, is 19. foot and a halfe. Without this Theatre there ſtandeth the foundation of two Buildings, but they are ſo much decayed, that you can find no end of them: neuertheleſſe, the Building marked F. for as much as you ſee of it, ſheweth that it was ioyned to other things. The wideneſſe wherein the F. ſtandeth, is 31. foote. The 2. ſmall places or ſancies holding vp the one ſide, are eyght foot and a halfe ; and on the other ſide, ten foot and a halfe. The Arches where the foure Columnes ſtand (which I take be made in that manner) are in length 27. foot and a halfe, and in bredth ten foot and a halfe. The bredth of the Building marked E. is twenty foot : the hollow places in the ſides, are 17. foote: the length of all together, is 60. foote, and is diſtant from the Theatre one hundred and one and fortie foot : and from the other Building, ſeuentie foote and a halfe.

The halfe of the olde foote.

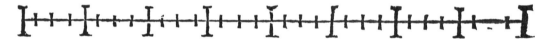

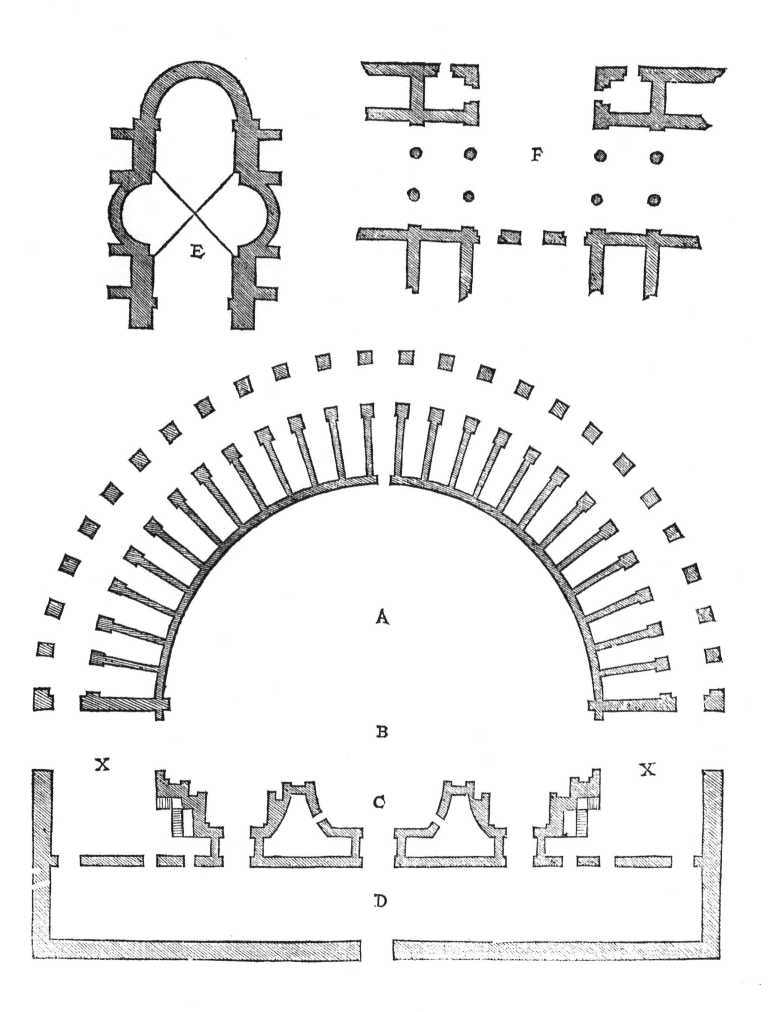

Of Antiquitie

THE Figure vnder this, marked A. I thinke to haue bene the Scene of a Theatre, it standeth betwéene Fondi and Terracina; but there is so little to be séene of the Theatre, that I measured it not: neither did I measure this part of the Scene, which is more decayed then it sheweth here but as I sate on horse-back, I made a slight draught thereof. The Doore marked B. standeth at Spoleto, and is very olde, made after the Dorica maner, which likewise I did not measure, but made onely the inuention and forme thereof. The Gate marked C. is betweene Foligus and Rome, out in the stréet: and although it séeme a licentious and vnséemely thing, that the Arch should breake the passage of the Architraue, Fréese and Cornice; yet neuerthelesse, the inuention disliked mee not. I measured onely the bredth and the length, the which I found to bee eighteene foote, and one and twenty foote and a halfe. I thinke it had béene a small Temple, or a Sepulchre; but be what it will, it sheweth well to a mans sight.

A

B

C

It is fayd, that this building was called, Porticus, of Pompeo: others fay,
that it was the house of Mario: but it
is called by the Common people, Cara-
bario: which building, as farre as I can
learne, was onely made for men to ease
themselues in: for there is no dwelling
in it at all: and although this building
at this day is almost decayed, yet it was
very great, and contayned many places,
as you see by many houses of this building which are found in the earth. Where
the Line standeth, is now the way to goe
from Campo Floro, to the Iewes place:
and where the Crosse is now, the houses
of Sancta Croce stand: where G. standes,
is the Iewes place: where the M, standeth, bee the Marcellarii: where the C.
standeth, is the Churchyard of S. Sal-
uatorie: and where the E. is cut through,
is the Fore-front of the houses of Cel-
sis: so that thereby you may see the great
compas thereof. The three round things
were Stayres to goe vp to the two emptie Roundles. And for that there is no
shew of Stayres to be seene in those two,
it is to bea conceaued, that they were o-
pen places to make water in, (for such
things are necessary.) The ground of
this worke is measured by the same Ell
that the Theater of Marcellus was
measured withall: which measure you
pou shall finde here, after the Obiliscen,
and (halfe an Ell shalbe thirty minutes.)
And first, the thicknesse of the Pilasters
is three Elles and a halfe: the thicknesse
of the Columnes is two Elles: the Intercolumnes, are on all sides, nine Elles
and a halfe: the Pilasters of the foure
Corners, are so much more then the outermost Corners stand ouer them: which
Corners were made with good iudgement, for they vphold the Corner by
strength, and with beauty of worke.
Hereby workemen may learne how to
make Corners with Columnes, and
with Pilasters bound together, that the
Corner may also be foure square, as the
Columne is, which giueth the Corner
more fastnesse, then if the same Corner
were drawne along the Pilaster: and
for the Corners which are drawne in, if
you see them ouer the side in Diagonall
maner, where the two round Columnes
couer the Corner, then they will seeme
vnperfit Corners, and specially, because
they are seene on all sides.

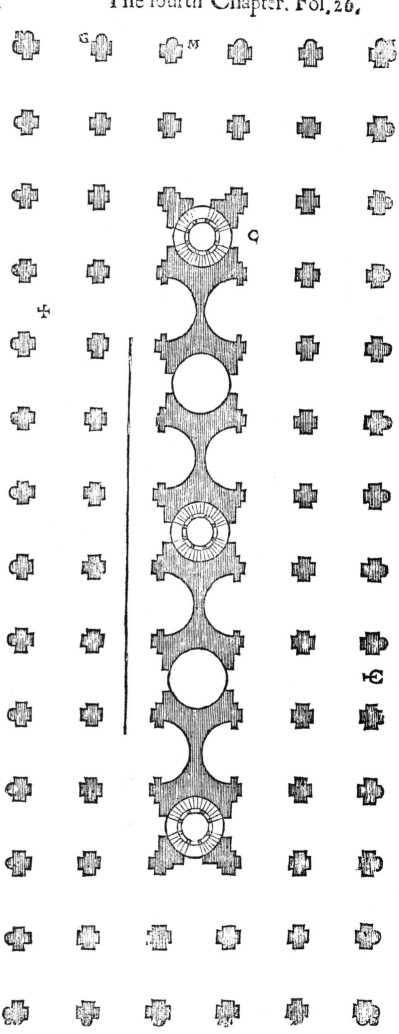

Touching the Ichnographie, I haue fayd inough; now I muſt ſpeake ſomething of the forme aboue the ground, although there is not much thereof to be ſéene: neuertheleſſe, there is yet ſo much ſtanding vpright (although it be hidden) that thereby the backe part therof without, is to be conceaued, which, in trueth, is an ingenious inuention, for a faſt worke, and eſpecially in the firſt order, which you call Dorica, although it hath neyther Architraue, Trigliph, nor Cornice: But yet there is the forme, and that very ſubtilly made, with great ſtrength and fayre Building (as well of hard ſtone as of Bricks) as you may ſée in the Figure following. The thickeneſſe and bredth are ſhewed before: the height of the Columnes with Baſes and Capitals, ſeuentéene Elles: and the height of the Arches, fiftéene Elles. The height of the Cuneo, that is, the ſhutting ſtone aboue the Arch, is 2. Elles: the height of the binding, which is in ſtead of an Architraue, is 2. Elles, and ſo much is the Facie aboue it. The ſecond order ſéemeth vnſupportable, for that there is a waight of Pilaſters ſtanding aboue an open hole: a thing which in trueth is falſe & erronious to ſpeake in reaſon. Neuertheleſſe, for that the firſt Order is ſo faſt and ſtrong, by meanes of the ſhutting ſtone aboue in the Arch; as alſo with the croſſe ſtone vpon it, with the faſt Facie vpon that, and by reaſon of the good ſhoulders of the Arch, which altogether ſhew to be ſuch a ſtrength (as in effect it is) that the Pilaſters that reſt vpon it. ſéeme not to oppreſſe the worke, as they would, if it were a ſimple Arch, with an Architraue, Fréeſe and Cornice: for which cauſe I blame not this inuention therein. The wideneſſe of this Arch is 4. Elles: the height is nine Elles: the bredth of the Pilaſters, is two Elles and an halfe: the thickneſſe of the Columnes, is an Ell and a ſirt part in Diameter: the height of the Columnes is eleuen Elles and an eyght part with Baſes and Capitals, and are made after the Corinthia manner. The height of the Architraue, Fréeſe and Cornice, is two Elles and thrée quarters. Although I can giue no particular meaſures of this Cornice, Fréeſe and Architraue, becauſe ſuch things are not to be ſéene, yet there is onely ſo much wall, that thereby a man may conceaue the Freeſes, Cornices and Architraue.

The third part of the Ell, wherewith this is meaſured.

Mong other faire Antiquities in Rome, there are two Columnes of Marble, all cut full of Histories, very good imbost worke. The one is called Antonianas Columne, the other Traians Columne : and for that Traians Columne is the wholest, I will speake somewhat thereof. This Columne, as men say, the Emperour Traian caused to be made, which is all of Marble, and made of many pieces; but so closely ioyned together, that they séeme to bee all one piece : and to giue the particular measure thereof, I will begin at the foote of the Basement thereof: And first, the degrée or step in the first rest, is thrée Palmes high, the Plinthus of the Base, is a Palme and eyght minutes high; the carued or grauen Base is as much: the flat of the Basement is 12. Palmes and sixe minutes high : the grauen Cornice is a Palme and an halfe high. The place where the Feston hangeth in, is two Palmes and ten minutes high : the whole Base of the Columnes, is sixe Palmes and 28. minutes, and is deuided in this manner: the Plinthus where the Eagle standeth vpon one corner (but you must imagine that there is one at euery corner) is thrée Palmes and ten minutes high : the Thorus aboue it, is thrée Palmes and eyght minutes high: the Cincte is ten minutes high. The height of the Columne, that is, the body, is 18. Palmes and 9. minutes: the Astragall with the Quadrants or lists vnder the Echine, is 10. minutes. The height of the Echine, is 2. Palmes and 2. minutes: the height of the Abacus, is 2. Palmes & 11. minutes: aboue vpon this Columne, there is a Pedestal of a round forme, through the which men crept fró the winding Stayres, and may goe easily round about, because the plaine ground thereof, is 2. Palmes and a halfe broad: the height of this Pedestall is 11. Palmes: but the Base is two Palmes, and the Cornice aboue, is a Palme high. The Crowne aboue the Pedestall, is thrée Palmes and a halfe high : the thicknesse of this Pedestall, is 12. Palmes and ten minutes : the thickenesse of the Columne aboue, is 14. Palmes, and the thicknesse below, is 16. Palmes: the roundnesse marked A. in flat forme, sheweth the thicknesse aboue : and the Circle marked B. is the thicknesse below. The widenesse of the winding Stayres, is 3. Palmes, and the Spill foure Palmes. The breeth of the Basement, is 24. Palmes and 6. minutes; in the which space are cut two Compartements, wherein is contained an Epitaph, vnder which many Trophees are cut. and in the Epitaph are these letters hereunder written.

S.   P.   Q.   R.
IMP. CAESARI DIVI NERVAE. F. NERVAE,
TRAIANO AVG. GERMANIC. DACICO
PONT. MAX. TRIB. POT. XVII. COS. VI. PP.
AD DECLARANDVM QVANTAE ALTITV-
DINIS MONS ET LOCVS SIT EGESTVS.

This Columne is historiographied with excellent good cut worke, and drawne along with Berries ; it is also flinted in Doricall manner : in the flintings the Figures are made in such sort, that rising vp or bearing out of the Figure, the forme of the Columnes and flinting, is nothing disparaged; betwene which Figures there stand some Windowes, which giue light to the winding Stayres : and although the said Windowes are placed orderly, yet they hinder not the Historie at all, and yet they are 44. in number, and I will shew the whole Columne in the Figure following: but these are the members thereof, openly written and set downe. All these members are measured with the olde Romane Palme, as you find it before vpon the round.

SENATVS

Of Antiquitie

I Haue before sufficiently spoken of the bredth of Traians Columne, and of the particular maner thereof, now I will shew the whole Columne proportioned as it is: So then, the Columne marked with T. representeth Traians Columne: but from whence the Obelisces spring or procéde, and how they were brought to Rome, and to what end they serue, I will not speake of, for that Pliny declareth it at large: onely I will set the measure here, and shew the forme of some things which I haue séene and measured within Rome: And first, the Obelisce, marked O. is without the Capena, and is all grauen and cut with Egyptian letters: the thicknesse thereof in the fote, is ten Palmes and a halfe: the height is 80. Palmes: and this onely was measured with the ancient Palms: but the other thré by it were measured by a moderne or vsuall Ell of 60. minutes, whereof the line that is betwéens the Obelisces, is the halfe, and is deuided into 30. parts. The Obelisce marked P. standeth in Vaticano (that is) at S.Peters, and is of Egyptian stone: in the top whereof (they say) the Ashes of the Emperour Gaius Cæsar stand: the thicknesse thereof below, is 4. Elles and 42. minutes: the height is 42. Elles and a halfe: the part aboue, is thré Elles and foure minutes thicke: and vnder at the fote standeth these letters.

DIVI CAESARI, DIVI IVLII. F. AVGVSTO. TI.
CAESARI DIVI AVGVSTI. F. AVGVSTO SACRVM.

The Obelisce marked Q. lyeth at S. Rochus, broken in the middle of the stréet in thré pieces, and men say likewise, there lyeth buried in the earth a Ladie called A la Augusta: the thicknesse beneath of the said Obelisce on each Facie, is two Elles and 24. minutes: the height is 26. Elles and 24. minutes: the thickenesse aboue, holdeth an Ell and 35. minutes: the Basement was all of one piece, and the Obelisce marked R. is in circo Antonino Caracalla, and is broken, as you sée in the forme. The thickenes of the Obelisce, is two Elles and 25. minutes below, and aboue one Ell and 33. minutes: the height is 28. Elles, and 16. minutes: and all the Pedestals are proportioned thereafter. And although (perabuenture) there are more of them in Rome, which I haue not séene, yet these which I haue séene, are here set downe to your sight, as being best knowne.

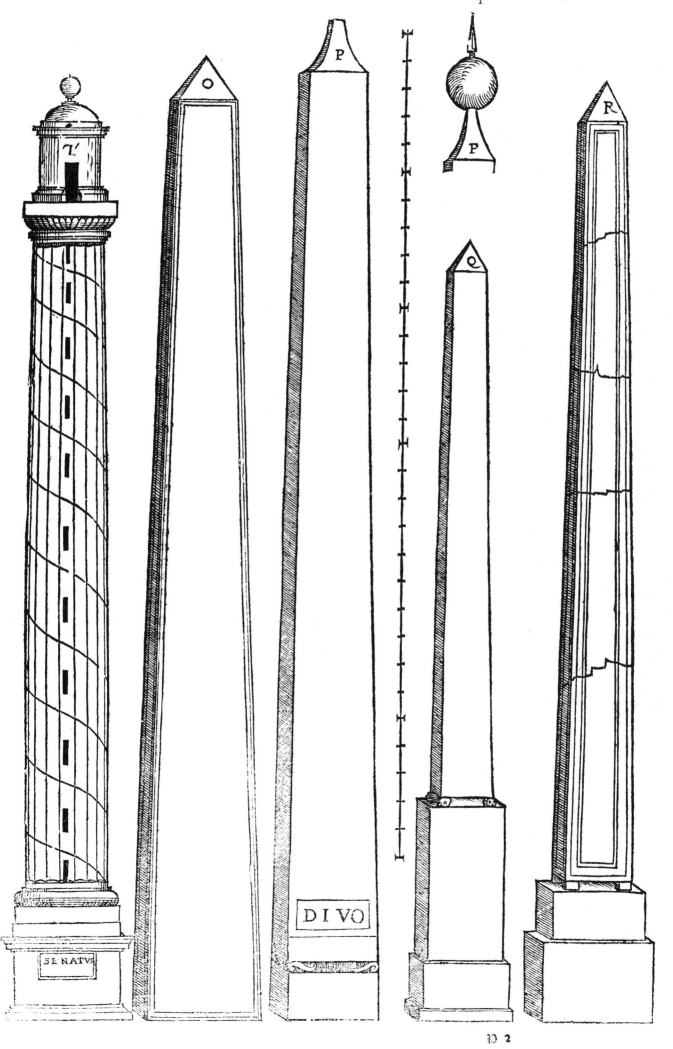

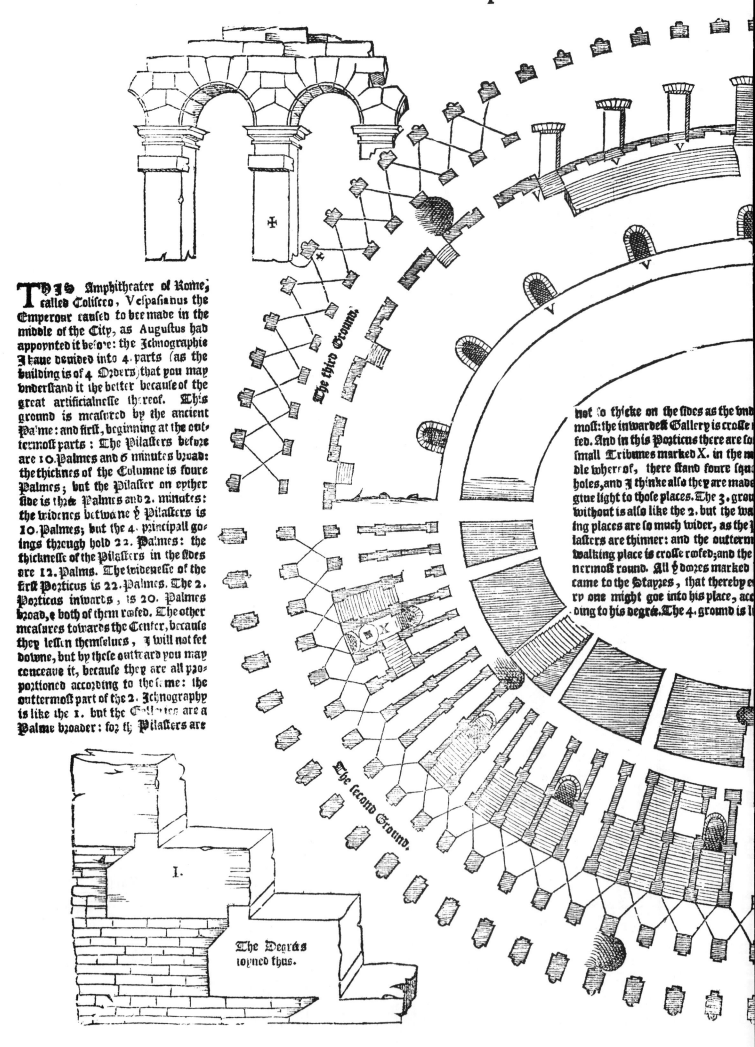

THIS Amphitheater of Rome, called Coliseo, Vespasianus the Emperour caused to bee made in the middle of the City, as Augustus had appoynted it before: the Ichnographie I haue deuided into 4. parts (as the building is of 4. Orders) that you may vnderstand it the better because of the great artificialnesse thereof. This ground is measured by the ancient Palme: and first, beginning at the outermost parts: The Pilasters before are 10. Palmes and 6. minutes broad: the thicknes of the Columne is foure Palmes; but the Pilaster on eyther side is three Palmes and 2. minutes: the widenes betwane the Pilasters is 10. Palmes; but the 4. principall goings through hold 22. Palmes: the thicknesse of the Pilasters in the sides are 12. Palms. The widenesse of the first Porticus is 22. Palmes. The 2. Porticas inwards, is 20. Palmes broad, & both of them roofed. The other measures towards the Center, because they lessen themselues, I will not set downe, but by these outward you may conceaue it, because they are all proportioned according to the same: the outtermost part of the 2. Ichnographby is like the 1. but the Galleries are a Palme broader: for the Pilasters are

not so thicke on the sides as the vndermost: the inwardest Gallery is crosse roofed. And in this Porticus there are some small Tribunes marked X. in the middle whereof, there stand foure square holes, and I thinke also they are made to giue light to those places. The 3. ground without is also like the 2. but the walking places are so much wider, as the Pilasters are thinner: and the outtermost walking place is crosse roofed, and the innermost round. All the dores marked came to the Stayres, that thereby euery one might goe into his place, according to his degree. The 4. ground is like

The third Ground.

The second Ground.

I.

The Degrees ioyned thus.

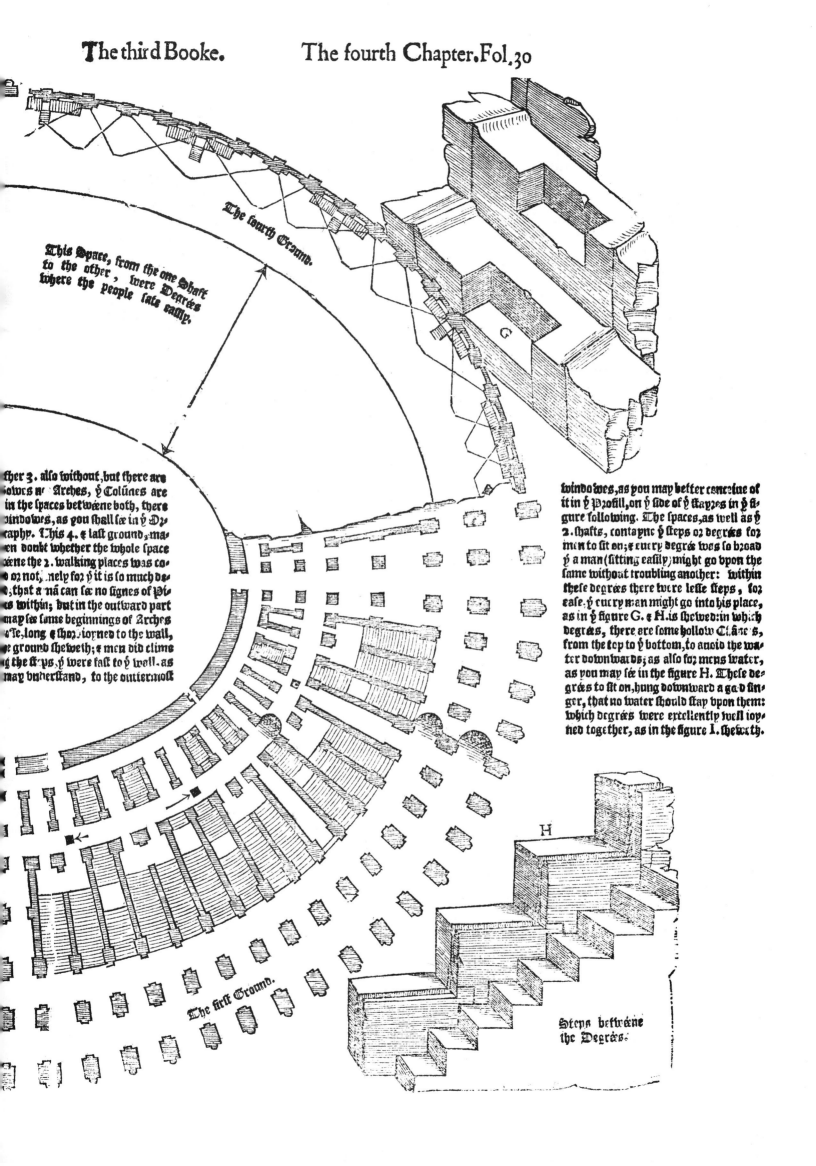

The fourth Ground.

This Space, from the one Shaft to the other, were Degrées where the people sate easily.

ther 3. also without, but there are
lowes no Arches, ẙ Colúnes are
in the spaces betwéene both, there
windowes, as you shall sée in ẙ Dꝛ
raphy. This 4. ẽ last ground, ma
en doubt whether the whole space
éene the 2. walking places was co-
o oꝛ not, nely foꝛ ẙ it is so much ꝺ
, that a ná can sée no signes of ꝓi
s within; but in the outward part
map sée some beginnings of Arches
Te, long ẽ shoꝛ ioyned to the wall,
e ground sheweth; ẽ men did clime
g the steps, ẙ were fast to ẙ wall, as
may vnderstand, to the outtermost

windowes, as you may better conceiue of
it in ẙ Pꝛofill, on ẙ side of ẙ stayꝛes in ẙ figure following. The spaces, as well as ẙ
2. shafts, contayne ẙ steps oꝛ degrées foꝛ
men to sit on; ẽ euery degrée was so bꝛoad
ẙ a man (sitting easily) might go vpon the
same without troubling another: within
these degrées there were lesse steps, foꝛ
ease, ẙ euery man might go into his place,
as in ẙ figure G. ẽ H. is shewed: in which
degrées, there are some hollow Clás e s,
from the top to ẙ bottom, to auoid the water downewards; as also foꝛ mens water,
as you may sée in the figure H. These degrées to sit on, hung downeward a gꝛꝺ finger, that no water should stay vpon them:
which degrées were excellently well ioyned together, as in the figure I. the forth.

The first Ground.

H

Steps betwéene
the Degrées.

I Haue shewed the Ichnographie of the Romish Colisco, in foure sorts, euen like as the building is of foure sorts or orders: now I must shew the Profill thereof, by the which a man may conceaue a great part of the inward things: therefore the Figure following sheweth the whole building aboue ý earth, as if it were cut through in the middle. In which Figure, first you sée all the degrées whereon the Spectators sate: there also you may perceiue how many wayes the goings vp were, which (in truth) were very easie to go vp & downe, so that in short time the Amphitheater was filled with a great number of men, without hindrance one of another. You may also sée in the outward part, how the thicknes of the Pilasters, and the walles vpwards lessened, which on the inside are drawne in, and being so drawne in, giueth the building great strength: and to shew it to be true, you may sée there, at this day, some part of the Facies without, yet whole, from the top to the bottome, and yet the inward parts are decayed, and that hath the drawing inward of the Centre done, which made the worke slighter, taking, as it were, a forme of a Piramides. But this is not obserued in the common building in Venice, but rather the contrary, because the walles without are in Perpendicular maner, and lessen inwards: and this they doe (for want of ground) to get the more space vpwards, but that which helpeth such buildings, is, that there are no Arches in it, nor Rofes, of any maner, that force the walles to gaue out, but the number of Beames which are layd and fastned in the walles, bind the walles and the roomes of the house together, and so such buildings stand fast so long as the Beames indure, which men from time to time renue: neuertheletle, these kinds of buildings last not so long as the ancient buildings did, made in such order as you sée in the Colisco, whereof I will speake agayne. And withall, (as I sayd) the innermost part being so ruinous, that men sée no part of the innermost worke, which is cut off by the line that hath Shafts or Arrowheads at the ends: and for that you sée no parts thereof at all, whether that the vppermost parts of the highest steps, vpwards to the top, were all couered with double Galleries, or that the Porticus was alone, and the other left open: therefore I haue made it in two maner of wayes: the one is (as you sée in the same Profill) ioyned with all the worke: and the other maner is, which standeth without the degrées or steps, which order also agréeth with the other, if you set it so, that the two Lists in the Pedestals méete each with the other: but for that you sée some remaynders of the crossed Rofes, which yet hang within on the walles, as the fourth ground sheweth, the which, I iudge, was onely a Porticus, and that the other part was vncouered to receiue the people, and being so must receiue them better then if the Galleries had béene double: Now to turne to the beginning of the degrees or steps, that I leaue nothing vntouched, as nére as I can, I say, by meanes of the ruines, and filling vp with matter fallen, the playne, or the place in the middle is so filled vp, that a man cannot marke how high the first degrées of the playne were eleuated: but by the instructions of those that haue séene the end, the first degrée was so high, that the wild and vntamed Beasts could not hurt the beholders: and there was also a Borstwering, and other stréetes, of a reasonable bredth to go round about, as it is shewed where it is marked with C. The two open places, the least and the greatest Arch, were to bring in light. The places standing vp about the degrées or steps which are couered and marked A. are Dores, whereby men went without, vp the Stayres to the Theater.

The Profill of the Amphitheater of Rome.

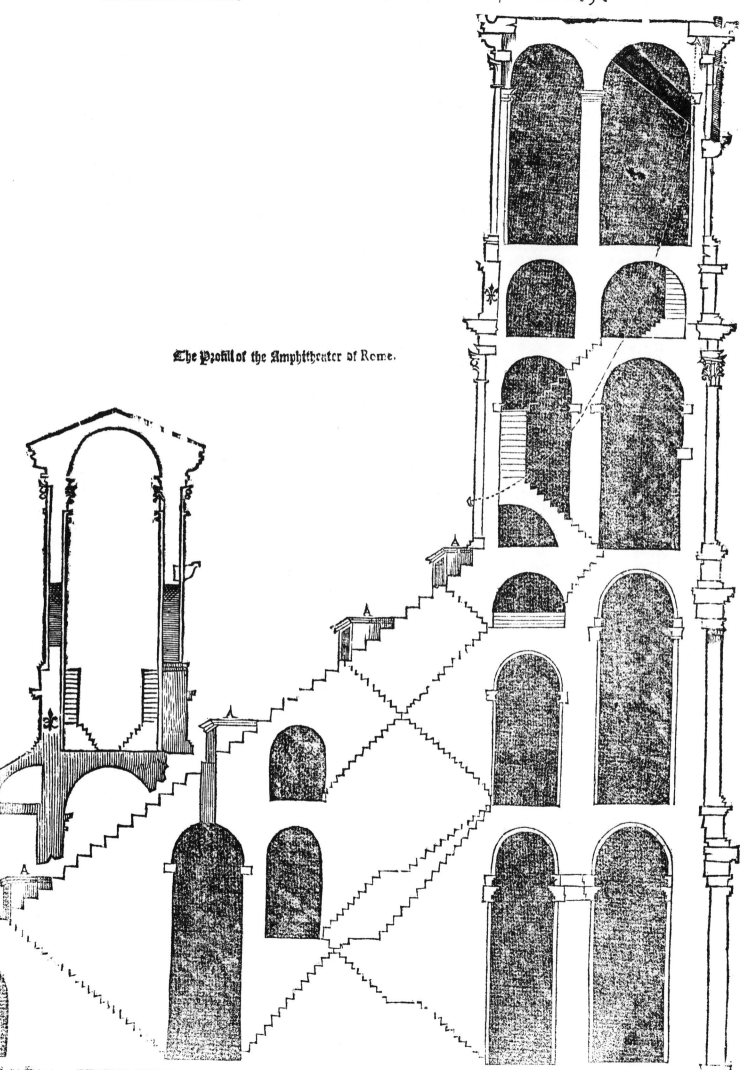

THe outward part, that is, the Orthographie of the Romish Coliseo, is made of foure stories: and the first story aboue the ground, is made after the manner of Dorica: and although there are in the Freese neither Trigliphes nor Metophes, nor yet guts in the Epistolie or Architraue; neither Fulmines and guts vnder the crowne, yet it may be called Dorica. The second Order, is after the manner of Ionica: and although the Columnes be not fluted, yet in effect they may be called Ionica. The third Story, is after the manner of Corinthia, but firme worke without cutting, vnlesse it be the Capitals, the which with their height are not exquisitely made. The fourth Story, is Composita; other call it Latina, because it was inuented by the Romanes: some others call it Italica. But it may well be called Composita, were it but for the mutiles which stand in the Freese, for that no other Story haue their mutiles in the Freese, but that. Many men aske why the Romanes made this Building of foure Orders, and made it not all of one forme or order as many others are, as that of Verona, which is all of rusticall worke, and that of Pola also. A man may answere thereunto, that the old Romanes, as rulers ouer al, & especially of those people, from whence the three former Orders had their beginning, would set those 3. generations one aboue another: & aboue all those orders, the Composita, as found by themselues, thereby signifying, that they as tryumphers ouer those people, would also tryumph with their workes, placing and mingling them at their pleasures. But omitting these reasons, we will proceed to the measures of the outtermost parts and Orthographie. This Building was elenated from the earth two degrees: the second degree was fiue Palmes broad, and the first two Palmes; the height was litt e lesse then a Palme: the Base of the Columne was not two Palmes, no more is the Dorica: the Columne is foure Palmes thicke and two minutes: the height is 38. Palms and 5. minutes, with Base and Capitall: the height of the Capitall is about two Palmes: the Pilasters on eyther side of the Columnes, are three Palmes and three minutes: the widenesse of the Arch is twenty Palmes, and the height is 33. Palmes: from vnder the Arch, to the Architraue, is fiue Palmes and sire minutes: the height of the Architraue is two Palmes and eyght minutes: the height of the Freese is three Palmes and two minutes: the Cornice as much. The Pedestall of the second Order, is eyght Palmes and ten minutes high: the height of the Columnes, with Bases and Capitals, is fiue and thirty Palmes, the thicknesse is foure Palmes: the Pilasters and Arches are like those beneath: but the height of the Arch is thirty Palmes: from vnder the Arch, to vnder the Architraue, is fiue Palmes and sire minutes: the height of the Architraue is three Palmes: the height of the Freese, is two Palmes and nine minutes: the height of the Cornice, is three Palmes and nine minutes. The Pedestall of the fourth Order, called, Composita, (here our Author hath forgotten the third Order, but howsoeuer, it differeth not much from the Ionica) the Pedestall of the Composita, is twelue Palmes high: the vnder-Base thereof, is foure Palmes: the height of the Pillars, with Bases and Capitals, is thirty eyght Palmes and sire minutes: the height of the Architraue, Freese, and Cornice, is about ten Palmes, deuided in three, one part for the Cornice, the second for the Freese, wherein the Mutiles stand, and the third for the Architraue. But for what cause, or reason, the workeman set the Mutiles in the Freese, (things, which, peraduenture, before that time were neuer made) I haue deliuered my opinion thereof in my fourth Boke, in the beginning of the Order of Composita. The Pillars of the fourth Order are flat, and rise but a little: all the rest are round Columnes, (that is to say) three fourth parts, rising out of the Pilasters: the Mutiles aboue the windowes vpheld some beames, the which are boared through with holes for men to draw cords to couer the hole Amphitheater, as well against the Sunne as the rayne: for what cause the Columnes are all of one thicknesse, and lessen not one more then the other (as it seemeth they should; and as Vitruuius would) as the second Order are lessened a fourth part, I haue also declared my opinion in the fourth Boke, and the ninth Chapter. In the treatise of making Columnes, longer or shorter; and that the particular members may also be noted, I haue marked them also by the Orthographie of the Coliseo, which are proportioned according to the principall, together with their Caracters whereunto they are likened.

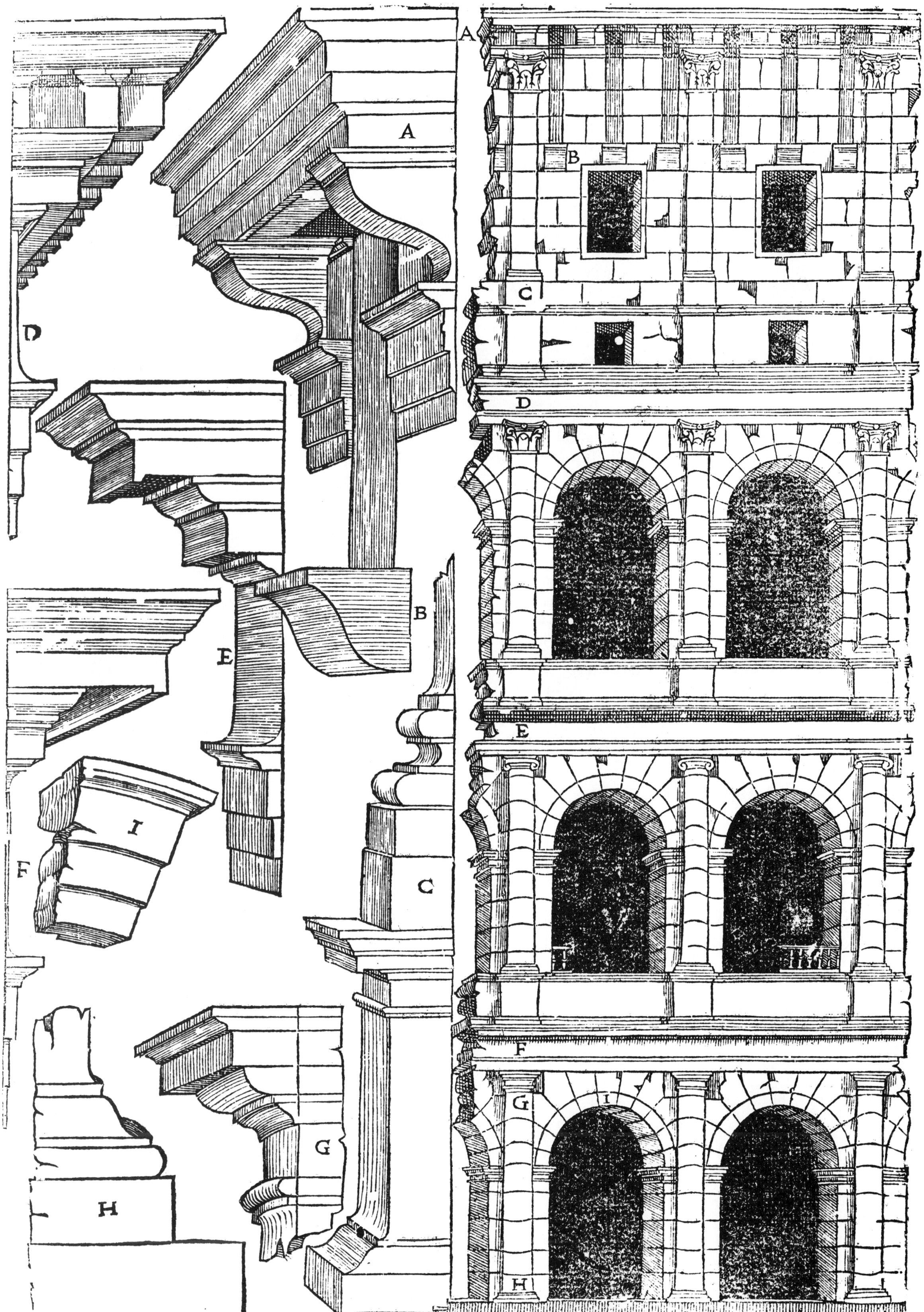
A
B
C
D
E
F
G
H
I

I C Vispello, a very old Towne in Italy, there is a very olde Porte or Gate, the worke whereof is Dorica, although it hath neither Trigliphes, Methopes nor Cuts: the two Towers on the sides thereof may bee called Moderne worke, in regard of the Ornaments aboue: both Towers are both of one fashion, although I haue left one of them out. The Ichnographie is vnderneath the Figure, and was measured with the ancient foote: and from one Tower to the other, are 60. and 10. foote: the middle Gate is 20 foote wide: each Posterne Gate is 10. foote wide: the Pillers betweene the 2. Ports or Gates, are 10 foote broad: the height I set not downe, but onely the invention, because it pleased me well. The Stayres vnder the Towers, with the ground, E. are by our Author made on both sides: but according to his ground, the Stayres must come as they stand aboue the ground C. or else not, then the ground must bee made like D. This, and other things more (although there consisteth no great matter therein) I thought good to note, that you may know that I haue set the towne peece by peece as I found them.

These Cornices, Basements & Bases, are reliques of Antiquitie: and that which is marked A. a piece of the Columnes with Architraues, Fri es
& Cornices; and also with the Basement aboue, which was all of one stone: the height thereof was 11. ancient foot, proportioned in that manner,
it was found without Rome by the Riuer of Tiber. The order marked B. was found in the foundation of S. Peters, and Bramant caused it to bee
buried againe in the ground, in the same place: all the members also were of one piece; it was 6. ancient foot high, & proportioned thereafter. The Base
marked C. is at S. Markes, very well wrought, of Corinthia worke, but not very great, it is a foot & an halfe high, and proportioned accordingly. The
Basement marked D. was found in a place called Capranica, very well wrought: the height of y Base, without Plinthus, is 2. Palmes, and
also proportioned thereafter. The Base marked E. was not very great: it was found among certaine ruines, and by reason of the Astragal s
which it had aboue the Thorus, therefore I esteeme it to bee Composita: and although I set downe no other proportion of all t e
particular measures, yet they are collected and set downe out of the great, into the small measure orderly.

E 2

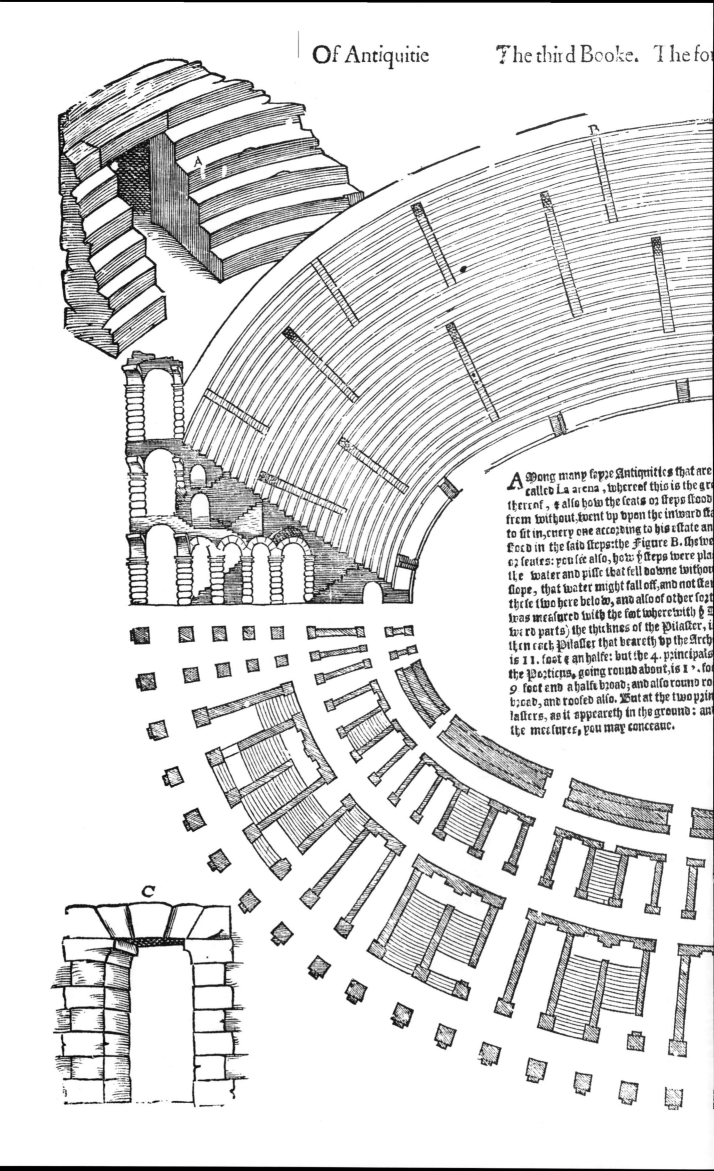

A Mong many fayꝛe Antiquities that are
called La arena , whereof this is the gr
thereof, & also how the seats oꝛ steps stood
from without, went vp vpon the inward st
to sit in, euery one accoꝛding to his estate an
stood in the said steps: the Figure B. She w
oꝛ seates: you see also, how ꝉ steps were pla
the water and pisse that fell downe withou
slope, that water might fall off, and not sta
these two here below, and also of other soꝛt
was measured with the foot wherewith ꝉ
ward parts) the thicknes of the Pilaster, i
then each Pilaster that beareth vp the Arch
is 11. foot & an halfe: but the 4. principals
the Poꝛticus, going round about, is 1 ꝺ. fo
9 foot and a halfe bꝛoad; and also round ro
bꝛoad, and roofed also. But at the two pꝛil
lasters, as it appeareth in the ground: an
the measures, you may conceaue.

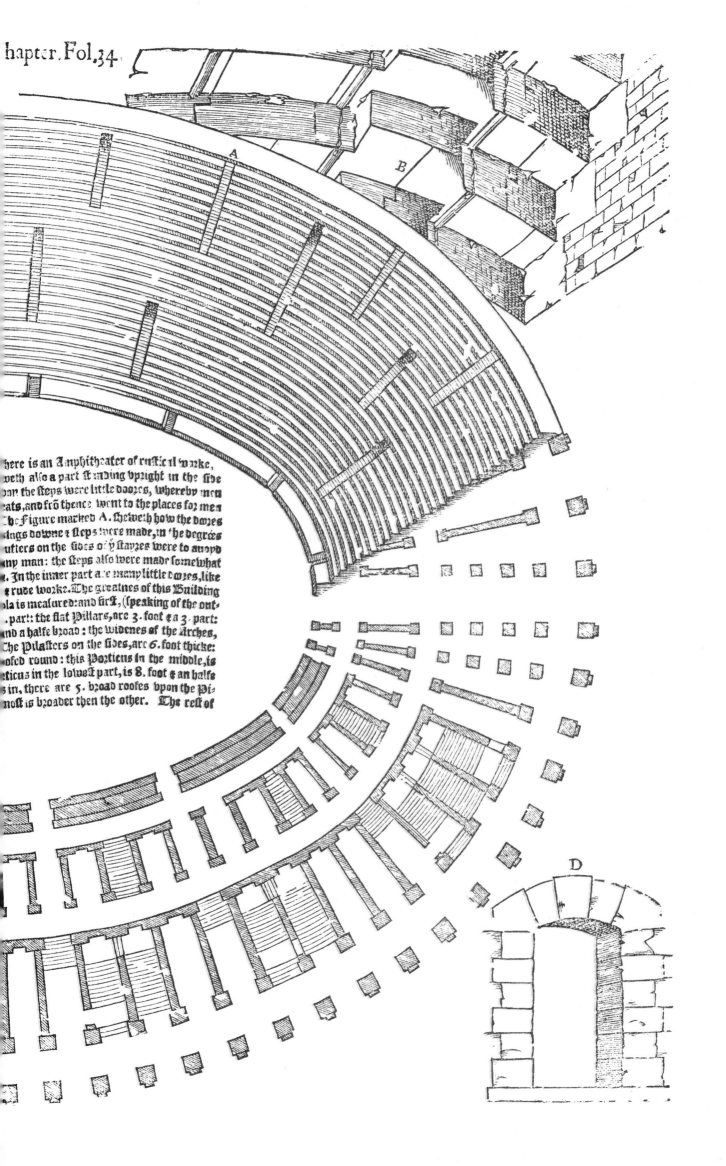

here is an Amphitheater of rusticall worke,
weth also a part standing vpright in the side
oon the steps were little doores, whereby men
eats, and fro thence went to the places for men
The Figure marked A. sheweth how the doores
ings downe & steps were made, in the degrees
ufters on the sides of y stayzes were to auoyd
ny man: the steps also were made somewhat
. In the inner part are many little coues, like
rude worke. The greatnes of this Building
la is measured: and first, (speaking of the out-
part: the flat Pillars, are 3. foot & a 3. part:
nd a halfe broad: the widenes of the Arches,
The Pilasters on the sides, are 6. foot thicke:
ofed round: this Porticus in the middle, is
eticus in the lowest part, is 8. foot & an halfe
s in, there are 5. broad roofes vpon the Pi-
most is broader then the other. The rest of

Touching the Ichnographie of the sayd Amphitheater, I haue set downe the principall measures, and partly spoken of that part which standeth vpright: now I will speake of the outward part, which worke can no otherwise bee called, then rude and rusticall, and haue likewise spoken of the thicknesse and breadth, therefore I will rehearse it no more: onely of the height I will say some thing: And first, the height of the first Arch is 23. foote: the height of the Pillars 27 foote: the Forme of the Architraue, Freese and Cornice, is 6. foote high: the Place brest high aboue the Cornice, is 2. foote and a halfe high: the height of the second Arch is 24. foote, and his widenesse 12. foote: the height of the Pillars is 24. foote and a halfe: the height of the Cornice, Freese and Forme of the Architraue, is 5. foote and a halfe: the Borstwering or Place brest high of the third Order or Story, is 4. foote and a halfe high: the widenes of the Arch is 9. foote and 3. quarters: the height of the Arch is 17. foote and a halfe: the height of the broad Pillers is 20. foote and a halfe: against these Pillars, as farre as a man may perceiue, there were Images, of good bignesse, set: the third and last Cornice is 5. foote high. But I will not set downe the particular measures of the Cornices, for that I haue set them downe with great diligence, according to the greatnesse in this small Forme, which shall be the first Figures in the side following, and there below, the Profill or cutting of the outermost part of the Amphitheater shall stand. And thirdly, there followeth the Orthographie of a péece of the sayd Amphitheater without, which is all wrought after the rusticall manner, with stones of Verona, being very hard: but the Cornices are somewhat better made: which Cornices haue diuers and seuerall Formes of the Romanes, and are very like vnto the Cornices of the Amphitheater of Pola. Touching the playnnesse of this Amphitheater, which by the Common people is called, La arena, (taken from arena) which is sand, which was therein strowed for certayne Playes or sports, which were there presented or Acted: and therefore I could not sée the ground thereof: but as it was told me by some old men of Verona, when the Playes were there made vpon the sand, then presently there came water, in the sight of all the beholders, which past through some Conduits, and in short space filled all the place full, so that there they might make battailes, and thrust one at another with Scutes and Boates, in the water, and the place dryed vp agayne, as at the first. This, and many other things, men may beléeue, if we consider the great magnificence of the Romanes, in the Antiquities of Verona. There are yet vpon the great Riuer of Adixe two fayre ancient Bridges, betwéene the which two Bridges, there was a most fayre and notable Spectacle, whereon there might stand a great number of people, to behold the Playes and sports there made in Boates, vpon the water: which Spectacle was made along by the water side, against a hill: and higher vpwards, aboue this Spectacle, there was a Theater, the Scene whereof, and the Spectacle ioyned together: (and for that, as I sayd before, the Theater was made very artificially in the hill, so is it aboue the Theater in the height of the hill) there was a great building, which surpassed all the other: but the ruines of these buildings are so many, and so cast downe in processe of time, that it would be great charges and losse of time to find them out: but for that in many places of the hill I haue séene some parts thereof, therefore it makes me wonder thereat. It was also, with good reason, that the Romanes made such things at Verona (for that, in my opinion, it is the best scituated place of all Italy) as well for playnes as hilles, and also for waters; and specially, the men of that Towne are very familiar and friendly people.

Of Antiquitie

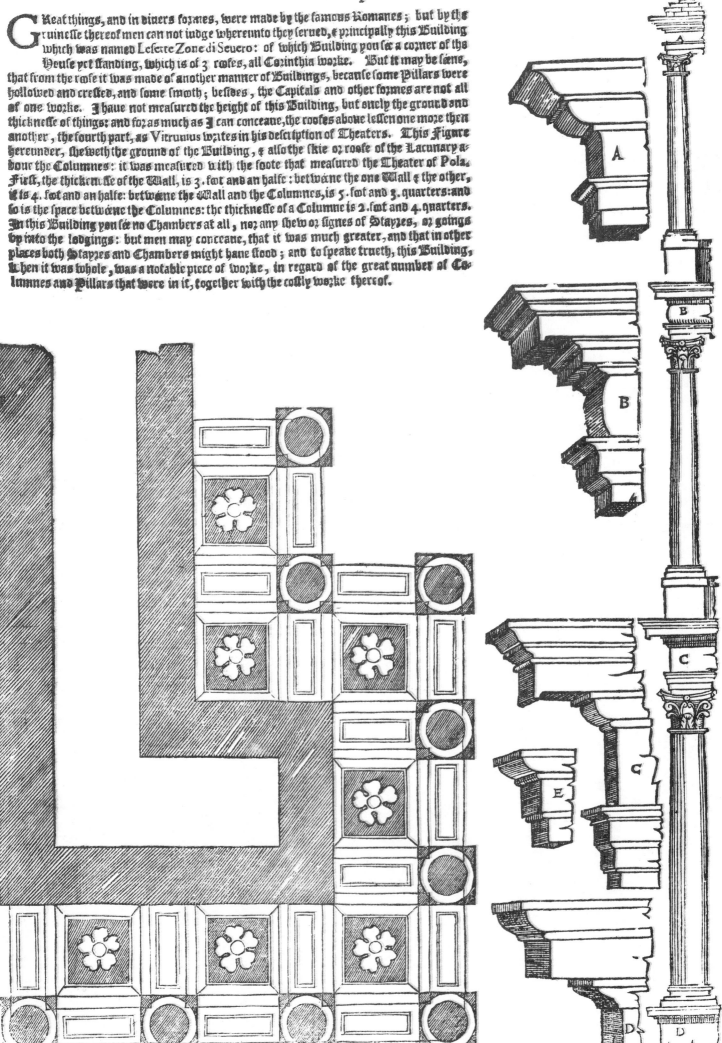

Great things, and in diuers formes, were made by the famous Romanes; but by the ruinesse thereof men can not iudge whereunto they serued, & principally this Building which was named Lesette Zone di Seuero: of which Building you see a corner of the House yet standing, which is of 3 roofes, all Corinthia worke. But it may be seene, that from the roofe it was made of another manner of Buildings, because some Pillars were hollowed and crested, and some smooth; besides, the Capitals and other formes are not all of one worke. I haue not measured the height of this Building, but onely the ground and thicknesse of things: and for as much as I can conceaue, the roofes aboue lessen one more then another, the fourth part, as Vitruuius writes in his description of Theaters. This Figure hereunder, sheweth the ground of the Building, & also the skie or roofe of the Lacunary aboue the Columnes: it was measured with the foote that measured the Theater of Pola. First, the thickenesse of the Wall, is 3. foot and an halfe: betweene the one Wall & the other, it is 4. foot and an halfe: betweene the Wall and the Columnes, is 5. foot and 3. quarters: and so is the space betweene the Columnes: the thicknesse of a Columne is 2. foot and 4. quarters. In this Building you see no Chambers at all, nor any shew or signes of Stayres, or goings vp into the lodgings: but men may conceaue, that it was much greater, and that in other places both Stayres and Chambers might haue stood; and to speake trueth, this Building, when it was whole, was a notable piece of worke, in regard of the great number of Columnes and Pillars that were in it, together with the costly worke thereof.

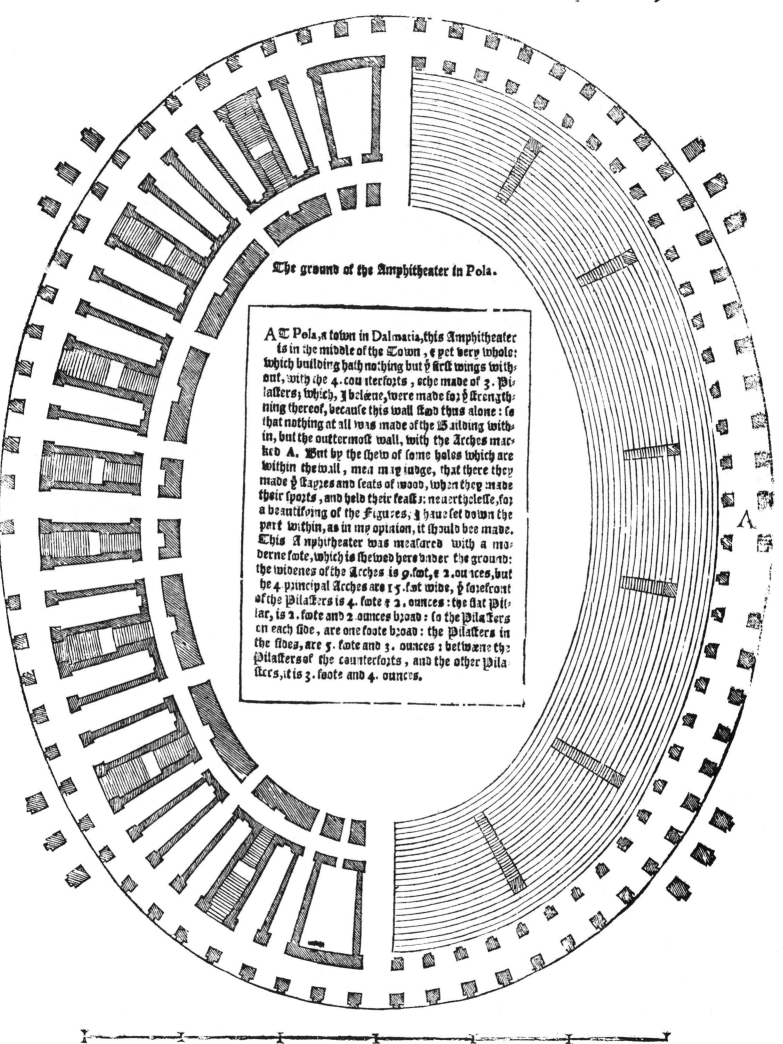

The ground of the Amphitheater in Pola.

AT Pola, a town in Dalmatia, this Amphitheater
is in the middle of the Town, & yet very whole:
which building hath nothing but the first wings without, with the 4. counterforts, eche made of 3. Pilasters; which, I beléeue, were made for the strength-
ning thereof, because this wall stood thus alone : so
that nothing at all was made of the Building within, but the outtermost wall, with the Arches marked A. But by the shew of some holes which are
within the wall, men may iudge, that there they
made the stayres and seats of wood, when they made
their sports, and held their feasts : neuertheleffe, for
a beautifying of the Figures, I haue set down the
part within, as in my opinion, it should bee made.
This Amphitheater was measured with a moderne foote, which is shewed here vnder the ground:
the widenes of the Arches is 9. foot, & 2. ounces, but
the 4. principal Arches are 15. fat wide, the forefront
of the Pilasters is 4. foote & 2. ounces : the flat Pillar, is 2. foote and 2. ounces bjoad : so the Pilasters
on each side, are one foote bjoad : the Pilasters in
the sides, are 5. foote and 3. ounces : betwéene the
Pilasters of the counterforts, and the other Pilasters, it is 3. foote and 4. ounces.

A

Touching the Orthographie, or the ground of the Amphitheater of Pola, I haue sufficiently spoken: but now I must shew the Orthographie of the part standing vp, beginning at the nether part: as touching the Basement, it hath no terminations of measures, (the cause why, is,) for that the Hill is not euen: for in the Hill the Pedestall is not onely lost, but also the whole first order of the Arches, with all their Cornices vpon them, and the Hill is the height of the plaine of the second Story; therefore I will set downe no height of the measure of the Basements: but will begin from thence vpwards. The height of the Pedestall vnder the Pillar, is 2. foot and an halfe: the height of the Pillar, or flat Columne with the Capitall, is about 16. foot: the height of the Arch, is 17 foot and an halfe: the Architraue is a foot and 9. ounces high: the height of the Freese, is 9. ounces: the height the Cornice, is one foot & 10 ounces: the height of the bord-bearing or place brest-high (if there bee any other) aboue the Cornice, is as high as ÿ Cornice: the height of the Pillar is 21. foot & 9. ounces, with the Capitall: the height of the Arch, is 18. foot and one ounce: the thicknesse of the Arch, is 1 foot and 9. ounces: the Architraue, Freese and Cornice, are of the same height that the vndermost is: the Basement marked X. is 4. foot and 4. ounces. From the Basement to vnder the Cornice, is 19. foot: the height of the Cornice is one foot and an halfe. And this is touching the Orthographie of the Amphitheater, the which Orthographie is on the next side, marked P. and for that (as in the Treaty of ÿ Ichnographie I haue sayd) the Amphitheater hath some Pilasters on foure sides, which were made for strengthening & counterforting of the walls: the which wall stood within, without any thing else; and therefore I meane to shew how it stood: the Figure market Q. sheweth the sides of this counterfort: & that part marked H. representeth a Pilaster: that part marked I sheweth the Profill of ÿ wall of the Amphitheater: betwæne the Pilaster H. and the wall or Pilaster marked I. is a going through of thrée foot and an halfe wide: so that two men may goe through together. These counterforts haue their ground in euery order or story, whereon the people might stand; but there are no stayres nor signes of stayres, but were made of wood, as may be seene by some holes before the windowes. And that the Cornices of this present Building may be the better vnderstood, therefore I haue set them there besides in greater forme, that a man may know their members, by their Caracters or Letters which they are marked withal. The manner of this Cornicement is much different from the Romish, as men may sée: and I, for my part, would not make such Cornices in my worke; but with the Theater of this Towne, I would serue my turne, because they are of a better manner of worke. I am of opinion, that this was an other workeman, different from the other, and it may be that this workeman was a high Almaine, because the Cornices are made much after the Dutch manner.

The halfe common foot, wherewith the Amphitheater is measured.

Of Antiquitie

AT Mount Caballo within Rome, where now the stone horses Praxitiles and Phidia stand, is the ruines of a most costly Pallace, whereof one part stood vpon the hill, but the part of the goings vp was made right against the descending of the hill, as you may see in the Profill hereunder. The Ichnographie of this building was measured with a common Ell, the third part whereof standeth hereunder. And first in the Niches or hollow places, marked T. and N. were found the figures of Tiberius and Nilus, which are now set in Beldenerie: the place marked A. is a stréete or way of 10. Elles broade: the part marked B. is 12. Elles foure square: the part marked C. is 36. Elles in length, and 18. Elles broad: the place D. is 36. Elles foure square: the walkes round about are 4. Elles broad: the place over-against C. B. is of the like measure. The widenesse of the foure payre of Stayres is 4. Elles each of them: the places E. are Courts, whereof each of them are 114. Elles long, and in breadth 62. Elles and a halfe. The Galleries F. are 13. Elles broad: the greatest Stayres, to goe vp to the playne of the Pallace, are 11. Elles wide: that part by the Corners marked K. is 12. Elles and a halfe broad, and long 16. Elles and a halfe: the parts H. are Counterforts to hold vp the Stayres. The place G. is a Court, which gaue light to the place within: the two goings in marked I. were to goe vp the Stayres, and the building began where the Stayres stand. The great stately Frontispice in the middle of the building, was of such breadth, as the middlemost part held without the Courts or Galleries. The two Figures, K. and ✠. which stand without the building, the one sheweth the Corner K. in greater and perfiter forme, and the other is a Corner of the Court D.

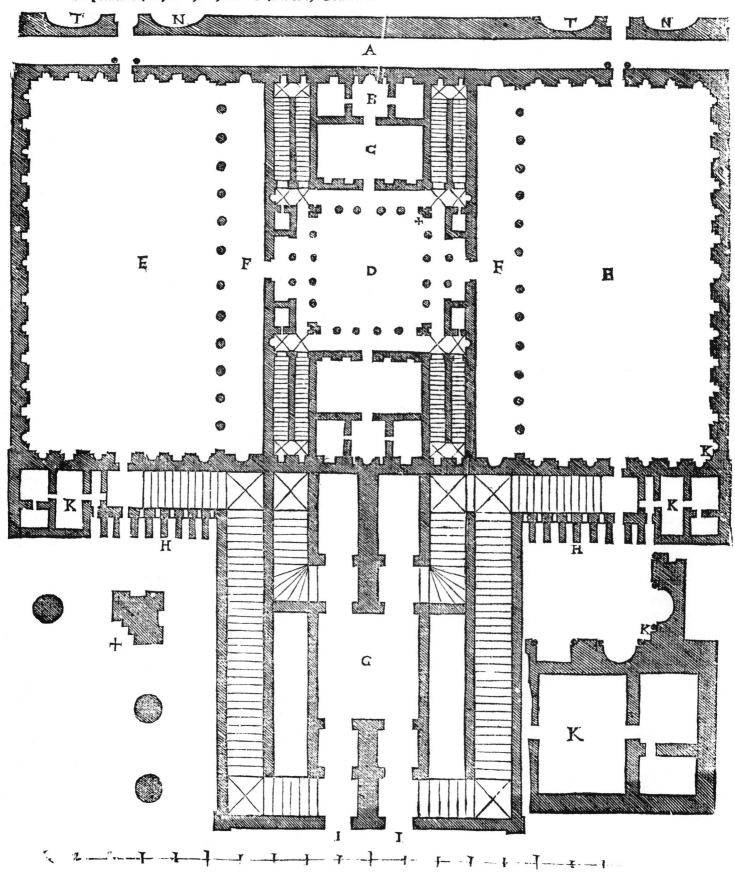

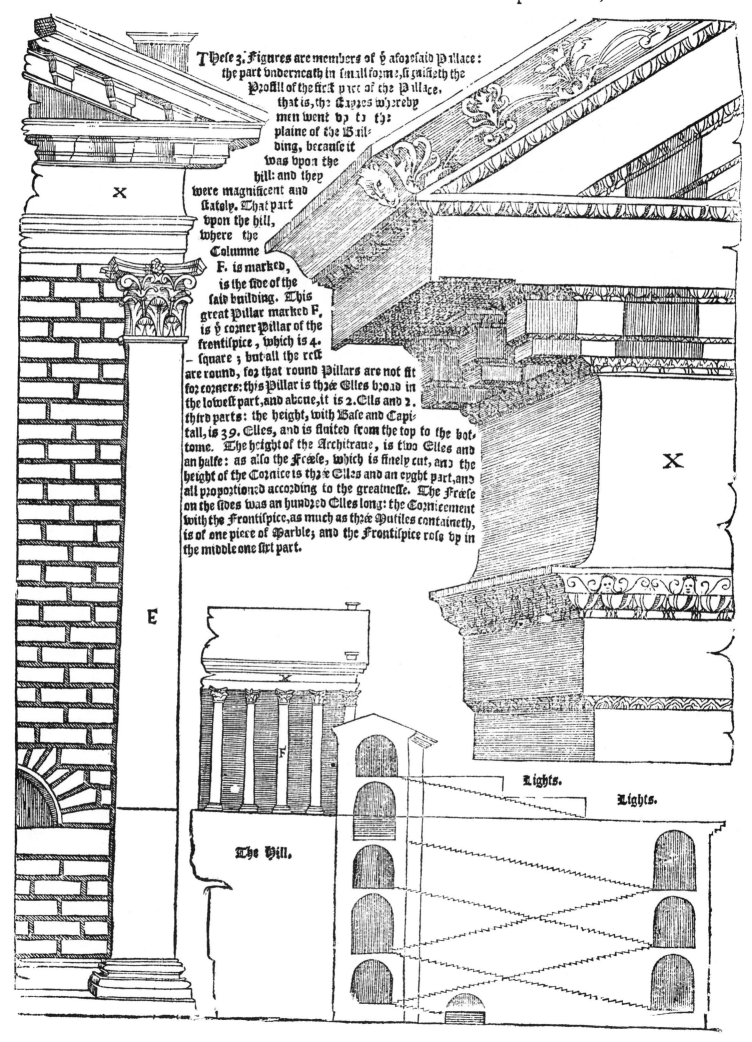

These 3. Figures are members of ý aforesaid Pallace: the part vnderneath in small formes, signifieth the Profill of the first part of the Pillace, that is, the Grezes whereby men went vp to the plaine of the Building, because it was vpon the hill: and they were magnificent and stately. That part vpon the hill, where the Columne F. is marked, is the side of the said building. This great Pillar marked F, is ý corner Pillar of the frontispice, which is 4. square; but all the rest are round, for that round Pillars are not fit for corners: this Pillar is three Elles broad in the lowest part, and aboue, it is 2. Elles and 2. third parts: the height, with Base and Capitall, is 39. Elles, and is fluited from the top to the bottome. The height of the Architraue, is two Elles and an halfe: as also the Freese, which is finely cut, and the height of the Cornice is three Elles and an eyght part, and all proportioned according to the greatnesse. The Freese on the sides was an hundred Elles long: the Cornicement with the Frontispice, as much as three Mutiles containeth, is of one piece of Marble; and the Frontispice rose vp in the middle one sirt part.

X

X

E

F

The Hill.

Lights.

Lights.

Among the ruines of Rome, there are many things found out, the which a man cannot marke nor imagine what they haue béene: a man also séeth there many ruines, which are now cast downe and ouerthrowns; whereby a man may conceaue the high mindes of the Ancient Romanes: amongst which Antiquities, this hereafter following, is one, as you may perceaue by that which yet standeth.   This Building is called the Basilica del foro transitorio: and a man may imagine the greatnesse thereof by the height of this Pillar, although you sée not the ending thereof vpwards; for the vppermost Cornice is not there in the worke, neither is there any pieces thereof among the ruines to be found,   whereby a man should conceaue what stood aboue such a Building.   This ruine was measured with a common or moderne Ell, which is deuided into 60. minutes: the halfe whereof standeth betwéene the Obelisées: this Columne stood 7. degrées eleuated from the earth, of indifferent height: the thicknesse of the Columne marked C. is 3. Elles in Diameter: beneath at the Base and in the vppermost part, vnder the Capitall, the Diameter is 2. Elles and 40. minutes: the height of the trunke or bare Columne, without Base or Capital, is 24. Elles and 55. minutes: the height of the Base below, is one Ell and an halfe: the height of the Capitall, is 3. Elles and 16. minutes: the height of the Architraue, is two Elles, and 23. minutes: the Cornice betwéene the Columne and the counter-pillar, which Cornice is marked D. is 1. Ell and 48. minutes: the Cornice aboue (as I haue sayd) is not found there: the counter-columne is flat, and is of the same proportion like the round Columne, and lesseneth also aboue, as the round doeth. The Capitall is formed like the Capitals of the Pantheon of the Rotund: the Base marked C. is placed there besides in better forme, and is proportioned in measure like the greater: likewise, there also you sée the Cornice D. in greater forme.   I haue set downe the measure of the greatest Columne C. now will I speake of the lesser, marked B.   which Columne vnder it, hath a very fayre Basement: the height whereof, is 6. Elles: the thickenesse of the sayd Columne in Diameter beneath, is one Ell and a third part; and it is lessened aboue accordingly, as the greatest is: the height thereof with the Base & Capitall is 13. Elles and 2. third parts: the height of the Base, is halfe the thicknes of the Columne beneath, and is fashioned like the greater: the height of the Capitall is one Ell & an halfe: which Capitall is very well made, and the forme thereof in great, is séen in my other 4. Booke, in the beginning of § Composita. This Columne is fluted, as the Figure thereof sheweth, and hath also a flat Columne of the same forme: the Architraue, Frése and Cornice aboue this Columne, are about 4. Elles: which Cornice hath the Mutiles without Dentiles, and is very like the worke of the Pantheon; and by as much as I could perceaue, this lesse Columne serued for an ornament of a Gate or Dore of the sayd Basilica.

The third part of the common Ell, wherewith this is measured.

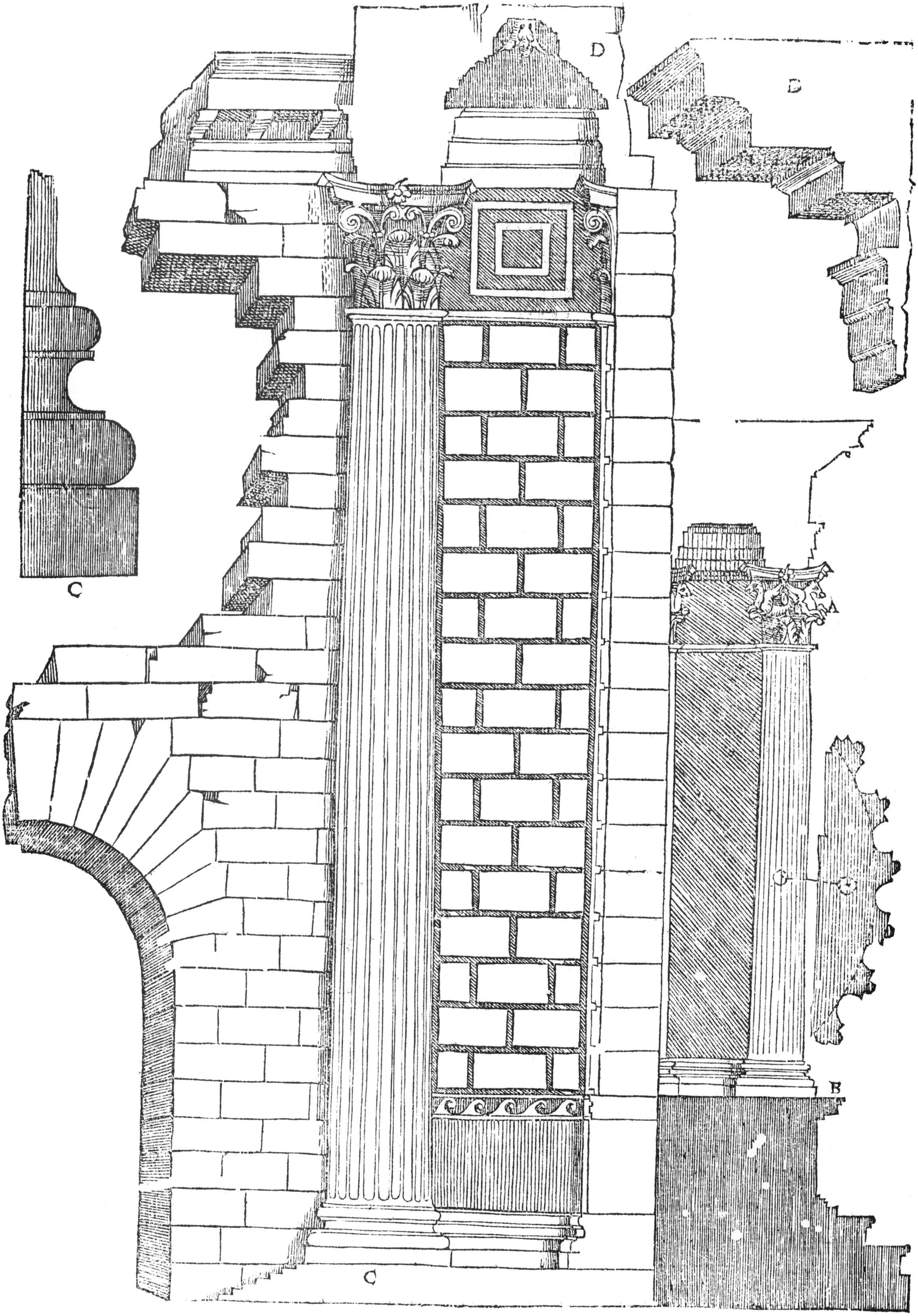
D
D
C
A
B
C

The Romanes (because of their great proud mindes) alwayes sought to build things of great maiestie, which might shew their great power both by Water and Land: and to that end they made the wonderfull Hauen of Ostia, for the ease of the Citie of Rome. which, in trueth (in regard of the commoditie and greatnesse of the Building thereof, and specially the great strength thereof) may well bee called wonderfull. It is of forme Hexagoniick, that is, 6. cornerd: and each Facie is 116. roodes long, and each rood is 10. Palmes: by these principall measures, you may vnderstand the greatnesse therof, euery Facie had a large walking place, with Galleries round about, & 4. Appertiments also, compassed with Galleries, and a walking place in the middle. Along the water side there were trunckes of Columnes orderly placed, wherein to the ships were fastened; and at the mouth of the Hauen, there were towers to defend it from the enemie in time of need. And for that you can hardly perceaue the Appertiments in so small a forme, therefore I haue placed them beneath in greater formes, and marked them with A. and B.

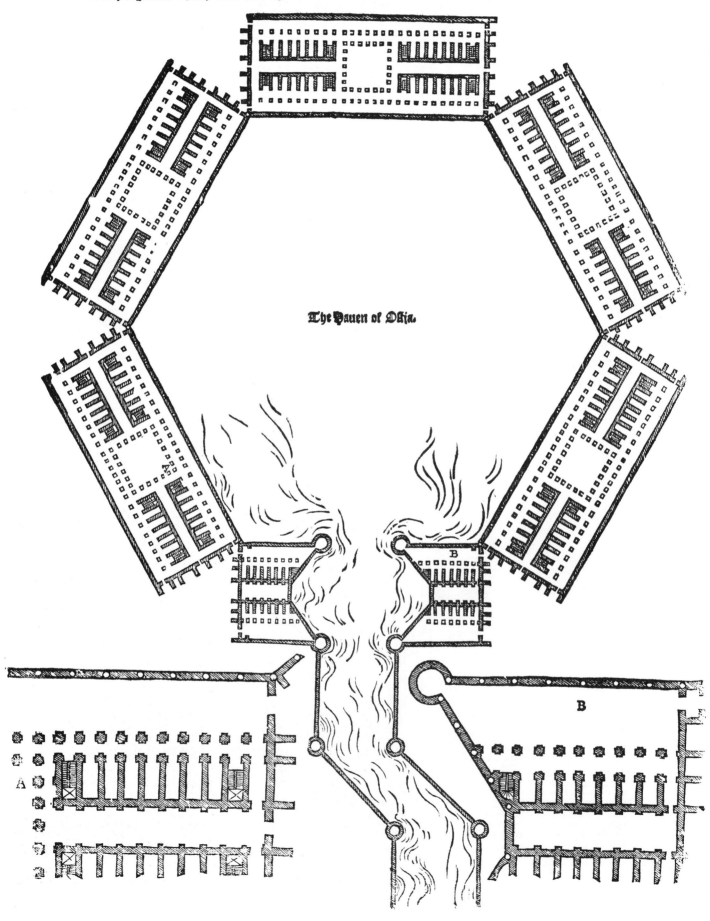

The Hauen of Ostia.

The Thermes of Titus are leſſe then the other, and therefore by the people they were called Thermi minori : netherthelesse, (after my opinion) they are well made: the Ichnographie of theſe Thermes is meaſured with the ancient Palme. Firſt, the Diameter of the round forme marked A. is about 150. Palmes: the part B. is in length 80 Palmes, and in breoth 51. Palmes: the part C. is 80. Palmes in length, and in breoth 60 Palmes. The forme D. is about 100. Palmes in Diameter: and the Portall E. is 50 Palmes: the part F. is 120. Palmes long, and 70. broad: the eyght ranked part marked G. is about 100. Palmes: the round part H. is 150. Palmes in Diameter. The part I. is 100. Palmes, and is almoſt two foure ſquares: the two parts, each marked with K. is 30. Palmes on eyther ſide. The part L. is 125. Palmes, in length, the breoth 30 Palmes. The roundneſſe marked M. is about 120. Palmes in Diameter. That part mar-

ked N. is 148. Palmes long, and 57. broad. The part O. is the ſame: the preſeruation of the water followeth after.

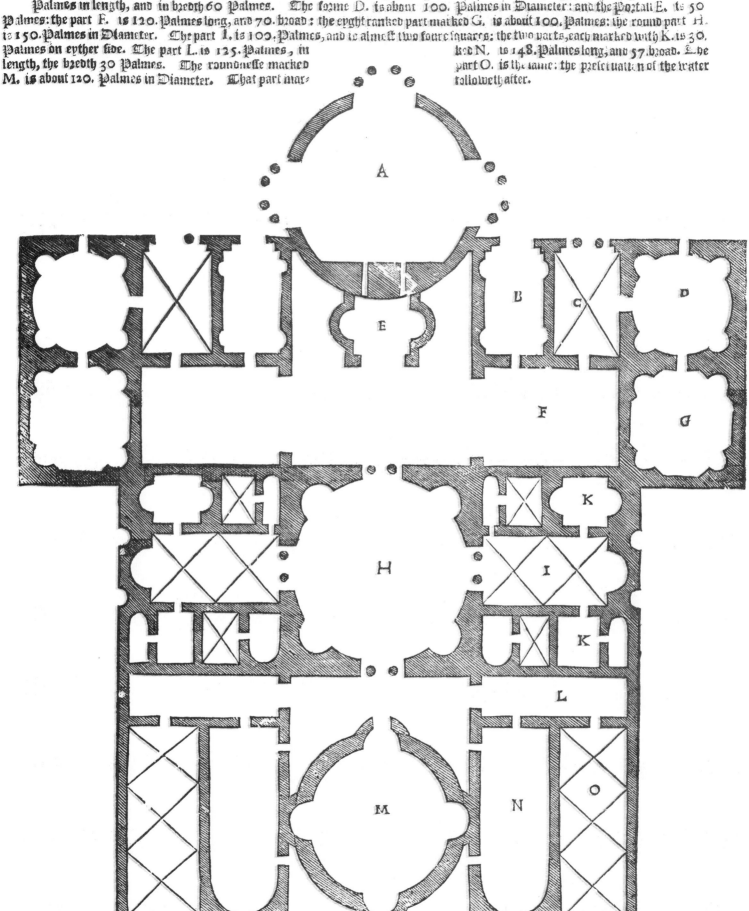

Of Antiquitie

The preseruing, or the place where the water of the Thermes of Titus, the sonne of Vespatianus was kept, is wonderfully made, and very Artificiall, and that is, for that the Arches of these preseruatiues are placed in such good order, that a man, standing in the going through of the one, seeth them all ouerthwarts : and this is the place which the people commonly call, The seuen Halles; and it was for this cause, because the spaces are seuen in number: and in them you see ouerthwarts, backwards and forewards, alwayes 7. in number: the thicknesse of the walls, is foure foot and an halfe: the widenesse of the Arches is sire foot: from one Arch to the other, are 27. foot: the widenesse from one wall to the other, is 15. foote, and they are round roofed, of an indifferent height. The walles and roofes are playstered with most hard plaister.

The old Romane Palme.

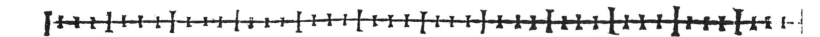

JN Rome and elsewhere there are many Bridges made by the Romanes, but I will here shew the inuention of foure onely, that you may see their manner of making of Bridges.

This Bridge is called Ponte S. Angelo, because it standeth vpon Tiber, by the Towne of Inghelenborch: by the ancient Romanes, it was called Ponte Elio, of Elio Adrianus.

This Bridge was wont to be called Ponte Tarpeio: others call it, Ponte Fabricio: and in our time it is called, Ponte de quatro capi.

This Bridge is called Pontus Milnius, but commonly it is called Ponte Molle.

This Bridge in former times, was called the Se-nates Bridge: others call it Ponte palatino: but now it is called Ponto S. Maria, and elso Ponte Sisto.

A Mong other Thermes which are in Rome, I finde this of Antoniano to bee better to bee noted then the rest, and although ẏ the Thermes of Dioclesian are greater, yet in this I find much fayrer correspondencie and knitting together in every part, then in the others: for that in the place C. they might make all kind of Playes or sports without any hinderance. And for that ẏ Thermes were specially made for men to bathe in, as they were vsed for diuers sports to be made in them, so was the preseruation of the water made behind ẏ builoing, marked A. where, by meanes of the Pipes, they were alwayes filled to serue for such vses.

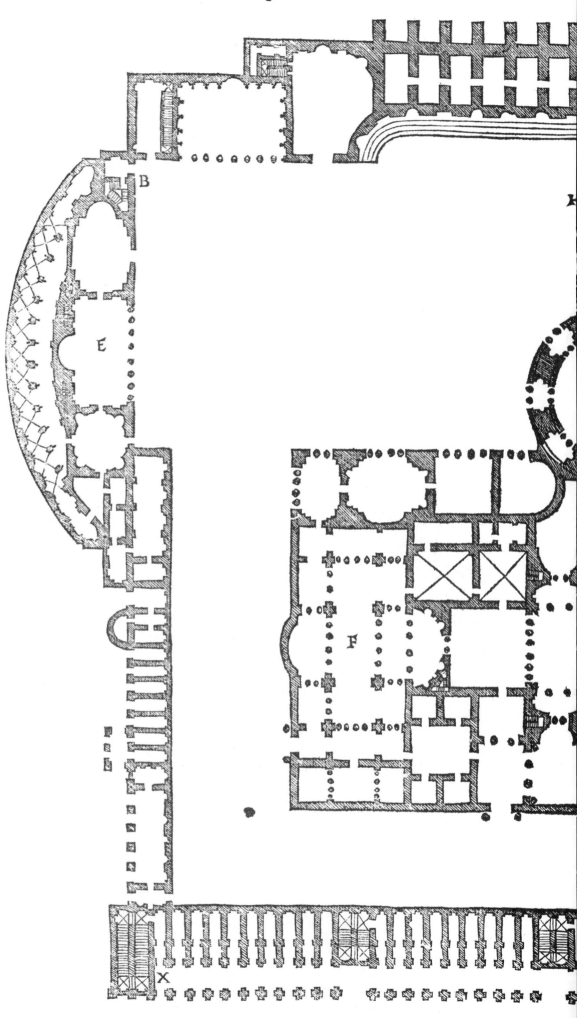

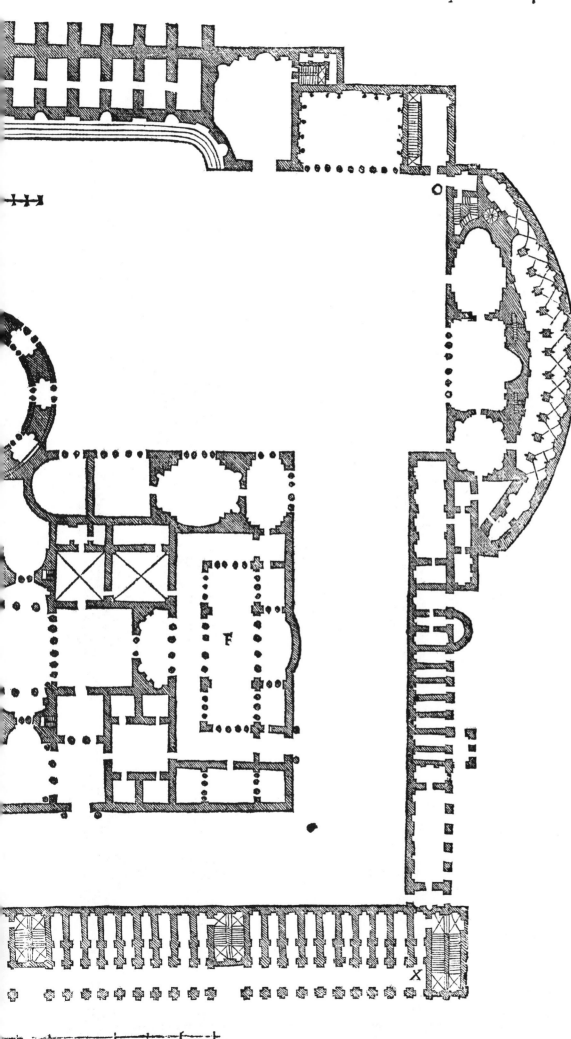

This ground is incalured with the common Ell, the third part whereof is hereunder set downe by the side of the Building. The line in the middle of the place, is 100. Elles, by the which you shall almost find all the measures, whereof, for breuitie, I will not speake directly, but onely of the principal things. First, one of the places for the keeping of the water, is thirtie Elles long: and 16. Elles broad. The part X. is 81. Elles long, and the bredth 44. Elles: the round Building D. is in Diameter 86. Elles. The place marked B.C. is 700. Elles long. The part in the middle, marked G. is in length about 105. Elles, and in bredth 60. Elles.

For that in the ground before set downe, by reason of the smalnesse of the figures, which could not be made greater in this Booke, a man can not so wel know the particular partes, therefore J haue in these two sides set downe some parts more plainly, as the ingenious workeman, by the letters wherewith they are marked, may see and find them, when he compareth them with the whole ground.

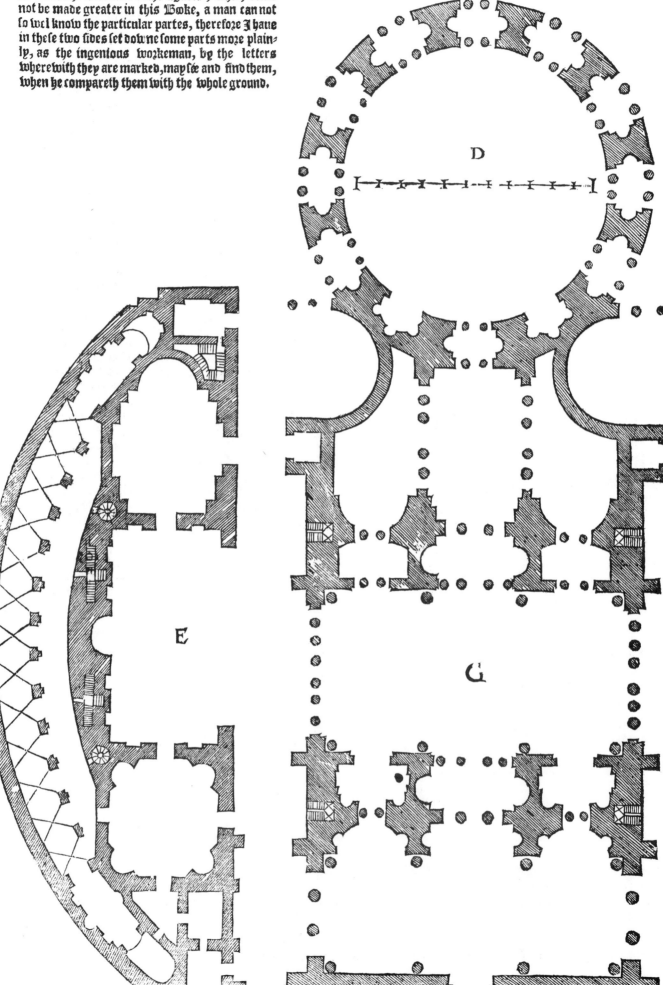

Lthough these Figures stand thus without order, and in many pieces; yet the wise workeman shall know, that they are members of the Thermes afore shewed, beholding the letters which stand in them (which comparing with the others) he shall find what parts they are. Also, he must know, that the parts H. and X. belong not to the part F. for the Figures hereunder are three severall parts; although, for necessitie sake, they are set one by another. I have also not set downe the particular measures: for the workeman shal better helpe himselfe with the invention, then with the measure.

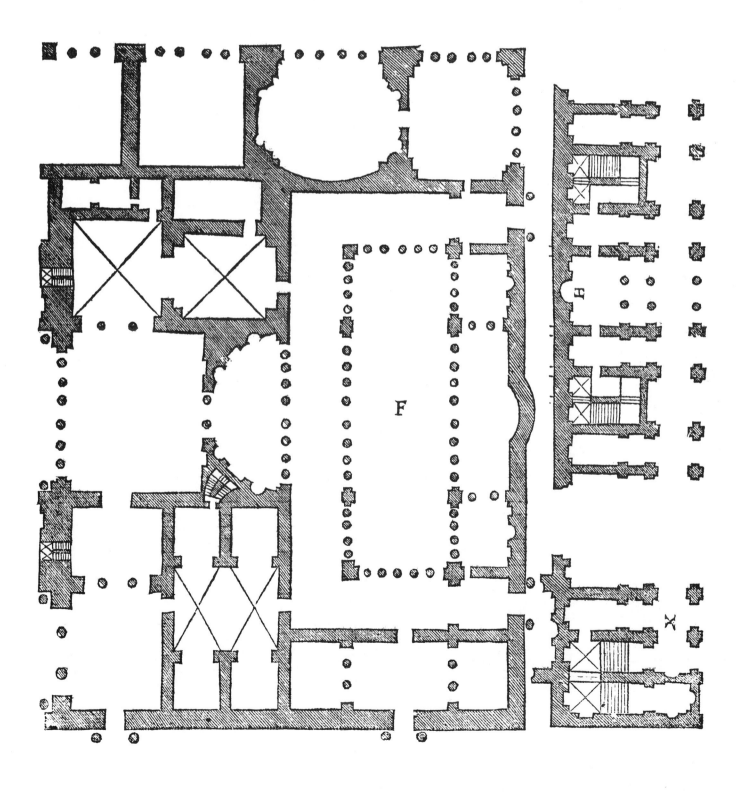

Of Antiquitie

About seuen miles from Alcaire there is a Piramides, whereof I will shew the forme, and also set downe the measure, as I had it from a Gentleman of Uenice, who measured the same himselfe, and was both vpon it, and within it. This Piramides was measured by Paces, and euery Pace is more then three ancient Palmes: the Base, on euery side, is 270. Paces, and is right foure square: it is all of hard stone, and you may clime vpon it without, (but not easily) vnto the top: for euery Pace is three Palmes and a halfe high: but there are not so many Playnes, that a man may easily set his foot vpon them: the number of the Paces or steps, from the Bases to the top, or the highest part, is 210. and they are all of one height; so that the height of the whole Piramides is as much as the Base. Many beléeue that this Piramides was a Sepulchre: for that within it, there is a place in the middle, whereon lyeth a great stone: thereupon men presume, that some great person hath there béene buried: but going in, vpon the left hand, you find a going vp of stone, which turnes about the Piramides within, through the which you goe vp the Station, in the top within. About the middle of this Piramides there is another going in, but it is fast shut: on the top of this Piramides, there is a faire flat or playne, about 8. Paces broad on euery side, whereby workemen know, that it was the same playne that was made at the finishing of the Piramides. Not farre from thence, there is a head of hard stone, with part of the brest all of one stone; the face whereof is 10. Paces long: and in this Figure there are some Egyptian letters: of this Pirami- des and head, Peter Martir writeth, and hath also séene and measured them, which differ not much.

ALthough the Gréekes were the principall founders and inuentors of good Architecture (as our Master Vitruuius, and many other Authors witnesse) neuerthelesse, by reason of their great warres, and their Land so often ouerrun and spoyled by the enemies, a man can hardly finde any good worke standing whole in all Grecia: but as some men haue told me, there are yet the ruines of a Building, which, as men conceaue, was of one hundred Columnes; whereof no man can by casting know the height.   But (with our Authors licence) for that he makes this by report, and hath no measure thereof, I haue onely set the fourth part of the ground by the halfe of the Building (which he hath thereto plased) whereby the workeman may conceaue the whole ground, and the whole Figure thereof.

By S. George Belabro, you may see this building hereunder, which was made by the Bankiers & Oxen sellers, in the time of Lucius Septimus Seuerus, and Marcus Aurelius Antonius: which Building is of Composita worke, well set foorth on euery side with grauing. Let no man wonder, that the Frise & the Architraue are couered with this table, for that there being much writing to bee set into it, the Frise was not great inough to containe so many letters: therefore the workeman made it so, and brake not the order of Architecture at all, leauing the full proportion therein in the corners.

I Will not set the measure of this Building at large, because it was lost after it was measured: but as I remember, the widenesse betweene the one and the other Pilaster was 12. old foote. The height of that widenesse was 20. fot: the thickenes of the Pilasters, with all the Columnes which are flat, is 4. fot and an halfe: and so much the Architraue, Frise and Cornice containeth.

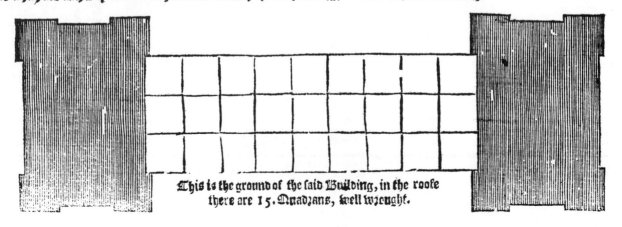

This is the ground of the said Building, in the roofe there are 15. Quadians, well wrought.

The works hereunder are the ornaments of the foresaid building, the which, in trueth, is as hmely set forth, as any other worke in Rome, for there is no space without grauing; and also well made: all things very correspondent, onely the vppermost Cornice; the which, in regard of the richnesse of the grauing, is much confused: it is also vicious from the Echine down-wards, for 2. causes; the one is, that betwæne the Echine with ý Ouale, and the Ouale, ξ the Dentiles, there is no parting of lift or cimatie: for it is very necessary to deuide the one frõ the

other, ξ especially when they are all cut. The other is of greater importance, ý vnder the Dentiles there are two works of one fashion ξ cutting, which I should not haue made so: but I say expresly it is not to be done, nor such things men ought not to doe.

(Doth rest.

The innermost part whereupon the rose or ſxling

The bottome of the Architraue.

In the furthest part of the rose, are 27. Quadrats.

THE Thermes of Dioclesian, in truth, is a most rich Building, by that which is seene in the ruines, which are yet standing aboue ground: besides, the Appertements of diuers formes, with rich ornaments, and the great number of Pillars that were there, are witnesses of their magnificence: by the deuiding this ground, and by the diuers formes therein, the ingenious workeman may bee well holpen. But a man can not denie, but that there is much discordance in it, which in our time would not bee borne withall: this I speake, not to correct such puissant Emperours, nor so many good workemen as were in those dayes: although they as then were not so skilfull, as a great number were at other times: but I say this onely, for the good of them that will not thinke scorne to read this my writing. It is true, that the fayrest part of a Building is the correspondencie thereof, and the appendances of the same, not troubled with things which trouble mens sight: therefore I said, if the way A. B. were like the way C. D. then the whole Building would stand better behind, in such sort, that all the wayes would be free, and not cumbred with any thing. Also the part of the Building in the middle marked A. which

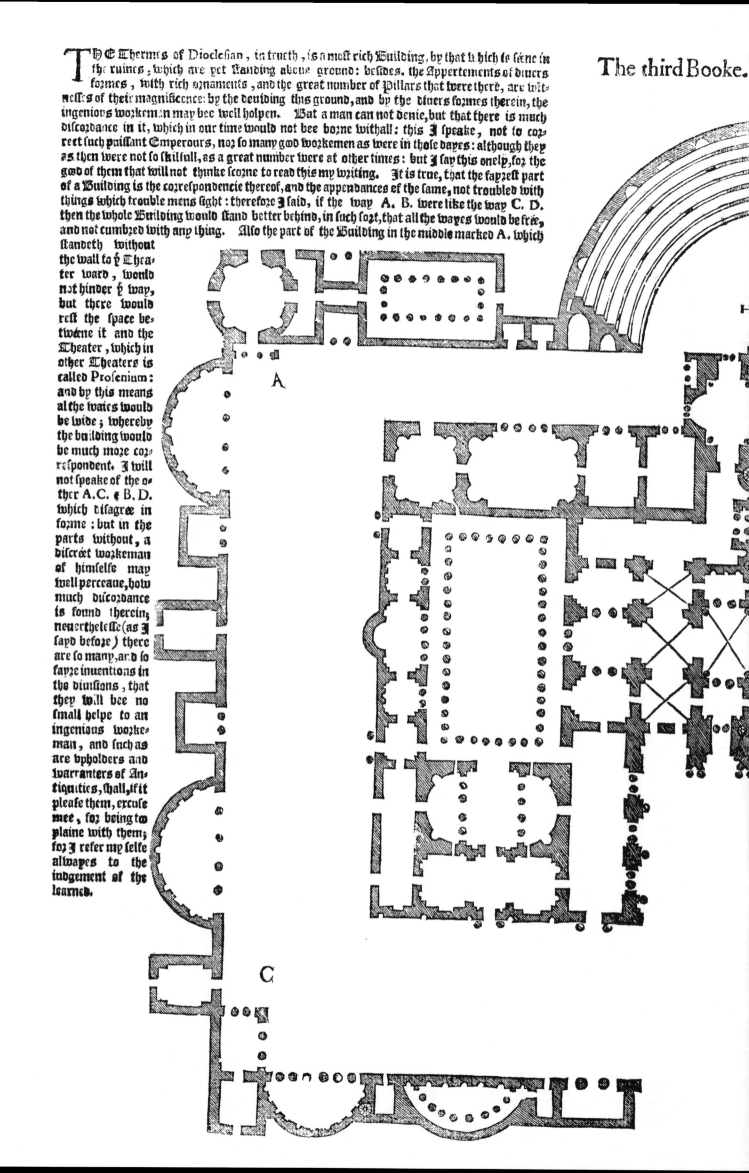

standeth without the wall to y Theater ward, would not hinder y way, but there would rest the space betwéene it and the Theater, which in other Theaters is called Prosenium: and by this means al the waies would be wide; whereby the building would be much more correspondent. I will not speake of the other A.C. & B.D. which disagrée in forme: but in the parts without, a discréet workeman of himselfe may well perceaue, how much discordance is found therein; neuerthelesse (as I sayd before) there are so many, and so fayre inuentions in the diuisions, that they will bee no small helpe to an ingenious workeman, and such as are vpholders and warranters of Antiquities, shall, if it please them, excuse mee, for being too plaine with them; for I refer my selfe alwayes to the iudgement of the learned.

This Ichnograhpie is meafured by the ancient Palme: but, for that in this ground I haue beene more curious of the inuention, then of any other thing, therefore I fet not downe the particular meafures, which, in truth, would be ouerlong to rehearfe: but I haue with great diligence fet this fmall forme in fo good proportion in forts, that the cunning Architector may in a manner find the meafures, ufing the fame fmall Palme, which ftandeth in the halfe Circle, deuided in 10. parts, and each part is 10. Palmes : fo the whole line is 100. Palmes : thus with a Compaffe in your hand, you may partly conceaue the meafure of this Building.　Touching the Orthographie, I haue not fet it downe at all, for 3. caufes : Firft, becaufe of the great ruines, there is little fight to be had thereof: the 2. becaufe of the difficultie to meafure the fame: the 3. for that, in truety, a man feeth this building was not made in that fortunate time of good workemen; for in it are many difcordances and vnfit things, but yet great and coftly ornaments.　But for that men in fo fmall a forme of Ichnographie can not perfectly fhew the forme of euery part and member, therefore hereafter I will fhew the part in the middle more plainely.

The ancient
Palme.

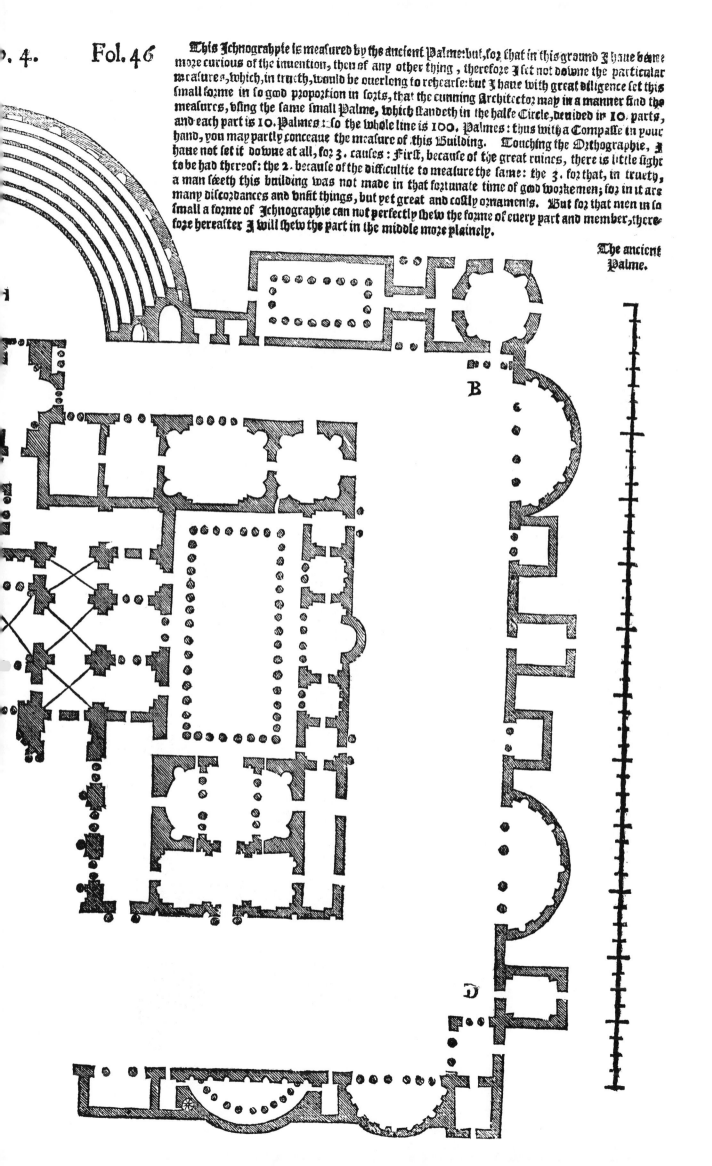

FO2 that (as J fap d) the ground of Dioclefians Therme, being placed in fo fmall a forme, can hardly be meafured from part to part; therefore J haue made a part thereof in greater forme, which ftandeth hereunder, and is like the middle thereof, as the letter A. fheweth : and the line in the midtle thereof, is alfo 100. Palmes, like the other; whereby a diligent workeman may almoft find all the meafures thereof with a payre of Compalfes.

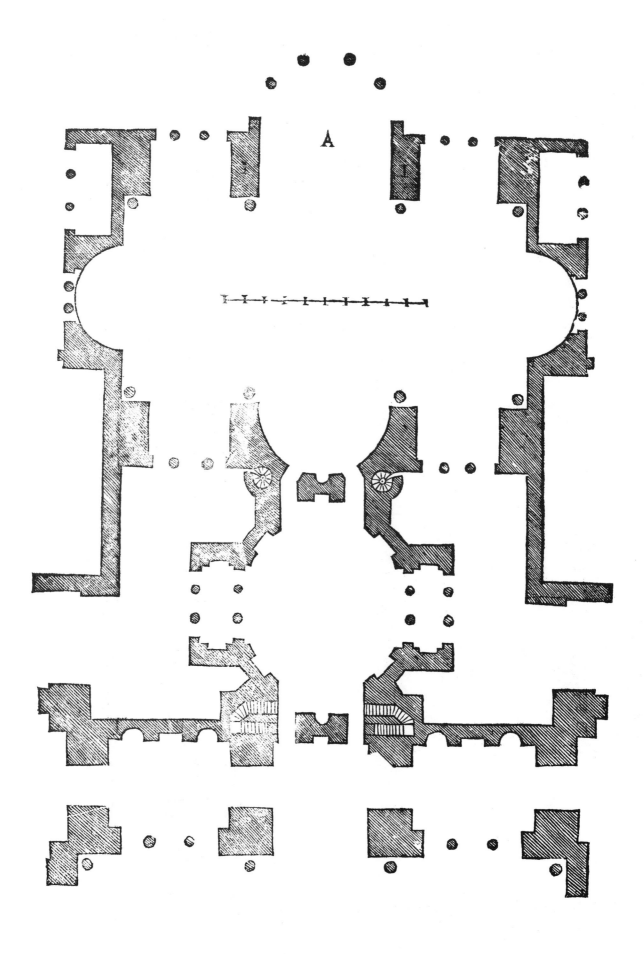

THe Therme made by Dioclesian, was vsed for diuers common and open sports, and specially to bathe in ; whereunto it behoueth to haue great quantitie of water, which was brought by Pipes a great way off; and it was kept in certaine Cesternes, which stod in the Thermes of Dioclesian, in this manner as is hereunder set downe : it was made with Pilasters, and aboue it was crosse rosed, with walles about them, of very good stuffe; which was so firme, that at this day it is yet to be séene: the thickenesse of the Pilasters is of each side foure foote : betwéene each two Pilasters is 12. foote of the old Romane foot, although the sayd Therme is measured with Palmes: and this line hereunder is halfe an olde foote.

The halfe ancient fot.

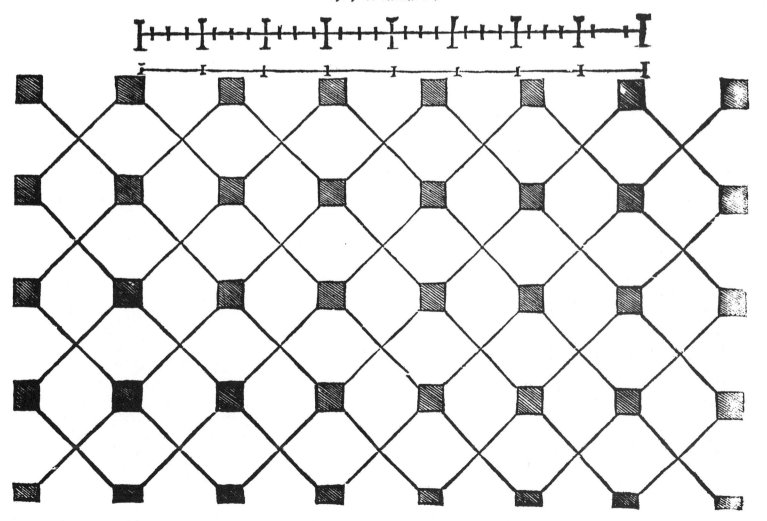

IN Rome there are many ancient Tryumphant Arches, among the which, this Building, by the greatest number, is accounted for a Tryumphant Arch: yet by the knowledge that men haue of it, it is thought to be a Porticus, or a Gallery, like vnto a Burse or Exchange for Marchants: it may be it was made by some one nation alone; as yet to this day in great Towres and Cities, euery nation hath a seuerall place, although they are not by that meanes deuided. This Porticus or Gallery stood in Nel foro Boario; and in ancient time was called, The Temple of Ianus: which is measured with the ancient Palme. This Building hath foure gates, as the ground hereunder doeth shew: betwene the one and the other Pilaster, there are 22. Palmes: round about this Porticus, there are 48. niches or hollow places: but there are no more then 16. to set Images therein; all the rest are but for shewes, as being not deepe inough cut into the wall: which places were beautified with small Pillars somewhat bearing out from the wall, as you see them, and were Corinthia worke, but now it is spoyled of all such ornaments.

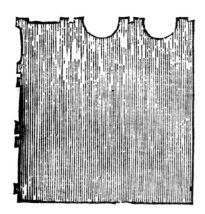

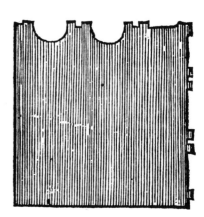

The ground of the Figure following.

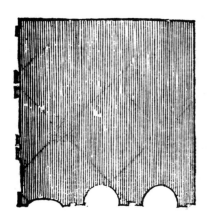

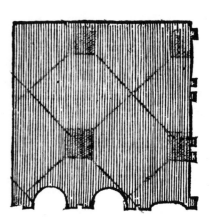

The height of the Arch is 44. Palmes : the height of the Bales beneath, marked E. is 1. Palme and an halfe. The Facie D. within the corners, is turned into a Cornice, and is the like height. The iudgement of the workman pleafed me well in ý piece, which is, that he made
no Cornice in the innermoft part, that might trouble the people that fhould be therein : the height of the other Cornices are not meafured, but
the formes of them diligently counterforted, follow hereafter.

The fiue pieces of Cornices hereunder set downe, are the ornaments of the Porticus aforesayd. The Base E. and the Facie D. were measured, and in this forme, the great measure set downe; but the other were counterfeited by sight, with their heights where they stand: and there is little difference betwéene the one and the other, for parts, and also in height. The Figure C. is the Facie vnder the first Niche or hollow place.

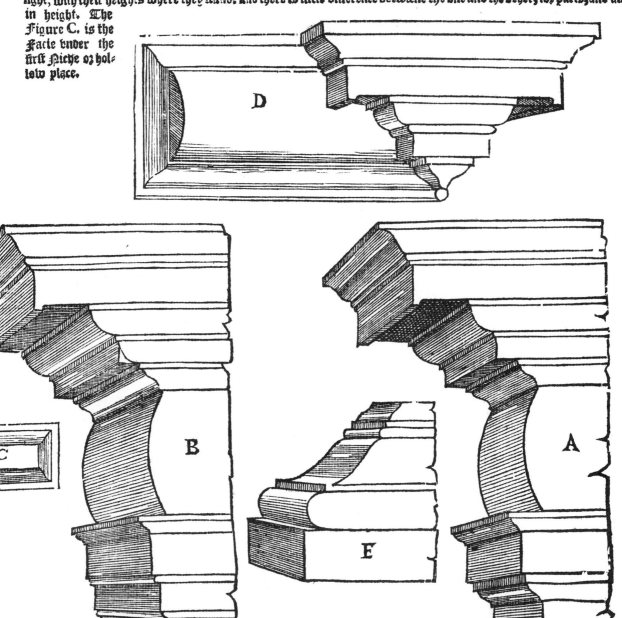

The Arch Tryumphant, next following, is called Titus Arch Tryumphant; whereof this Figure hereunder, is the ground, and is measured with the ancient foote. The widenesse of the Arch is 18. foote and 17. minutes. The thicknesse of the Columne, is a foote and 26. minutes and an halfe. The foote wherewith this is measured, is of 64. minutes, whereof the halfe is here set downe.

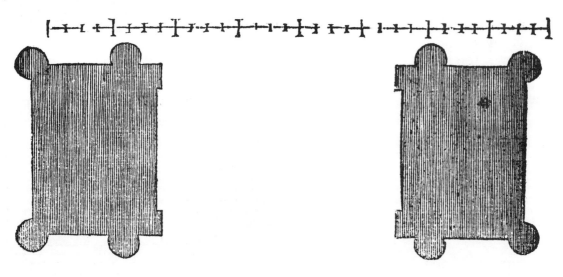

I haue ſpoken of the wideneſſe and thickneſſe, now I will ſet downe the height: And firſt, the height of the Bow or Arch is as much agayne as the breadth. The Baſe of the Pedeſtall is 2. foote 4. minutes leſſe in height. The Cornice of the Pedeſtall is 35. minutes high. The height of the Baſes of the Columnes is about one foote: all theſe parts, and alſo the Capitall of the Columne, well proportioned in meaſure, ſtand in the beginning of the Compoſita Order, in my fourth Boke. The flat of the Pedeſtall is foure foote and a halfe high. The height of the Columne without Baſe and Capitall 17. foote and 13 minutes. The height of the Capitall is 1. foote and 27. minutes. The height of the Architraue is one foote and 19. minutes. The Freſe is one foote and 17. minutes. The Cornice is 2. foote and 6. minutes high. The Baſement of the Epitaph is of the ſame with the Freſe. The height of the Epitaph is 9. foote and 12. minutes: the breadth is 23. foote: which members ſhall hereafter be ſet downe, and figured moe at large.

IT would be troublesome both to the writer and to the Reader, if I should set downe all the parts of these Ornaments, from member to member, as they are diligently measured; & that not onely with foote, but also with parts of minutes: but I haue taken the paynes onely to set the same downe out of the great into the small forme, in such sort, that he that is discréete, may with his Compasse find the proportion thereof. It is true, that the Ornaments of the most part of the Tryumphant Arches in Rome are much contrary to Vitruuius writing; and this, I thinke, is the cause, that the sayd Arches are, for the most part, made by the Rootes of other buildings, (that is, of as many sorts of péces as they could get:) and it may be, that the workemen in those dayes were selfe willed, and stood not much vpon obseruation, because they were things seruing for Tryumphs, and it may bee (as it hapneth oftentimes) made in haste. That part here on the side set downe, marked A. is the Base of the Epitaph. B. is the highest Cornice, Fréese, and Architraue: which Cornice, in my opinion, is very licencious for diuers reasons: The first, it is proportioned too high: from the nether Architraue, and aboue it, there are too many members, and especially Mutiles and Dentiles, which standing alike in one Cornice, are disliked by Vitruuius, notwithstanding it is very well wrought, and specially the Scima aboue: but had I such a Cornice to make (obseruing the right order) I would make the Scima lesse, and the Cornice more: I would leaue the Mutiles as they be, and I would not cut the Denticules, but the Cimated. The Architraue hereof pleaseth mee well inough. The two members marked C. shew the Facie and the Profill of the Mensola, which is the closing stone of the Arch. The members marked with E. are, in truth, rich for worke, but yet so rich, that the one darkeneth the other: but if the parts were so deuided, that the one were grauen, and the other playne, I would commend it more. And herein the workeman that made the Pantheon, was very iudicious, for that you sée no such confusion in his Ornaments. The worke vnder this Arch is very well made and deuided; it is also a fayre Compartment, and rich of worke. But it may be, that such as are too much conceited to commend Antiquities of Rome, will (perauenture) thinke that I am too bold to censure vpon that which hath béene made by such skilfull ancient Romanes; but in this respect I would haue them take my spéeches in good part, for that all my intent is, to shew it them that know it not, and such as will subiect themselues to heare my opinion: for it is not sufficient to make ancient things as they stand, but it is another thing with Vitruuius aduice to chose out the best and fayrest, and to reiect the worse. It is true, that the chiefest part of an Architector is, that hee mistaketh not himselfe in giuing his censure, as many doe, who being obstinate in their opinions, make all things as they haue séene them, and hereby couer their vnskilfulnesse, without giuing any other reasons of things: and there are some that say, Vitruuius was but a man, and that they also are men sufficient, to make and inuent new things, without regarding, that Vitruuius confesseth to haue learned it from so many skilfull men, partly in his owne time, as also by meanes of the writing of other worke men.

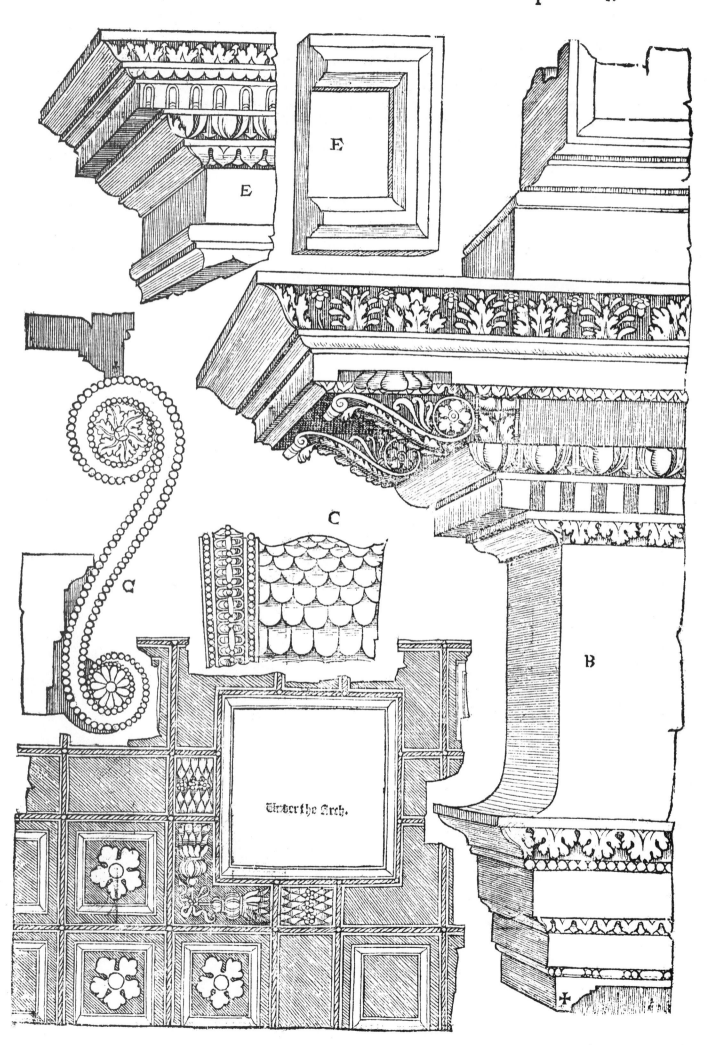

Under the Arch.

Beneath the Campidoglio there is a Tryumphant Arch, which by the inscription may be conceiued to be made in the time of Lucius Septimus Seuerus, and vnder his name, and by that which men marke and sufficiently find, it is made with Reliefs of other buildings: it is also well adorned with good cutting and grauing: it is richly wrought both on the sides, and also before and behind: it was measured by the old Romane Palme of 12. fingers, euery finger of 4. minutes, which in totall maketh 48. minutes. The widenesse of the Arch in the middle is 22. Palmes, 15. minutes and a halfe. The widenes of the Arches on the sides is 9. Palmes, 30. minutes. The thicknesse of the Arch in the sides is 23. Palmes, 25. minutes. The little Gates within the Arches are 7. Palmes and 30. minutes wide. The breadth of the Pilasters with the Columnes is 8. Palmes and 7. minutes. The thicknesse of the Columnes is 2. Palmes, 30. minutes. The thicknesse of the flat Columnes is 28. minutes. This Arch is now vnder the earth as farre as aboue the Pedestall, (for so high the earth is there raysed with the ruines) but there was a part left vncouered to measure it, but they could not come to the Base to take the measure thereof, because it was troublesome to remoue the ruines.

The ground of the Arch Tryumphant of Lucius Septimus.

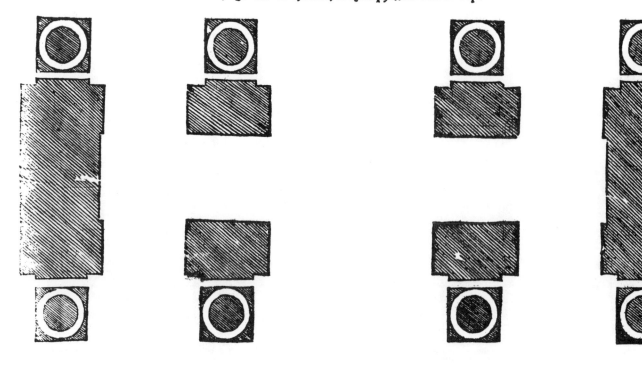

Efore, I haue set downe all the meafures of this Arch, touching the Ichnographie, that is, the thickneffe and breoth, now I will fpeake of the height. The height of the middlemoſt Arch, is 45. Palmes and 3. minutes. The height of the Arches befides, are 25 Palmes. The height of the Pedeſtall, is about 10. Palmes. The thickneffe of the Columnes, is 2. Palmes and 30. minutes in Diameter beneath: but aboue under the Capitall, they are 2. Palmes and 16. minutes. The height of them, is 23. Palmes and 25. minutes. The height of the Architraue, is one Palme and 30. minutes. The height of the Fraſe, is one Palme and 3. minutes. The height of the Cornice, is two Palmes and 14. minutes. The height of the Plinthus, aboue the Cornice, marked ✠. is 29. minutes. The Baſe aboue the Plinthus, is halfe a Palme. The uppermoſt Cornice, is one Palme and 2. minutes, and proportioned in a greater forme.

IMP. CAES. LVCIO SEPTIMO. M. FIL. SEVERO. PIO. PERTINACI AVG.
PATRI PATRIAE PARTHICO ARABICO, ET PARTHICO ADIABENICO
PONTIF. MAX. TRIBVNIC. POTEST. XI. IMP. XI. COS. 3. PRO.
COS. ET. IMP. CAES. M. AVRELIO. L. FIL. ANTONINO. AVG.
PIO FELICI TRIBVNIC. POTEST. VI. COS. PROCOS. P. P.
OPTIMIS, FORTISSIMISQVE PRINCIPIBVS
OB REMPVBLICAM RESTITVTAM IMPERIQ. POPVLI ROMANI PRO-
PAGATVM INSIGNIBVS VIRTVTIBVS EORVM DOMI FORISQ. S. P. Q. R.

IN the fide befoze, I haue fet downe all the heights and bzedths of the Arch Triumphant, of Lucius Septimus Seuerus: now I will fhew the particular, and feuerall parts thereof, as I faid befoze. There is no meafure of the Bafe of the Pedeftals; but it may be thought, that they containe as much at the leaft, as the Coznice of the Pedeftals: which Coznice is a Palme, and fo much the Bafe may hold: of which part, the fozme ftandeth heere in the middle, marked G. The Bafe of the Columne ftandeth thereby marked F. the which Bafe hath a ftone oz counter-Bafe vnder the Plinthus: and this may peraduenture be done, becaufe the Columnes could not reach to fuch a height as they fhould. The Capitall is here not fet downe, becaufe you fhall fee the like in the beginning of the Ozder, called Compofita, in my fourth Booke, foz this is Compofita wozke. The height of the Architraue, is one Palme and 30. minutes: the Fréefe is 9. Palmes and 3. minutes: which Fréefe, foz that it is full of grauing, fheweth of a fmall height where it ftandeth: and by Vitruuius wziting, it ought to ftand the fourth part higher then the Architraue; and this is leffe. The height of the Coznice, is two Palmes and 14. minutes: which in trueth is much too high, accozding to the propoztions of the other members; and it fheweth fo much the greater, becaufe it hath moze pzoiecture of height: and this makes me fpecially beléeue, that this Arch is made of diuers pieces of other buildings, becaufe of the fhzinking of the members. The fozme of the Architraue, Fréefe and Coznice, is marked with B. The height of the Bafe, aboue the faid Coznice, is halfe a Palme: the height of the laft Coznice, is a Palme and two minutes, and hath fuch a great pzoiecture, and hanging ouer, as you fée in the Figure: and in fuch place, I blame not the Coznice; but affirme that it was made with great iudgement: foz that the great pzoiecture makes the Coznice fhew greater, becaufe it is féene from vnder vpwards, and foz that there is like matter, it is not in baine foz the building. This Coznice here is marked with A. The Coznice which beareth vp the greateft Arch, is marked with C. whereof the Pzoiecture is much too great: and foz my part, in fuch a fubiect, I would rather giue iudgement that it fhould be high, that with the bearing out, it fhould not hinder the fight of the Arch. That wozke marked D. commeth right on the Facie, which goeth from Columne to Columne, aboue the two little Arches; and this accompanieth the Coznice C. The Coznice marked with E. is that which vpholdeth the fmal Arch, the which Coznice hath a Scima, which I fhould not make in fuch a piece of wozke: foz that all Coznices, whofe crownes haue not their iuft Pzoiecture, are vncomely: foz the fayzeft part of a Coznice, is, that the crowne bee of a good height, and of a good pzoiecture: wherefoze I fet it downe foz a common rule, that the crownes that are higher then their Scima, and thofe at leaft, that fhall haue as much Pzoiecture as height, fhall alwayes be commended by men of vnderftanding. This I thought good to fet downe, to aduertife them thereof that know it not.

Of Antiquitie

IN the kingdome of Naples, viz. betwéene Rome and Naples there are many Antiquities; for that the Romanes had great pleasure in those places: among the which, this Tryumphant Arch is séene, being yet all whole and fayre to sight: and therefore I thought it good to set it among the number of the rest of the Arches (which were made by the Romanes.) This Arch is at Beneuente, on this side of Naples, and was measured with a moderne Ell, whereof the third part is hereunder set downe. The Figure here below, is the Ichnographie of the same Arch; and to shew by whom this Arch was made, is néedlesse, because it may be vnderstood by the writing that standeth thereon. The widenesse of the Arch, is eyght Elles: the thicknesse of the Columnes is an Ell: the Pilaster vnder the Arch, is also as broad: the inter-columne holds thrée Elles: the height of the Arch, is almost as much againe as the bredth: the height of the Base of the Pedestall, with the vnder-Base, is one Ell, ten ounces and sixe minutes: the flat of the Pedestall, is two Elles, ten ounces and sixe minutes: the height of his Cornice, is nine ounces: the height of the Bases of the Columnes, is seuen ounces: the height of the Columnes, without Bases or Capitals, is nine Elles and foure ounces. The thicknesse of the Columnes beneath, is an Ell in Diameter, and aboue is lessened a sixt part: the height of the Capitall, is an Ell, fiue ounces and an halfe: the height of the Architraue, is 15. ounces: the Fréese is seuentéene ounces high: the height of the Cornice, is one Ell, thrée ounces and an halfe: the Plinthus, which standeth as counter-Base aboue the Cornice, is 19. ounces and a quarter high: the Base standing vpon it, is 11. ounces high: the height of the Epitaph, is foure Elles and two ounces: the height of the outtermost Cornice, is one Ell and thrée minutes: the height of the impost of the Arch, is halfe an Ell.

This Ell wherewith the Arch is measured, is deuided into 12. ounces, and each ounce into 5. minutes, which comes from 12. ounces to 60. minutes: and this is the third part of the sayd Ell.

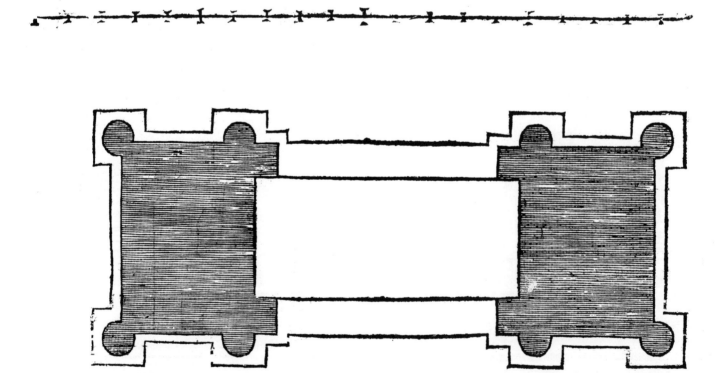

IMP. CAESARI. DIVI NERVAE FILIO,
NERVAE TRAIANO OPTIMO AVG.
GERMANICO PONT. II. MAX. TRIB. I.
POTEST. XVIII. IMP. VII. COS. VII. PP.
FORTISSIMO PRINCIPI.   S. P. Q. R.

The Ornaments of the Arch of Beneuenten, which I haue shewne in the leafe before, are here, according to the meaſure ſet downe, with the Originall. The Baſe of the Pedeſtall, and the Cornice thereof marked F. are, in truth, two peeces of good proportion, and fayre peeces for Cornicements. The Baſe of the Pedeſtall, together with the Counterbaſe vnder it, is one Ell, 10. Ounces and 6. minutes high: the Cornice of the ſayd Pedeſtall is 9. Ounces high: the Baſe of the Columne is 7. Ounces high, and is of Corinthia worke, very well proportioned according to the Columne, and ſtandeth heere marked with E. I haue not ſet the Capitall here: for that men (as I ſayd before) ſhall find ſuch a one in the beginning of the Compoſita, in my fourth Booke, becauſe this Arch is Compoſita worke. The Arch, Fræſe, and Cornice, which ſtand aboue this Columne, are here marked with C. which peeces are alſo well proportioned on the remnant of this building: and although that the Cornice is ſomewhat higher then Vitruuius would haue it, neuertheleſſe it is well proportioned of members, and the ſame flat is not in it that is found in other Cornices, which haue the Mutiles and the Dentiles ſtanding together: but this workeman, being circumſpect therein, would not cut the tæth in the Dentiles, although he hath ſet the forme thereof in the Cornice, to ſhunne ſuch a ſlaunder. The ſame conſideration the workeman that made the Panthern had, in the firſt Cornice aboue the Chappels, round about the Temple within: and therefore I counſell a workeman, to auoyde ſuch a ſcandall, and not to repoſe himſelfe vpon the doing of licencious and wilfull workemen, and excuſe themſelues, ſaying, Ancient workemen made it, and therefore I may make it as well as they. And although ſome will argue and ſay, Why, ſo many workemen, and in ſo many places of the world, (not onely in Italy) but alſo in diuers other places, haue made Cornices, with Mutiles, and ingrauen Dentiles , and that ſuch a cuſtome is now turned into a Law, yet I would not obſerue the ſame in my workes nor counſell others thereunto. The Counterbaſe, vnder the Epitaph, aboue the Cornice, marked B. is 19. Ounces and a halfe high: the height of the Baſe thereupon is 11. Ounces: the height of the Epitaph is 4. Elles 4. Ounces: the height of the Cornice is one Ell and 3. Ounces. I much commend the Baſe of this Epitaph. I commend the Baſe of this Epitaph, with ſo little proiecture, for the ſæing vp vnder it, but the Cornice whereof I will ſpeake, is much too high, according to the proportion of the Epitaph : but were it of leſſe height , and the Crowne more, and of more proiecture, I iudge, it would ſtand better, and I ſhould commend it more: alſo, if there were not ſo much caruing or grauing in it: for the members ought ſo to be deuided, that the one were playne, and the other grauen. But there are many workemen, and moſt at this day, that, to make men take pleaſure in their bad workemanſhip, make ſo many cuttings in it, that thereby they confound workemanſhip, and take away the beauty of forme from it: and if euer, in times paſt, that faſt and ſingle things, vncut, were by ſkilfull workemen commended, at this time they are not ſo. This Figure, marked D. is the Impoſt of the Arch , and is well knowne for ſuch a member ; the ſame Cornice changeth it ſelfe in a Facie, which goeth round, as you ſæ, and is halfe an Ell high : and although this Impoſt of the Arch ſheweth no Sculpture, yet is it grauen where it ſtandeth; but I forgot to draw it ſo.

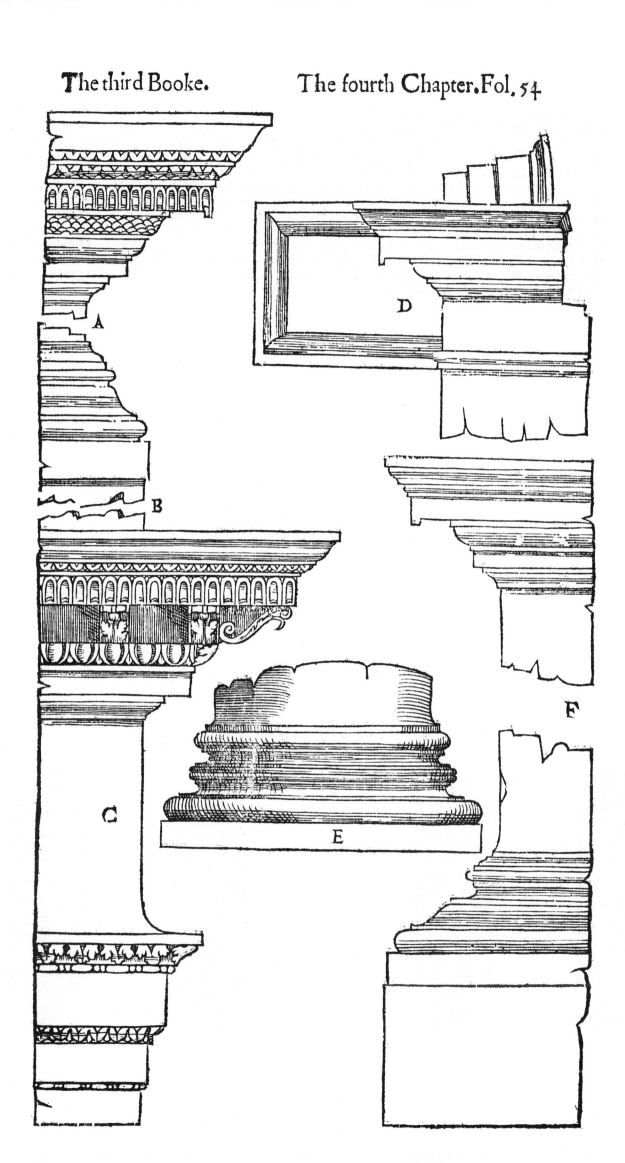

Of Antiquitie

Bʸ the Amphitheater of Rome, which by the people is called Coliſeo, there ſtandeth a very faire Tryumphant Arch, which is wonderfull rich of Ornaments, Images, and diuers Hiſtories, it was dedicated to Conſtantine, and is vſually called, Larco de Traſill. This fayre Arch, although it is now buried a great part within the earth, by meanes of the ruines, and riſing of the earth, is neuertheleſſe of great height, and the Gates and paſſages through it, are yet higher then two ſoure ſquares. This Arch (as is befoze ſayd) is paſſing fayre to the eye, and wonderfull rich of Ornaments & grauing. It is very true, that the Cornices are not of the beſt maner, although they be excéding richly grauen, whereof I will ſpeake hereafter. This ground hereunder, ſheweth the Ichnography of the ſayd Arch Trium-phant, and was meaſured with the old Romiſh Palme: the breadth of the greateſt Arch is 22. Palmes and 24. minutes: the wideneſſe of the leſſer Arches on the ſides is 11. Palmes, 11. minutes and a halfe. The thickneſſe of the Pilaſters are 9. Palmes and 4. minutes: the thickneſſe of the Arches in the ſides, is 21. Palmes and a halfe: thus the place with-in the Arch is almoſt ſoure ſquare: the thickneſſe of the Pedeſtals is 3. Palmes and 29. minutes: the thickneſſe of the Columnes is 2. Palmes and 26. minutes; which Columnes are ſtricked oz hollowed, by ſome called chanelo, and are whole round with their Pillars behind them.

The ground of the Arch Tryumphant of the Emperour Conſtantius.

THe widenesse and thicknesse of this Arch, is sufficiently set downe; now I will speake of the height thereof: and first, the Base of the Pedestall, with the Plinto, is one Palme and 30. minutes high. The height of the Bat, is 7. Palms and 5. minutes: the height of the Cornices of the Pedestals, is 42. minutes: the height of the counter-Base, vnder the Base, or the Plinthus of the Columne, is fiftie and two minutes: the height of the Base is 60. minutes: the height of the body of the Columnes, without Base or Capitall, is 26. Palmes and 25. minutes: the height of the Capitall, is 2. Palmes and 35. minutes, and is Composita. The height of the Architraue, is one Palme and 11. minutes: but the Freese is much lesse, and yet grauen; which, as I haue sayd, at other times is contrary to the doctrine of Vitruuius. The height of the Cornice is a Palme and 21. minutes. The height of the counter-base, vnder the second story, is 3. Palms and 9. minutes: from thence to the highest part of the Cornices, is 21. Palmes: but the height of that Cornice is 33. minutes. The Pedestals aboue the same Cornices were not measured, and thereon stood Images, and aboue the Cornices marked B. were Images placed against the 4. Pillasters, which represented the prisoners with whom hee went in tryumph. The letters which stand here, are aboue the Arch, in the place maked A. besides many others, which stand in diuers places of the Arch.

IMP. CAES. FL. CONSTANTINO MAX. P. F. AVGVSTO. S. P. Q. R.
QVOD INSTINCTV DIVINITATIS MENTIS MAGNITVDINE, CVM EXER-
CITV SVO TAM DE TYRANNO, QVAM DE OMNI EIVS FACTIONE,
VNO TEMPORE IVSTIS REMPVBLICAM VLTVS EST ARMIS, ARCVM
TRIVMPHIS INSIGNEM DICAVIT.

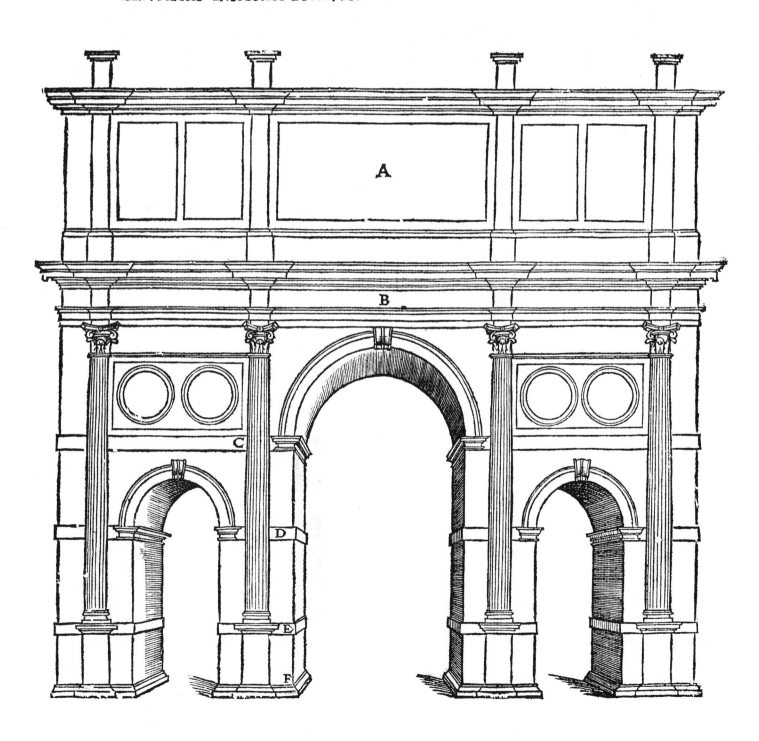

I Haue spoken of the proportion of the measures of the Tryumphant Arch of the Emperour Constantine : now I will speake of the seuerall parts and Cornicements, and set their measures downe. And first, the Base marked F. is of the Pedestall of the said Arch: the height whereof, is a Palme and 30. minutes. The height of the Plinthus vnder the Base is 28. minutes: the rest of the parts are measurably deuided, and proportioned accordingly. The height of the Cornices of the Pedestall, which stand marked vnder the Base E. is 42. minutes, and is also proportioned according to the principall. The counter-Base, vnder the Base of the Columnes (which I thinke were placed there accidentally)to heighten the Columnes, is 32. minutes high: the whole height of this Base of the Columnes, is 53. minutes: touching the height of the Columnes, I spake before, and also of the Capitals; of which Capitals, the forme standeth not here, for that the like doth stand in my fourth Booke, of the Order of Composita: the height of the Architraues, Freses and Cornices, is also spoken of before: and this Cornice is very seemely, for that there is no licenciousnesse in it, which is in some other Bases of this Arch ; as it is in the impost of the middlemost Arch, marked C. the which impost is greater and of more members and parts, then the great and principall Cornice, and is altogether confused in members, and that which is most intolerable, the Dentiles and Mutiles are one aboue the other : and although the Dentiles were not there, yet there needed not such a Cornice to beare vp an Arch. Herein the workeman of the Theater of Marcellus was more circumspect then this: for the imposts of the Arches of the said Theater, are the fayrest and best of shew for imposts that euer I saw, and such, as from the which a man may learne to make the like. The impost of the lesser Arches marked D. is one Palme and 23. minutes and an halfe high: the which impost would stand much better, if the two flats betweene the Astragall aboue, and the Echine vnder, were turned into playnnesse only; which then would serue for an Abacus , or also for a crowne, hauing the one Proiecture. The Base vnder the second story marked A. is 16. minutes high: the height of the vppermost Cornice, is 43. minutes, which height should bee to little in so great a distance, if it were not that the great Proiecture or Gallery, or ouerhanging holpe it not; because they are seeing vpwards, from vnderneath, which sheweth it to be much greater then it is: therefore I much commend this Cornice in this respect. And truely, all the Cornices, whereof the crowne hath more proiecture then height, answere alwayes better, and may be made thinner of stone, so that the members of the building endure lesse weyght: neuerthelesse, you must not make them of to many licencious proiectures: but you shall read hereof in Vitruuius, where he entreateth of the Order of crownes, after the maner of Ionica and Dorica: for he doeth there teach you clearely inough.

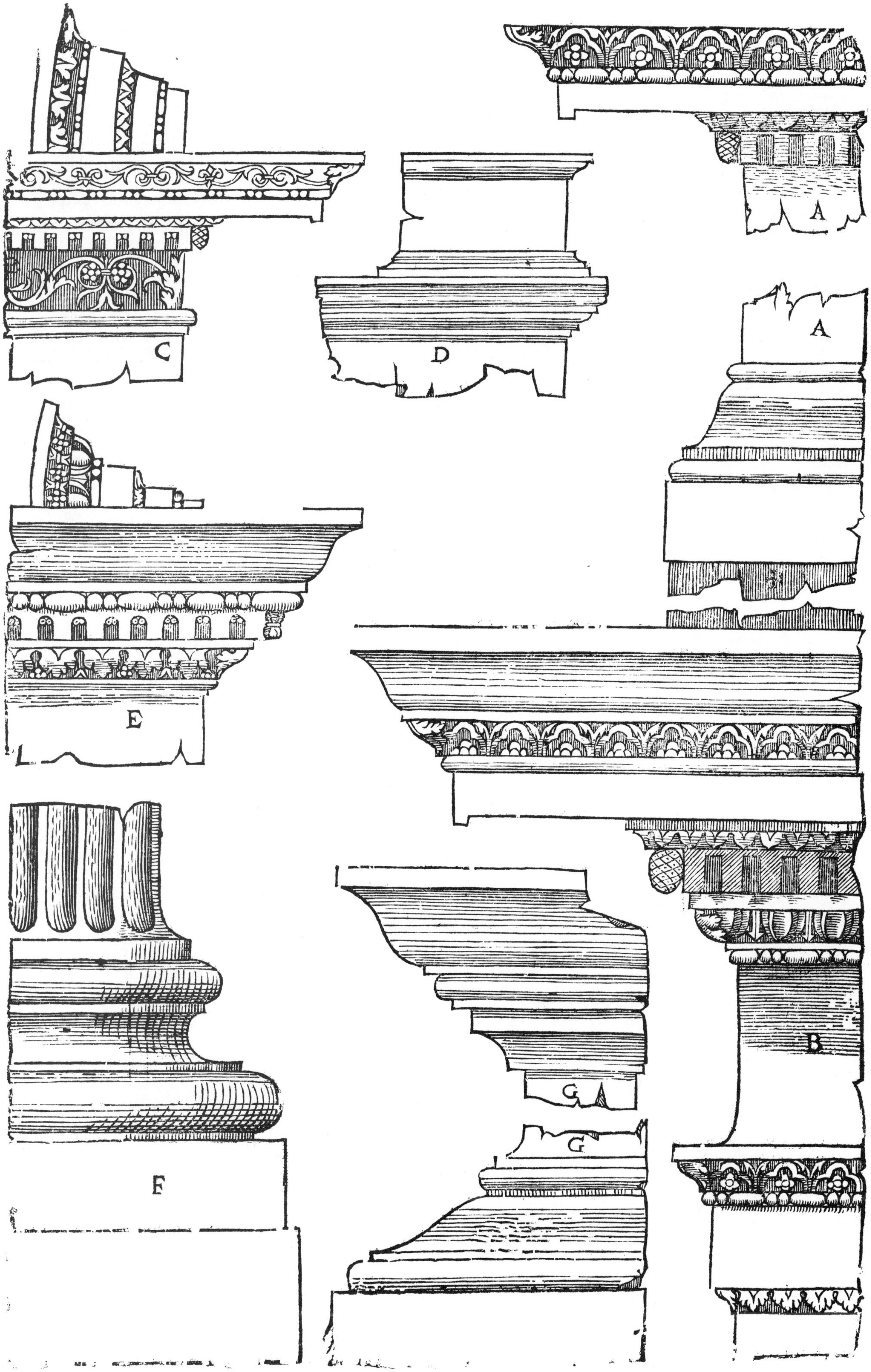

Thi
ure
ſtand
Foli
and t
gure
lio 5
houl
ſtan
this

Without Ancouen vpon the hauen, there is an head which reacheth it selfe a good way into the Sea, which was not made without great cost and charges : it was to defend the ships from the Leuant sea. Vpon the end of the height thereof, standeth an Arch tryumphant, all of Marble and Corinthia worke ; and there is nothing in it but the Capitals, which are done in very good worke : and in trueth, this building is so handsome, and of so good correspondencie, the members also agréeing with the whole body, that a man, although he vnderstand no Art, would neuerthelesse take pleasure in the beautie thereof. And those that vnderstand somewhat, séeing such congruitie, are not onely well contented, but also thanke the good workeman, that hath giuen vs somewhat in these dayes to learne out of this fayre and well made building : in the ornaments whereof, there is the order of Corinthia as well obserued and kept, as in any other Arch that is to be found, and by reason of the strength thereof, it is all whole ; onely it is vnfurnished of many ornaments. This faire Arch, as it is conceyued, Nerua Traianus caused to be builded : whereupon, in the highest part of the Arch (as it is sayd) his Image was erected, sitting on horse backe, séeming to threaten the clouds and people, ouer whom he loked and gouerned, lest they should rebell againe : which Image was of Copper excellently well made. There were also betwéene the Columnes, aboue the Cornices, certaine Images of Copper, as the letters in those places written, doe shew : there are also tokens of holes, which shewes that there were Rings of Copper, or other such like things hanging in them, which might bee taken from the Gotes, Vandals, or other enemies. This building was measured by the ancient foote, the ground whereof standeth hereunder. The widenesse of the Arch is ten foote : the thickenesse inwards is nine foote and two minutes : the thicknesse of the Columnes is two foote, 11. minutes : the Intercolumnes, or spaces betwéene the Columnes, is 7. foote, 5. minutes : the Columnes stand without the wall, 1. foote and 11. minutes : the height of the Arch is 25. foot and 1. third part : and this height, although it holdeth moe then two foure squares, is not therefore misshapen, when you behold the whole masse together : the height of the Pedestals with all their Cornices, is 5. foote : the breadth is thrée foote, 15. minutes and a halfe : the height of the Bases of the Columnes, together with the Vnderbases, are 1. foote and 36. minutes : the height of the Columnes to the Capitals, is 19. foote, 22. minutes and a halfe : the thicknesse vnder the Capitall, is one foote and 56. minutes : the height of the Capitall is 2. foote, 24. minutes, with the Abacus ; and the Abacus is 10. minutes : the sayd Capitall you shall find in my fourth Booke, in the beginning of the order of Corinthia : the height of the Architraue is one foote and 12. minutes : the height of the Frese is one foote and 18. minutes : the height of the Cornice is 1. foote and 22. minutes : the height of the Plinthus aboue the Cornice, is one foote, 6. minutes and a halfe : the height of the Base aboue the sayd Plinthus, is 30 minutes : the height of the Epitaph vnder the Cornice, is 6. foote and 22. minutes ; but the Cornice aboue it was not measured.

The halfe of the old Romish foote.

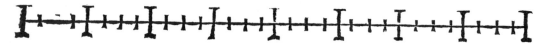

The ground of the Arch tryumphant of Ancouen.

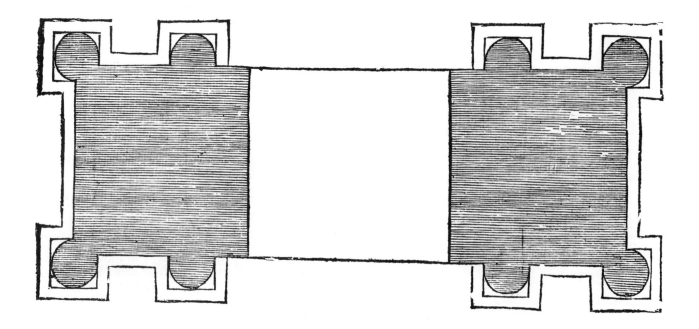

PLOTINAE AVG. CONIVGI AVG.   DIVAE MARTIANAE AVG. SORORI AVG.

Imp. Cæsari Diui Neruæ. F. Neruæ Traiano
Optimo Augusto. Germanico Dacico. Pont.
Max. Tri. Pot. xix. Imp. xi. Cos. vi. P. P. Pro-
videntissimis Principibus.   S. P. Q. R.
Quod accessum Italiæ, hoc etiam addito. Ex Pe-
cunia sua, Portu tutiorem Nauigantibus reddiderit.

IN my opinion, I haue sayd enough of the measure of the Arch of Ancona, yet that the parts of the Cornices may be the better vnderstood, I will shew them here greater: and first, I will set downe the lowest parts, as they stand aboue the ground of the worke. The height of the Pedestall, marked G. is sayd to be of 5. fot, with all the Cornices thereof: but the height of the Plinthus of the Base, is 18. minutes: the Base aboue the Plinthus, is 19. minutes, and a third part high : the Cornice of the Pedestall, is 20. minutes , and a third part high; so much doeth the stone also hold, standing thereby, marked F. which, by my aduice, is placed there , to heighten the Columnes, and sheweth not badly, but more, because it is set forth with a list round about it; whereby the Base differeth from the Plinthus : and so, in my opinion, standeth well. The Base, which is Corinthia, together with the Cincte of the Columne, is 43. minutes high : and the Proiecture, is 16. minutes and an halfe in breadth: the thicknesse of the Pedestall, is 3. foote, 15. minutes and an halfe: the thicknesse of the Columne, is 2. foote, 11. minutes : and there stand 13. hollowings , or chanels, without the Pilaster: the widenesse of one chanell, is 7. minutes and a halfe: and the List which parteth them, is 2. minutes and a halfe. The height of the Capitals are the thicknesse of the Columnes below, without the Abacus: which Capitall hath a very fayre forme, whereby we may be perswaded and beleeue, that Vitruuius doctrine is false, and that Vitruuius vnderstood the height of the Capitall without Abacus : (and for this cause) for that the most part of the Capitals that I haue sene and measured, are most of such height, and higher , and specially the Capitals that stand in the Rotund: whereof, in the beginning of this Booke you may see one. The height of the Architraue aboue the Columne, is one fote and twelue minutes. The height of the Frese, is one foote and eyghtene minutes. The height of the Cornice, is one foote and two and twenty minutes. These three are marked together with an A. The Plinthus aboue the Cornice is one foote , sixe minutes and an halfe high : The Base vpon it, is thirtie minutes : the space wherein the letters are written, is sixe foote and two and twenty minutes, and is marked with ✳. The Impost of the Arch is marked D. the height whereof is 1. fote and fiftene minutes : but the vppermost Cornice, as I haue sayd, was not measured. The height of the Mensole in place of the closing stone, marked B. aboue the Arch, is three foot and 30. minutes : and hath a foote and 14. minutes without the wall, in the vppermost part; and in the parts below, it comes out a foot. The foure tables with the Cornices vpon them, which stand betwene the Columnes, are thought to be placed there, for holding vp of halfe Images: the forme whereof, standeth here marked E. and is there also by the Profill on the side, whereby a man may see how they are wrought: for they are full of worke, euen to the Center. The height of the Cornices, standing aboue them, is 32. minutes: and although I haue not shewed all the Proiectures & heights from part to part, yet I haue with great diligence reduced them from the great, into a small forme , and were (as I sayd before of the rest) measured with the old Romane foot.

Of Antiquitie

The Towne of Pola in Dalmatia, is adorned with many Antiquities: besides the Theater & Amphitheater, whereof I spake before, there are other Buildings, whereof now I will speake. There is an Arch Trgumphant, of Corinthia worke, rich of ornaments, for Figures, works, and strange deuices; so that from the Pedestal vpwards, there is no worke nor space left vngrauen, not onely before, but also on the sides, and within, and vnder in the Arch, wherein are many and diuers workes, so that it would require long time to declare them particularly: therefore I will shew such parts thereof as are necessary for a workeman, for inuention and Arte. The ground of the Arch following standeth hereunder, measured with a Moderne or common foote, whereof the halfe is here set downe. The Arch is 12. foot and a halfe wide: the height is about 21. foot. The Pilasters in the sides inward are 4. foot thicke. The thicknes of a Columne is one foote, 9 ounces and a halfe. The Intercolumns is 2. foot, 3. ounces and a halfe. The Pilaster of the Arch is one foot, 2. ounces broad. The height of the Plinthus vnder the Base of the Pedestall, is one foote. The Base is 4. ounces high. The flat of the Pedestall is 3. foot: the Cornice 4. ounces. The Plinthus marked D. vnder the Columnes is 4. ounces. The height of the Base with the Plinthus is 10. ounces and one quarter. The height of the Columne is 16. foote, one ounce and 3. quarters. The height of the Capitall is 2. foot and one ounce. The height of the Architraue is one foote and one ounce. The height of the Fr*se is one foote and 2. ounces. The height of the Cornice is one foote and 10. ounces. The height of the Plinthus aboue the Cornice is one foote and 2. ounces. The height of the Base of the Pedestall, and also of the Plinthus vpon it, is one foote and 2. ounces: but the height of the Base alone is 10. ounces. The height of the flat of the Pedestall is 2. foote and one ounce. The Cornice is 6. ounces. The Cauet aboue the Cornice, (which Vitruuius, as I thinke, calleth Corona lisis) is 5. ounces: and this is the measure of the ground following.

The halfe common foote.

This is the ground of the Arch triumphant of Pola.

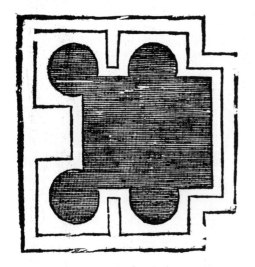

The meafure of this prefent Arch is fet downe before: in this fide following, the particular parts fhall bee fhewed.
These great letters hereunder, ftand in the Frée ſe, marked Y.

SALVIA. POSTVMA. SERGI, DE SVA PECVNIA.

Thefe vnder marked, ftand in thré Pedeftals, marked X. H. A.

L. SERGIVS. C. F.   **L. SERGIVS. L. F. LEPIDVS. AED.**   **C. SERGIVS. C. F.**
AED. II. VIR.   **TRI. MIL. LEG. XXIX.**   **AED. II. VIR. QVINQ.**

IN the fide before, I haue fpoken of the vniuerfall meafure of the Arch triumphant of Pola, and haue alfo fhewred the figure thereof, and partly fet downe fome of the richeft and faireft ornaments of the fame: Now I will fet downe the particular meafures of the parts thereof: and firft, I will begin with ý nether parts, as that was placed firft aboue the ground.   The height of the Plinthus vnder the Bafe of the Pedeftall, is one foot; although that vnder it there lieth another of much more height, but it is vnder the earth: the height of the Cimatie turned about aboue it, with the Aftragalus, is 4.ounces: the flat of the Pedeftall, is 3. fot high: the Cimatic aboue, it is 4.ounces, & fo much alfo is the vnder-Bafe, aboue the Cimatie: the height of the Bafe of the Columnes, is 10.ounces, and is very well cut and grauen: and although the forme is Dorica, yet the delicate works thereof fhew that it is Corinthia: the Columnes are fluted or chaneled from the top to the bottom; and there are alfo many hollowings without the Pilafter, as the figure hereafter doeth fhew.   The height of the Capitall with the Abacus, is two fote and one ounce: the which Capitall is higher then the thicknefle of the Columne beneath.   Neuertheleffe, it is very well, and fheweth pleafing to fight; it is alfo richly wrought, as it is here fhewed in the figure thereof: and alwayes, as the Capital of Corinthia is in fuch proportion a-gainft the Columne, I would thinke it better to the view of workemen; then if with the Abacus it had but the height of the Diameter of the Columne: and although Vitruuius writeth thus (as is before fayd) yet may his text be falfified. The height of the Architraue, is one foot and one ounce: the height of the Frœfe, is one foote and two ounces: the height of the Cornice, is a fote and ten ounces: which Cornice is very licencious, although it be rich of worke, becaufe fuch rich-nefle of worke confoundeth it: but that which is moft vnfeemely in it, is the Echine with the Ouale aboue the Seima, a thing, in trueth, much vnfightly : and that, which is more worthy laughter, is, that the faid Echine in the vpper part, is cut through, without being couered with any lift, that it might not bee confumed with the water. But there hath al-wayes béene licencious workemen, as there are yet in our dayes, who, to pleafe the people, make much grauing in their workes, without refpecting the qualities of the orders, and will alfo in Dorica worke, which fhould bee faft and ftrong, vfe much grauing and cutting, as in Corinthia worke, which, by their folly, afketh many ornaments. But wife and iudicious workemen will alwayes obferue Decorum: and if they make worke after Dorica maner, they will follow good Antiquities : which, for the moft part, agrée with Vitruuius precepts.   If they make any worke after the Corinthia maner, then they couer them with Ornaments, as that kind of worke requireth.   This I haue fet downe, to aduertife thofe thereof that know it not; for they that know it, néede not my aduice.   Now to come to the pur-pofe againe: Aboue this Cornice there is a Bafement, which maketh out thrée Pedeftals; the Plinthus vnder the Bafe-ment, which is there fet againft the proiecture of the Cornices. (for otherwife, in looking vp, it would darken the Bafe) is a fot high; aboue it ftandeth the Bafe, whereof the height is 10. ounces: the flat of the Bafement, is 2. fot & 1. ounce high: the Cornice aboue it, is halfe a fote high; which Cornice is very féemely, and the parts thereof deuide themfelues very well from each other, for that betwéene the two carued members there ftandeth one playne aboue: the Cornice is that member or part, called Corona lifis, as I vnderftand Vitruuius, whereof the height is 5. ounces. Aboue thefe there are fome ftones that fhew to no end at all, but it may be thought, that fome things ftœde vpon them: the height of thefe ftones is 10. ounces: the height of the Impoft of this Arch is 10. ounces; the which Impoft is very licencioufly made : and although thofe 3. members one aboue the other, are diuers, yet they are like each other in proiecture: and therefore in the worke they ftand to no good effect: the other parts you fhall know by the Caracters in the great Arch.

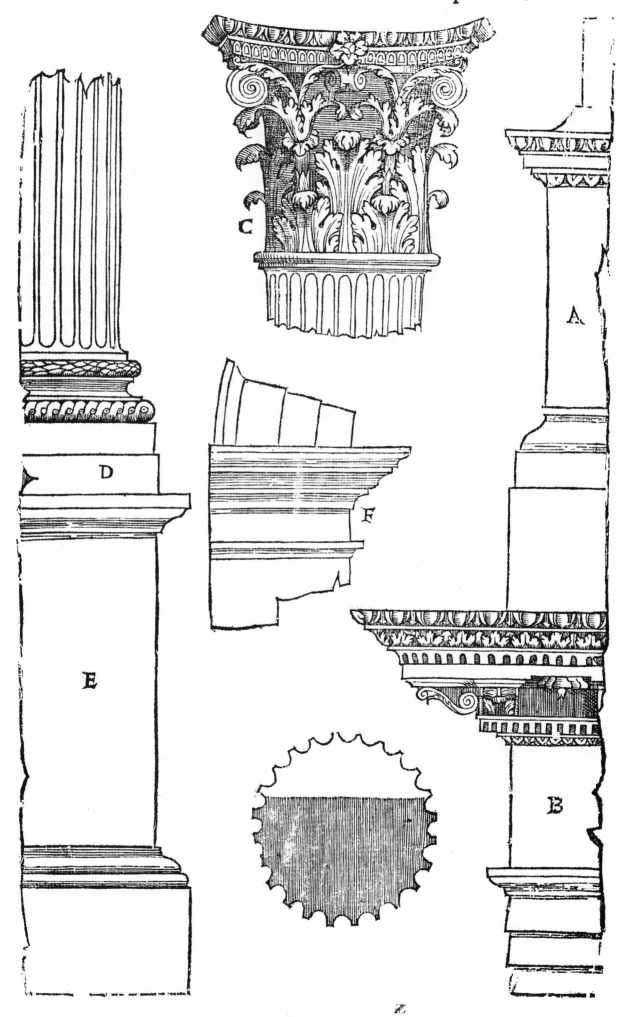

IN Verona, there are many tryumphant Arches; among the rest, there is one Gate, called Castel Vecchio: the which, truely, is of good proportion: this Arch, as men conceaue, was wrought both before and behind, and also on the sides: it had two goings in, as you may perceaue by the ground which is yet seene, although I shewed but one side onely. This building was measured by the same foot, wherewith the Arch of Pola aforesayd was measured. The widenes of this Arch is ten foote and an halfe: the thicknesse of the Columnes, is two foot and two ounces: the intercolumnes, are 4. foot and 3. ounces: the Pilaster or Pillar of the Arch, is 2. foote and 2. ounces broad. The thicknesse of the Arch in the sides inward, is 4. foot and an halfe: the widenesse of the Tabernacle betweene the Columnes, is two foot and ten ounces: and thusmuch for the widenesse and thickenesse: but comming to the height, the Base of the Pedestall of the Columnes, together with the Plinthus, is one foote and three ounces high: the flat of the Pedestall, is foure foot, three ounces and an halfe: the Cornice is ten ounces and an halfe: the height of the Base of the Columnes, is one foot: the height of the body of the Columne, without Base or Capitall, is 17. foote and three ounces: the height of the Capitall, is two foot, foure ounces and an halfe. The height of the Architraue, is one foot and an halfe: the height of the Freese is one foote, 7. ounces and an halfe: the height of the Cornice, is one foot and ten ounces: and although that in this Figure there is the Frontispice, yet you see it not in the Arch; for from the first Cornice vpwards, there is nothing at all: neuerthelesse, although the wall is this yeere consumed, yet you may see there some signes, whereby a man may conceaue that the Frontispice hath beene there. The vppermost Cornice is not there, and therefore I set no measures, according to all Antiquities: but I haue made one, with such measure and formes, as my selfe would haue made it, hauing for a common rule, that the vppermost things stand the fourth part lesse, then the nethermost: this Cornice therefore, shall be the fourth part lesse then that which standeth vnder it, and is thus deuided, that the whole height should be set in foure parts and an halfe: the halfe part shall be for the Astragal with the list, and the fourth part shalbe for the Scima. The Proiecture must be like the height, & so shall this vppermost Cornice be made in maner aforesaid. Betweene the Columnes stand Tabernacles, wherein there were Images, whereof the widenesse is two foot and ten ounces: the height is seuen foote, and the depth thereof in the wal, is one foote and ten ounces: the height of their Basement, is 4. foot, with the Base and Scima: the little Pillars on eyther side, are halfe a foot thicke: the Architraue is 7. ounces and an halfe: the Freese is 6. ounces high: the height of the Cornice without the Scima, is 4. ounces: the height of the Timpanum of the Frontispice, is 8. ounces. Aboue these Tabernacles are small tablets, with other Cornices: the which tablets are two foot broad, and hold one foot in height: the height of each Cornice is 11. ounces: the height of the opennesse of the Arch, although it be somewhat bigger below, is yet twise higher then broad: for the widenesse thereof, is 10. foote and a quarter: and the height is 25. foote and an halfe. The Capitall vnder the Arch, is as high as broad: the worke of this Arch is Composita, and brauely set out with Images of Marble and Copper, as you may perceaue in the voyd places.

This is the ground of the Arch following.

This forme of the Arch Tryumphant of Castel Vecchio in Verona, is made as it is here set downe: and although from the Frases vpwards, there are no signes of ornaments; neuerthelesse, it did stand so. And for that the parts hereof are so small that you can hardly vnderstand them, in the next side they shall bee set downe in a greater and playner forme. This Arch tryumphant (by that which is found written within the inner parts thereof) by some is sayd, that Vitruuius caused it to be made: but I beleeue it not, and that for two reasons or causes. First, that I see not in the Inscription, that it saith, Vitruuius Polio: but it is possible that it was another Vitruuius that caused it to be made. The second reason is this, that Vitruuius Polio, in his writing of Architecture, doeth vtterly condemne and reiect Mutiles and Dentiles, standing together in one Cornice, and such a Cornice is found in this Arch. And therefore I conclude, that Vitruuius, the great and learned Architector, made it not: but bee it as it will, this Arch hath a good forme and proportion.

These letters are vnder the Tabernacle in the Pedestall.
C. GAVIO. C. F.
STRABONI.

These letters are cut in the inward side of the Arch.
L. VITRVVIVS. LL. CERDO
ARCHITECTVS.

These letters are also in the Pedestall of the Tabernacle.
M. GAVIO. C. F.
MACRO.

Ecause I haue not fully written the particular meaſures of the members of the aforeſayd Arch, neither haue I ſhewed it in ſuch forme that a man may conceaue the particular meaſures: therefore you may ſee them here ſet out in greater forme, and in ſuch ſort as they are: and firſt, the height of the Plinthus , vnder the Baſe of the Pedeſtall, marked G. is a foote and three ounces. The height of the Baſe aboue vpon it, is 6. ounces. The flat of the Pedeſtall, marked F. is 4. foot, 3. ounces and an halfe high. The Cornice vpon it, is 10. ounces and an halfe high. The Baſe of the Columne, is one foote high. The Plinthus of this Baſe turneth into a Corona liſis ; which me thinkes , is very pleaſant: for that I haue ſeen ſome Greeke Pedeſtals ſo. The Columne is ſtrycked, chanelled or hollowed, from the top to the bottom. The height of the Capitall of this Columne , is one foot, 4. ounces and an halfe : but the forme is not here, becauſe it is ſhewed in the beginning of the Order of Compoſita : which Capitall, in effect, is Compoſita, although the Arch may be wholly accompted to bee Corinthia: and this Capitall ſtandeth in that place, maked C. Alſo, in the ſame place you ſee the Capitall of the impoſt of the Arch, which is marked with D. But the little Capitall of the Tabernacle betweene the Columnes, is here marked H. And the Cornice alſo, with the Baſe, marked E. is that which is vnder the Tabernacle. The Figure C. is the table aboue the ſayd Tabernacles , and the Figure marked D. is the Architraue, Freſe and Cornice, of the Frontiſpicium of the Tabernacle. The Figure marked with B. is the worke which goeth about the Arch: the Cornice marked A. is the principall Cornice aboue the Arch; the which, in effect, is very comely, and well wrought: yet it is vicious, as I haue often ſayd; that is, the Mutiles and the Dentiles therein are by Vitruuius reiected, with many ſtrong reaſons. But in this, many men affirme, that ſithence Vitruuius time, many workemen haue made Mutiles with Dentiles, in moſt places of Italy, and there round about , ſo that now there is no queſtion made thereof; but euery man hath libertie to make that in his worke which he findeth and ſeeth in Antiquities: whereunto I anſwere, that diſprouing the ſame, they haue proued their cauſe to be good. But if they will acknowledge Vitruuius for a learned Architector, as moſt workemen affirme, then (reading Vitruuius with good iudgement) they muſt confeſſe and acknowledge, that they haue done amiſſe therein.

The halfe of the foot, wherewith the Ichnographie, and the Orthographie, together with the ornaments of this Building, are meaſured.

Of Antiquitie

IN Verona, at the Gate Dei Leoni, there is a Trpumphant Arch, with two like goings through, which I neuer saw in any other place besides, but many with 3. Arches: which building, although it hath the figure of 6. windowes, yet go they not through, nepther yet very déepe in the wall: whereby you may iudge, that some round Images stoode in them. Aboue the first Cornice this building is hollow, in maner of a Nich or seate, but not very déepe in the wall, but yet with helpe of the proiecture, or striking out of the Cornice, men might stand there to doe some thing or other, while the Triumph lasted: but for that this concerneth the workeman very little, I will speake of the measures. And first, the opening of the 1. Arch is 11. foote wide, and 18. foote high: the Blocke vnder the Pedestall, is one foote high: the Base of the Pedestall is 3. Ounces: the flat of the Pedestall is 2. foote and one Ounce high: and the Cornice is 3. Ounces: the height of the Bases of the Columnes is 8. Ounces and a halfe: the height of the Columnes, without Bases or Capitals is 12. foote and 1. third part: their thicknes is 1. fot, 4. Ounces: the height of the Capitall is 1. foote, 8. Ounces: the height of the Architraue is one foote, 5. Ounces: the height of the Fréese is one foote, 8. Ounces; and so much is the height of the Cornices: from the Cornices to the second Roofe is 3. foote and a halfe, whereon there are certayne Mutiles, whereupon Images had stoode, made fast to the 7. Pilasters, betwéene which, little windowes, beautified with small pillars, stand, but not much bearing out: the widenes of a window is 2. foote, 2. Ounces: their height is 4. foot, 8. Ounces: the height of the greatest Columnes is 5. foote, 4. Ounces, with Bases and Capitals which are flat, not not much rapsed vp. The height of the second Architraue is 6. Ounces and a halfe: the height of the Fréese is one foot and a halfe: the height of the Cornice is 10. Ounces and a halfe: the Corona licis aboue the same Cornice, is 10. Ounces high. The Base of the second Pedestall is one foote; the flat of it selfe is 3. foote, 7. Ounces and a halfe high: the Base of the second Columne is 8. Ounces: the height of the Columnes is 8. foote, 3. Ounces and a halfe. The thicknesse of the sayd Columnes is 10. Ounces and a halfe: the height of the Capitail is one foote, one Ounce and a halfe: the height of the Architraue is one foote and one Ounce: the height of the Fréese is 1. foote, 2. ounces: the height of the Cornice is one foote, whereon there standeth some part of the wall, but a man cannot perceiue what it might be. This Arch is not very thicke, nepther beautified on the sides; for that behind this Arch there is another, standing so néere together, that a man can hardly goe betwéene them both, as I will shew hereafter when I speake of the other figure: the windowes stand not in any good order, but somewhat vnséemely: for the 2. windowes are not right in perpendicular vpon the sharpe poynt of the Frontispice, but some part aside, which sheweth not well: and for that I could not endure such disorder, I haue placed them orderly. The Capitals of these Arches are part Composita, and part Corinthia, as hereafter I will set downe in Figure.

Louing Reader, Corottus, a Paynter in Verona, hath counterfeited this Arch: the Cornice vnder the Timpanum is not there: for he placeth there certayne order of figures resting vpon the Architraue: the which Architraue, you must vnderstand, is betwéene the 2. Columnes ouer each Arch, and is somewhat flat, because of the writing following.

Ouer this Arch, on the right hand, these letters following stand.

T. FLAVIVS P.F. NORICVS, IIII. VIR. ID. V. F. BAVIA. Q. L.
PRIMA SIBI, ET POLICLITO, SIVE SERVO, SIVE LIBERTO MEO,
ET L. CALPVRNIO VEGETO.

Of Antiquitie

HEre before, I spake of the vniuersall measure of the sayd Arch, and thereunto set downe the forme, according to the proportion of the same, but cannot giue perfectly the particular parts in so small a forme. Of which members, for that there are diuers ornaments in them, I will in this leafe declare them: touching the height and thicknesse, I will speake no more; for I haue done it already: but I will onely shew which they are. The Figure marked G. is the first Pedestall, with the Bases, and the beginning of the Columnes, the which is hollowed: all the members are proportioned according to their greatnesse. The Capitall marked E. hauing the Architraue vpon it, followeth vpon the first Columne, as the hollowing sheweth. The Figure marked D. is the Architraue, Freese and Cornice together, which stand aboue the first Columne: which Cornice, by the authoritie and example, which is by me in many places alledged, the iudicious Reader may know, whether they be erroneous or good. The Capitall marked F. is that, which vpholdeth the Arch vpon the fouresquare Pillars; these two Capitals are called, Latine worke, and very fayre. I will not, as I haue said, speake of the measures, for that this Figure is proportioned after the principall, and with great diligence transported from the great into the small.

The halfe of the common foote, wherewith the aforesayd double Arch, with the following ornaments, is measured.

AS I sayd before, the Arch is very rich of ornaments, and among them, some very fayre and perfect ; some also very vicious & ill made: and in trueth, I finde nothing that more misliketh me, then the Cornice marked D. in the other leafe, for the reasons beforeshewed : but all the rest before set downe are of good proportion, as well the workes as the Cornices. And as the parts of the first story are, so are these following of the second story. The Mutiles marked H. are in the beginning of the second story above the Frontispicie : vpon which Images (as I haue declared) there were Images fastened against the flat Pilasters. The window marked I. is the forme of one of the Windowes with the Cornice vpon it, and therefore iust of his measure. That Capitall and the Base marked K. is of the same windowes, shewed in greatest forme, that the members may be the better vnderstood. That Base and Capitall marked L. is the little Pillar betwéene the Pilasters and the window: and in trueth, in these two Bases, that is, that of the greatest of the small Pillars ioyned with the lesser, the workeman was very iudicious to accord or agrée the one with the other, that the greatest Pillar should haue his due Base, and the lesser should alsohaue a lesse Base, according to proportion, which I commend much. The Architraue, Fréese and Cornice, marked C. sheweth that of the second story, above the small Pillars: this Cornice is very séemely, and not confused with cutting. The Pedestall marked B. sheweth that of the last story, whereof the Base marked M. doth rest: also the Capitall which standeth above, is his companion, and is truly Corinthia, the which is confirmed to the principall, for worke and fashion, and in my opinion, very séemely. That Architraue, Fréese, and Cornice, marked A. sheweth the last Cornice: the Architraue is not vicious, because it hath onely two Facies; for if it had thrée, it would, by the farre distance, stand cumbred: the Cornice with the Mutiles, liketh me well, because it hath no Dentiles ; and is also well deuided with members: neither is it confused with much grauing, but hath a séemely Proiecture, which beaueth vp the height thereof a little.

The halfe of the common foot.

This Arch tryumphant was made before the Arch aforesayd, which the table sheweth, wherein there standeth P. TVALERIVS. Q. CECILIVS. Q. SERVILIVS: P. CORNELIVS. it is thought it was set vp in the time of Hanibal. This is measured with the same measure that the other is : the widnes of each Arch is 11. foote: the height is 17. fote: the Pilasters of the Arch are one foote, 8. ounces broad: betwéene the 2. Pilasters are 5. foote, 4. ounces: the sides, eche holdeth 3. foot. The Cimatie vnder the C. in place of an Architraue, is 6. ounces and an halfe: the height of the Fréese, is one foote, 7. ounces and an halfe: the list aboue thé Fréese is 2. ounces: the Cimatie vnder the Dentiles, is 4. ounces and a quarter: and the Cimatie aboue it, is one ounce and an halfe. That Astragall is one ounce. The Cimatie vnder the crowne, is one ounce and a third part: the crowne is 3. ounces and an halfe high: the Cimatie thereof, is 2. ounces and a quarter. The Scime is 3. ounces and an halfe high : but the list is 2. ounces : the Proiecture of all, is as much as the height. The Basement aboue this Cornice, is one foote, one ounce and an halfe in height: the thicknesse of the hollowed Columnes, is 1. foot, 3. ounces: the height without Capitals, is 7. foot, one ounce and an halfe. The Capitall is 10. ounces high. This Columne hath no Base nor Cinthe. Carettus, who also counterfeited this Arch, séeth but foure places where Historeis are grauen, and 5. Columnes in this third story: in the second story but 4. windowes, and 5. Pilasters: and aboue them, 5. Columnes: the third Cornice you cannot come vnto.

This figure B. is the Architraue, Fræfe & Cornice aboue the windows, and the height of the firft Facie is 8. ounces, & a 3. part. The fecond Facie, is 9. ounces & an halfe. The Tenia is thréé ounces. The Fræfe is 1. foot and 4. ounces high: ý breadth of ý triglypts is one foot: the lift thereabout is a 3. part of an ounce. The other aboue that, is 1. ounce and a 4. part. The Cimatie vnder ý Dentil, is 2. ounces and a 4. part. The height of the Dentile is 4. ounces and a 3. part. The Cauet aboue it, is 1. ounce. The Aftragals are 3. quarters of an ounce: the Cimatie aboue it, is 1. ounce and a quarter: the height of ý Corona is 4. ounces: the Cimaty is 2. ounces: the height of the Scime is 4. ounces: the lift is 2. oúces & an halfe: the Projecture of all, is like the height: ý whole height may be called Dorica, only the graue Aftragall: but it was a toy of the workemans braine. Many other things are in Verona, whereof I will not fpeak, becaufe they are very licencious; &

fpecially the Arch triumphant, called Dei Burfari, becaufe it is barbarous workes.

Hauing spoken of many Antiquities, and placed them in Figure; it is requisite that I also shew some of those that were made in these dayes, and specially, of Bramants worke, although I haue not altogether omitted it, hauing shewed the wonderfull worke of S. Peters Church, and other things belonging to holy Temples. And in truth, a man may well say, that he restored good and perfect Architecture, as yet, by the meanes of Iulio P. M. many fayre pieces of worke were made by him in Rome, do witnesse; of the which, this set here, is one: this is a Gallery made in Beluedere, in the Popes Court, wherein are two fayre things to be séene: the one is, the strength thereof; the which, for that the Pilasters are of so great bredth and thicknesse, will last, while the world endureth: the other, for that there are so many accompagments so well set out, with good inuention, and excellent proportion: this worke is measured with the ancient Palme. The bredth of the Arches, is 18. Palmes: and so much are the Pilasters: the bredth of the Pilasters is deuided into 11. parts: one part on eyther side of the Pilaster, which beareth the Arch shall haue, which is two parts: other two parts shall be giuen vnto one Columne, that is 4. parts: 2. parts shall be giuen to the little Pilasters of the Niches, or hollow seates, and 3. parts to the Niches themselues: so are the 11. parts distributed. The height of the Pedestals shall be halfe the widenesse of the Pilasters. The height of the Base of the Pedestals, shall haue one part of the beforesayd 11. parts. The Cornice is the 9. part lesse then the Base. The height of the Columnes, with Bases and Capitals, are of 9. Diameters, and thereunto also the seuenth part. The Base is halfe the thickenesse of the Columnes. The Capitall is of the same thickenesse: and the seuenth part for the Abacus. The height of the Architraue, Fréese and Cornice, is as much as the Pedestall without his Base. And this height is deuided into 11. parts, foure for the Architraue, 3. for the Fréese, because it is vngrauen, and 4. for the Cornice, as the halfe Circle of the Arch is drawne; then the heights of the lights will be double: after that, the imposts being drawne in their places, the which are of halfe a Columne thicke, and so the Niches or seates, and the Quadrans aboue them, haue their certaine proportion.

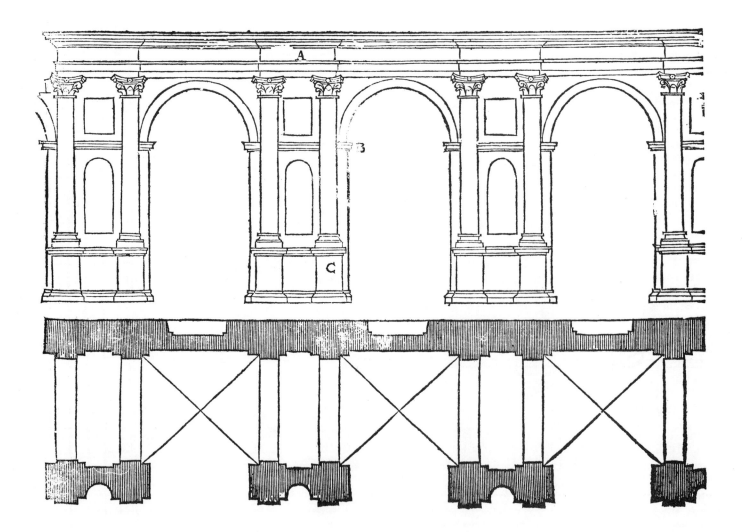

Ecause I could not (by reason of the smalnesse of the Figure) perfectly shew the parts of the Gallery aforesayd, therefore I haue shewed them hereunder in greater forme: the part C. is the Pedestall of this Gallery, and vpon it the Base of the Columne standeth, proportioned according to the great: the part B. sheweth the impost of the Arch, with a part thereof. The Figure marked A. sheweth the Architraue, Freese & Cornice aboue the Columnes. The generall measures, touching the height, are already shewne, therefore not to be mentioned againe: for they are proportioned after the great. In this Cornice the workeman was very iudicious, that he suffered the Corona to go through vnbroken; and suffered the other parts of the Corona to beare outwards, which is very seemely, and the crowne the stronger, and keepeth the whole worke from water: with which inuention, the workeman may helpe himselfe in diuers accidents; for the reaching out of Cornices stand not alwayes well, but in some places well, and in some places ill; and the bearings out vntolerable, where the Columnes on the sides haue no Pilasters: of these bearings out, I will say more in the fourth Booke, in the handling of foure maner of Simmetrie of Columnes.

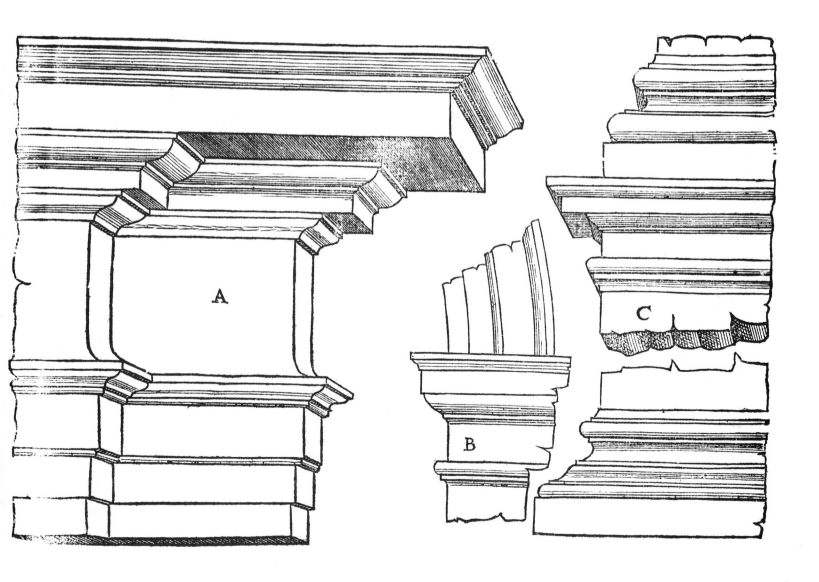

IN the leafe before, I shewed a piece of worke of Bramants making: and now I will shew another of his workes, from whence a wise workeman may helpe himselfe much, by meanes of the diuers and sundry ornaments that are in it. In this Gallery, the workeman would shew three stories or orders one aboue another, viz. Dorica, Ionica, and Corinthia: and in trueth, the orders were faire, well set out, and placed: notwithstanding, that the Pilasters of the first story or order being Dorica, were somewhat too weake, and the Arches too wide, to the proportion of the Pilasters; and therewith the weight of the wall of the Ionica order standing vpon it, was an occasion that it was broken, ruinated and decayed in short time. But Balthazar of Siene, a skilfull workeman, repayred the decayed ruines, making counter Pilasters, with vnder-Arches: therefore I haue said, wise workemen may learne of this building; not onely to imitate fayre and well made things, but also to beware of errors, and alwayes to consider what weight the nethermost story is to sustaine: therefore I counsell a workeman rather to be timerous, then ouer-bold; for if he be timerous, he will alwayes chuse the surest way, and make his worke with consideration, and will vse counsell, yea of such as are lesse skilfull then himselfe, of whom sometime men often learne: but if he be high-minded, and trusteth too much to his own skill and knowledge, then he will scorne another mans counsell, whereby oftentimes he deceyueth and ouer-shooteth himselfe; so that oftentimes his worke falleth out badly. Now I will turne to speake of this Gallery, and set downe some notes of the proportion thereof. The widenesse of the Arch shall bee deuided into eyght parts, whereof three parts shall be for the breoth of the Pilasters, and the height of the Arch shall containe 16. of such parts. The forepart of the Pilasters shall be deuided into foure parts, whereof two parts shall be for the Pilasters of the Arches, and the other two shall be for the thicknesse of the Columnes: the height of the Pedestals shall containe halfe the widenesse of the lights: the height of the Columnes shall bee eyght parts of their thicknesse, with the Bases and Capitals. The height of the Architraue, Freese and Cornice, is a fourth part of the length of the Columne. The second story shall bee lesse then the first by a fourth part, viz. That from the Pauement of the Dorica story, to the highest of the Cornice, shall be deuided into 4. parts, and 3. of them shall be for the whole story of the Ionica worke, and so shall all the parts particularly bee lessened in themselues a fourth part. The like also shall be done with the third story, which is Corinthia, in regard of the second order, although it standeth not here, because the Figure is drawne too great: but not to put the Reader in a maze or doubt at the Columnes which stand here in the middle, as desirous to know how they end at the top; you must vnderstand, that you shall finde such inuention in the fourth Booke, in the Order of Dorica in the side H 2. that although that those Columnes are Ionica in the sayd Booke, notwithstanding, you may make them Corinthia. And that the workeman might the better vnderstand the members and Cornicements of this worke, I haue shewed them in greater forme, and proportioned them according to the principall: I speake of the members of the first story: for a man could not easily come to measure the other.

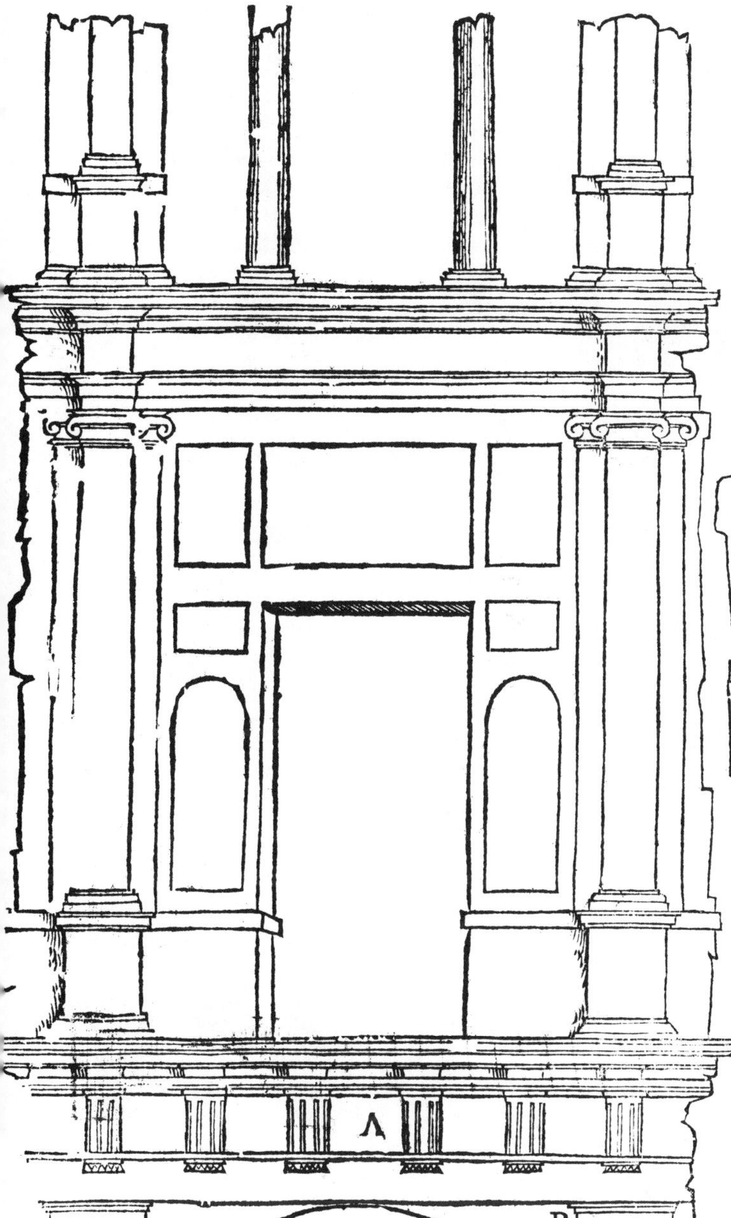
A
B
C
D

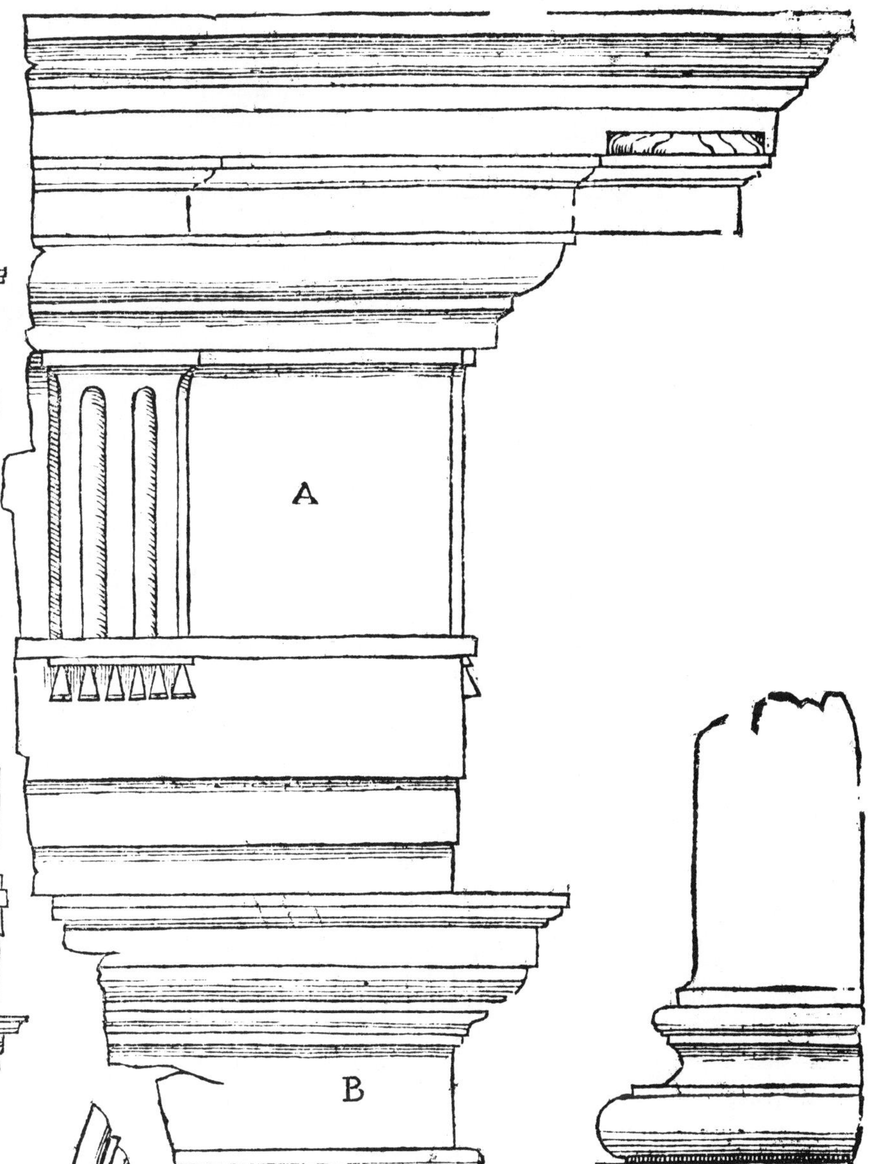
A
B
C
D

A T Beluedere, at the entry of the Popes Court, through the Gallery, which I haue set downe before, for the pla= ces alwayes goe vpwards, there is a going vp which is very fayre: at the head wherof, you come to a plaine, which hath the forme of a Theater; the ground whereof is shewed vnder this: and thereto I haue set the Profill, that you may vnderstand it. Here I haue kept no account of the measures, desiring onely to shew the inuention of the stayres, and the halfe Circle as it standeth. This halfe Circle is very much eleuated from the Court of the Popes house to the Palace-ward: and behind the halfe Circle, you find a great playne with fayre appertements; at which place, you goe through the two Gates, which you see in the sides of this halfe Circle; in which places there are many faire Ima= ges, and among the rest Laocoon, Apollo, Tyber, Venus, Cleopatra, and Hercules.

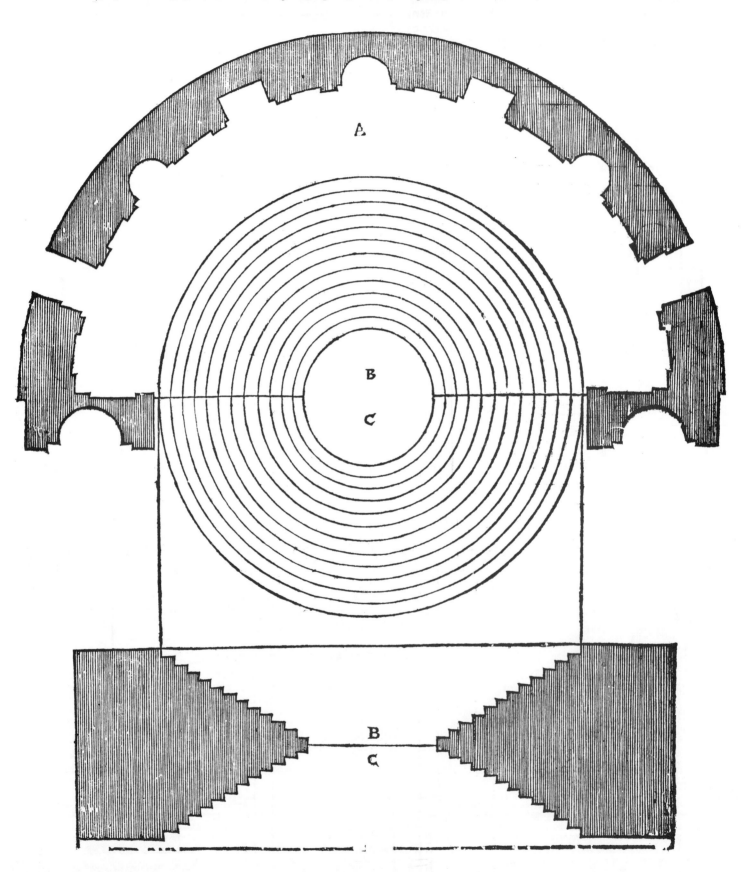

This is the Orthography of the ground shewed Folio 69. and as I haue sayd, I will not speake of the measure thereof, but onely of the inuention: and although that here on eyther side, onely one Pilaster, with his Columnes, is shewed, yet is it not vnlike some Galleries, whereof I haue spoken before, and that appeareth by the double Columnes, together with the Niches or hollow seates, with the Quadrans aboue them. In Beluedere there are many other things, which I haue showne, & among other things, there are wonderfull winding Stayres, in the ground whereof, there standeth a Fountayne, flowing exceedingly with water, the which going vp is all full of Columnes in the innermost part: which Columnes are of foure Orders: viz. Dorica, Ionica, Corinthia, and Composita: but that which is most wonderfull and ingenious, is that betwéene one and the other Order, there is no difference or distance, but men goe from the Dorica to the Ionica, and from the Ionica to the Corinthia, and from the Corinthia to the Composita, with such cunning, that a man cannot perceiue where one Order endeth and goeth into the other: so that I am of opinion, that Bramant neuer made a fairer nor costlier piece of worke then this.

Of Antiquitie

Without Rome, at Monte Mario, there is a very fayre place, with all things belonging to a place of pleasure, of which particular parts I will rather refrayne to speake, then not shew them sufficiently, onely I will speake of a Gallery, with the Facies thereof, made by an excellent workman Raphael Durbin, who hath made diuers appertements and beginnings to other workes, as the Courtill, although that it is fouresquare, yet he had fashioned it round, as the foundation partly sheweth. That Vestibulum marked A. and the two places, B. and C. stand not in such forme, but I haue placed them there to fill vp the ground: for the part C. endeth in an hill, as also the part E. but in the other side of the Gallery marked F. there is no halfe Circle, and that was left out, not to pinch some of the appertements, but to accompany other members by it. The order of this Gallery is very fayre: the roofe whereof is concordickly altred: for that the middle part is with a round tribune; and those two on the sides are crosse-wise. In which roofe, and also in the walles, Ian van Vdenen hath made wonderfull great pieces of paynted worke: so that regarding the fayre and excellent workemanship of Architecture, with the beautifying of paynting, together with diuers ancient Images, this Gallery may well be called, one of the fayrest that euer was made. And whereas it is spoken of an halfe Circle which doth not answere the rest, neither the workeman not willing to leaue it vndecked or vnfurnished, his Disciple Iulio Romano, in the Facie thereof, paynted the great Gyant Poliphemus, with many Satyres round about: which worke, Cardinall de Medicis, that after was Pope, by the name of Clemene, caused to be made. The measure of this Gallery I will not set downe, but the inuention shall suffice the workeman, for that all things are proportioned according to the great; and hereafter you shall sée it made vpright, together with the Facie of the Gallery, but the Niches or hollow seates on the sides are not there.

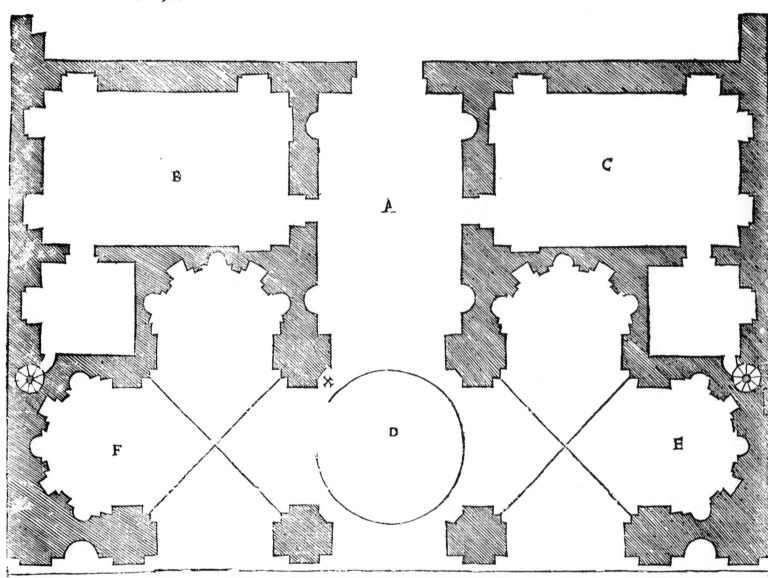

By this part following, marked B. A. you may conceiue the roofe of the aforesayd Gallery, the fayrenesse whereof consisteth much in the corner marked ✠ (the which giueth to vnderstand also the thrée others, being well placed) and shew well in the beauing vp of the tribune in the middle, going alwayes binding with the duplication of Pillars, to each Facie of the Pilasters: which Pillars (in regard the Coronas remayne whole) make not the Pilaster shew bare, but rather such breaking of Pilasters into two Pillars, maketh a large séeing vpwards, and stands (neuerthelesse) in manner and place of a firme Pillar: for the Base of the sayd Pilasters follow also. And for that in the Figure following in the Pilaster, there is but one Pillar with a péece shewed, yet to make it better to be vnderstood, is, that each Facie of the Pilasters within the Gallery is to be deuided into thrée, of the which a man may make two flat Pillars, and at the corners one Intercolumne: so that (as it is sayd) although there are two flat Pillars with one Intercolumne, yet, altogether, it is but one Pilaster.

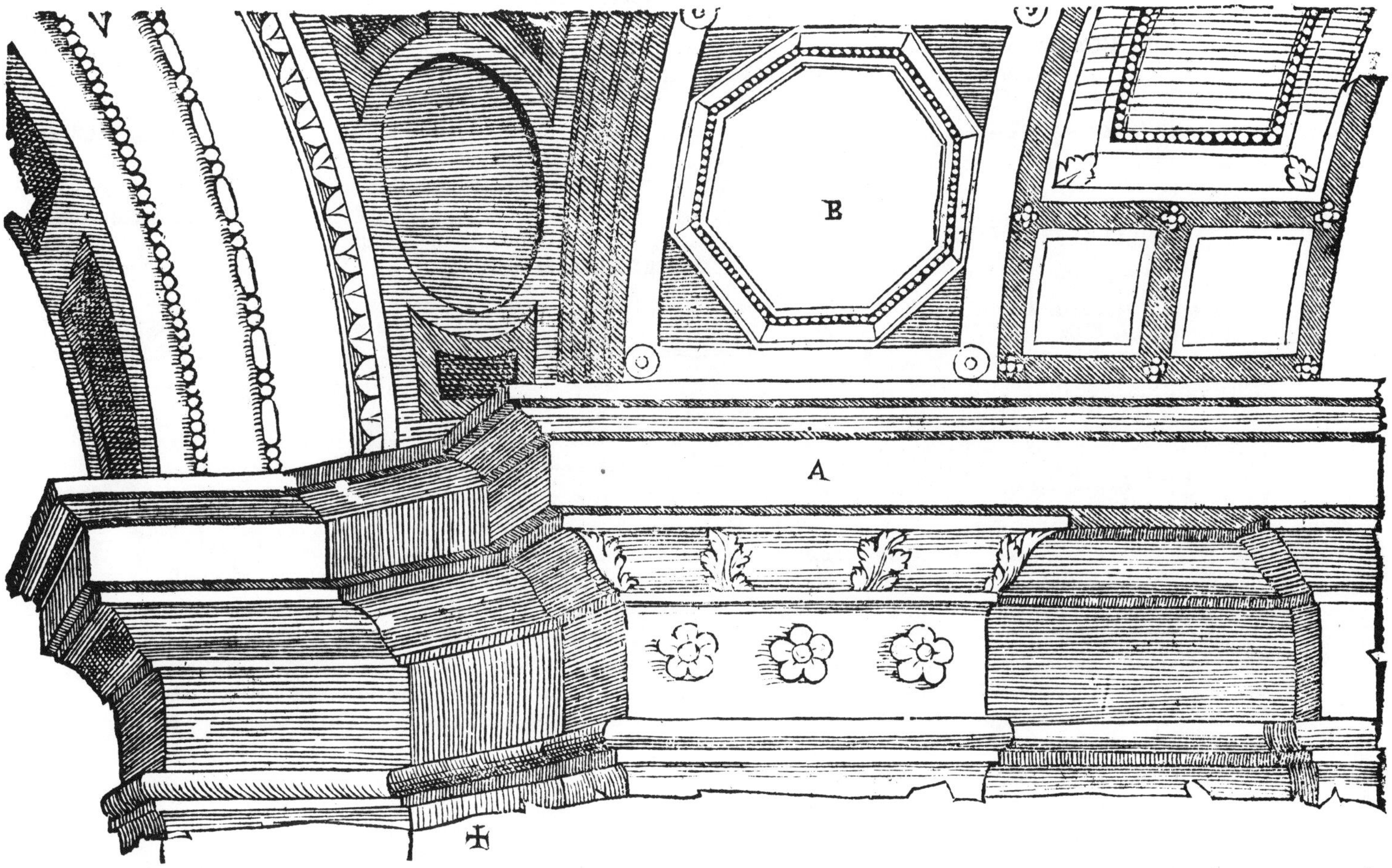
V
B
A
✠

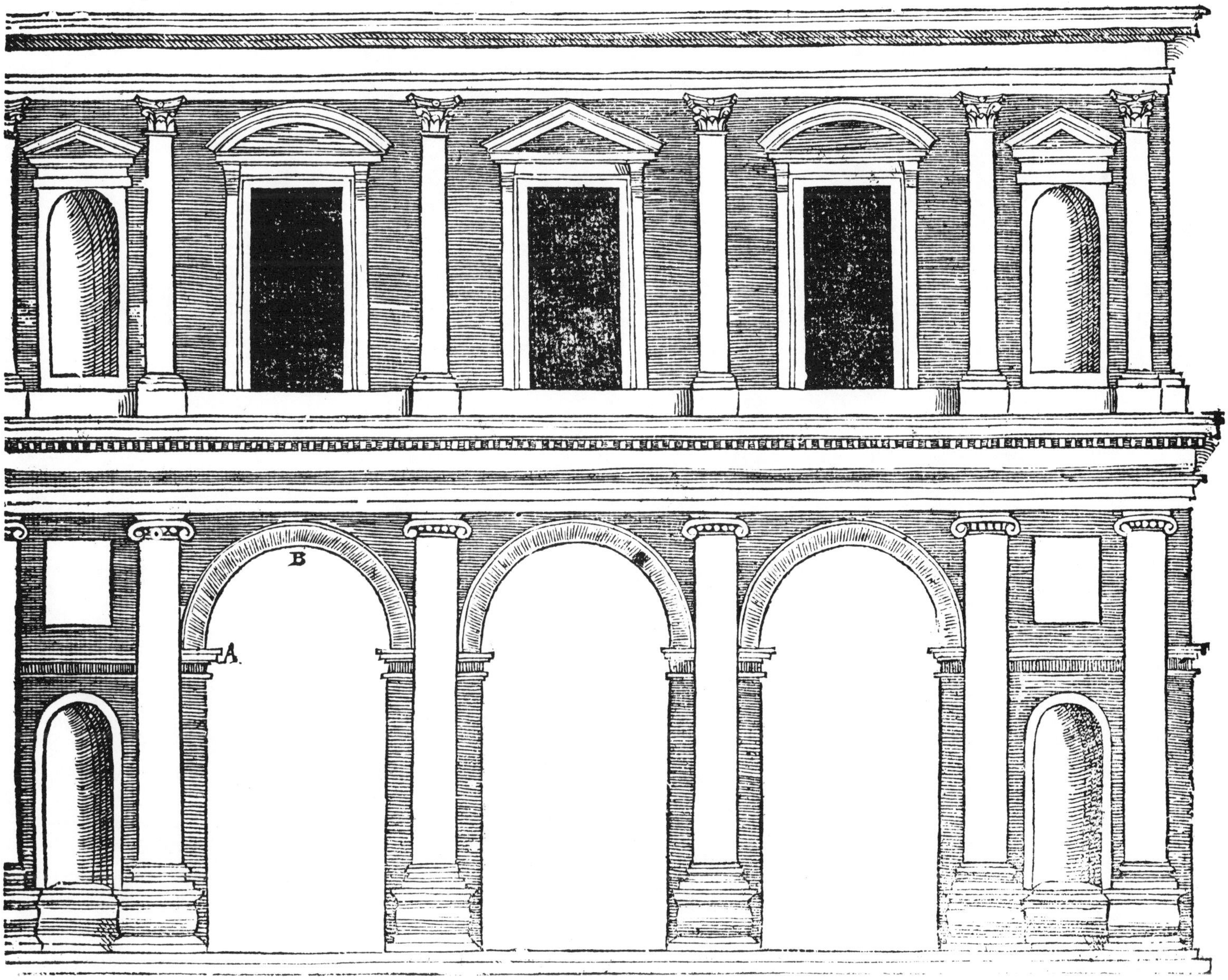
B
A.

AMong other Cities of Italy, Naples is called, La Gentile, and that not onely in respect of the great Barons, Lords, Earles, Dukes, and great numbers of Gentlemen therein, but also, because it is so well furnished with stately Houses and Palaces, as any other parts of Italy. And among other pleasant places that are without the Citie, there is a place called Poggio Reale, which King Alphonsus caused to be made for his pleasure, in that time (then most fortunate) when Italy was in peace, and now vnfortunate, by reason of the discords therein. This Palace hath a very faire scituation, and is well deuided for Roomes, for that in each corner thereof might bee lodged a strong company of men: in the middle there are sixe great Chambers, besides the Roomes vnder the ground, together with some secret Chambers. The forme of this faire building in the ground, as also, the building that standeth vpright, is here set downe in the next leafe: the measure thereof I set not downe vnto you, onely, because I will shew vpon the inuention: for a workeman may imagine of what greatnesse he will haue a Chamber, being all of one greatnesse; and then from those Chambers he may imagine all the measures of the rest of the building: which building the Noble King vsed for his pleasure, because men accustomed to dwell in the Countrey in the Summer time. The Court of this Palace is compassed with double Galleries: and in the middlemost place, marked E. men go downe a payre of Stayres into a fayre eating place, in which place, the King and his Lords vsed to banquet and eate at pleasure; in which place he caused certayne secret places to bee opened, whereby in the twinckling of an eye, the place was full of water, so that they sate all in water: likewise at this Kings pleasure, all ẙ water voyded out of the roome againe, but there wanted no shifts of clothes to put on, nor yet rich and costly beds for them to lye in, that would rest themselues. O voluptuous Italians, how are you impouerished by your discords! I will not speake of the most beautifull Gardens, filled with all kind of flowres, with diuers compartements of the Orchards and Trees of all kind of Fruits, with great abundance of Fish-ponds and Fishes, of places and cages of diuers Birds both great and small, of fayre stables, filled with all sorts of Horses; and of many other fayre things, which I will not speake of, for that Marcus Antonius Michaell, a Gentleman of that Towne, very learned in Architecture, hath seene it, and hath written of it at large in a Latine Epistle, which he sent to a friend of his. But to turne againe to the parts of the said Palace, which is right foure square, it is within, Galleried round about, one aboue the other: in the foure Corners, within the thicknesse of the walls, stand the winding stayres to goe vp into the building. The foure Galleries without, marked B. are not there, but for the commoditie and beautifying of the house, they would stand well there.

Iŋ this Figure hereunder, I haue ſhewed the Oꝛthographie both within and without: the part marked A. ſheweth the part without: the part marked B. repꝛeſenteth the Galleries within: the part C. ſheweth the ruines within. I haue not ſet downe the couering oꝛ roofe of this houſe: foꝛ accoꝛding to my opinion, I would haue plaiſtered ſuch a building, that it might onely be vſed foꝛ a walking place, to behold the countrey about.

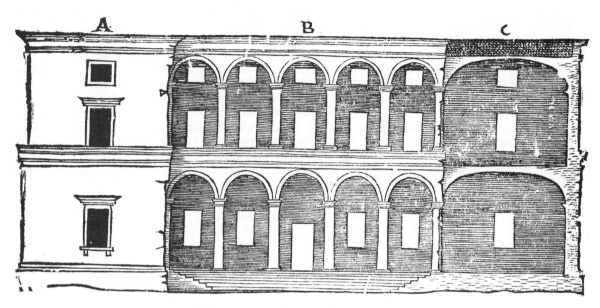

The grcund of the Poggio Real of Naples.

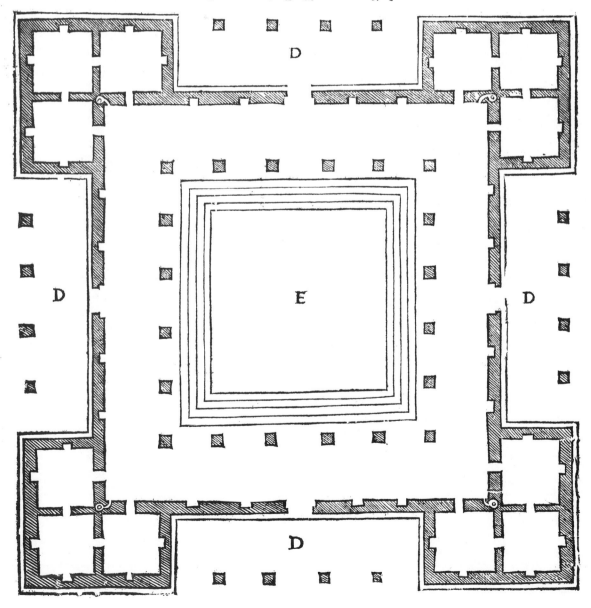

Onſidering the fayre Building of Poggio Real, I haue thought good to ſet downe ſuch an other here in this place; but in other forme for appertements, and peraduenture with more eaſe, for that the places are all of one greatnes, which is not ſo good a forme: but it is neceſſary that the firſt ſhould be greater then the ſecond. In this place I make you no place for lights within, for that it is a place in the countrey, being not cumbred on the ſides; it hath light inough on all the foure corners: but ſome men may ſay, that the Hall with the foure Chambers, becauſe they haue no light but through the galleries, are darke, for it is no perfect couer: to which I anſwere, that the houſe being made to be vſed in the time of great heat, hauing no place in the middle, the Hall and the Chambers will alwayes be cold, by reaſon the Sunne cannot come vnto them. Theſe places will be very pleaſant at noonetime, for that the ſaid places haue not ſo great lights as the other dwellings; yet haue they ſo much light as they need: ſuch like may be ſeene in Bolonia, which are made in this manner with Galleries, and daily inhabited. This Building is ſo diſpoſed, that the corner places being of great thickeneſſe, the reſt ſhall be ſtrong inough, yea, although the walls haue no great thickneſſe, in regard they are all counterforts one to the other, yet ſhall they be of ſufficient ſtrength. I will not ſpeake of the meaſures, for that this being proportioned, the ſkilful workman may imagine (according to his pleaſure that cauſed it to be built) firſt the greatnes of the roome, then deuide it into ſo many feet or other meaſures, thereby to meaſure all the reſt of the building, as the ſituation of the place may beare it. Then this building, aboue all things, ſhall be placed, that the Sunne may riſe vpon one of the corners, and ſo ſhine vpon all the ſides thereof: for if it ſtands with one ſide to the Eaſt, and the other to the Weſt, then it will follow, that the North ſide ſhall neuer enioy the Sunne-ſhine vpon it, which were rumaticke and vnwholeſome.

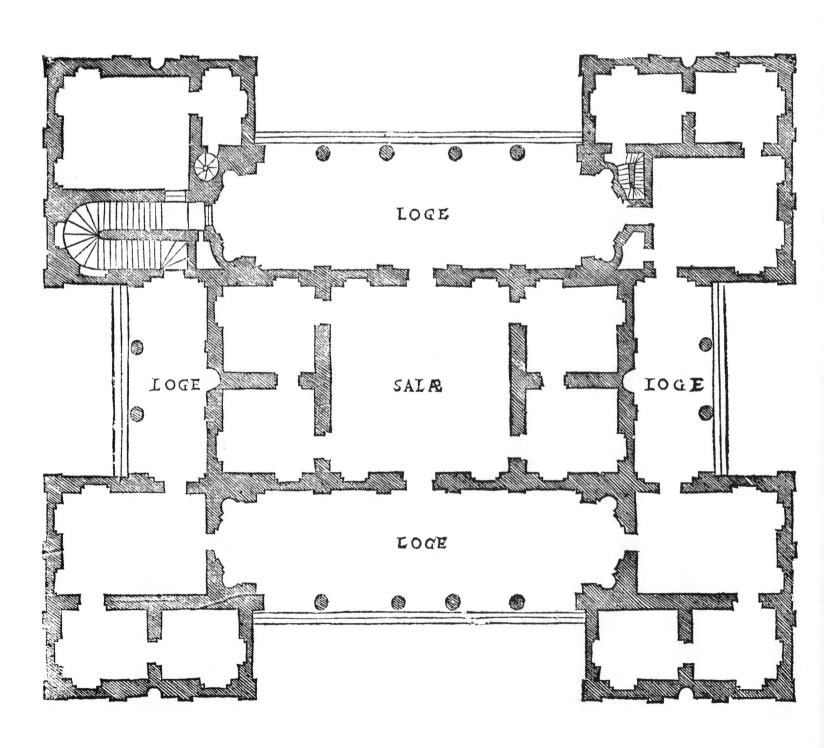

Men may build in diuers and sundry sorts vpon the ground aforesayd: but for that this is a place of pleasure, I thought good, for the brauenesse thereof, to make it after the Corinthia maner. I will not trouble my selfe to speake of the measures nor heights; for in my fourth Booke, in the Order of Corinthia, O 2. you shal find a Treatise, which, together with the iudgement of ý wise workman, will serue to set down this measure. And, for that in this Facie there is no shortening at all, whereby you may know the Galleries, the flat and closed places eche from other; therefore I will set downe the two highest sides at eche end: you must conceaue it to haue flat Pillars from beneath vpwards; that part betwéne both, which is lower, you must suppose hath two Galleries, one aboue the other, the Columnes whereof would be round: the same is to be vnderstood to be both behind, and on both sides. Men may also make aboue the Galleries a Tarrace or Pauement, to defend the raine, the Gallery being made with a Leane-to, or Raile out of the Cornices of the first order of the Figures aforesayd: and so also the Hall in the middle, together with the 4. Chambers of ý second story, would haue more light. For 2. causes I haue made the small windows aboue the great, in the first story. The I. is, if you will make the windowes so low, that a man sitting, may easily sée out of them, then (if you should make the windowes no higher then the doore) there would bee to much space betwéne the windowes and the roofe of the house, which would greatly darken the house: and otherwyse the windowes bring much more light into the Hall. The 2. is, that the Chambers by the Hall néd not bee of such height, but you may make hanging Chambers therein, whereto those windowes will serue. I might speake of many other things, which I referre to the iudgement of the workeman.

A T firſt, J was not minded to ſet this ground, noʒ yet the building of the 100. Columnes, placed in M. 1. in this Rocke; foʒ that they are things which the Authoʒ hath made by repoʒts and heare-ſay, which J eſteeme not woʒ-thy to be ſet by things that are counterfepted and meaſured: yet that it ſhould not be ſayd, that J haue publiſhed this Booke lame and unperfect, and not full as the Authoʒ made it, which might haue giuen ſlandereus and enui-ous perſons occaſion to ſcoʒne and ſcandalize this Booke; therefoʒe J haue not onely ſet this héere, but alſo added this o-ther Figure following by him ſet downe in the leaſe R. 3. And now to turne to this ground, our Authoʒ ſapth, that in Jeruſalem (as it was told him) on a hill, there is a building cut out of a reaſonable greatneſſe, in manner hereunder ſet downe: and foʒ that by meanes of the wideneſſe of the middlemoſt part, the roofe ſhould not fall in, therefoʒe the two Pilaſters were left in the middle, and withall, two of a middle ſoʒt by them, with two leſſe alſo befoʒe, underholding the roofe, which altogether were cut out of the rocke with inſtruments. Jn the firſt entry are foure little Chappels. Jn the middle there are 18. and behind there ſtand 2. and a dooʒe locked, which ſheweth, that men went further: the grea-teſt Chappel is wide the length of a man, whereby you may iudge the greatneſſe of the building. This place hath no light, noʒ can be perceaued that it had any light. The Chappels are taken out, as the Figures A. and B.

FOr that our Author before,
ſpeaketh of an Arch triumphant in Verona, called Dei
Borſari, which he termeth to
be barbarous and confuſed of
parts and members, as (according to the writing of Vitruuius of good Antiquities)
in effect it is: Neuertheleſſe,
for that Iohannes Carottus
(which our Author alledgeth)
hath ſet it downe for an ornament of Verona, in his booke
of Antiquities, much better,
and with more deliberation
then all ẏ reſt of the Figures
by him made (for in trueth,
ẏ reſt are very groſſe: Therefore I thought it good to ſhew
it here to the curious Reader
that he may ſee and alſo note
(by Vitruuius rule aforeſaid)
what is good or ill in it, which
may peraduenture pleaſe
ſome of this countrey better
then another, becauſe they vſe
to ſeeke for much worke in
their Architecture. And for
ẏ this Figure was to great
in forme, therfore I haue here
ſet downe but the halfe; and
you muſt conceaue the other
ſide, that is, an Arch with
windowes and other orna-
ments, like theſe: the foot of
Verona, wherwith this building is meaſured, ſtandeth
here on the ſides in halfe proportion: of which foot, one
ſmall ſtandeth in the Pedeſtal, vnder ẏ great Columne;
whereby the meaſure is to be
conceyted: for the ſaid Carottus giues no other war-
rant of all his Figures (but
onely of the Figure of the
wonderfull ſpectacle, as hee
termeth it) with the Theater
aboue it: but aboue all, with
the goings vp to the hill,
where a Temple of Ianus
ſtandeth, as our Author ſheweth afterward in Folio L. 3. in
this preſent Booke. Of this
building, Carottus ſaith more
then of all the reſt: and for
that I may ſatiſfie the Reader at full, of all that is ſayd
in this Booke, therefore I
haue cauſed this figure to bee
printed alone, becauſe it was
to great, and (in my opinion) to groſe, to ſet hereby.
    Vale.

The halfe foote of Verona, wherewith this building is meaſured.

The end of the third Booke.

Tranſlated out of Italian into Dutch, and
out of Dutch into Engliſh, at the charges
of *Robert Peake* and are to be ſold at
his houſe neere Holborne Conduit, next to the Sunne
Tauerne. 1611.

The fourth Booke.

Rules for Masontry, or Building

with Stone or Bricke, made after the fiue maners
or orders of Building, *viz.* Thuscana, Dorica,
Ionica , Corinthia and Composita : and
thereunto are added examples of Antiquities; which, for the most part, agree
with the instructions of *Vitruuius*: with
some Figures more, added vnto them,
which were not in the first, and some
deuices of the Author , which are
corrected, and hereunto
annexed.

Translated out of Italian into
Dutch, and out of Dutch
into English.

LONDON

Printed for Robert Peake,
and are to be sold at his shop neere
Holborne conduit, next to the
Sunne Tauerne.

ANNO DOM. 1611.

To the wel-willers of Architecture.

Vitruuius *sayth, that such as haue built without learning or instruction (although workemen) could neuer make any famous or commendable pieces of worke: no more can others, being no workemen, such as haue followed the letter or writing onely, and made no proofe: of which, some haue presumed to father their doings vpon Vitruuius: yet in diuers places of their writings, which are found, they could not close vp their rules orderly, but haue left many things doubtfull, and (more) haue esteemed that to be good and commendable, which in worke is not to bee endured. The cause of this errour, is, that the last Booke of the sayd Vitruuius, wherein the Figures are, was lost: whereby men might haue knowne and found out his meanings: so that hereby it appeareth, that some Antiquities haue beene very bare in their workes, and especially, in their Orders of Dorica, because Vitruuius nameth no Dorica Bases: but in stead thereof, speaketh of an Attica. Now it may be, regarding that he there speaketh not of any Order of Attica, therefore they durst not make any Dorica Bases or Columnes: on the contrary, others possibly contemning the darknesse of the writer, (or for want of knowledge) haue so far exceeded their Author in many things, that they haue not onely forsaken and left the examples and reasons of good Antiquities, but also (more then that) haue made their workes vnseemely, and ridiculous to mens eyes, as may be seene in diuers ancient works: whereby, gentle Reader, many workmen, well seene in both, haue beene cumbred therein, and especially in this our time. Bramant of* Castle Durant, *Balthazar of* Scienne, *and many others, for that (not onely by meanes of* Iulius the 2. Pope, *but) also by others, good Architecture was bettered in their times: who, after long disputation and searching of many, aswell Authors and Commentaries, together with the examples of good Antiquities, haue with authority (to make an end of all doubts) not only added this* Spira Attica, *of the Dorica, but also as many orders as now are vsed, beginning at the Thuscan, as the grossest and slenderest of all the rest, and haue reduced the same into a certaine and common forme, together with their ornaments and measures: which rules* Sebastian Serlius, *a workeman and scholer of the sayd* Balthazar, *hath written, and set out in figures; so that, leauing the obscurities of* Vitruuius, *we may make an incorrigible worke. And for that all those that loue workemanship, vnderstand not the Italians, therefore (in my opinion) I haue translated the most certayne and best rules out of Italian into Dutch, and out of Dutch into English; onely the names of all Procels, Bases, Capitals, Cornices, &c. which are not named in Dutch nor English, for that* Bastian, *by* Vitruuius *termes, vseth the common and moderne Italian words, which by some should be as hardly vnderstood as the Latine. But I would commend him, that seeing we take vpon vs to follow* Vitruuius *writings, that we giue him the name of* Vitruuius, *that the learned might bee vnderstood of the workeman, and the workeman also vnderstood of the learned. And for that the workeman might the better read it, I haue printed it in our ordinary Dutch letter. And although this fourth Booke of seuen was first set out, because it is the best, yet the other also are no lesse fit and conuenient to further Architecture or Art of Building, as in the ensuing Epistle you shall see.*

Sebaſtian Serlius to the Reader.

Louing and friendly Reader, after I had collected certaine rules of Architecture, thinking that not only thoſe of deepe conceyt would vnderſtand them, but that alſo each indifferent man of wit might conceaue them, as he is more or leſſe addicted to ſuch an Art; which rules are deuided into ſeuen Books, as hereunder ſhall be ſet downe: but for that this Art requireth it, therefore I thought it requiſite to begin with this fourth Booke, and to ſet it out, firſt, which is more to the purpoſe, and more neceſſary then the reſt, for the knowledge of many ſorts of Building and ornaments thereof, to the end that euery one may haue ſome knowledge of this Art, the which is no leſſe pleaſing to the mind of thoſe workmen that thinke vpon things that are to make, then alſo to mens eyes when they are made. Which Art, by the wiſedome of the famous and excellent ſpirits that are now in the world, doth flouriſh in theſe dayes, as the Latine tongue did in the time of *Iulius Cæſar*, and *Cicero*. Then with glad and ioyfull heart receyue at leaſt my good will, (though the effect enſueth not) which, in trueth, I haue (to pleaſure and ſatisfie your minds) in this reſpect.

In the firſt Booke, I will entreat of the beginning of Geometry, and of diuers cuttings through of lines, in ſuch ſort, that the workman may yeeld reaſon for that he worketh.

In the ſecond Booke, I will ſhew in Figure, and by reaſon, as much of Perſpective Art, that if the workeman will, he may declare his conceyt or purpoſe, by reaſons and figure.

In the third Booke, workmen ſhall ſee the Ichnographie, that is, the ground: the Orthographie, that is, the rayſing vp of a Building before. The Scenographie or Sciographie, that is, the inſight, by ſhortening of the moſt part of the Buildings that are in Rome, Italie, &c. diligently meaſured, and ſet by them in writing, with the places where they are, and their names.

In the fourth, which is this, I will ſpeake of fiue maner of Buildings, and of their ornaments, as Thuſcana, Dorica, Ionica, Corinthia and Compoſita, that is to ſay, mingled. And by theſe, the whole Arte is learned.

In the fift, I will ſpeake of diuers kinds of Temples, ſet downe in diuers formes, that is, round, foureſquare, ſix-cornerd, eyght-cornerd, Ouall-wiſe, and croſſe-wiſe, with their ground, heights and ſhortenings, diligently meaſured.

In the ſixt, I will ſpeake of all dwellings, which, at this day, may bee vſed, beginning at the meaneſt houſe or cottage, and ſo from degree to degree, proceeding to the moſt rich, fayre and princely Palaces, as well in Countrie villages, as in great Cities or Townes.

In the ſeuenth and laſt, ſhall be ſet downe many accidents, which may happen to workemen in diuers places, ſtrange maner of ſituation, repayring of decayed houſes, and how we ſhould helpe our ſelues with pieces of other buildings, with ſuch things as are to be vſed, and at other times haue ſtood in worke.

Now then, to proceed readily herein, I will begin with the greateſt and ruſticke order of Building, that is, the Tnuſcan, being the playneſt, rudeſt, and ſtrongeſt, and of leaſt grace and ſeemelineſſe.

The Author to the Reader.

THe ancient workemen in times past (as Vitruuius affirmeth) dedicated their workes and Buildings to the gods, according to their natures, strength or weakenesse; so is the forme called Dorica ascribed to the gods, Iupiter, Mars, and valiant Hercules, taking such formes from strong men. The forme called Ionica, is ascribed to the goddesse Diana, Apollo and Bacchus, as of the nature of Matrons, that is, of wise & sensible women, which are both tender and strong: for Diana, by her feminine nature is tender, but by vsing to hunt, shee is strong: Apollo, by reason of his beauty, is tender; but being a man, he is strong: the like of Bacchus. But the Corinthia is taken of mayds, and they ascribe all to the goddesse Vesta, and her chaste mayds: yet at this time I thinke it good to proceed in another sort, nothing differing from the ancients aforesayd. My meaning is, to follow the maner and customes of the Christians, that I (as far as I may) will ascribe holy Buildings to God and to his Saints: and profane buildings, as well publicke as priuate, I will ascribe to men according to their professions. So say I then, that the Thuscan maner (after my opinion) is fit for strengths, for Gates of Cities, Townes and Castles, places for treasure, munition and Artillery to keepe them in; for prisons, hauens of the Sea, and such like things, seruing for the warres. It is true, that rusticke and playne worke, that is, such Buildings as are made of rough stones, and others that are made somewhat smother, according to the pleasure which the Stone-cutters take therein, are sometimes mixed with Dorica, and sometimes with Dorica and Corinthia. Neuertheles, for that the Thuscan order is the roughest set foorth, farre more then the other are, I am of opinion, that the Country Bulding is more like vnto the Thuscan, then any of the rest: which you may playnely see to haue bene obserued by the Thuscans, as wel in their chiefe Cities and Townes of Florence, as without in their Country Villages, in so many rich and fayre Buildings, made after the rusticall maner, as may be seene in all Christendoome, mixed with such a slight manner of worke, as the workeman thought good. Therefore I conclude, that such Buildings are more agreeable to Thuscan order, then any other. Therefore, altering somewhat from Antiquities, and some others of ours, I will in diuers sorts shewe of such workes, viz. how to make Gates of Cities, Townes, or Forts; as also, in publike and priuate places, Houses, Galleries, Windowes, Niches or seates, hollowed in worke, Bridges, Water-courses, and such like seuerall Ornaments, as may happen into a workemans hands to doe. Men may also (not differing from the ancient rules) mixe this rusticall maner with the Dorica, and also with Ionica; and sometimes with Corinthia, at the pleasure of those that seeke to please their owne fantasies, which a man may affirme to bee more for pleasure then profit: therefore the workeman ought to proceed with good aduice, especially in publike buildings, wherein comelinesse is commendable.

In the beginning of this Booke, I obserued the Comedians order, who (when they intend to play any Comedy) first send out a Prologue, who in few wordes giueth the audience to vnderstand what they intend to entreat of, in their Comedie. So I, meaning in this Booke to entreat of fiue maner of Buildings, viz. Thuscan, Dorica, Ionica, Corinthia and Composita, haue thought good, that in the beginning thereof, men should see the Figures of all the seuerall kinds whereof I purpose to entreat of. And although that in the Columnes and their ornaments, all the measures and proportions are not set downe, but onely the principall, by generall rules; yet will I not fayle, as occasion shall serue, to set them downe in particularities: but this is done, as I sayde, to shew in generall rules for an Introduction onely, the better to be vnderstood of euery workeman, and in the beginning will obserue Vitruuius order and termes, marked on the sides with A. B. C. that euery workeman may name them according to his country speech. And first, the Stilo bato, or Thuscan Pedestall, I meane the flat, without Crowne or Base, shall bee a perfect fouresquare. The perfect Dorica shall be as much more as the drawing of a line from corner to corner, of the perfect fouresquare, placing it vpright. The Pedestall Ionica, shall be of one fouresquare and an halfe: the Pedestall Corinthia, shall be a fouresquare and two third parts thereof. The Pedestall Composita shall bee of two perfect fouresquares. Also, wonder not, that the Chapter next ensuing is the fift, which others would esteeme the first: for that the first Booke doeth contayne a Chapter of Geometry: the second of Perspectiue, shall be of two Chapters: the third of Antiquities, shal be of one Chapter, which maketh foure Chapters: so that, this considered, the next shall be the fift.

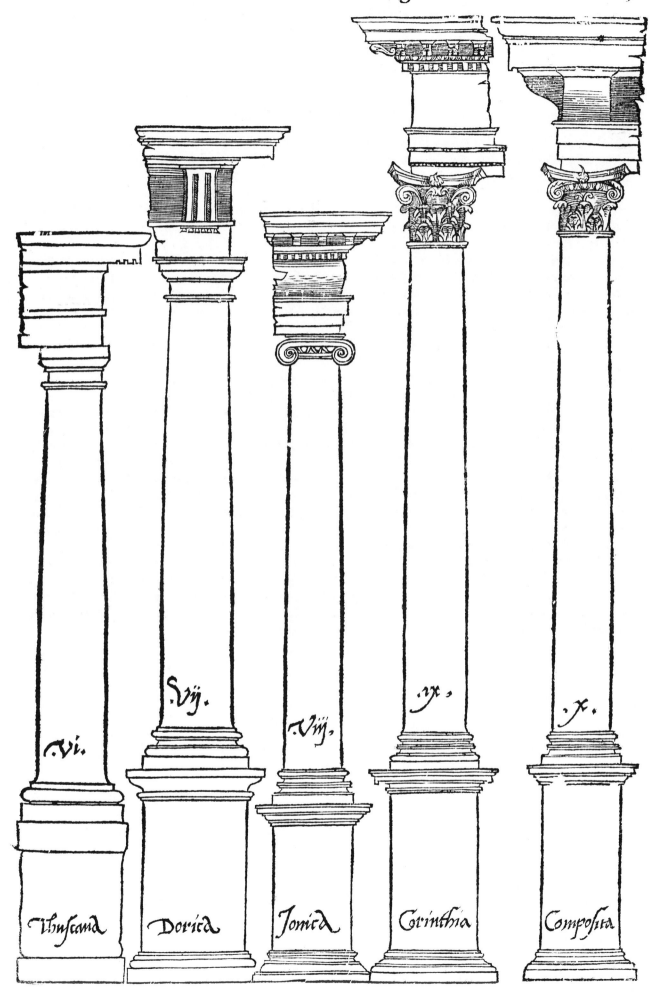

.vi.

.vij.

.viij.

.ix.

.x.

Thuscana   Dorica   Ionica   Crinthia   Composita

Of the order and maner of Thuscan workes, and
the Ornaments thereof.

The fift Chapter.

IN Vitruuius *fourth Booke and seuenth Chapter we find, that a man should make a Thuscan Columne of seuen parts high, with Capitall and Base, which measure should be taken from the thicknesse of the Columne below. The height of the Bases or Basement, should be the halfe of the thicknesse of the Columne, which shall bee deuided into two equall parts, whereof one shall be the Plinthus, the other deuided in three, two parts thereof shall bee the Thorus, the third the Cincta. The Proiecture you shall make in this maner : Fi st, make a Circle as great as the Columne is thicke below, placing it in a fouresquare : without the foure square draw another Circle, close about the corners of the foure square, which shall bee the Proiecture. And although all other Bases haue their Plinthus foure square, yet this of Thuscan must be round, as Vitruuius teacheth. The height of the Capitall must bee like the Base : that deuide into three parts : one part shall be the Abacus : the other shall be deuid d in foure parts, three for the Echino, the fourth for the Annulo or Cintho, which may be called, a Girdle, Band, ar List in English. The third part resting, shall bee for the Hypotrachelium, or Freese. The Astragall with the Cincta, is halfe the Freese; but that deuided in three, two shall be for the Round the third his List, the bearing out must bee as the height : and although this List is here named with the Capitall, yet it is a part of the Columne, which Columne ought to be made thinner aboue a fourth part; also the Capitall in the vppermost part shall not be greater then the Columne below. The maner to lessen the Columne is thus : Let the body of the Columne be deuided in three parts : the third part below shall hang at the leade, and the other two third parts you shall deuide into as many equall parts as you will : then at the third part of the Columne draw halfe a Circle, and from the lines that hang there, from the outtermost corners of the Capitall inwards, measure the eyght part, which in all shall be a fourth part : from vnder the corner (where the Columne is thinnest) you shall draw two lines by a leade, to the halfe circle, and those parts of the circle outwards, you shall set below, in as many euen parts as the two third parts of the Columne holdeth : which being done on both sides, then there shall be as many Paralels or crosse lines, drawen from the one poynt of the halfe circle to the other, each line being marked with number, from the top downewards, and the like vpon the lynes that deuide the Columnes; which numbers being orderly placed, then it is certayne, that the first line shall agree with the thinnest part of the Columne aboue : after, take the second line of the halfe circle, and set it vpon the second line of the Columne, then the third vpon the third, and the fourth vpon the fourth : when that is done, there must be a lyne drawne from the Base of the halfe circle, to the lyne 4. and from the lyne 4. to the lyne 3. and from the line 3. to the lyne 2. and from the line 2. to the lyne 1. also a lyne : and so from the second side of the Columne : and although that the lynes in themselues are right, yet they make a crooked lyne, which the iudicious workeman knoweth how to regeire and moderate at hi will on all sides in the gathering of the lynes. And although this rule is made for the Thuscan Columne, which is lessned aboue a fourth part, yet it may serue for all sorts of Columnes; and the more the deuiding of the Columnes and the halfe Circle are in number, so much the lessening will dimynish.*

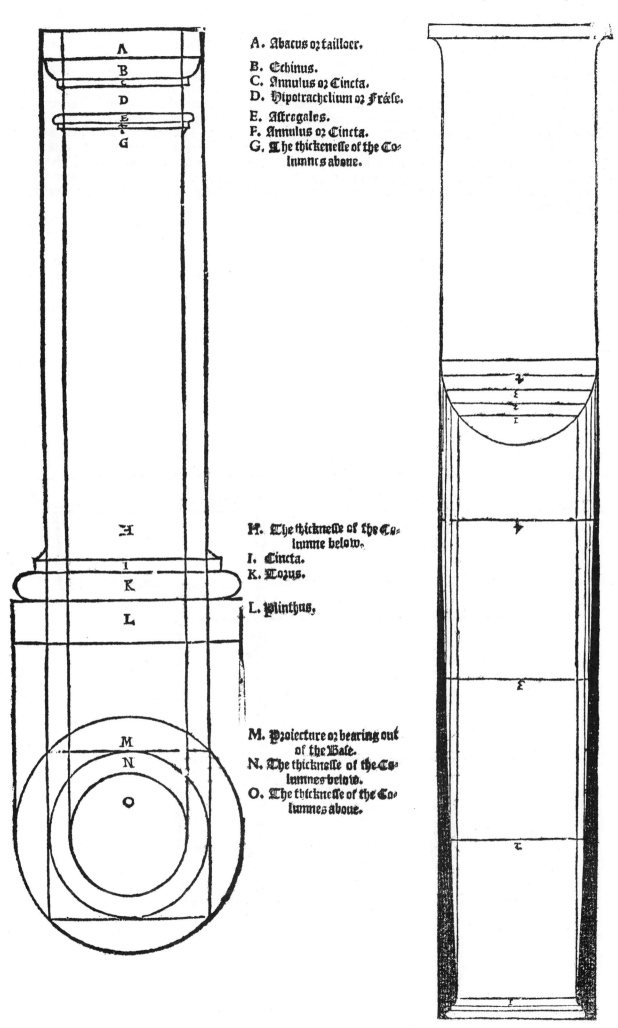

A. Abacus or tailloer.

B. Echinus.
C. Annulus or Cincta.
D. Hipotrachelium or Frése.

E. Aftregales.
F. Annulus or Cincta.
G. The thicknesse of the Columnes aboue.

H. The thicknesse of the Columne below.
I. Cincta.
K. Torus.

L. Plinthus.

M. Projecture or bearing out of the Base.
N. The thicknesse of the Columnes below.
O. The thicknesse of the Columnes aboue.

The Columne being finished with the Capitall and Base, then the Architraue, Frése and Cornice are to bée set thereon. That Epistolum or Architraue must be as high as the Capitals, and the Tenia or List, the sixt part thereof. That Sophorus or Frése of the same height. The Cornice also, with her members, must bée the like: and the same being deuided in foure parts, one part shall be for the Cimatie, two parts for the Corona, and the last for the Facie vnder the same. The Proiecture or bearing out of them all, must be at least so much as their height. And vnder in the Corona you may cut channels or hollowings, great or small, as the worke is, at the pleasure of the workman. But, for that this worke is grosse, and plaine of members, a man (in my opinion) may take vpon him to adde some parts vnto it, which may séeme to belong vnto the same; which must be done when men desire to make the worke shew better, as you sée in this herevnder set downe. I commend also those crownes that haue most Proiecture or bearing out, without their fouresquares; especially, when the stones are fit to beare it: Which Proiectures are both commodious, and beautifie the worke: commodious in this, that the walking place vpon them will bée broader, and it will also kéepe the worke from water: beautifying in this, that when men behold the worke with convenient distance from it, it will shew the greater; and where the stones bée scanted, by reason of their smalnesse, the Proiecture will supply that want, by shewing greater.

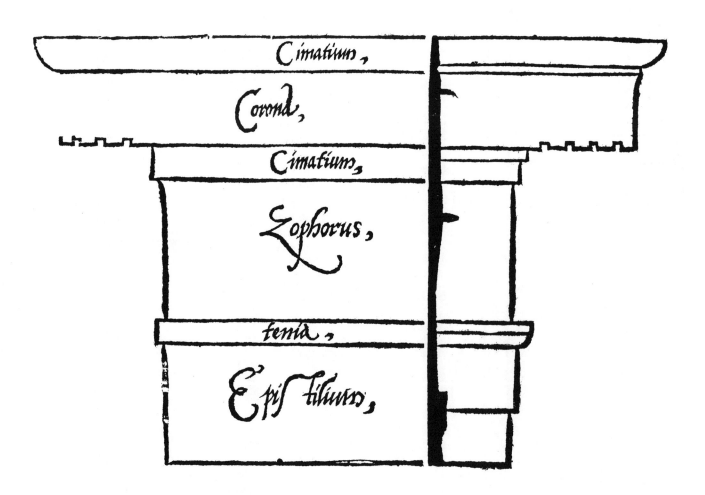

Cimatium,

Corona,

Cimatium,

Zophorus,

tenia,

Epistilium,

Although I said before, that the Thuscan Columne (according to Vitruuius rule) ought to be of seuen Diameters high, with Bases and Capitals, which proportion is approued good; neuertheleße, for that the first Columnes (as you haue heard in my small Booke) were made in sixe parts, taking the measure from mens feet, which is the sixt part of the same: And also, for that ye Columnes called Dorica, are now of seuen parts, the ancient workmen hauing another part vnto them, to heighten them, therefore, in my opinion, by the same autho- ritie, for that the Thuscan Columne is stron- ger then the other, I iudge, it might be made lower then the Dorica; and, by my aduice, be made but of sixe parts, with Bases and Ca- pitals, this you may hold for a common rule. And, for that neither Vitruuius, nor any o- ther workeman that I haue seene, haue set downe no rule for the Stilobato or Pedestal, and in Antiquities, as far as I can see, were by workemen made, as neceßitie required; whether it were for raysing of Columnes, or to a going vp with stayres, to Galleries, or by any other occasions: Therefore, not be- ing copelled thereunto, I am of opinion, that euery workeman should to each kind of Co- lumne set a conuenient and seemely Pede- stall, as reason requireth, and as hee seeeth cause: It is certaine and well knowne, that the Pedestall at least must bee fouresquare, that is, the body thereof, without Base or Cime, therfore the Thuscan Columne being the best of all, the Pedestall thereof ought to be a perfect fouresquare: the forepart thereof ought to be as broad as the Plinthus of the Base of the Columne: the height should bee deuided into foure parts, one part whereof shall be set vnder, for the Plinthus, and one for the Cime, which members shall be vncut: so then, if the Columne bee of sixe parts, the Stilobato or Pedestall shall bee of sixe parts also in it selfe, according to the proportion of the Columne.

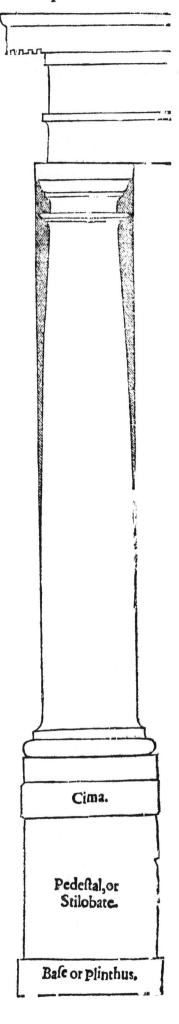

Cima.

Pedeſtal, or
Stilobate.

Baſe or Plinthus.

Of the Thuſcana

I Haue promiſed in this Booke, onely to intreat of the ornaments and different maner of Buildings: therefore I will not, at this time, ſhew how men ſhould place the Gates of Townes and Forts, with their ſides, places to lay out Cannons, with other circumſtances of defence, leauing ſuch care to the workemen belonging to warres, according to the ſituation and accidents of time and place. But I will ſhew you, that when the Gates of the Citie, Towne or Fortreſſe are placed, how men, in my opinion, ſhould ſet them forth, ſetting downe ſome Figures thereof. You muſt vnderſtand, that each Gate or Port is to bee after the Italian maner, and ought, of neceſſity, to haue a Poſterne Gate, which are called Porten van Secourſe, which are the ſmall Ports on the ſides. But to obſerue the Semetry, that is, a due meaſure, they ought to be made in this manner. The meaſure of the Gate is thus, as much as the breoth of the light ſhall be, the halfe whereof ſhall ſerue for the height. The breoth of the light is deuided into ſixe parts, whereof one part ſhall be for the breoth of the Pilaſters on eyther ſide of the Gate: the flat of the Pillars thereof ſhall be as broad as the third part of the light, and the height, with Capitals and Baſes. The height of the Baſes ſhall be a third part of the breoth of the Pillars, and ſo much alſo the Capitals, obſeruing the rule ſet downe in the firſt Columne. That Epiſtolium, Zophorus, and Corona ſhall be altogether of ſuch height, as the breoth of the Pillars, by the rule aforeſayd. Betwane the one Pillar and the other, the Poſternes or ſmall Gates ſhall bee, and the wideneſſe ſhall bee as broad as the flat Pillars. The height ſhall be twice as much as the breoth: the Pilaſters ſhall be the third part of the ſayd Poſterne. The eleuation or rayſing vp aboue the gate, ſhall bee at the workemans will. But the proportion of the Faſtigies or Frontiſpicie (which is called with vs, the ſpanning, couer, or roofe) I will ſhew in two ſorts in the order of Dorica.

A Pilaſter.

ANd for that the workeman ought to be copious of inuentions, to pleaſe himſelfe and others, the Gate of the City, Towne, or Fortreſſe, may be ſet out in this maner, obſeruing this rule : that ſo broad as the going through of the Gate is, the height ſhall be as much, and halfe as much agayne, that is, 2. parts in bredth, and 3. parts in height.

The Pilaſters ſhall be the 8. part of the wideneſſe of the Gate: and the Columnes ſtand for the round Columnes and flat Pillars , being the fourth part of the Gate. But for that the Columne is a third part ſet into the wall, and is bound faſt with other ſtones, more for ſhew then bearing, it is to be made 7. parts high, and alſo of 8. at the workemans will, which will ſet forth the Gate with more ſhew. The wideneſſe of the Poſterne ſhalbe the halfe of the middle Gate, the Pilaſters alſo (as the greater) that is the halfe. The height thereof ſhalbe ſuch as the Facie that beareth the Arch, and it ſhalbe the Supercilie, or Architraue thereof, as we call it: and if you find not a ſtone all of one péece fit for it, then you ſhall make the Cunei or Pennants as you ſée them héere in the Figure. And thus the proportion of the Poſterne ſhall bee, that is, 3. parts in bredth, and 5. of the like parts in height. The Cunei or Pennants of the Arch, ſhall be 15. In the Baſes, Capitals, Architraue, Fréſe, and Cornice, you muſt obſerue the rule aforeſayd; and the eleuation in the middle ſhall be at the workemans will, as I ſayd of the other : and all ſuch workes, the groſer they be made, and boſſ out, the ſtronger they are for fortification.

Of the Thuscana

A Man may make Gates of Townes and Forts in another maner, both playne and stronger, following the order hereunder set downe: and the proportion or the widenesse of the Gate shall be as much as the height is vnder the Facie, which beareth vp the roofe: and from the Facie vpwards, as much higher as the halfe Circle; yet alwayes at the workemans will to be increased or diminished, and especially, as he is by accident restrayned. The two Posternes are to be made, as I haue before shewed: Their widenesse must be the halfe of the middle Gate, and so much of the wall shall be left betwéene the great Gate and the two small: which height shall be doubled with the bredth, and the Facie, which vpholdeth the Arch, shall also hold vp the Cunei of the small Gates. Yet must wee take such order, that the Facie shooting through, should bee the Supercilie, which, as I sayd, may bee altered at the will of the workeman, without altering them from the Figure.

fascia.

Iuers kinds of ornaments, many times, put the workeman in mind of things which he peraduenture would not haue thought of: Therefore the Figure ensuing will serue the workeman to good end in building, as occasion shall serue: as in the wall of a fortresse, where the wall being of a good thicknesse, this worke within it would first serue for a place to stand drie in, making the walking place aboue broader; and easily for defence in time of warre: and for more securitie, it might within be filled vp with earth. It might also be the workemans chance, to build about an Hill: and to frée himselfe thereof from the waters, that alwayes with the rayne fall from it, make the earth to sinke, it is therefore necessary for the workeman to set the like buildings against such an Hill, whereby he shall be assured from such suspicion, and it will also be a great strengthening to the worke. The like inuention Raphael Durbin vsed at Monte Mario, a little aboue Rome, in the Vineyard of Clement the seuenth, by him begun in the time of the Cardinall Ieronimi Genga: and without Pisera, for the defence of water against a Hill, was made the like.

Ancient workemen, in this kind of ruſticall worke, haue vſed many and ſeuerall kinds of Buildings, as you may ſée hereunder, wherewith a workeman may helpe himſelfe in many things, as neceſſitie requireth : the meaſure ſhall be, that the light ſhall be a perfect fourcſquare, and the wall betwéene both, ſhall be a fourth part leſſe. That Supercilie or Architraue, ſhall haue the fourth part of the light, and ſhall be made of Pennants which run vpon the Center in vnequall numbers : and aboue the Supercilie ſhall be layd an halfe Circle, deuided in nine equall parts, the lines being alſo drawne vpon the Center. The Cunei or Arch-ſtone being formed, and the thrée pieces layd betwéene it, with the Facie aboue it, will in this ſort be an euerlaſting worke. But for that the Cunei of the Architraue muſt lye faſt, it ſhall be needfull to fill the halfe Circle with Brickes. And for the more beautifying, you may vſe Rootes, as the ancients vſed to doe, as you may, at this day, ſée in Rome at S. Coſmians and Damian ; which, although the ſtones be old , yet it is very ſtrong.

AS in the beginning I said, the workeman may vse this Gate in diuers places, but not for Fortresses, for the passage through serues not for Artillerie, or other great preparation for wars; neuerthelesse, this part may well serue for the outtermost Port or Gate : The proportion shall be, that the light or opening shall be twice so high as the bredth. The Arch-stones of the halfe Circle shall be nine; drawing vpon the Center of the Circles. The Facie vnder the Arch shall be the seuenth part of the Gates; from the Facie downewards to the Pauement, shall bee deuided into seuen parts and an halfe, and shal be sire stones broad: three whereof, shal be each a part and an halfe, the other three of one part: and thus the seuen parts and an halfe are deuided. The height of the middlemost Arch-stone, or the closing stone, which you will, shall be halfe as broad as the Gate. The Facie aboue the Arch-stone, must bee as broad as a foot, that is, the thinnest part of the sayd Stone: but the middlemost Arch-stone, and also the foote vnder, shall be a fourth part broad;

Of the Thuſcana

*T*He proportion of this Gate, viz. the opening is twiſe as high as broad: the Pilaſter and the Arch are a fift part of the bredth of the light: the great Pillar ſhall be once ſo broad againe, and the height of fire bredths. The height of the Baſe ſhall be a fourth part, and the Capitall a third part, and ſo great the Capitall or impoſt vnder the Arch ſhall bee. The Facie in the place of the Architraue ſhall be as high as the Capitals: the Freeſe alſo as much, and alſo the Cornice, following the rule aforeſapd: the reſt map bee found with the Compaſſe.

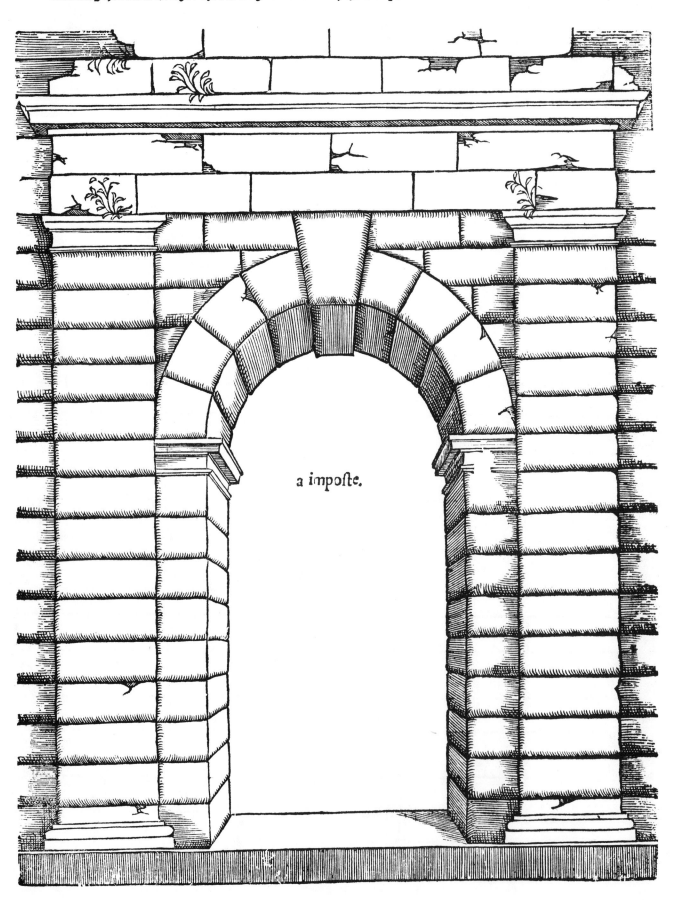

a impoſte.

ALthough the Gate hereunder set downe is much different from the fashion of the rest, yet, for that it is Thuscan worke, and ancient, I thought good to set it here, the which, in former time, was in Rome, En Capo de la militia Traiana, although by the decayes thereof, now not to bee seene: the two Niches or seates that stand by it on the sides, are out of their places, with which the ingenious workeman may serue his turne withall, if he place them where they should stand. The proportion of them (by the rule aforesayd, may easily be found: touching the gate it selfe, I will set downe no measure, for it is very easie to be found.

Of the Thuſcana

This maner of Gate is couered by the ſirt part of the Circle, and is very ſtrong woꝛke, yet the Pennants will not agrée with other Buildings of Stone: therefoꝛe if a man will make ſuch woꝛke, it would ſtand well in a wall of Bꝛicke. Touching the pꝛopoꝛtion, J will not ſpeake, foꝛ that it is eaſie with a Compaſſe to ſind the meaſure thereof. But the Piches oꝛ ſeates, placed by it to ſill vp the place, the woꝛkeman may, at his pleaſure, ſet where he thinketh beſt, and they may not onely ſerue foꝛ Piches, but alſo foꝛ windowes: if they ſhould bee vſed foꝛ Piches to place Images therein, it is neceſſary, that the height ſhould ercéed the double pꝛopoꝛtion of the bꝛeath oꝛ ſomewhat moꝛe, that they may be moꝛe ſit and coꝛreſpondent foꝛ Images to ſtand in, which is alwayes reſerred to the woꝛkeman.

IN times past, the Romanes vsed to mingle Dorica, Jonica, and sometime Corinthia, among their rusticall buildings; but it is no errour, if a man mixe one of them in a piece of rude worke, shewing in the same, nature and Arte, for that the Columnes mixed with rough stones, as also the Architraue and Fræse, being corrupted by the Pennants, shew the worke of nature: but the Capitals, and part of the Columnes, as also the Cornice, with the Frontispice or Geuell, shew workes of Art. Which mixture, in my conceyt, is a good sight, and in it selfe sheweth good strength, therefore fitter for a Fortresse then for any other Building: neuerthelesse, in what place soeuer the rusticall worke is placed, it will not doe amisse. In such mixtures Iulius Romanus tooke more delight, then any other man, as Rome witnesseth the same in sundry places, as also Mantua, and without Rome, the fayre Palace called vulgariter El. Te. Which, in trueth, is an example in these dayes, both of good Architecture and paynting. The proportion of this Gate is to bee made thus: the widenesse must be of double proportion, that is, twice so broad as high, iust vnder the Arch. The Pilaster shall be the seuenth part of the widenesse, and the Columnes twice as thicke as the Pilasters: the height with the Capitall shall be eyght parts. The Capitall, Fræse, Architraue and Cornice, shall bee made as is sayd before: also, the Fastigium, Frontispicium or the Geuell shall also bee shewed in Dorica order. The halfe Circle of the Arch, shall bee deuided in eleuen parts, for the stones of the Arch; but the closing stone shall bee greater: the which stone the workeman may, at his will, hang somewhat out. The Facie which do th vphold the Arch, shall bee halfe the thicknesse of the Columnes: from thence downewards, you shall deuide it into nine parts, whereof two parts shall bee for the nether part of the Columnes, the other seuen deuided into equall parts, shall be the stones which bind the Columnes, drawing crosse ouer them. And the ruder per this worke is bossed out (yet artificially) it would, in that case, shew more workemanlike, especially the stones that bind the Columnes and also the Pennants.

C 2

It is not sufficient that the worke should be strong, but it must also be made artificially, to please mens sight. Where-fore this building of stone is not onely very strong, but also ingenious and pleasing: with which inuention, the work-man may serue his turne in many things. The proportion shall be, that the opennesse in the bredth, shall be once, and halfe as much as in height: the halfe Circle is deuided into 9. parts and an halfe, because the middlemost stone is one fourth part broader then the rest. The height of the closing stone, is halfe the opennesse of the light. The flat Facie vp-holding the Arch, is the sixt part of the light: from the Facie downewards are 7. parts made: the Facie aboue the Pen-nants, shalbe as broad as the closing stone vnder it is, which may be made hanging out vnderneath the eyght part of his bredth. Touching the binding of the other stones with the Pennants, you see it playnely in the Figure.

Of the Thuscana

For that pleasure is sometimes turned into beautifying, and sometimes to ornaments surpassing necessitie, to shew Art, according to the wealth of the builder: This invention is made for pleasure, strength and beautie: for pleasure, in regard of the openesse thereof: strength, for that betwixt both, there is good store of wall, well bound together: and for beautie, because it is rich of ornaments; with which invention a workeman may helpe himselfe much, in divers things, as I have sayd. The proportion thereof shall bee, that the closed or massie worke shall bee as broad as the opening: which opening shalbe of twice so much height. The Pilasters shall be the eyght part of the widenesse, and the Columnes the fourth part. The inter-Columnes, that is, the widenes betweene the two Columnes, shall be the thickenesse of one Columne. The height of the Columnes, with Bases and Capitals, shall be of eyght parts. In the Architrave, Frese, Cornice, Base and Capitall, the rule aforesayd shalbe observed. The Pennants and other bindings are seene in the Figure: and although the Columnes surpasse the rule two parts; yet, because they stand neere together, and are made fast in the worke, more for beautie then strength, it may passe well inough, by the authoritie of ancient workemen.

IT is an excellent thing in a workeman to be full of inuention, in regard of the diuersitie of accidents which belong vnto building: for sometimes a man shall find store of Columnes, but so low or short, that they serue not for that purpose, for which men would vse them vnto, vnlesse the workeman deuise some meanes to helpe them. Therefore, if the Columne be not so high as it will reach to the Facie, that lyeth like yᵉ rose of this Gallery, then with these maner of Pennants a man may rayse it higher, if on both sides it hath good strong shoulders: touching the wayght aboue, it will be very chargeable, therefore to make it without binding of iron barres, it would not be sure: but it is lesse to be feared, if the Gallery were not so broad, but that it might be couered with stones that were all of one piece, or else to make strong beames therein. The proportion hereof shall be, that the widenesse of the Arches shalbe the thicknesse of 4. Columnes, and the height twise as much. The least space betweene the Columnes, shall be of the thicknesse of 3. Columnes, and the height, of the thicknesse of 6. Columnes, and each widenesse shall be once agayne as high as broad. The Columnes, if they be ouer-burdened with wayght, should be of the measure before set downe; the rest are clearely to be seene in the Figure: but touching Bases and Capitals, I haue sayd sufficient at the first, in the treaty of the first Columne.

Of the Thuſcana

AS this Arch is very ſtrong, conſidering the concordance of the binding, ſo alſo it is ingenious and pleaſing to view. Which invention ſhall not onely ſerve for Galleries of ſuch work, but for Bridges over Rivers; Conduits to carry water from one Hill up to another, and ſo to a Conduit. The proportion is, that the wideneſſe from one Pilaſter to another, and alſo the height, ſhall be to the Facie that beareth the Arch. The Facie ſhall be the ſeventh part of that wideneſſe or height: from the Facie townewards is devided to ſix parts: the halfe Circle into nine parts and a quarter; for the cloſing ſtone is the fourth part more then the other: the reſt may be found with the Compaſſe.

IT may sometimes fall out, that a workeman should need many holes in great walles, for the building of his House, whereunto this worke belongeth, to carry the wayght for strengthening thereof: and were there not so much need of light, some of them might be filled vp with Bricke. The proportion shall bee this, that the space of the lights and the massie wall, shall be both of like breedth, and twice so high as broad, although all such things are to bee increased and diminished at the workemans pleasure. The like worke is yet to be seene in Rome, being not very old made, but such as are in these dayes made, and stronger. The example whereof is at S. Cosmas and Damianus.

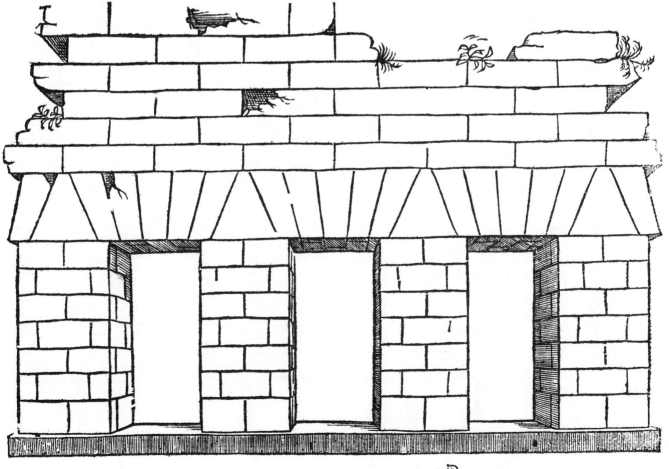

D

Of the Thuscana

IT is said, that sight preserues memory, whereby oftentimes that is made, which workemen would not haue made, if it had not beene made before in some other place, and so, at some times, you shall see in a Court or elsewhere a side of a Wall, that shall haue neyther Dore nor Windowes in it, and yet it is well set out in this rude maner and boorish kind of worke: by which invention, a workeman may helpe himselfe: In which places a workeman may set Images, or other reliques of Antiquitie. Touching the measures and proportion thereof, I will not set it downe, for I leaue it to the workeman for to heighten or make broad, as occasion serueth.

For that the moſt part of the Supercilies oʒ Architraues, as we call them, that are ſet ouer Gates oʒ other things, by reaſon of the widenes (if ẏ ſtones be not of a good bigneſſe) may yéld to the waight, whereby in time, they bʒeake and decay, as you may ſée in many places: Therefoʒe you ſhall, although it bee in great diſtance (ſo that the ſhoulders on the ſides be ſtrong) make ſuch woʒke of péces, as hereunder are in diuers wayes ſet downe: which, without doubt, will be very ſtrong: and the heauier the waight is aboue, the longer it will laſt.

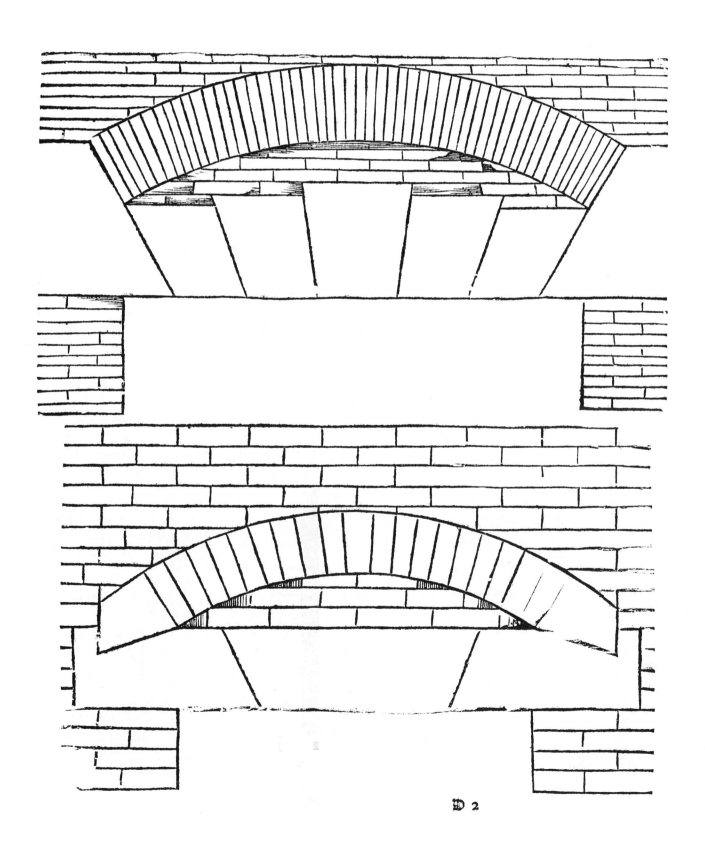

Of the Thuscana

ALthough that in Vitruuius writings there is no mention made in what maner men in ancient times made places in Palaces and common houses to make fire in, yet men find in olde buildings some shew of Chimneyes, to giue a way to voyd smoke, neyther can I find by any workeman the truth of any such matters: neuerthelesse, for that men many yeeres since haue vsed, not onely to make fires in Halles and Chambers, for their ease, but are also wont to make diuers ornaments in, and ouer such places; and for that I intend in this Booke to speake of all the Ornaments that a workeman may haue cause to vse in building, therefore I will shew some formes of Chimneyes or fire places, after the Thuscan maner, as shalbe needfull in such buildings: the one delicately made without the wall, the other rusticall worke, made within the wall.

The first rufticall workes were made in this manner, that is, péeces of ftone roughly hewen out; but the ioyning together were proportionably made.

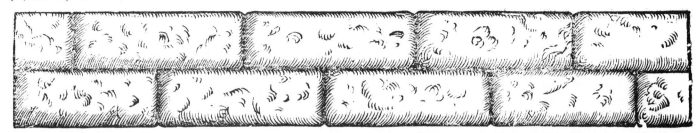

After, they deuided the ftones in more proportion and fhew, with flat lifts, and for more beautie, and for ornaments fake made thefe croffes in them.

Other workemen brought in wrought Diamonds, and made them decently in this manner.

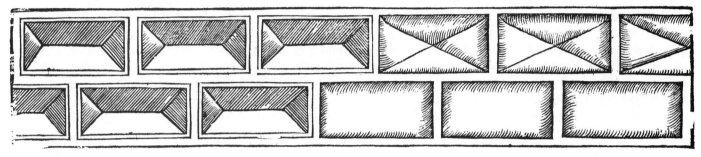

And in proceffe of time, things altered: workemen for flat Diamonds, fet flat tables, and rayfed them fomewhat higher, as in this Figure is to be féene.

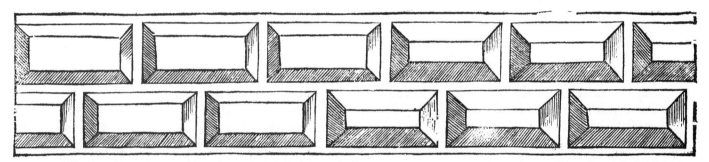

Some other workemen vfed more differences and féemelyer worke, neuertheleffe, all fuch workes haue their originall from rufticall worke, which is yet commonly called, Workes with poynts of Diamonds.

Héere endeth the maner of Thufcan worke, and now followeth the order of Dorica.

The ſixt Chapter.

THe Ancients (as we haue heard) conſidering the ſtate of their gods, ordained Dorica worke, and dedicated the ſame to *Iupiter, Mars,* and *Hercules*: but we build Temples, and dedicate them to *Chriſt, Paul, Gregory,* and ſuch holy perſonages, that were not onely profeſſed Souldiers, but alſo valiantly and boldly loſt their liues, and ſhed their bloud for the faith of CHRIST. All ſuch belong to Dorica, and not to their gods onely, but to men of armes, and ſtrong perſonages, being of qualitie more or leſſe: for whom, if a workeman make or build houſes or palaces, they muſt be Dorica: and the nobler the man is for whom ſuch worke is done, the ſtronger and ſtatelyer they ought to be; and the more effeminate that they are, the more ſlenderer and pleaſanter the building ſhall be, as I will ſhew when time ſerueth. But now we will come to the maner of the worke. *Vitruuius* ſpeaketh of this Dorica worke, in his fourth Booke and third Chapter: but touching Baſes of Columnes, hee ſpeaketh thereof in his third Booke; although ſome are of opinion, that he ſpeaketh & meaneth of the Baſes of Corinthia, for that they haue bene much vſed on the Corinthia Columnes, and Ionica. And ſome alſo thinke, that Dorica Columnes had no Baſes, hauing reſpect to many ancient buildings; as the Theater of *Marcellus,* one of the fayreſt workes in *Italy,* being the middle downewards Dorica: which Columnes had no Baſes, the body of the Columnes reſting vpon a ſtep, without any other ſupport. There is at *Carcer Tulliano* the ſignes of a Doricall Temple, the Columnes whereof are without Baſes. You may alſo ſee in *Verona* an Arch tryumphant, of Dorica worke, where the Columnes are without Baſes. Neuertheleſſe, for that workemen haue in former times made the Corinthia Baſes in another maner, as I will ſhew hereafter: Therefore I affirme, that the Baſes Atticurga, which *Vitruuius,* in his third Booke, ſo nameth, are the Dorica Baſes: and this wee ſee, *Bramant* hath obſerued in his Buildings which he made in *Rome*: which *Bramant,* being the light and Inuentor of good and true Architecture, which from Antiquitie to his time (being vnder Pope *Iulius* the ſecond) had beene hidden, we ought to beleeue. Then this Baſe of Dorica ſhall be the height of halfe the thickneſſe of a Columne: the Plinthus the third part of his height: of the reſt there ſhalbe foure parts made; one ſhall be for the Thorus aboue: the other three ſhall be ſet in 3. euen parts: the one for the Thorus aboue, the ſecond for the Trochile or Scotia: but the ſame being deuided in ſeuen parts, one part ſhall be the vppermoſt liſt, and another the vndermoſt. The Proiecture or bearing out of the Baſe, ſhall be of halfe the height, and ſo ſhall the Plinthus of each Facie hold a thickneſſe and a halfe of the Columne. And if the Baſe ſtandeth below our ſight, the corner vnder the vppermoſt Thorus, (being of it ſelfe darkened) ought to bee ſomewhat lower then the other. But if the Baſe ſtandeth aboue our ſight, the corner aboue the nethermoſt Thorus (alſo of it ſelfe darkened) ſhall be greater then the other. Thereto alſo the Scotia, darkened by the Thorus, in ſuch caſe ſhalbe made more then the meaſure appoynted. And in ſuch caſes the workeman muſt be iudicious and wary, as *Vitruuius* would haue him to bee learned in the Mathematicall ſcience, that doth ſtudy his Booke.

Torus ſuperior,
Supercilium,
Scotia   ſiue trochulus,
Aſtragali,
Scotia
Plinthus.

And for that Vitruuius hath deuided this order of Dorica by models, making the Columne of two models in thicknesse, and the height with Capitals and Bases of 14. Models; so then, the height of the Base is a Modell: the bodie of the Columns is 12. models: and the Capitall one modell, which is 14. models in all: The height of the Capitall shall be deuided in 3. parts, whereof one shall be for the Plinthus, or Abacus, wherein also the Cimatie is to be vnderstood: the second, the Echino with the Annulo: the third, the Hypotrachilo or Freese, which Hypotrachilo shall bee in thicknesse the sixt part lesse then the Columne below. The bredth of the Capitall in the vppermost part shall be in each Facie 2. Models and a sixt part: and this is according to Vitruuius wryting. Although I am of opinion, that this place is falsifyed touching the Proiecture, which, in effect, is very lame, in respect of that we see in Antiquities; therefore, after this Capitall, I will make another after my fantasie, with the particular measures thereof, better described, for that Vitruuius doeth it too briefly.

The Capitall being deuided into 3. parts, as I sayd before, I say also, that the Plinthus or Abacus should also be deuided in 3. parts, one part for the Cimatie with her Rule, List, or Fillet: but the same thicknesse deuided in 3. shall bee the List, and the other two the Cimatie. The Echinus shall also be deuided in 3. parts, and 2. third parts being for the Echinus, and the rest for the Annulo, which shall also be deuided in 3. parts, giuing each of them one. The Freese shall bee as the others. The Proiecture of each part shalbe like the height: and so doing, it shall bee made by more certaine rules, better, and more easily for shew.

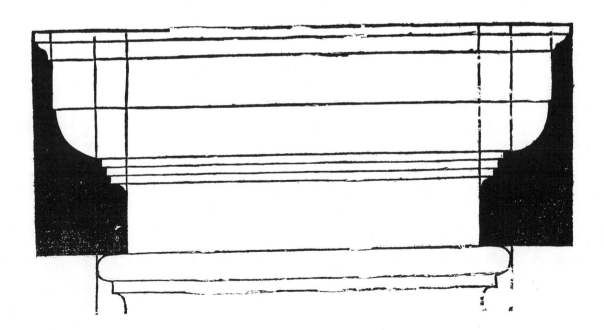

Of the Dorica

Upon the Capitall you place the Epistilia or Architrane, the height whereof shall be one Modell, and deuided in 7. parts, one shall be the Tenia or List: the Guttes or small Lists vnder the Tenia (which Vitruuius nameth Sub tenia) are in all, the first part of a modell: which height being deuided into 4. parts, the 3. parts shall bee the Guttes, and the other the List. The Guttes shall bee sixe in number, hanging vnder the Trigliphes. The height of the Trigliphes or Trigliffe shall be one Modell and an halfe, and the bredth one Modell: which bredth deuided in 12. on eyther side there shall be one left for the halfe Channels or hollowings, and of the 10. parts resting, 6. shall bee for the flat of the Trigliphes, and 4. for the Channels or hollowings in the midd. And from the one Trigliph to the other, there shall be the space of a Modell and a halfe: which space shall be right 4. square (by Vitruuius named, Methopha.) In which spaces, as you please, you may set, cut, or graue, Oxe heads, with Dishes; and that, not without secret signification. For in ancient time, when the vnbeleeuing folke sacrificed Oxen, they also vsed Dishes, & Platters thereunto, placing such things round about their Temples for ornaments. Vpō the Trigliphs, you must place their Capitals: the height whereof shall be one sixt part of a Modell. Aboue the Trigliphs or their Capitals, the Corona must bee placed with 2. Cimaties, the one aboue, the other below: and they both together deuided into 5. parts, 3. for the Corona, and two for the Cimaties. But the height of them all, shalbe of halfe a Modell: vpon the Corona, you must place the Scima: the height whereof is halfe a Modell, and to it you must adde one eyght part for the List thereof aboue. The Proiecture of the Corona shall bee of 3. parts: two be in one Modell: in the ground of the Corona, right aboue the Trigliphes, the Guttes were orderly set, as you see them in the Figure hanging beside. Also, betwéene the Trigliphes are cut Fulmines, that is, winged lightning: or you may leaue the spacies bare. The Proiecture or bearing out of the Scima must be like the height thereof: euen so, each part of the bearing out of the Corona shall haue their Proiecture like their height. But the more Proiecture the Corona hath, if the stone may beare it, the more statelyer it sheweth. This, we sée, that the ancient Romanes did obserue, as shall be shewed when time serueth, both in Figure and measure.

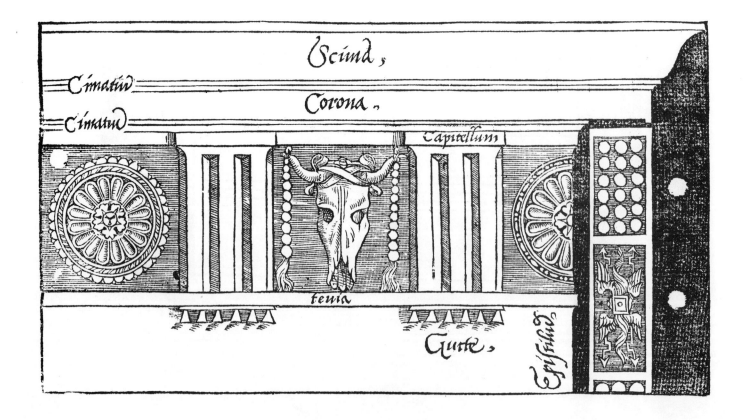

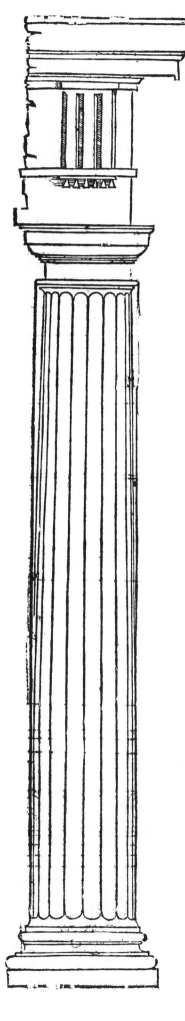

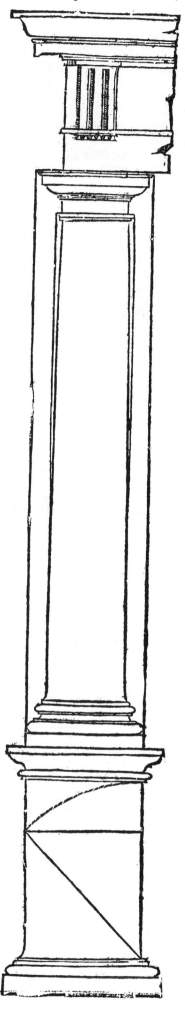

IF you will stricke or channell the Columnes, you must make 20. in number, in maner hollowed, and from the one side to the other: in the spaces of the strikes there must a strayght line bee drawne, which shall bee the side of one 4. square: which 4. square being made, placing the one foote of the Compas in the Center, and with the other touching both the one and the other end of the line, drawing it about, it will make the right hollowing, which shall be the fourth part of a Circle, as it is hereunder shewed. And if, for the raysing vp of Columnes, or for other occasions, it were necessary to haue the Stilobatum or Pedestall being not high enough, to be made higher, then the flat of the Stilobatum shall bee like the Plintho of the Base of the Columne: and the height, that is, the euen or flat shalbe thus: of the bredth shall be made a perfect 4. square; and from the one corner to the other, a line drawne for Diagonus, and the length of the Diagonus shall bee the height of the flat, as you may see it here beneath, which being deuided into 5. parts, there shalbe one part set aboue for the Cimatie, with that belongeth thervnto, and one other part shalbe giuen to the Base; and so this Pedestall shalbe of 7. parts, as the Columne is. And although this Proiecture of the Capital is contrary to Vitruuius rule, because it is Perpendicular with the Plintho of the Base: yet for that I haue seene the like in some Antiquities, and haue also placed some of the like sort in pieces of worke, I thought it not amisse to set this here, for the vse of those, that will make y like, although some of Vitruuius schollers, not hauing seene the like in any Antiquities, will contradict it: but if they marke the Abacus of the Corinthia, whose Proiecture also hangeth on the Plinthus of the Base, they will not so hastily reiect this Proiecture.

Of the Dorica

F**O**₂ that I find great difference betwéne the wzytings of Vitruuius, and the things of Rome, and other places of Italy; therefoze I haue héere set downe some, which are pet extent in wozke to be séne: which, although they bée of small fozme, without numbers oz measures, pet they are propoztioned accozding to the great, and with great diligence reduced into small fozme.   The Capitall R. was found without Rome bpon a Bzidge, standing ouer Tiber.   That Capitall V. is in Verona, in an Arch tryumphant. That Capitall T. is in Rome, in a Dozical Temple, called Al carcer Tulliano.   That Capitall P. was found in Pesaro, with diuers other commendable Antiquities: the bearing out whereof, although it be great, pet it sheweth well to the epe.   The Basements, oz Bases, and Capitall A. are at Rome, in Al foro Boario.   The Coznice, Capitall, and Impofta of an Arch marked B. are in the Theater of Marcellus.   The Coznice, Fráse, and Architraue, are also in Rome, in Al foro Boario: which I haue shewed, that wozkemen may chuse that, which liketh them best.   Hereafter I will set downe some particular measures necessary foz the wozkeman.

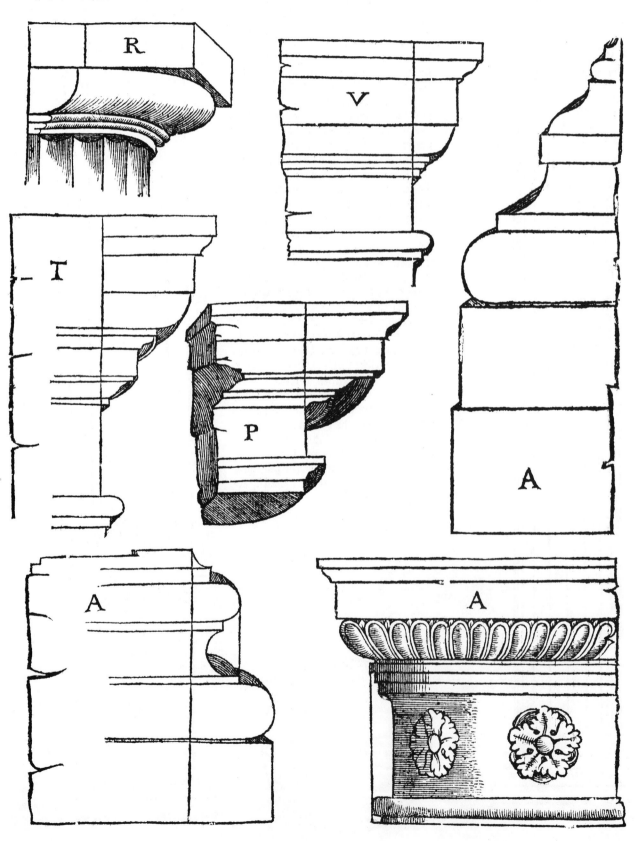

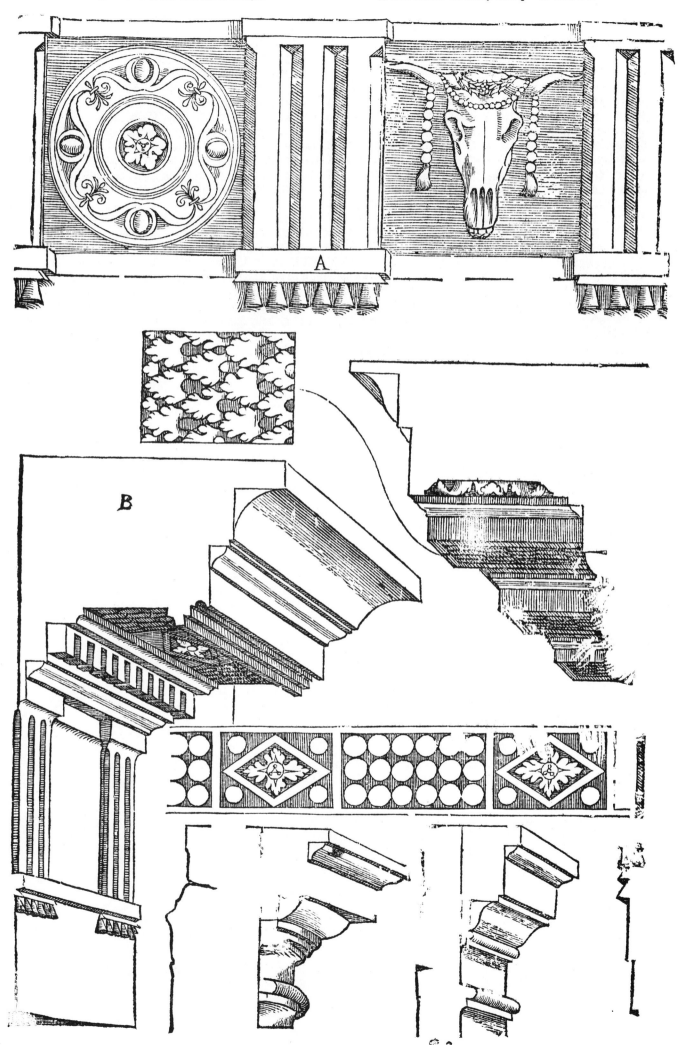

A

B

Of the Dorica

The parts of the Trigliphes and Methophes being in this order unprepared, and yet very necessary, I will take paynes to declare so well as I can. First, although Vitruuius affirmeth, that the Models of the worke Peraftilos, viz. of sire Columnes, may be distributed and deuided into 35. parts: yet I find not, that the parts may stand so, for this cause, that giuing the middlemost inter-Columne 4. Methophes, and the other spaces 3. the sayd number will not make the whole: but, as I conceaue, if you set 42. as you may see and reckon in this Figure following, as also in the worke Thetrustilos, that is, of 4. Columnes: the Booke saith, that the Forefront of the whole worke should be deuided into 23. parts, which, I assure you, cannot stand so, if you will giue the middle space 4. Methophes, and the other two eche of them 3. But, by my aduice, there should be 27. as you may see in the Figure following. Then, if the principall of the Temples be deuided into 27. parts, the Columnes shall bee 2. Models thicke, the middlemost inter-Columnes shall be of 8. Models, that is, the thicknesse of 4. Columnes, and the inter-Columnes besides, shalbe each of 5. Models and an halfe, that is, two and a quarter, and a quarter and halfe: and so shall the 27. bee distributed. And aboue each Columne his Trigliph being set, & the Trigliphes deuided with Methophes, according to the rule aforesayd: then the middlemost space shall haue 4. Methophes, and thols on the sides shall haue 3. The height of the Columne, Capitall and Architraue, &c. shall be also made according to the rule: but the height of the Fastigium or Geuell shall bee the ninth part of the length of the Cimatie, that is aboue the Corona, setting the measures under the A, upwards to the undermost Cimatie of the Corona B. The Acroteria or Pedestall marked A. upon the Fastigium shalbe halfe the height of the Fastigium or Geuell, that is, of the euen or flat, which Vitruuius calleth Timpanum, and they shall be as broad as the Columne is aboue, and the middlemost must be an 8. part higher then the other. And for that this Doore or Gate is of Dorica, and is hard to be understood, therefore I will shew in the best sort I can, both in writing and Figure. Vitruuius saith, that from the Pauement to the Laconary, that is, from the ground of the Gallery, to the roofe of the same under A. must be deuided into three parts and an halfe, and two parts shall be for the height of the lights: so sayth my Author, in my opinion. But for that a man cannot so well in a small Figure explaine the particular measures, I will make it more greater and perfecter in the next leafe.

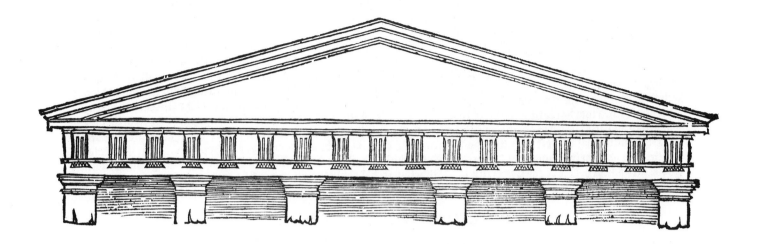

Tympane.

A

Of the Dorica

Auing made (as is before sayd) three parts and an halfe from below vpwards, 2. parts shall bee for the height of the light, which height being deuided in 12. one part shall be the bredth of the Antipagmentum or Pilaster, and the light shall be 5. parts and an halfe broad : but if the light vnder be of 16. foot, the Pilaster shalbe lessened a 3. part in the vppermost part: and the same Pilaster shall also be made thinner a 14. part aboue. That Supercilie or Architraue shall be of the same height, in the which the Cimatium Lesbium with the Astragall is to bee made : which Cimatie shall be the 16. part of the Supercilie, I meane the Astralogus Lesbium, as it is shewed in the Figure A. It seemeth, that the Author meaneth onely the Cimatie aboue the Supercilium : but as it is seene in some Antiquities, therefore it is so made, in regard of the Antipagmentum. Vpon the Supercilium, in stead of a Freese, you shall set the Hyperthyrium as high; in the which, the text sayth, men cut the Cimatium Doricum , and that Astragalum Lesbium in the Scima Sculptura, which is confused. But here I let my selfe to vnderstand, that the meaning of the Author is broken, where he sayth, Sima Sculptura : he would haue sayd, Sine Sculptura, that is, without cutting or grauing; and that is, Cimatium Doricum, together, with the Astragalum Lesbium : the proportion whereof standeth in the Figure marked A. D. Now, for that the text saith, that the Cimatic of the Corona shalbe of like height of the vppermost of the Capitals, which being so, then the Corona will be very great: to which (according to the Authors meaning) I haue giuen as much Proiecture as the height of the Supercilie is. Although such Crownes will neuer be handsome or seemely in worke, neuerthelesse, to intreat of the Ornaments, I thought good to set downe my opinion herein, and to shew it in Figure.

Corrections of the aforesayd text, by S. Serlie.

I Haue perused Vitruuius writing narrer, and with more deliberation, where hee speaketh of the Cimatie Dorica, and the Astragalo Lesbium, in the Sima Sculptura : and I find, that Sima Sculptura is meant of flat cutting, rising very little: now, for that I haue found many such like in Antiquities, viz. where the Astragals, Leaues, and Egges, &c. haue but small or little Proiecture or rysing vp , therefore I set this for instruction of Translators, to be corrected touching Dores .

A Nd for that our Author hath set this correction of the Cimatie and Astragall here, wherein, in my opinion, there consisteth no great matter, I thinke it not amisse to helpe him a little in this matter touching doores, wherein consisteth much. For where Vitruuius saith, that you must deuide the part from the Pauement to the Lacunary in 3. parts and an halfe, it must be vnderstood, aboue towards the Timpanum marked B. and then the doore would bee well, and the Corona would be like the Plinthus of the Capitall. Now, for that the text is so different in other places, as in the middle of the Models, whereof Cæsarianus sayth, that he hath found 3. or 4. sorts; so it is to bee feared, that this also is not well vnderstood. Thus much I haue (with your licence) thought good to set downe here, that the building should not be left vnperfect, as our Athor doeth. For although he sets downe the Figures of more doores, yet hee sheweth not how they shall stand in the Building aforesayd.

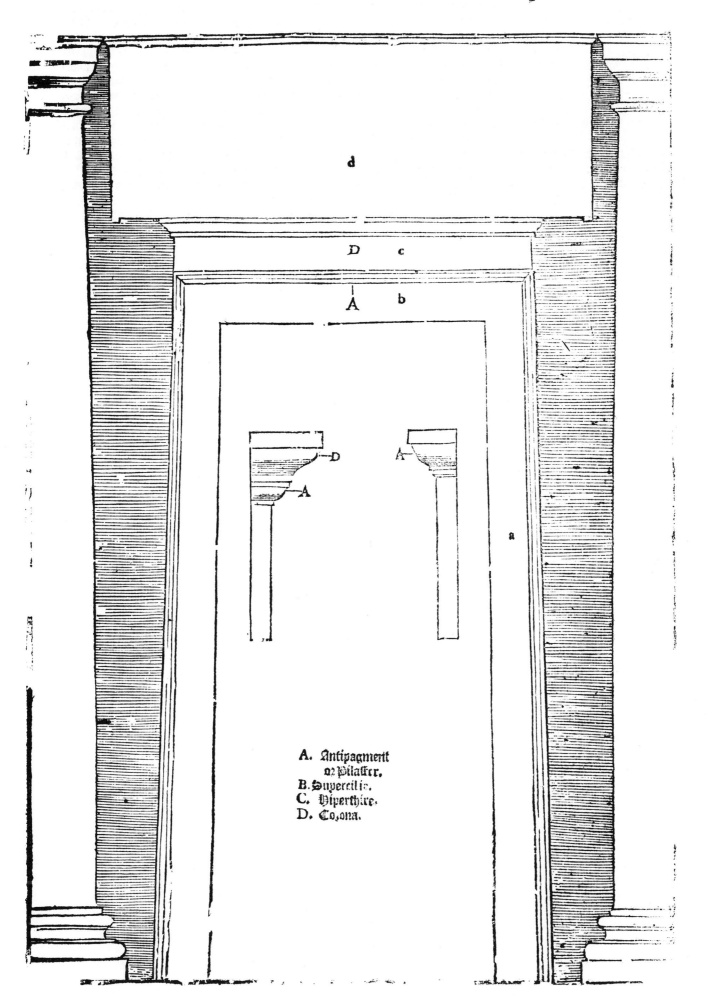

A. Antipagment
    or Pilaster.
B. Supercilie.
C. Hiperthire.
D. Corona.

Of the Dorica

FOr that men in our time doe not vse Dores lessened aboue, as they did in ancient time ; which I, for some reason, doe not discommend , yet some skilfull workeman haue many, which most part of common workemen like not. If then the workeman will make a Thiromatum or Dore simply, with little beautifying, after the Dorica order, then he may obserue this order and measure hereafter following , whereof the light or that which is open, shall be twice as high as broad. The Antipagmentum or Pilaster shall be the sixt part of the breadth of the light : without the Antipagmentum you must make an Echine with two Lists, which shall be the fift part of the Pilasters or Antipagmentum, although in the Gate, spoken of before, it is the sixt part : neuerthelesse, for that I haue seene in Antiquities, in a meane Gate of 12. parts, I haue done it here also, as I promised : you must not make the Echinus of the 4. part of the Circle, but it must be flatter and lower, which Vitruuius calleth, Cimatium Lesbium. The rest of the Pilaster shall be deuided into 9. parts, whereof 5. shall be for the greatest Facie, and 4. for the lesser Facie. Aboue the Antipagmentum, that is, the Supercilium, the Cornice shall be set of the same height that the Supercilium is, and shall bee deuided in 3. euen parts: the first, for the Cimatie with the Astragall : the second , for the Corona, with her Cimatie : and the third, for the Scima : But there is also the eyght part added thereunto, and the Proiecture bearing out or shooting ouer, shall be according to the rule aforesayd, set downe in the beginning of this Boke.

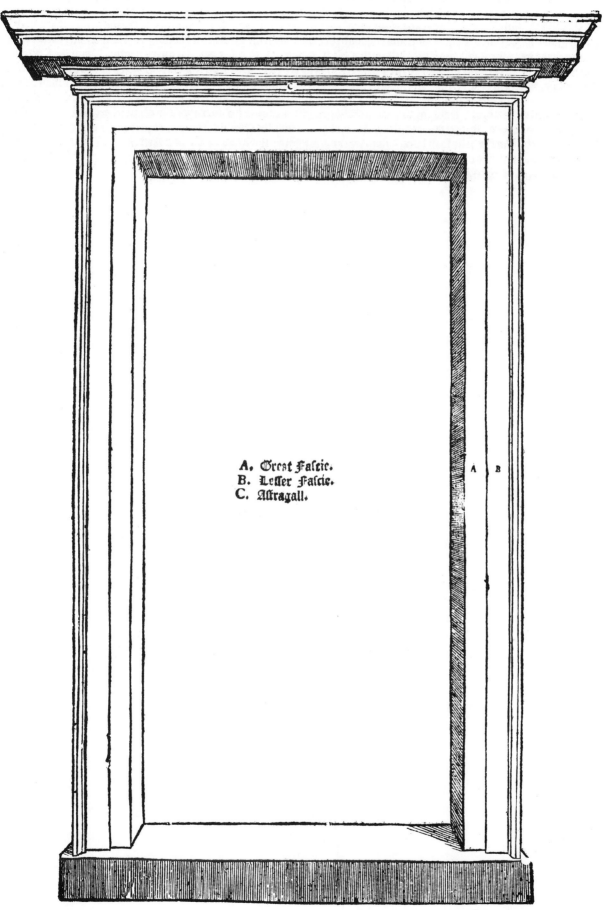

A. Great Faſcie.
B. Leſſer Faſcie.
C. Aſtragall.

Of the Dorica

ALthough that in the Order of Dorica Vitruuius maketh mention of one Doore or Gate onely, and darkly inough (in my opinion) as J shewed before, J thinke it requisite, that men shall not onely vse one sort of Doores or Gates, but also of diuers sorts and fashions, to beautifie a piece of worke, and to please diuers minds : Therefore, when a man will make a handsome Gate, he may follow this Figure: that is, to set the breoth of the Doore twice in the height; and the Pilaster must bee made of an eyght part of the light, and the Columnes of the third part of the breoth; which shalbe set 9. times in the height: and although it be more then the measure set down, yet it is not false, because some part is made vp in the wall: also some Antiquities vse it, which in such cases are not ouercurious. Vpon the Columnes you must set the Architraue as high as the Pilasters or Supercilie. The Fréese shalbe 3. parts of the thicknesse of the Columnes, vpon euery Columne there shalbe Trigliphes set, and from the one Trigliph to the other, there shall be thrée Trigliphes and fiue spaces deuided. The other particular members, as Base, Capitall, Fréese, Triglipy and Cornice, follow the rule aforesayd. Now, for that some Fastigies, Frontispicies, Couerings and Geuels, are higher then Vitruuius sets them downe, their common rule shalbe, that you deuide the Cornice from one corner to the other, as from A. to B. in 2. parts, and the halfe shall hang downewards, strayght by the Lead to C. and then the one foot of the Compasse set vpon the C. and the other foot of the Compasse on the corner A. drawing it about tt the corner of the Cornice B. that vpper part of the Circular line, shall be the due height of the Fastigium or Geuell.

The fourth part of the Circle.

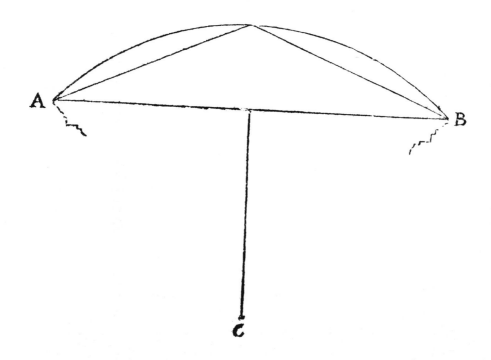

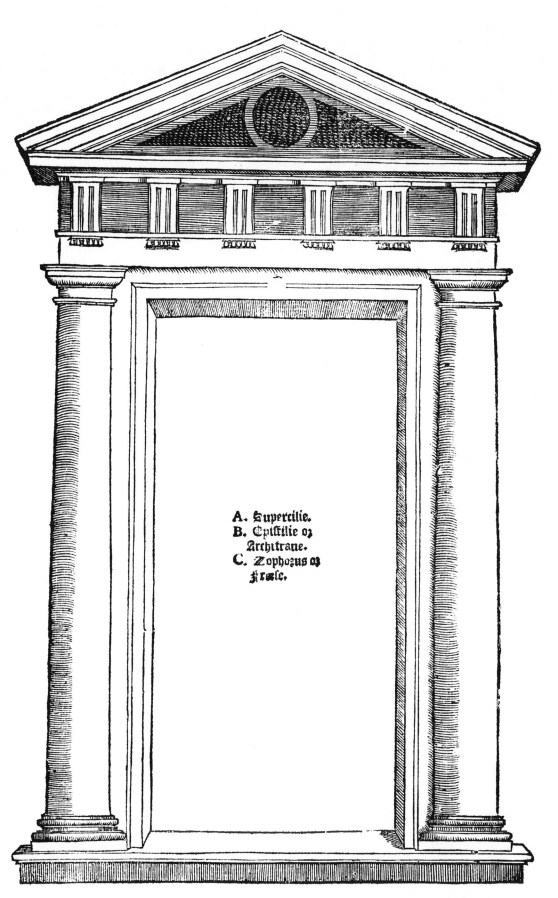

A. Supercilie.
B. Epistilie or
　　Architraue.
C. Zophorus or
　　Freese.

Of the Dorica

ALteration oftentimes is better and moze esteemed, then perfect simple fozme in her owne nature: therefoze it is the moze pleasing, when a piece of wozke is made of diuers members and parts, although of like nature, as you may perceyue in the Figure following, wherein there are Trigliphs and Mutiles, all in one ozder: which, in effect, J neuer saw in any Antiquities oz wzitings. But Balthazar of Sienne, one that read and sought out all Antiquities, may, peraduenture, haue seene some, oz at least himselfe was the Inuentoz thereof, placing Trigliphes aboue the Dooze, where they beare least stresse, and the Mutiles aboue the firme part of the Pilasters, which beare all the waygbt of the Fastigium, and in my concept, seemely, and was much commended by Clement the seuenth, who, assuredly, was a man excellently seene in all Artes. This part shall haue the light double propoztioned; but the Pilaster shall be the 7. part of the height, and the Supercilies the halfe thereof. The bzedth of the Trigliphes and Mutiles, is the halfe of the Supercilies, and the height a double bzedth, making 2. Mutiles ouer one Pilaster, and 4. Trigliphs ouer the Dooze: the spaces shall be all 4. square. Aboue the Mutiles and Trigliphes, you must set the Capitall oz Abacus: the height oz thicknesse whereof, shalbe a 4. part lesse then the bzedth of the Trigliph, ano the Cimatie the 3. part of the Abacus: The height of the Cozona with her Cimatie, shalbe as bzoad as the Trigliph is, and the Scima also as much: the bearing of the Cozona befoze, shall bee as much as the space from one Abacus to another, that in the ground there may be perfect foure squares: But the Pzoiecture oz ouer-bearing both on the right hand and on the left, shalbe halfe so great as befoze. The Pzoiecture of the Scima and the Cimatie, shall be each accozding to their height. That Fastigium iu the highest part, shall be a fift part of the widenesse, from the one cozner of the Scima in the right line, to the other.

Mutiles.

Of the Dorica

ALthough a man may make diuers kinds of Gates in Dorica worke, yet for that at this day men couet after nouelties, especially, when they are made by rule and reason, although the Columne, Froese and other members are
mixed with rusticall Building, yet herein you may see forme and fashion: and whereas I haue sayd, that a man
should vse rustical and boorish workes in Forts and Fortresses; now this may serue for a change, but not without,
for receiuing of shot in them, &c.   The light thereof is also double in height: the Columnes two times so broad as the Pilasters, being 14. Models high, with Capitals, Trigliphes, Fastigium, &c.   Let the Reader doe his pleasure further
herein, for me thinkes there consisteth little herein, and there is inough sayd as before.

My meaning was, in the beginning of this Booke, to speake onely of the ornaments of the fiue Orders of Buildings, as of Columnes, Pedestals, Epistiliums, Zophorus, Cornices, Gates, Windowes, Niches, & such like things. But, after that I determined to augment and enrich this Volume, in shewing diuers Facies or foreparts of Edificies, Temples, Palaces and Houses, &c. And for that, when as the Columne standeth vpon the ground, they are commendable; yet oftentimes it falleth out, that men haue not their Columnes thicke inough, nor long inough, as they desire, so that it is necessary to place Pedestals vnder them: therefore I haue made this order following, the proportion whereof shall be as followeth: that the widenesse shall be double in the height: the Pilaster with the Arch, shalbe a 12. part of the widenesse: the Columne as thicke againe: the inter-Columne halfe the widenesse of the light or Dore: the widenesse of the Niches, 2. Columnes thicke, and 4. in height: the Pedestals, 4. Columnes thicke in height: his bredth, and the rest, as is before sayd. The Columne, with the Base and Capitall, shalbe 9. parts high: the Epistilium is halfe a Columne thicke: the Trigliph of the same bredth, and twice so high with the Capitall. The Trigliphes placed as you see them, the Corona and the rest of the members shalbe made as is before shewne. The height of these Geuels somewhat exceed Vitruuius writings: but I haue seen such an other, somewhat higher, in Antiquities, being made of the sixt part of the Corona in length. The Acroteria shalbe of height and bredth like the Columne aboue, without Cornice: and the middlemost a sixt part higher, as also the Columne a 9. part, being made fast in the wall.

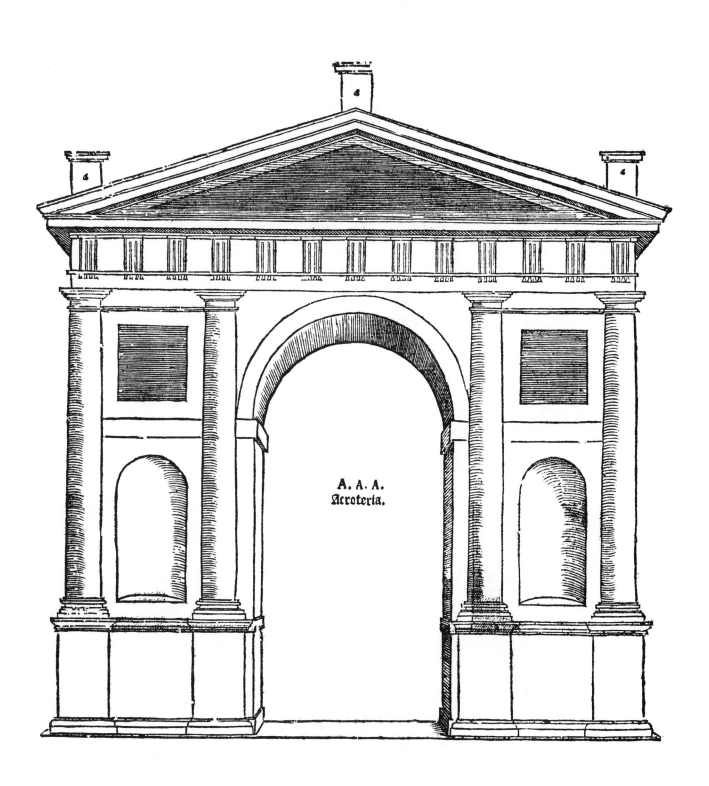

A. A. A.
Acroteria.

This Figure following, may be vſed by the learned workeman for divers things, and may bee altered according to the accidents that ſhall happen: it will alſo ſerue for a Painter to beautifie an Altar withall, as men at this day doe in Italy: it may alſo ſerue for an Arch tryumphant, if you take away the Baſement in the middle. Likewiſe, you may beautifie a Gate withal, leauing out the wings on the ſides: ſometimes, for ſetting foorth a Window, a Niche, a Tabernacle, or ſuch like things: which proportion ſhall be made thus, The openneſſe or wideneſſe ſhall bee deuided in 5. parts, and one of them ſhall be the thickeneſſe of the Columnes: the Facies or Liſt round about ſhall bee halfe a Columne thicke. The height of the light ſhall be the thickneſſe of 7. Columnes, and the Baſe and Capitall together, of the thickeneſſe of a Columne, and in all, ſhall be eyght parts high. That Pedeſtall ſhalbe 3. Columnes thicke in height, the bredth or forepart like the Plinthus vnder the Columne. The inter-Colũnes on the ſides ſhall be one Columne thicke, and in the Corners ſhall ſtand the fourth part of a Columne: the wings on the ſides, wherein the Niches are, ſhall be of the thickneſſe of a Columne and a halfe, but the Niches a Columne broad, and 3. in height. The Architraue ſhall haue the halfe thickneſſe, and the Trigliph alſo as broad, but the height without the Capitall ſhall bee a 4. ſquare, and two 3. parts; whereby, placing the Trigliphes on the right ſide, and on the left, right aboue the Columnes, and betwéene both 3. Trigliphes, and 5. Methophes more: the deuiſions ſhall rightly come to be 4. ſquare in the ſpaces. The Corona and the Frontiſpicie, and all the other parts, as well below as aboue, ſhall be made as is taught in the beginning. And for that the Trigliphes on the ſides differ from Vicruuius doctrine; yet, notwithſtanding, I haue ſéene them in Antiquities ſtand vpon the corners, the workemen may, at their good pleaſures, make them in worke, or beare them out, as occaſion ſhall ſerue. Further, I had no meaning to ſet any grounds or platformes in this fourth Booke, for that it is intended to be intreated of elſewhere; yet ſuch forefronts as are hard to be vnderſtood, I wil ſet the Ichnographie or ground, for more light to the Reader.

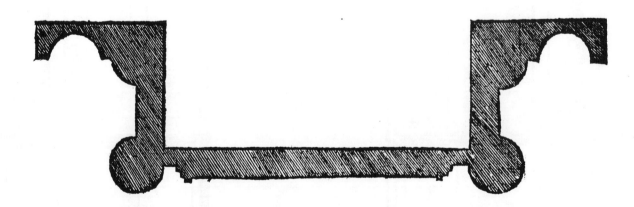

Although in Antiquities, as farre as is found, when workemen had placed the Epistilia vpon the round Columne, they set nothing else but the Fastigium vpon that, vsing the same order in Churches and Temples, and not in any other buildings: Neuerthelesse, I will not omit to set downe some maner of Houses without Arches: for if you will make Arches with their fouresquare Pillars and round Columnes before them for beautifying of the worke, séeking to make much light in your Gallerie, the Pillars with the Arches will hinder a great deale of light: Then if you will set the Arches onely vpon the round Columnes, that were altogether false, for that the foure corners of the Arch would surpasse the roundnesse or body of the Columnes: therefore I intend, to make some Houses and other Buildings without Arches, both of this order, and also of the other. This shall therefore be made in this maner, that the greatest inter Columne shall be the thicknesse of foure Columnes, and the smallest of one and an halfe. The height of the Columnes shall be of nine parts, with Bases and Capitals: the Architraue, Fréese, and Cornice, &c. shall bee made according to the former rule: the widenesse of the windowes are of two Columnes thicknes: the height a fouresquare and two third parts: and their Pilasters one sixt part of the light, hauing the Cornice aboue, like the Capitall. The dore shall be of the breoth of thrée Columnes, and seuen in height: and so shall the lights of the windowes, and of the doores, bee all one height. The Trigliphes and Methophes shall bee deuided, as you may perceiue. The second Story shall bee lesse or shorter by a fourth part, according as Vitruuius giueth counsell: so also, shall the Architraue, Fréese, and Cornice bee a fourth part lessened: the windowes thereof, with the Pilasters, should bee as broad as the lowest. The ornaments in the Niches shall stand in Perpendicular, with the Columnes: and the hollowings of the Niches, shall be as broad as the inter-Columnes: their heights shalbe of two foure squares and an halfe: the third Story shall be shorter a fourth part then the second: The Architraue, Fréese and Cornice accordingly: but being together deuided in thrée parts, one shalbe for the Architraue, the second, for the Fréese and Mutiles or Mogdilions, and the third, for the Cornice: You shall find the particular measures hereof after the Composita: the windowes shall also be as broad as the lowest, but the Niches shall be a fourth part lesse: the rest you shall lightly find.

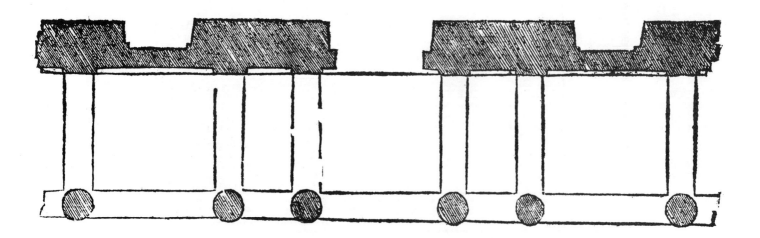

ALthough in the Thuscan Order, in the Facie 13. I haue shewed the like inuention, this, notwithstanding, differeth: for that this Gallery would bee round rosed, and where the Arches are, the crossings would be made as you see in the ground. And for that the Columnes cannot vphold the sides, alwayes giuing out, therefore aboue the Columnes, you shall lay or fasten Iron bindings, in the sides, as you see it in the platforme, but they will last longer, if they be made of brasse. The proportion of this Facie shall be made thus: The greatest Intercolumnes shall be 4. Columnes thicke, and the least two. The height of the Columnes, with Bases and Capitals, shall hold 7. times their thickenesse. The Epistilium shall bee three foure parts of a Columne thicke: aboue the which, there shall be a halfe Circle made, the breadth thereof shalbe halfe a Columnes thicknesse: vpon the Arch you shall set the Cornice of the height of the Epistilium. Betweene both the Arches there shall be the maner of a window made, the widenesse whereof shall be like the Intercolumnes vnder it: and the List or edge, as broad as the Arch. That Cauet or Trochile, and the Echine aboue the windowes, and part of the Cornices, shall, neuerthelesse, beare out somewhat aboue the windowes, for to beautifie the same. The widenesse of the Dores shall bee two Columnes, and one fourth part. The Pilaster or Antipagmentum, shall bee a sixt part of the light: the height of the light shall reach to the Supercilie, iust vnder the Capitall of the Columne: which forme of Capitals shall follow aboue the dores and windowes. The light of the windowes shall bee in breadth two Columnes in thicknesse: but these thicknesses aforesayd, in these cases, are to be vnderstood as the Columnes fall out. The length of the light shall be a foure square and a halfe: The Niches shall also be of the same height. The Roofe aboue, or the second Stage, as you will terme it, shall bee lesse or shorter a fourth part, deuided in this sort: The Podium or part brest high, of one Columne and a halfe in thicknesse. The rest shalbe deuided in fiue; one of them shall be Architraue, Freese and Cornice. The Niches with the Ornaments shall stand in Perpendicular aboue the windowes, betweene the Arches, but shalbe in bredth fiue parts: two parts shall be the Columnes, the rest the Niches with the Pilasters. The Cornice aboue the Niches shall be the bredth of one of these Columnes: and the Bases, the halfe bredth thereof. The windowes betweene the Niches, shall in the light contayne one fourth part lesse then the dore, and of double height: but of the rest of the Ornaments (for that this worke is somewhat mixed) you shall find further satisfaction in the Ionica and Corinthia. The Trigliphes in this composition, betwixt the one and the other, will not make their Methopes right foure square, because I haue set three Trigliphes aboue each window, and as many ouer euery of the Niches, as you may see in the figure: wherein, if there be any thing wanting in the measure, or else what, I alwayes referre my selfe to the rule set downe in the beginning.

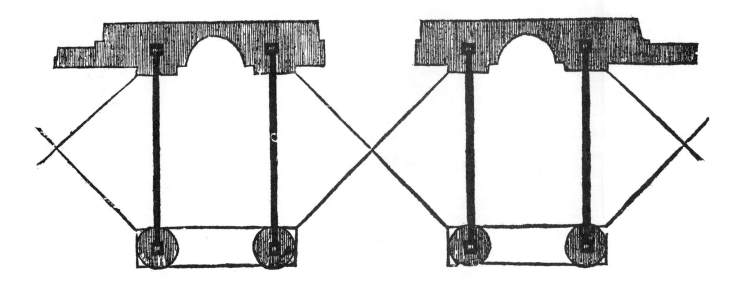

Of the Dorica

FOr that sometimes, some men will haue altogether Arches and Galleries, and for that it is confused worke, to place Arches vpon round Columnes, yet a man may make foureſquare Pillars vnder them with Baſes and Capitals, like the other. And although this houſe is whole, which is but little for a man that hath a great liuing, yet you may ſet it forth in 5. Arches, alſo in 7. Arches. The Deuiſion whereof may be, that each Intercolumne may be of the thickneſſe of foure Columnes. The height of the Columnes with Baſes and Capitals of ſire parts: and aboue them the Arches to be ſet of the breadth before, of halfe a Columne: the openneſſe ſhall bee of double proportion. Aboue the Arches you muſt place the Architraue, Fraſe, and Cornice: the height of them all ſhalbe of 2. Columnes thickneſſe: and being deuided in 3. parts and a halfe, one part ſhalbe the Architraue, halfe a part for the Fraſe, and one part for the Cornice: for the other part, you ſhall follow the rule aforeſayd. The dore ſhalbe two Columnes outward: the Pilaſter, the ſirt part of the light: but the Cornices of the dore, and the windowes, ſhall haue the height of the Capitals. The windowes ſhalbe a Columne and a halfe bearing out: and their length or height, ſhall be taken in Diagonall maner. The corner Columnes ſhalbe as broad as the other: but they ſhalbe of 8. parts and a halfe high. The ſecond ſtory aboue this, ſhalbe a fourth part leſſe: the corner Columnes, with Architraue, Fraſe and Cornice, leſſened accordingly: The windowes aboue the Arches, with the Pilaſters, ſhalbe as wide as thoſe below: but the height of the 2. foureſquares, and the Fraſe about them, ſhall bee as broad as the Supercilium: the Cornice alſo as much: The ſmall windowes a-boue them, are made for two purpoſes: The firſt, the Roomes being high, as they ſhew outwardly, will make the cham-bers and other roomes much lighter. Secondly, for neceſſity a man may make hanging chambers in them, and then thoſe lights will ſerue to good purpoſe. The third ſtory ſhalbe leſſe then the ſecond a fourth part: and the ſame being deuided in 5. parts, one part ſhalbe for the Architraue, Fraſe and Cornice: and that part deuided in 3. one part ſhalbe for the Architraue and Fraſe, and the third for the Cornice: and in the Fraſe, the Mutiles and Mogdilions ſhalbe deuided, as you ſee them. The lights of the windowes ſhalbe as the others, but they ſhall bee a twelfth part higher, becauſe they are further from the ſight: the Pilaſters, Fraſe and Cornice, ſhalbe like the other. The Frontiſpice and Arches ſhall be made, as I haue ſayd, in the dores and gates of the Order of the Dorica: for beautifying, or to place another row of Arches in it, you may ſet Acroteries or Pilaſters vpon them, which will paſſe well in the making of their fire places, or chimneyes for auoyding of ſmoke. The ſpaces betweene the windowes, that remayne white, are left to bee paynted, as the workeman will, or at the pleaſure of the owner of the houſe. But for more ſecurity of this building, it ſhalbe ne-ceſſary to place theſe Iron bands in it, or at leaſt, ouer the Gallery, as is taught before.

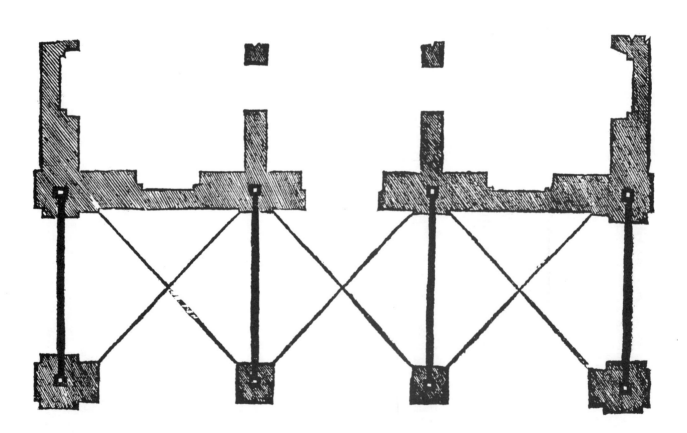

Pilasters.

Of the Dorica

IN the famous Towne of Venice, because houses stand néere together, they are forced to make their lights as they may, so that their Boilding differeth much from that Building of Italy : notwithstanding , the workeman may giue them light inough, obseruing Antiquities, which shall be thus made and deuided : You shall deuide the widenesse of an Arch in 2. parts and an halfe: whereof one shall be for the bredth of the whole Pillar: the thickenesse whereof shalbe the halfe, the round Columnes also as much : the height of the Arch shalbe of one 4. squars, and two 3. parts : you may also make them of two 4. squares, heightning the rest accordingly. The Impost or Capitall vnder the Arch, shall haue the halfe thickenesse of the Columne, according to that which is shewed before, of the Theater of Marcellus. The Doore shall be of thrée Columnes thicke in widenesse, the height of a foure square and two 3. parts: the Pilaster or Antipagmentum shalbe of the 8. part of the light: the Corona shalbe like the Capitall: but the Cima being set vpon it, you shall make the Fastigium as is before sayd, and aboue it giue more or lesse light, as the house requireth. If the building stand in a field or an open place, you make shops, which shall well fall out with the building: aboue the Columnes, the Epistilium must be set of halfe a Columne thickenesse: the bredth of the Trigliphes also as much : the height shall be made more or lesse, at the workemans will, that the spaces may be 4. square; whereupon you must set the Cornice of a 6. part higher then the Epistilium : the particular parts and measures, you shall make according to the rule before set downe. The story aboue shall be a 4. part lesse, making a Plinthus vnder the Columne, of such a height, as the Proiecture of the Cornice beareth: the rest must be deuided in 5. parts, one part shall be the Architraue, Fréese, and Cornice, (which, as before is taught) shall also bee deuided in thrée parts. The Columnes which vphold the Architraue, shall bee nine parts high, the lesser Columnes which vphold the Arch, are thinner then the rest a third part: the spaces in the middle, vnder the Arches shall bée twice so wide as the sides; so then, the Cornices being placed vpon the Columnes which beare the Arch, and the halfe Circle made vp to the Architraue, also, the eyes or holes besides the Arch, then it will bee excéeding light: and where there wanteth a Chamber, you may shut the middlemost lights, and the sides shall serue for windowes. Neuerthelesse, this order being obserued both without and within, it will not stand much amisse ; for the place shut vp, shall be for a Fire place or Chimney, which ought alwayes to bee made betwéene two windowes , like to a mans face, where the windowes are the eyes, and the Chimney the nose, which alwayes drawes the smoke.

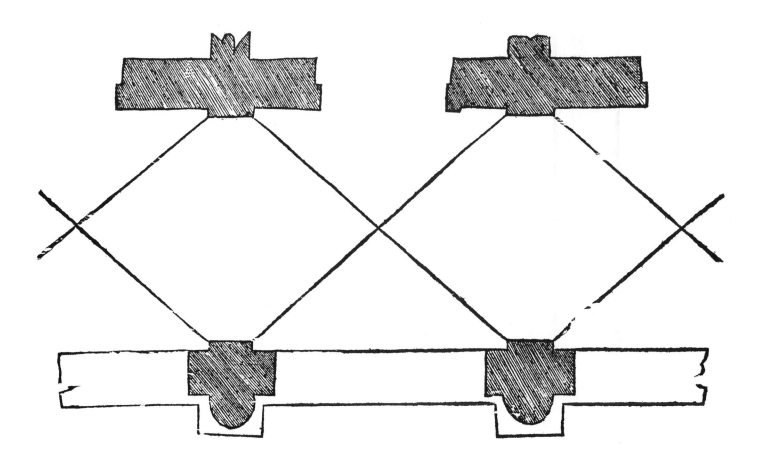

Of the Dorica

To deuide this present Facie, sayth the Author (for otherwise he maketh no preface) you shall deuide the breadth in 14. parts, and one of these parts shall be for a Columne: the middlemost inter-Columne shall be of 6. parts, and the other each of 3. parts: the windowes shall be of a Columne and an halfe: the height of them, two 4. squares and an halfe. The Pilasters shall be of the sixt part of this light: the windowes in the first story are of the same breadth: the nethermost, shall be a perfect 4. square, and the other of a 4. square and an halfe. The port or Gate shalbe 5. Columnes wide, that the Columnes may haue a fast foundation: the height of this Gate is a 4. square, and of two 3. parts: the Arch-stones, and the rest, you shall see sufficiently in the Figure: from below vnder the Arch, vntill you be aboue the Facie, shall be 2. Columnes thicke. And although that all other stories or buildings, being one story aboue another, would alwayes bee shortened a fourth part: yet in this case, (by my aduice) for that the compartition of the Columnes, being aboue this rusticke worke, and that the rough worke should not take too much place when it is of sufficient strength, it is requisite that it should bee of the same height. Aboue the first order, as you shall make a Podium of a Columne & an halfe high, whereon you must set the Columnes in order (as it is taught) the height without the Podium shall be deuided in 5. parts, whereof 4. shall bee for the Columnes, the other for their ornaments, whereof the Trigliphes shalbe deuided, as you see, obseruing the rule aforsayd. The middlemost shalbe dealt thus, that the small Columnes shall be the halfe of the greater, and the middlemost inter-Columne shalbe as broad againe as those that stand on the sides, which shall be like eyes of the windowes. Aboue the windowes, to make more light, you shall make the eyes, and aboue the smallest spaces in the middle, you shal make that you see here in the Figure, for to accompany the same eyes. And although there rest particular parts, you shall alwayes seeke them forward, where you shall be assured to find them. The third order or story, and that which belongeth thereunto, shall also be made lesse a 4. part; but the windowes as broad as the lowest, as also their heights, and all other things; you may easily find with the Compasse. The raysing vp in the middle without the Frontispicium, shall bee halfe the third order in height: for the rest, a workeman may adde and diminish at his pleasure.

BEfore, I haue shewed in two figures, how to make the Facies or forefronts of Houses after the Venetians maner: but for that in such works men would willingly haue some places bearing out, which are, for the most part, made ouer the water, for fresh ayre of the water, whereon the most part of buildings haue their fayrest forefronts or Facies; as also, to see the tryumphes oftentimes made there in Boates and Ships : to which purpose, the sayd bearings or iuttyings out serue well, and yet neuerthelesse, are vnseemely things, and haue no other supporters but the Mogdilions : Now, such things as haue not their foundation strongly layd and made, hurt the walles of the house or building, whereof ancient workemen were very carefull, and made no such bearing out, but onely Cornices : therefore I say, if a man will make any such things in any building with good aduice, it is necessary that the first wall should bee so thicke, that it may stand so farre out as the flat of the bearing out requireth, as may bee perceyued in the round : and for that the middlemost wall standeth out more then the sides, if you will not make it so thicke, then you may make a strong Arch within, to vphold the middlemost, although it be hollow and of small weyght. This bearing out, is to bee vnderstood aboue the Facies of the rusticall worke : which being made, then the compartement of the Facies shall bee aboue this, so that the middlemost part shall be of three portions, and the sides of three and an halfe, I meane within the walles, as the ground sheweth. The height of this second order or story, shall be like the vndermost, according to the rules aforesayd : and first, you shall make the Podium of an indifferent height, to leane vpon : then that which resteth shall be deuided in fiue parts, one of those shall bee the Epistilium, with the rest of his parts. The widenesse of the middlemost part, must be thus : the opennesse with the Arch must be as great againe as the sides, and the height doubled ; so the Architraues being set vpon the Columnes, for the vpholding of the Arch, all the Windowes shall bee vpon a rowe : likewise also, for more commoditie of light and ornament, the eyes of the Windowes shall bee made. These ornaments, together with many other things, if a man, in regard of cost, will not make them of Marble, or of other stones, they may be set foorth with painting. The third order or story shall also bee a fourth part lesse then the second : and so euery other part thereof accordingly, following the rule aforesayd : and although the Ionica be set before the Dorica, which ancient workmen sometime haue done, you shall find the proportion thereof hereafter in his place.

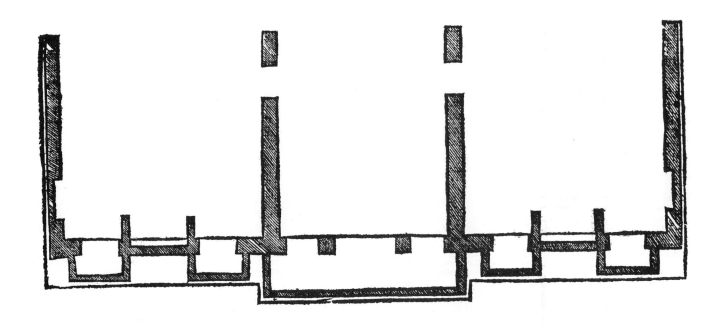

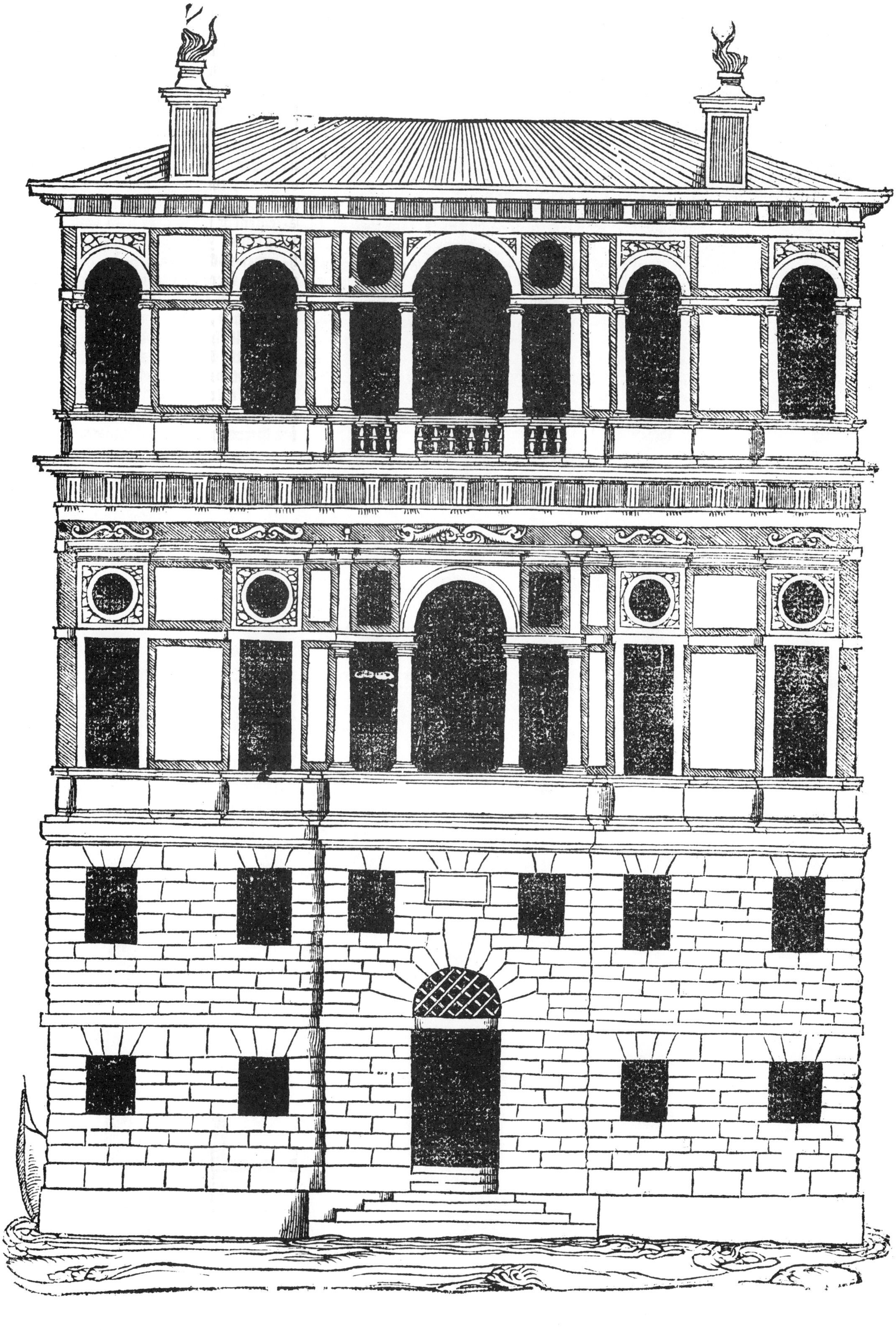

Of the Dorica

Although the workeman hath séene so many inuentions in this Dorica worke, yet they will not further him or ornaments of Chimneyes: but I will set two sorts thereof here in Figure, one indifferent whole, & in the thicke-nesse of the wall, for a small round Chamber or House: the other, for a greater place without the wall, drawne with Mogdilions: for if a small Chamber should be cumbred with a Chimney, it is requisite to make it wholy within the thicknesse of the wall, and the height of the opening being made, according to the situation of the place, shall be deuided into foure parts and an halfe, and shall be the bredth of the Pilaster, but the Architraue shall containe the halfe: the Tenia or List, going round about, shall bee a seuenth part, and all his other Lists of the same bredth: the Tri-gliphes and Mogdilions, shall be halfe the bredth of the Architraue, but their height you shall take in this manner, that the Mutiles stand aboue the Pilasters, and the Trigliphes deuided betwéene both, the Methopes may haue their fouresquare of the bredth of the Architraue, but yet the Methopes or spaces betwixt the Mogdilions, shall not bee fouresquare. The Capitals of the Mutiles and Trigliphes, shall bee so high as halfe the bredth of the Trigliphes. The Corona, with the Scimatie and Scima, shall bee as high as the Architraue; and being deuided in two parts, one part shall be for the Corona; of the other you must make thrée parts, one for the Cimatie with the List, the other shall be for the Scima with his List. The bearing out of the Corona shall be so great or little, that the spaces betwéene the Capitals of the Trigliphes in the ground of the Corona, may be fouresquare, for that, if men will sit round about it, they may haue their place of sight. The Proiecture of the Scima with the Cimatie, shalbe made like that height which standeth aboue, at the discretion of the workeman. But if the Chimney be very small for a little roome or Cham-ber, then a man shall make the Pilaster of the seuenth part of the height of the opening.

Architrave, or Supercilie.

Of the Dorica

This other Chimney without the wall, shall be made thus, when the height and widenesse of the place, according to the situation, is appoynted, the same height, from the ground vp to the Architraue, shall be deuided in 4. parts, one part for the Architraue, Freese, & Cornice, their parts being made according to the rule aforesayd: and whereas they shew greater, that is, because men see them vnderneath, the bredth of the Modiglions shall be the 7. part of their height: the Capitals the halfe of that breadth, and shalbe deuided as it is said of the Doricall Capitals: some lessen the breadths of these Modiglions vnderneath the fourth part, that the foote of them may giue out a fourth part, so that the Plinthus vnder the foote, is as broad as the vppermost part. But if you will make such Modiglions all of one breadth, I would commend it in a great worke, for that the vndermost drawing to the wall, & going from our sight, lessen themselues: for that the part which receaueth the smoke, is Piramides-wise, which wil not stand well in a great height. You may set it vpon the first Cornice higher or lower, as you will, or according to the situation of the place. This building of Chimneyes may be made in great forme: but if you will make them small, then you shall deuide the height from the Pauement to the Architraue in 5. parts, whereof one shall be for the Cornice: the breadth of the Modiglions shall be the ninth part of that height, the Capitall of halfe the breadth: and thus it will bee more seemely in an indifferent meane forme. This I speake by experience, for that I haue obserued this greatest measure in small formes in making of Chimneyes, but they proue too great.

The end of the Dorica order: and here followeth the Ionica.

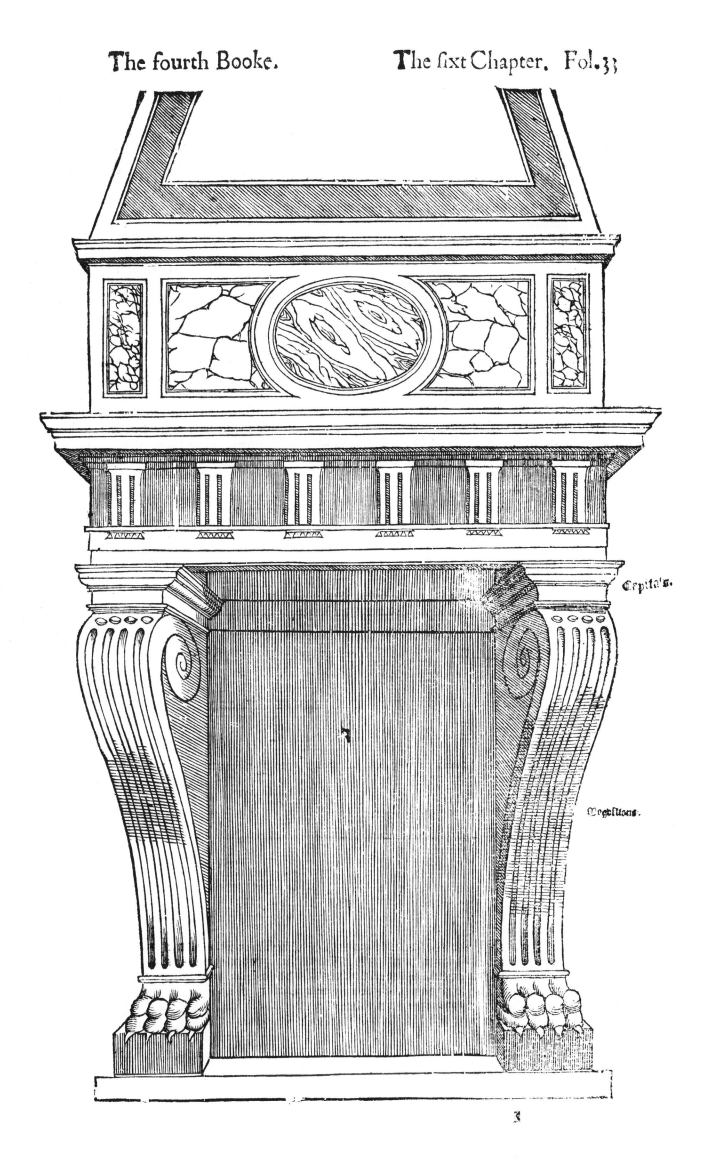

Capitals.

Modilions.

Itruuius speaketh of Ionica, in his fourth Booke and 1. Chapter: and as I also said, the ancient Pagans tooke this kind of worke from women, and ascribed it to *Diana, Apollo, & Bacchus,* &c. But we that are Christians, hauing a Temple to make of this worke, we will dedicate it to such Saints as are of nature, eyther weake or strong : so likewise, common workes are fit for peaceable people, men, neyther great workemen, nor all too simple in workemanship : and such workemen are fittest for such worke. Now let vs come to the measures : the Ionica Columne, by a common rule, must be of 8. parts, with Capitall and Base : although that *Vitruuius* sayth, it must be of 8. parts and an halfe; so may men sometimes make it of 9. parts and more, as some indifferent workemen haue affirmed. But this, I say, shall be made of 8. parts, which must hold his thicknesse below, and so shall their Bases be of halfe the same thickenes, which *Vitruuius* setteth downe diligently, in the 3. Booke, and in the third Chapter of the same Booke, in this maner, that the Base aforesayd, must be of halfe the Columnes thickenesse, but the Plinthus must be of the third part thereof: which Plinthus taken of, you shal make seuen parts of the rest; whereof three shall be for the Thorus, and foure shall bee for the two Scoties or Trochiles, with their Astragals and Lists, so that each Trochile must haue his Astragall. The Astragall shall be the eyght part of the Trochile, the Lists halfe the Astragals. Although each Scotie with the Appendances are all of one height, yet the vndermost shalbe greater; for it shall shoot out vnderneath, to the outtermost part of the Plinthus. The Proiecture on eyther side, shall be one eyght part, and one sixt part: so that the Plinthus on eyther side shall be one fourth part, and one eyght part more then the thickenesse of the Columnes. Now, for that the Cincte or List is suppressed by the greatnes of the Thorus, I am perswaded that it ought to be made the halfe greater then the other. Obserue in all the members and parts with discretion, as should be vsed in the Dorica.

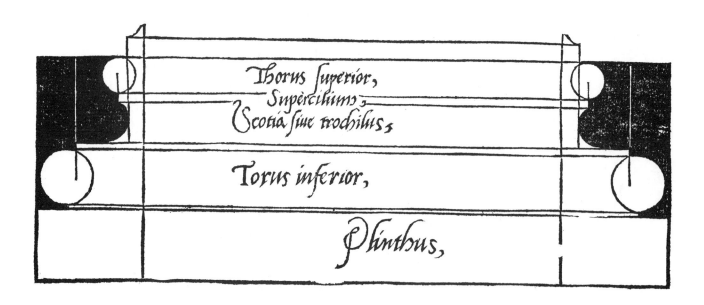

FOR that the Base of the Ionica Pillar, written of by Vitruuius, contenteth not the greatest workemen, because the Thorus is very great, and the Astragall small, vnder so great a member, according to the iudgement of expert workmen, that haue oftentimes disputed the same, with reuerence, and much respect of such an Author; I will frame one here according to my opinion. The Plinthus being made, as I sayd before, the rest shalbe deuided in three parts, whereof one part shalbe for the Thorus: the other vnder that Thorus deuide in sixe parts; one of them for an Astragall, the Cinthe the halfe thereof. The Cinthe or Supercilie vnder the

Thorus, muſt be as broad as the Aſtragall. The reſt is for the Scotie or Trochile: the other three parts that reſt, ſhall alſo be deuided into ſixe parts: one for the Aſtragall, one halfe for the Cinthe, and the vndermoſt alſo the like: the reſt is for the Scotie comming at vnderneath, as is before alleaged.

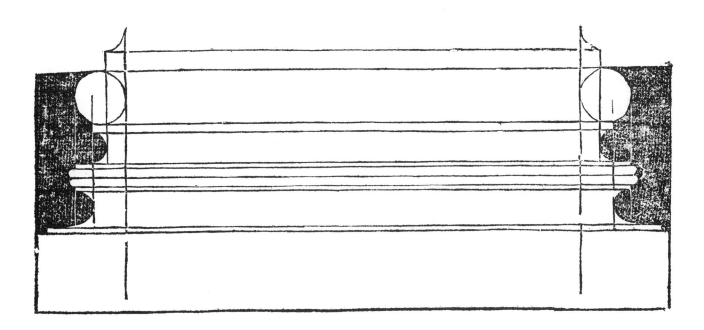

The Ionica Capitall ſhall bee made in this maner: the height ſhall be the third part of a Columne, and the former part of ỹ Abacus the breadth of a Columne in thicknes: to it alſo muſt be added the 18. part, which in the whole, ſhall be nineteene parts, but inwards a part and a halfe: at eyther end the line Catheta muſt be drawne, which ſhall containe 9. parts and an halfe, which is the halfe breadth of the Capitall: one part and a halfe ſhalbe for the Abacus, which Corners you muſt make like the right or left ſide, for both are ancient: the 8. parts that are hanging vnder the Abacus, ſhall be for the Volutes. And for that it would be troubleſome in this ſmall Figure, eſpecially to ſet downe before your eyes the numbers, therfore in the Leafe following, I will ſhew it better in great, and therewithall the maner how to make the ſtrickes in the Columnes, with the Figure of the ſide of the Volutes, and of the Capitals. But if the Columne be of 15. foote downwards, then it ſhall be leſſened a ſixt part aboue, as it is written of the Thuſcan order: but if it bee of 15. foote vpwards, then I referre you to Vitruuius, touching the ſame, in his third Booke and ſecond Chapter.

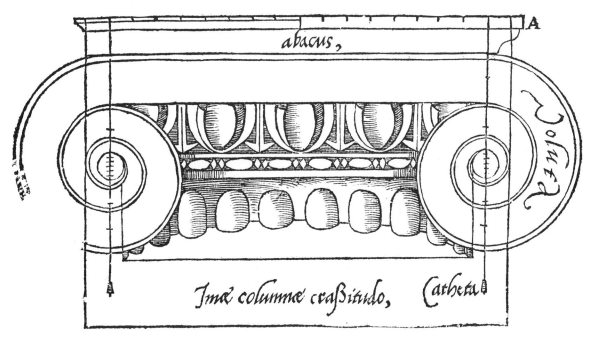

Of the Ionica

WHen the Capitall of this Ionica is made, you muſt make the Uolutes, which ſhall bee made by the line, called Catheta, which wee heere call, The right Lead: and when you leaue the Abacus vnderneath foure parts, then the firſt part ſhall be for the eye, and ſo there yet reſteth three parts from the eye downewards; and ſo in all, they make eyght, as is before ſayd: the eye ſhall be deuided in ſixe parts, and the numbers ſet therein, as it is hers ſet downe; then plac one foote of the Compas vpon the poynt 1. and the other foot vnder the Abacus, drawing netherward, vp to the Catheta, to the eyght part; then letting the ſame foote of the Compaſſe ſtand, bring the other foot of the Compaſſe to 2. and draw it vpwards againe to the Catheta. Then hold the foot of the Compaſſe there, bringing the other foote to 3. drawing it then downewards againe to the Catheta: keeping that foote there alſo, bring the other vpon the poynt 4. then drawing it againe to the Catheta, holding the Compaſſe there, the foot will come vpon 5. ſo drawing about, doe likewiſe to 6. and then it comes to ſhut with the eye; there you may make a roofe, if you pleaſe. The reſt of the particular members you ſhall eaſily find with the Compaſſe. The ſtrickes of the Columnes, which wee call Chanels or hollowings, ſhall be 24. in number, and one of them ſhall be 5. parts: whereof 4. ſhall be for the Guttes or Chanels, and the 5. for the Liſt, by Vitruuius called Strix: and ſo from one ſide of the flat of the Liſt to the other, you ſhall draw a ſtrayght line, the middle whereof ſhall be the Center of the hollowing out. But if the workeman pleaſe ſometimes to make a thinne Columne to ſhew thicke, then there muſt bee 28. ſtrickes: the Abacus of this Capitall is as broad on the ſides, as before: which ſides are proportioned according to that, which is ſayd before. Friendly Reader, I haue layd this Uolute, according to my ſimple vnderſtanding, becauſe Vitruuius writing is hard to vnderſtand, and which is more, promiſed the ſame Figure in the laſt Booke, together, with diuers other ornaments, which Booke is not to bee found.

S. Serlii vpon the ſpeach aforeſayd.

LOuing Reader, there are many things which cannot fully, from poynt to poynt, bee ſhewed in Figure, vnleſſe the workeman muſt helpe himſelfe by practiſe, like as the Cincte or band of theſe Uolutes: which (if the Capitall bee very great) will ſtand well: if the bredth contayneth the fourth part of the eye, and if the Capitall bee of indifferent greatneſſe, then it muſt be made of a third part of the eye: but if the Capitall be ſmall, then it muſt bee the halfe of the eye, alwayes at the workemans diſcretion: for I haue ſeene it ſo in Antiquities, although they differ. The thickneſſe being marked aboue, vnder the Abacus, then you muſt place the Compaſſe a little below the figure 1. from aboue the Catheta downewards: then agayne, you muſt place the Compaſſe a little aboue the figure 2. drawing your line from beneath vpwards to the Catheta.

Now, whereas I haue ſayd, that the laſt Booke promiſed by Vitruuius, is not found, by meanes whereof, diuers opinions are ſpred abroad touching the ſame, ſome affirming, that in Vitruuius time, there were many vnſkilfull workemen (as there are now alſo) hauing better fortune, then good vnderſtanding: (others) that preſumption, vnter to vnſkilfulneſſe, beareth ſuch ſway among common workemen, that vnderſtand not themſelues, it is thought, that Vitruuius refuſed, or at leaſt, would not publiſh it, in regard of the vnthankfulneſſe of ſuch as neglect good learning. Some alſo affirme, that it was too hard a matter for him to place them in figures; which I can hardly iudge to bee the mind of ſuch an Author. But whereas ſome affirme, that this laſt Booke was ſo pleaſing and acceptable, in regard of the figures there at large ſet out, and he being ouer-carefull in looking vnto it, was robbed thereof, among other riches and treaſures, by vnſkilfull perſons: this I beleue beſt, is as warre, which is enemy to all good Artes, which yet, at this day, is eſpecially to be lamented, for that men by the figures, might haue made diuerſities of worke in the right matter.

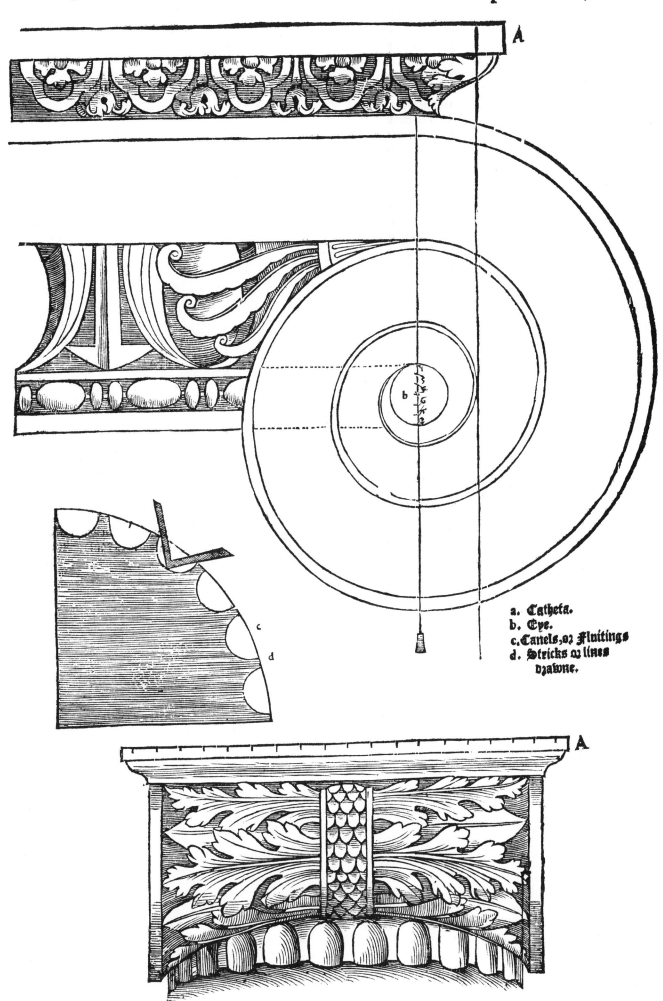

a. Catheta.
b. Eye.
c. Canels, or Fluitings
d. Stricks or lines
   drawne.

Of the Ionica.

I Haue declared hereafter, according to Vitruuius writing, how to make Ionica worke, as farre as my learning shall serue. Now, I will shew how some Antiquities in Rome, of that worke, are made, yet standing. The Capitall M. standeth yet in the Theater of Marcellus, whereof I will set downe some general measures: the forehead of this Abacus is like vnto the Columne below. The Volutes giue out a sixt part of the Abacus, and so farre out as the halfe of the Abacus: the height of the Capitall is a third part of the Columne below; but for that some workemen thought that Capitall to be but barely set foorth, they haue added the Freese which you see in the Capitall, vnto it, making the height of the Capitall of 2. third parts, of the Columnes thickenesse below, wwich Capital is at this day to bee seene in Rome, with others of the like.

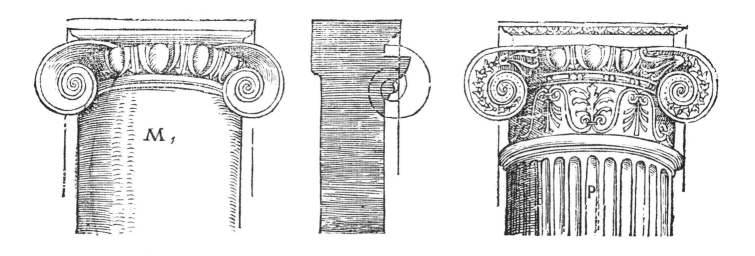

A Nd for that it may sometimes happen to the workeman, to make a fouresquare shutting with Ionica Capitals, so that some workmen haue erred in placing of the Volutes; to helpe or ease you of that errour, it shalbe needfull to make the corner Capitals, as you see them in this ground: of such Capitals, there was the like found in Rome , which caused many to study, where it was made, in such maner, for it was called, The confused Capitall: but at last, after long disputation, it was concluded, that it had stood in an open corner, shutting vp the order of the Columnes marked A. But if the workeman haue flat Columnes to place against the wall, in this Corner, that the Volutes may come alike on both sides, the workeman may place them, as in the ground B. is set downe.

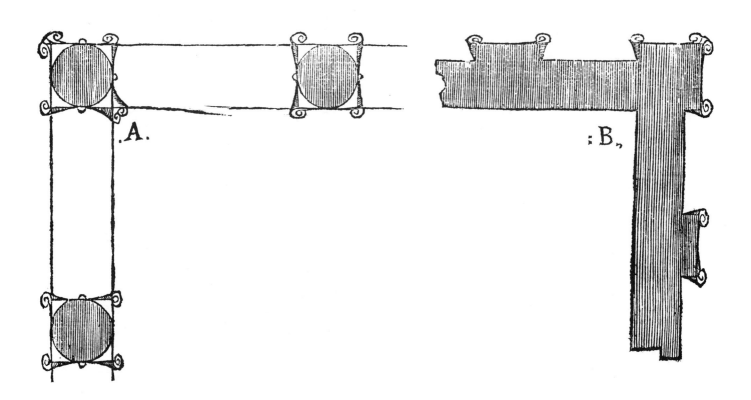

The Epiſtilium oʒ Architraue is made thus: If the Columne be of 12. to 15. foote high, the Architraue ſhalbe the halfe of the Columne beneath: if it be of 15. to 20. foote high, then it ſhalbe deuided in 13. parts: one ſhalbe the height of the Architraue; and from 20. to 25. foote, the Columne ſhall be deuided in 12. parts and a halfe: one part ſhalbe giuen to the Architraue: If the Columne be of 25. to 30. foote high, then the Epiſtilium ſhall be the twelfth part of that height: If the Columne be higher, you muſt increaſe the Architraue moʒe: foʒ the further it goeth from a mans ſight, ſo much moʒe it loſeth of the greatneſſe. The Architraue being made of his due light, and deuided in 7. one ſhalbe the Cimatic: the Pʒoiecture thereof, alſo as great. That which is ouer, is deuided in 12. thʒee ſhalbe giuen to the firſt Facies, foure to the ſecond, and fiue to the third. The thickneſſe of the Architraue vnder, ſhalbe like the Columne aboue, in the thinneſt part: but the thickneſſe of the Architraue aboue, ſhalbe like the thickneſſe of the Columne below. The Zophoʒus oʒ Fréeſe ſhall haue the meaſure accoʒding to the length of the woʒke: but if there be ſomewhat to cut oʒ graue in it, then it muſt be made a fourth part higher then the Architraue: but if it be made playne, without cutting oʒ grauing, then it muſt be a fourth part leſſe. The Cimatie muſt be ſet vpon the Fréeſe, which muſt be the ſeuenth part of the ſame Fréeſe; and the pʒoiecture alſo as much. Aboue the Cimatie muſt the Denticules be placed, in height, like the middlemoſt Facie: and the Pʒoiecture like the height. The bʒedth of their téeth muſt be double in height. The intercutting oʒ hollowing betwéene the téeth, ſhalbe a third part leſſe. The Cimatie is the ſirt part of the Dentile. The Coʒona, with the Cimatie thereof, is the greatneſſe of the middlemoſt Facie. The Pʒoiecture of the Coʒona, with the Denticules, is as much as the height of the Fréeſe, with the Cimatie. The Scima is an eyght part higher then the Coʒona. The rule oʒ liſt thereof ſhall be a ſirt part, and the pʒoiecture like the height. Alſo our Authoʒ affirmeth, that all Ecphoʒes oʒ coʒners will ſtand well, when their Pʒoiecture is like the height.

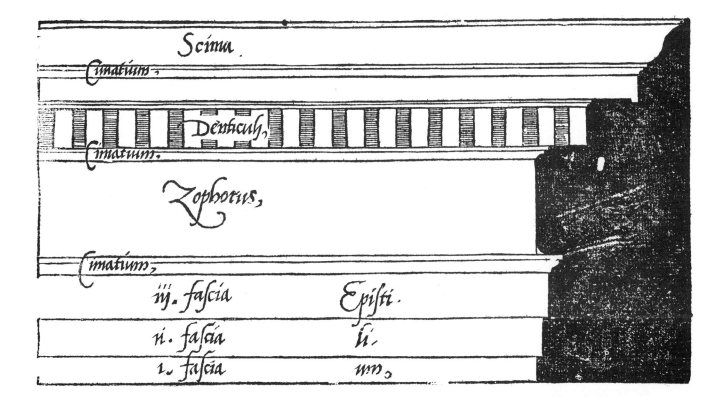

Of the Ionica

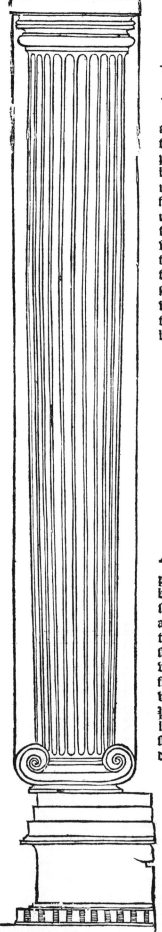

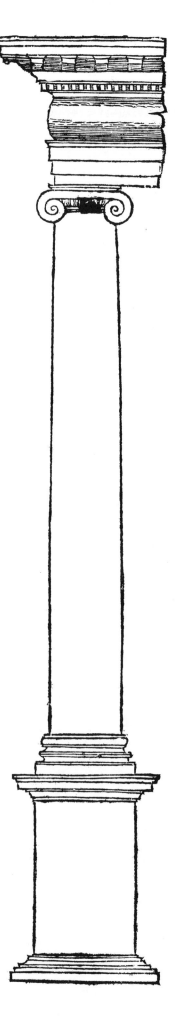

Foz that the works of Rome differ from the writing of Vitruuius, I will frame another Columne, whereof the Architraue, Fréese and Coznice, shall be the foarth part of the height of the Columne: which 4. part deuided in 10. parts, thzée shall be foz the Architraue, deuided after the rule afozesayd: 3. foz the Fréese, and 4. foz the Coznices: which 4. shall bee deuided in 6. whereof one shall be giuen to the Denticules, one to the Cimatie which vpholdeth the Mutiles, and two to the Mutiles and the Cozona; the rest to the Scima. The Pzoiecture of all, shall be at least as much as the height: vpon such a Coznice was found writtcn, A Sante Sabina, at Rome, in a building of the ozder of Ionica.

And if sometimes it be necessary to rayse vp Columnes, being not compelled oz pinched by any thing thereabout, then the propoztion of ÿ Pedestal shall be thus; it shall be as bzoad befoze as the Plinthus of the Columne: but the height of the flat of the Pedestall shalbe a fouresquare, and a fourth part: which deuided in sixe parts, one shall be foz the Base, and one foz the Coznice, which in all is eyght parts: so shall the Pedestal be of eyght parts like the Columne. This must alwayes be vnderstood in common, that it is left at the discretion of the wozkeman.

By reason of the great difference, which I finde in things of Rome, from those which Vitruuius writeth of; therefore I haue here shewed some of them, that are best knowne at this day, extant in Rome to be seene in worke. The Cornice, Freese, and Architraue marked T. is in the Theater of Marcellus, in the Ionica order, aboue the Dorica; the Pilaster with the Base thereupon, also marked T. is in the same order, vnder the Ionica Columne. The Cornice for the impost of an Arch, also marked T. is of the same order, and vpholdeth the Arch. The Cornice with the Mutiles marked A. was found at S. Adrians, and S. Laurence, in Rome. That Architraue marked F. was found in Nel Friulle: which Architraue, for that it had three Facies without Astragals, I iudge to be Ionica. Here is nothing said of the measures hereof, for I haue diligently reduced them from the great into the small: which measures are easie to be found with the Compasse.

Of the Ionica

ALthough that the Thiromatum Ionicum, that is, the doore by Vitruuius deſcribed, in my opinion, not proportioned to anſwere the building (as it ought to do:) therefore I will ſpeake thereof, according to my knowledge: I ſay then, that Vitruuius writing is not right, touching the height of the light of ẏ Thiromatum Doricū, viz. from the Pauement to the Lacunary, there were 3. parts and an halfe made, and two parts thereof were for the height of the light, whereby the Corona was very high, as alſo of the Dorica. But there followeth yet another errour, viz. making the Gate or doore 5. parts high, ſetting three parts thereof below, as Vitruuius ſaith, alſo leſſened in the vpper part, like the Dorica: then I finde, that the wideneſſe thereof commeth to be broader then the inter-Columne in the middle, making a Temple of 4. Columnes, with the meaſure which Vitruuius hath ſet downe in his 3. Booke, as I haue ſet it downe here in Figure, that workemen may ſée the correſpondencie of this Gate or Doore, with the Temple thereof; which, in my opinion, is not full, for this cauſe, for, if the doore of the Dorica, which order of Columnes is lower then that of Ionica, hath the height of 2. foureſquares, and a little more, I ſay, the Ionica doores, whoſe Columnes are higher, ought to be higher alſo for light, then the Dorica. But it is not ſo much, according to Vitruuius Booke, which ſayth, 5. parts in height, and 3. parts in breadth: but let all this be ſpoken with reuerence of ſo great an Author. Neuertheleſſe, taking the parts in Vitruuius Booke, which may be to ſome purpoſe, I will make another Figure thereof, without leſſening it aboue: but he that for his pleaſure will leſſen it aboue, obſerueth the Dorica order.

The Tranſlator.

WHat Vitruuius ſayth, touching the height of the light of the Doore or Gate of this Dorica building, there is ſuffi-ciently ſpoken: but touching the wideneſſe of this Gate or Doore, where he ſayth, that the height or openneſſe thereof ſhould be deuided into two parts and a halfe, and the wideneſſe thereof, to haue one part and a halfe: it may be (as it is in other places) that the place is falſified; and it may alſo be, that it is a quarter too much: for if it be made of 10. in height, and 5. in breadth, the light then being of 2. foureſquares, would bee reaſonable, ſo the Intercolumnes were as wide as from the Dorica: for it is of foure Diameters, and this but of thrée Columnes wide, and the Antipagmen-tum would not be darkened; ſo that leaning out but a quarter, this building would thereby be made perfect.

I Say, that the light of this doore ought at least to be of 2. fouresquares high, the Antipagmentū or Pilaster shalbe the 12. part of that height, made in such maner as is said of the Epistilium Ionicum, & thereto the Astragals shalbe added, as it is shewed in the Figure E. If a workeman will cut any thing in the Fræse aboue the Supercilium, then it must be a 4. part higher then the Supercilium: but if you leaue it plaine, it must be a fourth part lesse. The Corona, with the other members, shall be as high as the Supercilium, deuided as you see it in the Figure F. The Ancones or Prothirides, shall be broad aboue, like the Pilaster, but in the nether part, like the height of the hanging light, shalbe lessened a fourth part, from the which the leaues hang, as you see in the Figure F. That part of the Circle, in stead of the Fastigium, shal haue his height made in this maner; with a Compasse you must reach the two corners of the Scima in the vppermost part, and one foot of the Compasse sinking to the point of the crosse, with the other foot, the part of the Circle being drawne, shalbe the height, which will be the third part of a Circle: which maner of making or not making of a Fastigium, shalbe alwayes referred to the pleasure of the workeman; it may also serue for windowes.

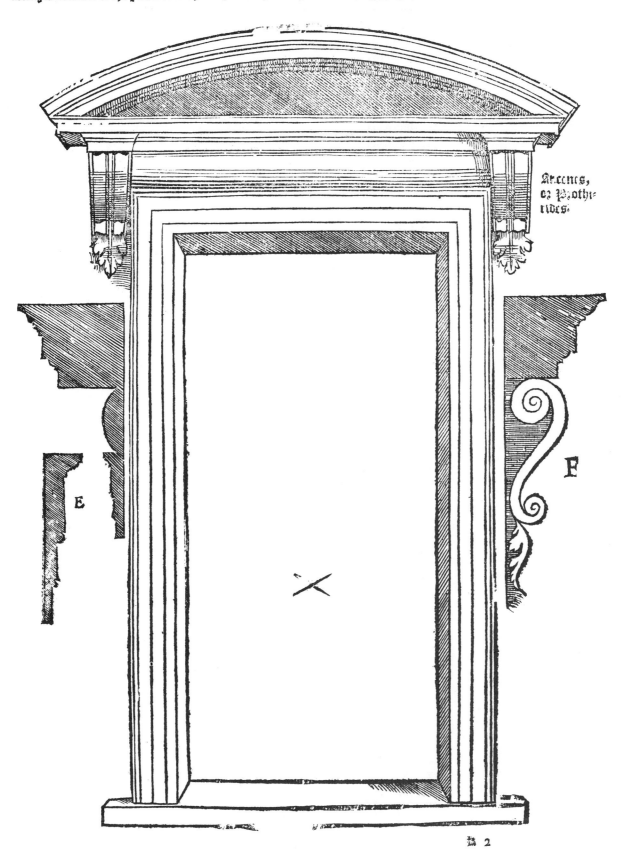

Ancones, or Prothirides.

E

F

X

The light of the Gate following, is more then of double proportion, viz. of two fouresquares and a quarter : the flat of the Pilasters shall be the 8. part of the breadth of the light, and the Columnes shall be twice as thicke: the same Columne shall be lessened aboue a sixt part: the height shall be of 9. parts, with Bases and Capitals, according to the measure aforesaid. And although these Columnes hold a part more then the rule aforesayd, yet it is not therefore trueth, for that the 2. third parts stand onely without the wall, bearing no other waight then the Frontispicium : further, if by any accident these Columnes should exceed 9. parts, yet were it not to be blamed: for they are onely set for an ornament, being made fast in the wall. The height of the Architraue shall be like the Supercilies ouer the doore: the Frise shall be cut, and shall be made higher, as is before: if it be not cut, you may lessen it so much lower : the Cornice shall be higher, like the Epistilium or Architraue : with the other parts you must handle, as it is said in the beginning of this order. The Frontispicis shall bee referred to the will of the workeman, eyther to make it higher or lower, by any of the aforesayd rules. By this inuention, a workeman may helpe himselfe in many things, making the light high or low, as need shall require ; as sometimes of a fouresquare, or of two third parts: but if the workeman bee not otherwise compelled, I should best commend the double proportion, that is, of two fouresquares.

Of the Ionica

ALthough I haue set this rusticall Gate in the order of Thuscana, and not onely in many places applyed it to the Thuscana, but also mixed it with the Dorica, yet I haue placed it here with the Ionica: although it is not therefore to be set in all buildings that are made after the Dorica, neuerthelesse, to good intent and purpose, as without in the countrey, in such a case also, it is not to bee discommended in a Citie or Towne, for a Marchants or Lawyers house; in which places it is tolerable. But in what place soeuer a man will make it, in a maner of bearing ouer, then the proportion of this worke shall be thus: the light vp to the Arch shalbe two fouresquares, and the Pilaster the 8. part of the bredth of the light: the Columne shall hold the fourth part thereof, but the height shalbe 9. parts with Bases and Capitals. The Arch of the halfe shalbe deuided in 13. parts and a quarter, because the middlemost stone shall hold a quarter more then the rest. The Architraue, Freese and Cornice, are together the fifth part of the Columnes: of which three pieces, the workeman shall make 11. parts: 4. for the Architraue, 3. for the Freese, and 4. for the Cornice. The height of the Podium shalbe the bredth of the light. The Cornice and the Base, may be taken out of the aforesayd Stilobato: but the other Base, Capitall, Architraue, and Cornice, shalbe made as it is sayd in the beginning. The Arch, stones and the other that bind the Columnes, you may see in the Figure.

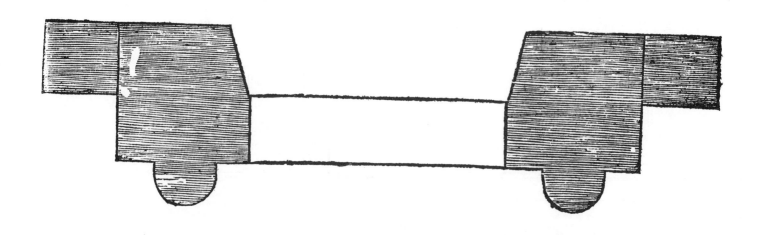

Lthough the height of this Arch is not of double proportion, as the most part of those which I haue shewed, yet it is not false, but is made by good discretion, for that it may some time fall out, that in the compartition of a Facies, vpon occasion of any necessary height, and to make the Arches vnequall, which should be so to place the principall gate in the middle, which in such case should not attayne to such height: but if we be not constrayned by any necessity, I more commend the double height, then any other proportion. The widenesse then betwéene one Pilaster and the other shalbe 3. parts, and the height 5. but afterwards the widenesse being deuided in 5. then the whole Pillars which stand before the 2. Pilasters, haue 2. parts, and the thicknesse of the Columnes shalbe of one part: the Pilasters shall each of them be of halfe a Columne in thicknesse: likewise the Arch, and the Impost which vpholdeth the Arch, are of the same height made, as it is shewed in the Theater of Marcellus marked T. The Columnes shalbe 9. parts high, with Bases and Capitals, made according to the rule, in the beginning of this Chapter set downe: the doore in the middle shalbe halfe the widenesse betwéene the Pilasters: the height shalbe found in this maner: The Pilaster being made of the sirt part of the light, the Cornice like the eyes of the Impost, placed aboue it, and the Scima vpon that, making afterward the Fréese the fourth part lesse then the Antipagmentum, then the height will find it selfe, which will be litt'e lesse then two fouresquares. The Frontispice shalbe made according to a rule set downe in the Dorica: the Architraue, Fréese and Cornice shalbe made in height, of the fourth part of the heights of the Columnes, by the rule a-foresayd. The Story aboue shalbe lower by one fourth part: so shall the Architraue, Fréese and Cornice bee of the fift part of that height, which shalbe the fourth part of the height of the Columnes; but touching the deuision of the particular members, you shall find them in full measure in the Order of Composita. The windowes being made with Arches, shalbe in bredth like the doore: likewise the Pilasters and the Arches, but their height shalbe two fouresquares and a halfe, which is to giue more light in the chambers. The Columnes shalbe flat, and one fourth part shorter then the lower. The bredth of the Niches betwéene the Columnes and the windowes, is one Columne and a halfe, the height of foure Columnes thicknesse. Thus of any parts or members that bee resting, you shall find meanes to make them by the prescription of the aforesayd rules of that order: for of this Corinthia, you shall find the measure in the beginning of that order. Aboue this story, he that will, may make a walking place, well defended from water: and that the height of this Podium were of reasonable height to leane vpon, or to rest vpon with a mans armes, these Facies would bee a great beautifying to the building, and much ease to the inhabitants.

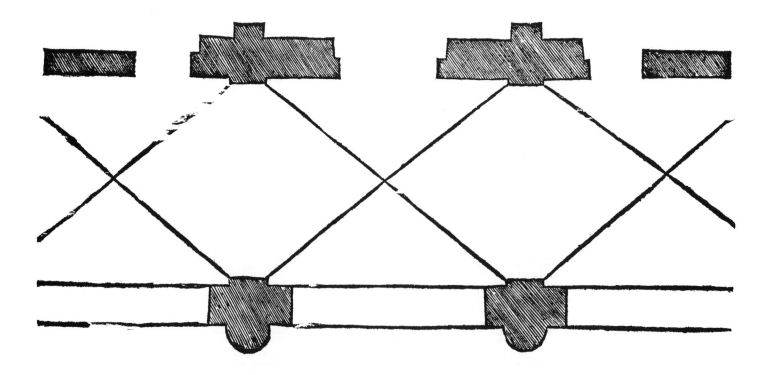

Sometime, as is sayd, a workeman shall find a great number of Columnes, but so low, that they will not reach high inough for his worke, if he cannot helpe himselfe therewith, and apply such members, to serue the building which he hath in hand: therefore if the height of the Gallery riseth higher then the Columnes, then in the middle of the Facie you may make an Arch, being vpholden by the Architraue, which shalbe aboue the Columnes, which Architraue shall bee the Impost or vpholding of a round roofe. But where the Arch shall be, there shall be a Crociere, as the workeman may see in this ground: and for strengthening thereof, let there be Iron or mettall barres layd ouer, as it is taught in the Dorica Order. But the deuiding of this Facie shalbe such, that the middlemost Intercolumne shalbe of 6. Columnes thicknesse: and the height of the Columne, with Bases and Capitals shalbe of 8. parts: the Architraue holdeth as much as the Columne is in thicknesse aboue: likewise the Arch: aboue the which the workeman shall make a Cornice, which height shall hold a fourth part more then the Architraue, without the Thorus vnder, with the List: which Cornice shall also serue for a Capitall vpon the Pillars, aboue the Columnes, and shalbe of the same breadth that the Columne is aboue. The Intercolumnes on the sides shalbe of 3. Columnes in thicknesse: the height of the doore shalbe so, that the Architraue vnder the Arch shall serue for the Cornice aboue the doore, changing partly her members, as it is figured. Under the Cornice there shalbe a Freese set, which shalbe a fourth part lesse then the Architraue, the Supercilies with the Pilaster of the same height. But as much as shalbe vnder the Supercilies, to the stayres, of that halfe, the breadth of the light shalbe made; and so the light shalbe of two souresquares. The windowes shall stand as the eyes of the doore stand, and their widenesse shalbe of two Columnes thicknesse, but the height shalbe taken in Diagonall maner: the second Order or Story shalbe a fourth part lesse then the first; the Podium being taken of a reasonable height, that which resteth shalbe deuided in 5. parts, foure whereof shall be for the height of the Columnes, the other for the Architraue, Freese and Cornice, obseruing the giuen measures of such a Story. The breadth of the window in the middle, is with the Antipagmentum as wide as the light of the doore, but the light shalbe double in height: in the Ornaments aboue, workemen may follow and obserue the rule set downe. The windowes on the sides shall be like those that stand below, and their height like the greater: the raysing vp in the middle aboue the second story, shall also be a fourth part lesse then the other, and euery part thereof lessened accordingly: for the light thereof, the order of the lowest story is obserued: but the making of this third story, or the not making thereof, is at the pleasure of the workman.

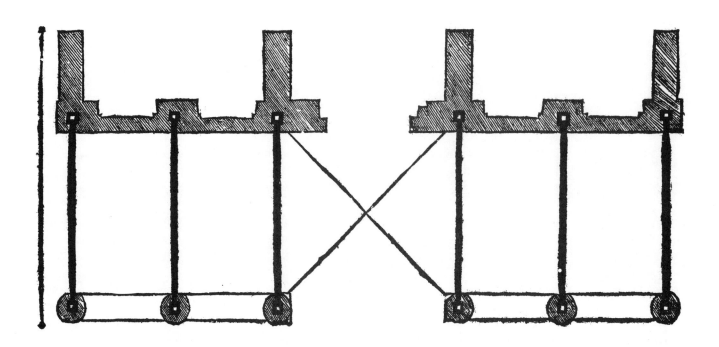

Of the Ionica

AS it is said in the beginning of this Booke, the maner and order of the Ionica being made after the Feminine kind, it is so likewise a materiall thing, that hauing a Chimney to make of that order, wee must, as néere as we can, make some shew of that sexe therein: the proportion whereof shalbe thus, that ý height of the openneffe, being placed, it shalbe from the ground of the Chamber or Hall, to the Architraue, eyght parts high, and that shall be according to the placing of the Columnes, which shall be such like, monsters or strange formes (as we call them) made in this maner, which shal serue for Mogdilions. The Architraue, Frése and Cornice, shall be the fourth part of the height, as it is before sayd. The table vpon the Capitals, which couereth the Architraue and the Frése, I iudge, that ancient workemen haue vsed to finde more space to write in, and also, for that they were desirous of nouelties: which table, whether it be made or not made, is referred to the will of the workeman. The second order, with the Dolphins, is made for two causes, the one is, to make the mouth of the Chimney, which doeth recepue the smoke wider: the other is, to make a Piramicall forme, making the necke of the Chimney in a Chamber, but it is still at the will of the workeman, to make them more or lesse, or not at all.

Of the Ionica

This other maner of Chimney is very eafie for fmall rœmes, and they are vfed to be made lower then a mans fight, that the fire, which is enemy to mens eyes, may warme the reft of a mans body. The widenefse of this Chimney is a full fourefquare : the Pilafter fhall haue a firt part of the widenefse: the Cimatie the feuenth part of the Pilafter. Of the reft you may make 12. parts, 3. fhalbe giuen to the firft Facie, 4. the fecond, and 5. the third Facie: and for more beautifying, a man may alfo make the Aftragals, as you fee them here in the fides. The height of the Volutes fhalbe like the 3. Facies without the Cimatie, and of them muft be made 3. equall parts, one part for the Frefe, with the chanelature or hollowing, and the other for the Echine, with the Aftragall and Lift, the third fhall bee giuen to the Volutes, which fhall hang on the fides like the Cimatie, but the leaues fhall hang downe as low as the Architraue. The height of the Corona, with the two Cimaties, and the Scima, are like the fecond and third Facie, together with the Cimatie : but the Proiecture of Corona, Cimatie, and Scima, each of them hold as much as the height. This like forme I haue made in worke, very well liked of : but, as is fayd of the other, if by occafion of worke it taketh ouermuch place, then you may make the Pilafters of the 8. part of the widenefse, fo will they be much more feemely of themfelues. That part made ouer for an Ornament, is alfo at the workemans will, for this Chimney is to ftand in the thicknefse of a wall, fo that this Ornament, of this Order, would ferue for a window or dore.

Here endeth the Ionica Order of building : and there followeth the Corinthia.

The eyght Chapter.

O F Corinthia worke, *Vitruuius* ſpeaketh onely in his fourth Booke, and the firſt Chapter, in a maner as if he would ſay, that the ſame, which is ſayd of the Ionica Columne, is in Corinthia worke: and in his ſecond Chapter hee ſpeaketh of Mogdilions among the Coronas, therefore not giuing any other rules or meaſures of the other parts: but the ancient Romanes vſing this order of Corinthia much, (as alſo the reſt) made the Baſes of theſe Columnes, with a great number of members or parts full of workes of which Baſes to ſet downe ſome rules, I will ſpeake of one of the fayreſt buildings in Rome, that is, the Pantheon, called by the name of, Our Lady de Rotonde, ſetting downe all the meaſures thereof. The Columne of Corinthia worke is made by a common rule, conſiſting of 9. parts in height, with Capitals and Baſes: the Capitall whereof, ſhall be as high as the Columne is thicke below, but the Baſe ſhall be of halfe the thickeneſſe of the Columne. Of this halfe, or height of the Baſe, there ſhall be foure euen parts made, whereof the one is for the Plinthus, the other three ſhall be deuided in fiue equall parts, whereof one part ſhall bee for the Thorus aboue, but the Thorus vnder ſhall be a fourth part thicker: ſo that which reſteth ſhall be deuided into 2. euen parts, whereof one part is for the Scotie below, with the Aſtragall, and two Liſts or borders: that Aſtragall ſhall be the ſixt part, and each liſt or border the halfe thereof: but the liſt or border vnder the nethermoſt Thorus, ſhall bee a third part more then the other. The Proiecture of the Plinthus ſhall ſtand aboue in another order of Columnes, making them like the Ionica order; but if the place be beneath vpon the ground, then the Proiecture ſhall be like the Dorica order. Alſo, according to the place where the Baſes ſhalbe placed, ſo the workeman muſt adde or diminiſh, as is before ſayd: for as theſe Baſes ſtand beneath the ſight, it will ſtand well; but if it bee placed aboue the ſight, then all the places that are vſed by the other members, with their ſeuerall diſtances, ſhall be made greater, then by this rule is preſcribed. And the higher they be ſet, ſo much the leſſe and fayrer ſeeme the members: herein the workeman of the Rotonde was well aduiſed, for that hee made the Baſes aboue the firſt ſtory within, with two Scoties, but yet with one Aſtragall alone, in ſtead of two.

Torus ſuperior.

Scotia.

Aſtragali.

Scotia, ſiue Trochilus

Torus inferior.

Plinthus.

The deriuation of the Capitall Corinthia, was from a Mayd of Corinthia: but for that Vitruuius in his fourth Booke and first Chapter describeth his petygrée, whereof I will not trouble my selfe to speake of, thus much I will say: If a workeman had a Temple to make for the Virgin Mary, or any other Saints that were Virgins, or Houses or Sepulchers for persons of honest life and conuersation, then a man might vse this maner of worke. The height of this Capitall shall bee like the thicknesse of the Columne below: the Abacus the seuenth part of that height. Of the rest there shalbe thrée parts made: one for the leaues below; the other for the leaues in the middle; and the last for the Volutes, as we may call them. But betwéene the Volutes and the middlemost leaues, there is a space left to the lesser leaues, from the which the Volutes grew. The Capitall marked B. shall bee vnderneath like the Columne aboue: vnder the Abacus, there is a Cintha made, the height whereof shall be halfe the Abacus: of which Abacus, thrée parts being made, one shalbe for the Cimatie with the Lists, and the rest for the Plinthus. Vnder the foure corners of the Abacus, the greatest Volutes are made; and in the middle of the Abacus, there is a flower as great as the Abacus is thicke, vnder the which the least Volutes shalbe made; vnder the greatest, and also vnder the smallest Volutes, the middle leaues shalbe set, betwéene the which the least leaues shall grow out, and out of them the Volutes spring. The middlemost, and also the vndermost leaues, shall each be 8. in number, standing betwéene each other, as the figure C. sheweth. The widenesse of the Abacus, from poynt to poynt, shalbe two Diameters of the Columnes below: which Diameter shalbe placed in a 4. square, & a Circle drawne without the foure square, which shall touch the foure corners: then, without this great Circle, another foure square being made, and deuided in Diagonall, that is, crosse-wise, those lines will shew to be two Diameters in length (as Vitruuius teacheth.) But from the line B. C. you shall make a perfit Triangle: and vpon the corner X. shall be to make hollow the Abacus: from the spaces, betwéene the great Circle and the small, there shalbe foure parts made, one part shal rest aboue A. and thrée shalbe thus taken away: the one foote of the Compasse being set vpon X. the other vpon A. drawing about from B. to C. where the crooked line shall reach on the two sides of the Triangle, there shalbe the termination of the corners of the Capitals. The example is in the figure D. in this maner. The Abacus shall come in Perpendicular, with the Plinthus of the Base.

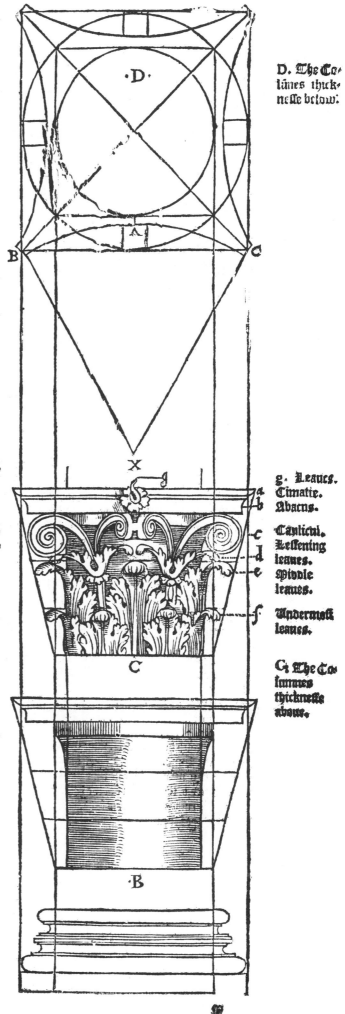

D. The Columne thicknesse below.

g. Leaues.
Cimatie.
Abacus.

Canlicul.
Lessening
leaues.
Middle
leaues.

Vndermost
leaues.

G. The Columnes
thicknesse
aboue.

Touching the Architraue, Fréese and Cornice of the Corinthia, as I haue sayd in the beginning of this Chapter, Vitruuius setteth downe no measure thereof, although he setteth downe the originall of the Mutiles, which may bes made in all maner of Cornices, as wee sée in Antiquities : but to procéed orderly, and not to leaue Vitruuius writing too much, I will set the ornaments of Ionica in this Chapter, adding thereto the Astragall in the Architraue, and an Echinus vnder the Crowne, as some Arch-Architects in Rome haue done. So I say, when the Architraue is made as it standeth by the Ionica, vnder the middlemost Facie, there shall be an Astragall made of the eyght part of the same Facie, and vnder the vppermost Facie also, one of ý eyght parts of the sayd Facie wrought with Lead, as you sée : after that, when the Fréese is set with the Cimatie, and thereto the Denticules with the Cimatis, then you must place the Echine aboue it, of such height as the first Facie is, the which with the Projectures and cuttings, shall shew more then the middlemost Facie : aboue the Echine, you must set the Corona, Cimatie, and Sima, as it is sayd in the Ionica Order.

Some Romish workemen, procéeding with more boldenesse, haue not onely placed Echines aboue the Denticules, but also made Mutiles and Dentiles together, in one Cornice, which is much condemned by Vitruuius in his fourth Booke, and second Chapter : for that the Dentiles represent certaine téeth, by Vitruuius called Asseri, and the Mogdilions are for the supporting of other ends of wood, by the sayd Author called Cantery : which two kind of beames may not stand together in one place ; and I, for my part, could neuer endure Dentiles and Mutiles in one Cornice, although Rome aboundeth therein, and diuers places of Italy also : but procéeding orderly in this worke, I find a generall rule, that is, that the height of the Columnes with Bases and Capitals, shalbe deuided in 4. parts, whereof one is giuen to the Architraue, Fréese and Cornice, and such a height agréeth with the Dorica : the fourth part shalbe deuided in 10. parts : 3. shall be for the Architraue, as aforesayd, 3. for the Fréese, and 4. for the Cornice. But of those 4. there are 9. parts made, one shall bee for the Cimatie aboue the Fréese, 2. for the Echine with the List, 2. for the Mutiles with their Cimatie, 2. for the Corona, and the 2. last parts for the Sima, with her Cimatie, which shall be the fourth part of the Sima. The Project of all shall be as aforesayd : you may also make this Architraue, Fréese and Cornice, of the first part of the height of the Columne, as Vitruuius sayth in his fift Booke, and seuenth Chapter of the Theater.

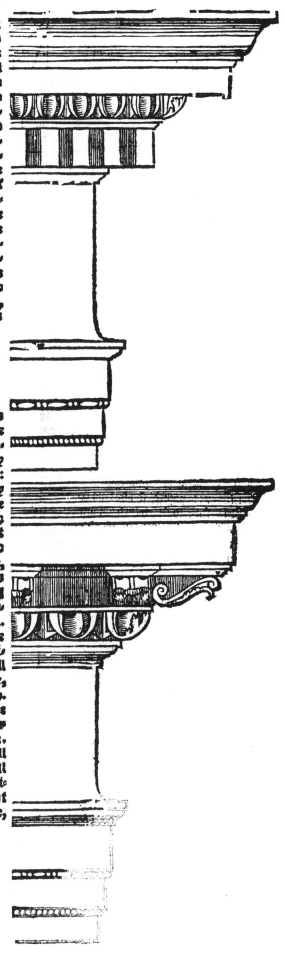

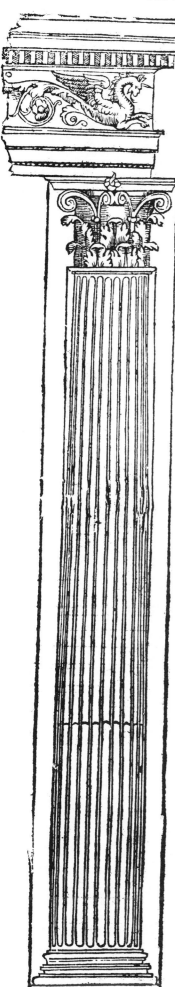

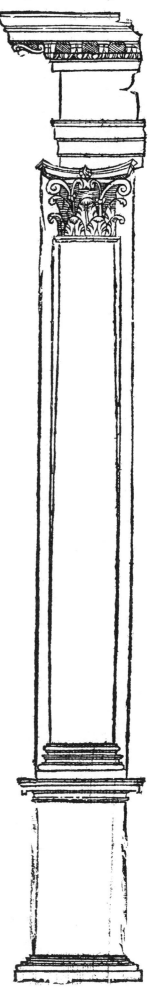

The leſſening of the Corinthia Columne ſhall be made, as it is ſayd of the other: and alſo thereafter as the height is, but of 16. foote downewards: it ſhalbe leſſened aboue the ſixt part, by the rule aforeſaid: and if it bee ſtriked or chaneled, then you ſhall make it like the Ionica; but from the third part netherwards the caruing or hollowing ſhall be full, as you ſee it in the Figure on the ſides. The Corona is without Mutiles, whereof the Architraue is halfe the Columnes thickeneſſe: the Frèſe, for that it is cut, is the fourth part more then ẏ Architraue: and the Cornice without the Cimatie of the Freeſs, is as high as the Architraue: the height of all together is ſomewhat leſſe then the fift part of the Columne: neuertheleſſe, if the Proiecture of the Corona bee well made, then it will ſhew to bee higher then it is, and ſhall bee leſſe wayght vpon the building: wherefore, that the ſkilful workman may chuſe out thoſe parts, that beſt ſerue his turne, that he may not exceed Vitruuius doctrine, and the good Antiquities, which men, by his writing, acknowledge, if by any accident this Columne had néed of a proportioned Pedeſtal, being not let by any occaſion, then ẏ proportion thereof ſhalbe thus: the bredth ſhalbe deuided in 3. parts, whereof 2. parts ſhall bee for the height, that is, one fourth parts, and 2. third parts, (I meane the flat) which height ſhall be deuided in 7. parts: one for the Baſes, one for the Cornice aboue, which ſhall in all be 9. parts, proportioned according to the Columne: but of the particular members of the Baſes and Cornices, I will hereafter ſhew more, with ſome Antiquities, whereof men may take ſuch meaſure as ſhall beſt ſerue their turnes.

Of the Corinthia

Among other Antiquities of the Corinthia, which are ſeene in Italy, I thinke the Pantheon of Rome, and the Arch tryumphant, at the Hauen of Ancona, are the fayreſt and beſt to be ſeene : of which Arch, the Capitall hereunder marked A. is with great care proportioned after the great : which height is contrary to the writing of Vitruuius : neuertheleſſe, it had good correſpondencie ; & it may be, that Vitruuius meant, that the height of the Capitall ſhould be one Columnes thickeneſſe without the Abacus : but the text herein is falſified, for that I haue not onely found this Capitall, but others more of ſuch proportion. The Columnes hereof are chanteled, as it is ſhewed here : the Pedeſtall with the Baſe vpon it, is a member of the ſame Arch, alſo proportioned in the ſmall : the Cornice hereunto added, was found at Al foro tranſitorio in Rome : that marked with A. is very handſome, for a Corinthian Cornice without Mogdilions : that marked with B. is a little fayrer ; but that with C. is the vnhandſomeſt, becauſe of the double parts, which haue no good grace from the Corona downewards : and alſo, for that the Corona, vpon ſo much Cornice, hath ſo ſmall Proiecture. The Baſe of the Pedeſtall marked D. in my opinion, is very fayre, and alſo the Baſement with E. I thinke hath béene a thing that hath continued in ſome building : which things, altogether, men may applie to the order of Corinthia ; and in the Ionica I haue ſéene the like. The Architraue V. is in Verona, in an Arch tryumphant, which Facies ſtandeth contrary to Vitruuius writing : yet I haue ſet them here to ſhew ſuch difference.

A

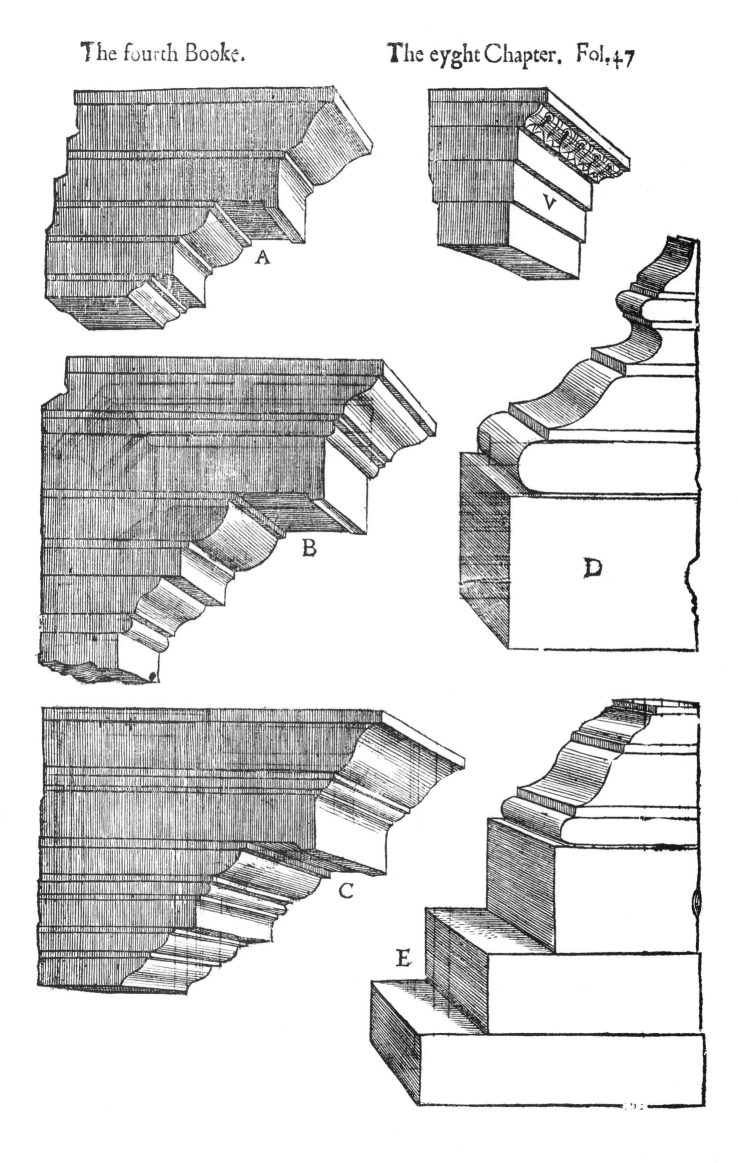

Of the doores of Corinthia worke, Vitruuius speaketh nothing at all; but I will speake of the Antiquities which are yet to be seene. The Gate or doore marked S. Y. is at Tiuoli, vpon the Riuer of Auiene, in a round Temple, made after the Corinthia maner, which doore is lessened aboue the eyghteenth part. The height is aboue, 2. 4. squares: the rest of the members are proportioned after the great. The window T. and X. is in the same Temple, and lessened aboue like the doore: the Pilasters or Antipagmentum are all proportioned, which a man may find with the Compasse. The doore following, marked P. Z. is that of the Pantheon in Rome, also Corinthia worke; which is 20. ancient Palmes broad: the height 40. And it is sayd, that the Antipagmentum is all of one piece, and I also haue seene no other. The Antipagmentum of this doore is the bredth of the 8. parts of the light thereof, and in the sides it is of a good thickenes. But for that you cannot see the first, without seeing a part of the sides, therefore it seemeth to such as looke on it, to be broader then in effect it is. And this doore, because it is so high, comes in Perpendicular, and is not lessened as the other aforesayd: all the other members are proportioned according to the greatnesse. The Base aboue the Gate, is like that of flat Columnes aboue the first order, which I haue set downe by the Corinthia.

Of the Corinthia

The doore hereunder set downe, is at Palestina, and is Corinthia: the widenesse is 2. fouresquares: the Antepagmentum or the Pilaster is broad the sixt part of the widenes, deuided in maner aforesaid. The Sophore or Freese is the fourth part more then the Supercilie. The Corona and the rest, are like the Supercilie, deuided as you see in the Figure. The Prothyrides or Ancones, with that which is vpon them, hang so slightly or losely, as you see. The Frontispicie is made, as in the order of Dorica, in the second Facis, is sayd.

ALthough this Doore differeth from all the other, that euer I saw in any Antiquitie, neuerthelesse, it is very pleasing to the sight, and sheweth well: which Doore is without Spoleta, about halfe a mile without the way, in an ancient Temple, made of the Corinthia maner; of the proportion and particular members, I will say nothing; for hee that seeketh neere, may find it with a Compasse.

Of Corinthia

OF this Order of Corinthia, which is pleasing vnto all men, I will make more sorts of buildings, setting downe some generall rules, to satisfie those that take pleasure to read this worke: and for that ancient workemen, in times past, that desired to make their things strong and euerlasting, made Pillars (wherein the Pilasters are closed) which beare vp the Arches of a great thicknesse; for that cause, the Forefront or Facie ensuing hath the Pillar (that is, the whole body) as broad before as the widenesse of the Arch is; but the thicknesse is 1. fourth part lesse. The thickenesse of the Columnes shall bee a sixt part of the Pillar. The Piches betwéene the Columnes are 2. Columnes thickenesse in bredth: their height is somewhat lesse then 2. fouresquares. The height of the Pedestals of 3. Columnes thickenesse. The height of the Arch shalbe made of 2. fouresquares. The height of the Columnes with Bases and Capitals, shalbe 9. parts and a halfe. The bredth of the Arch with the Pilasters, shalbe of halfe a Columne. The Impost which beareth the Arch, shalbe of the same height, made, in maner, like that of the Theater of Marcellus, in the Order of Ionica: which Impost shall serue for a Cornice aboue the dore: but the height of the dore shalbe made thus: Under the sayd Cornice, the Supercilie shalbe also made of the like height; and from thence downewards there shalbe 2. equall parts made to the Stayres; whereof, one shalbe the bredth of the light, and likewise the Cornice of the dore, as the eyes, shall come with the windowes, and the Cimatie of the Pedestall shall also come in like sort vnder the windowes. The light of the windowes shalbe taken Diagonall wise: and the Antepagmentum a sixt part of the light. The particular members of the Pedestall, Base and Capitals, shalbe made, as in the first part of this Order it is sayd. Aboue the Columnes, the Architraue, Fréese and Cornice shalbe set, deuided in such maner as is shewed in the beginning. The height of the second Story shalbe a fourth part lesse then the first, and all the members lessened accordingly, as you may sée and measure it in the figure: the eleuation aboue this I estéeme not for a whole Story, but much lower: the height thereof is as much as the widenesse of the Arch below, and the Cornice which serueth for Architraue, and Fréese, shalbe the sixt part of the height of that Story; which measures you may take from the Capitall Dorica: and for more Ornament, a man may set a Fastigies aboue: but setting it in the middle, it would hardly agrée with the flat small aboue the Piches, vnlesse it ran round, whereby the worke should be changed, and shew better to the sight.

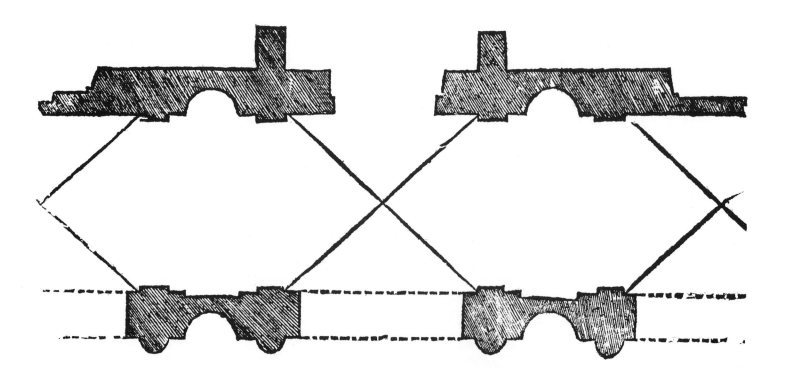

Of the Corinthia

When a workeman will build a Temple, the higher the ground or Pauement is eleuated, so much statelyer the building will shew, for so right ancient workemen haue done, although they vsed other formes of Temples, much different from this here set downe: for they made a body alone, but wee, that are Christians, make our Temples in three parts, setting one part in the middle, and 2. parts on the sides : and sometimes the Chappels are made without the sides, as you see in the ground. The widenesse of this Facie shall be of 32. parts: one whereof shalbe ÿ thicknes of a Columne: the middlemost inter-Columnes shall containe 7. parts: the greatest inter-Columnes on the sides shall bee 4. parts and an halfe. The inter-Columne with the Niche shall be 2. parts: and so the 32. parts shalbe distributed. The Arches with the Pilasters shall be halfe a Columne broad : the widenesse of the Doore shalbe of 3. parts and an halfe: the height of 7. parts: the Impost vnder the Arch is as broad as the Arch. The height of the Pedestall is 3. parts: the height of the Columne, with Capitall and Bases, is 9. parts and a halfe. The Architraue, Freese and Cornice shalbe the fourth part of the height of the Columnes: and so for the particular members and parts resting, the first rule shalbe obserued. The windowes, Niches and other ornaments, a man may conceaue in the figure and measure. The second storie shalbe a fourth part shorter then the first, and all the members lessened accordingly : but the Architraue, Freese & Cornice, shalbe placed in 3. equall parts, as I sayd of the other. The Fastigies shalbe made, as Vitruuius hath shewed in the order of Dorica. The 2. sides that stand for beautifying and vpholding, shall bee the fourth part of a Circle, whereof A. and B. is the Center; and aboue each Arch that parteth the Chappels, a man may set such things, which will be a great vpholding to the middlemost worke, and also along vpon them, the water may fall from the vppermost roofe to the nethermost.

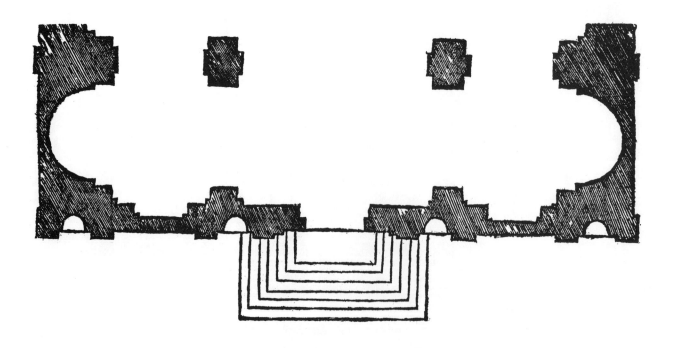

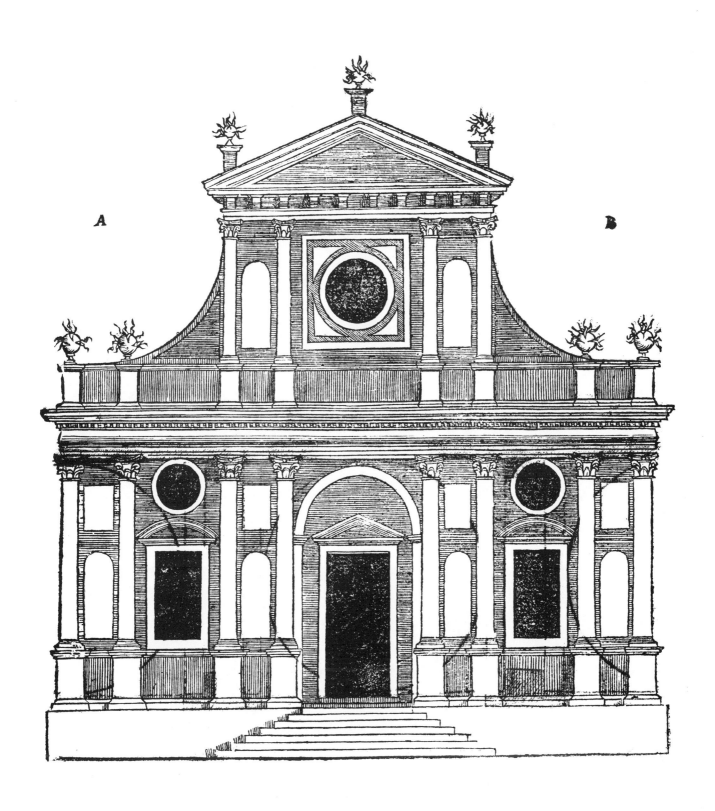

The deuiding of this worke enſuing ſhalbe thus, that the Pillar ſhalbe the third part of the witeneſſe of the Arch, but the thickeneſſe of the ſirt part: the thickeneſſe of the Columne alſo as much. The height with Baſe and Capital of ten parts and an halſe: the Arch, Pilaſter, and impoſt of the halfe Columne: the meaſure of the Impoſt a man may take from the Dorica Chapter, altering the members: the ſame ſhall alſo ſerue for a Cornice aboue the doore, and for ſupporting of the windowes aboue the ſhops: the height of the Arch (for ſometimes vpon occaſion, a man ſhall be forced to haue it ſo low as you ſée) ſhall be of 3. parts in the breoth, and 5. in height: and the doore alſo ſhall haue the ſame proportion. The Antepagmentum ſhall be the ſirt part of the light; and if the workeman will make the height of the Arch of double proportion, the doore alſo will be of ſuch proportion: but the Columnes ſhoulo néd a great ſtone vnder th Baſes, with which things ancient workemen holpe themſelues. The height of the Architraue, Fréſe, and Cornice are of 2. Columnes thickeneſſe, as it is ſaid in the ſirſt part of the rules, or in maner of ſome Antiquities afore ſhewed. And for that the ſpace vnder the Arch to the ſoller, which is euen with the flat of the Cornice, ſhould be to great to make croſſewiſe, in ſuch caſe my aouice ſhould be, to make an Arch right behind the Columne, and to make each ſpace kettlewiſe, as you ſée in the ground. The height of the ſecond ſtory ſhalbe one 4. part leſſe then the firſt, ocuided in this maner: the Podium ſhall bee as high as the thickeneſſe of two of the loweſt Columnes, and from thence vpwards ſhall be made 5. parts, one for the Architraue, Fréſe and Cornice, and 4. for the Columnes: the Arches with the Pilaſters ſhall be of halfe a Columne; and for the reſt, you ſhall obſerue the generall rule: and if the Facie ſtandeth in any place or market, as it is ſhewed by the winkels or ſhops, it will be eaſe and comely to make a leaning about the vppermoſt Cornice: but for ſafety from rayne, ſnow, and froſt, aboue all other things, it ſhall bee requiſite to make a roofe or pauement well cloſed and leaning forward, becauſe of the water: but it will be ſurer, if it be couered with lead. And although good workemen condemne and ſhun the ſetting of a Columne in an emptie place, which I alſo commend not, neuertheleſſe, for that I haue ſéene the like matter vpon the Porticus of Pompey in Rome, but made after the Dorica maner, therefore I haue preſumed to ſet the like, if it may ſerue any mans turne.

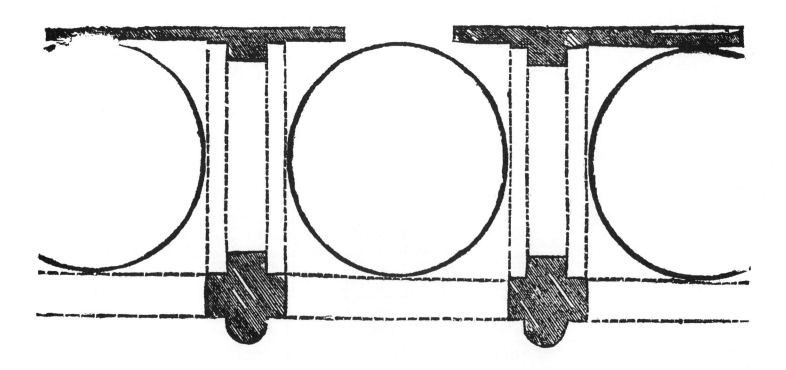

Of the Corinthia

FOr that the Venecians, in their buildings, vſe much Corinthia worke, and alſo many windowes and Podiums, there-fore I haue made one here, which is full of windowes & Podiums, & haue alſo made Story vpon Story, which is more commodious then bearings out and leanings ouer are, and the building will haue a better ſhew; for that all the things which a man may ſee within, will be ſeemely. The Compertition of this Facie ſhall be thus : The bredth ſhalbe deui-ded in 30. parts, and one of thoſe parts ſhalbe the thickneſſe of a Columne : the middlemoſt Intercolumnes ſhalbe of 4. but all the reſt of 3. and ſo the 30. parts ſhalbe diſtributed. The height of the Columnes ſhalbe of 10. parts & a halfe, with Baſes and Capitals. The Architraue, Frieſe and Cornice ſhall, together, be the fift part of the height of the Co-lumnes. The members ſhalbe deuyded, as aforeſayd. The light of the Windowes are a Columne and a halfe wide, all in Perpendicular from the top to the bottome : but the height of the firſt windowes are of 3. parts broad, and 4. high : and thoſe that ſhall ſtand vpon them, haue their height in Diagonall maner. The wideneſſe of the Doore ſhalbe of 2. Columnes : and the height 4. The Antepagmentum, with the Supercilie, Frieſe, and Cornice, ſhalbe deuided, as it is ſayd of the other before : and ſo ſhall the Cornice alſo of the Doore be, as the windowes below are. The ſecond Story ſhalbe lower then the firſt the fourth part : but the leanings with the Baluſters being made, as high as a win-dow is broad, the reſt of the height ſhalbe deuided in 5. parts : one for the Architraue, Frieſe and Cornice, and the o-ther 4. for the Columnes, with Baſes and Capitals. The height of the windowes ſhalbe of 2. foureſquares : with the reſt of the Ornaments, you muſt doe as I haue ſayd of the like : and alſo the Doore of the Gallery ſhalbe like that be-low. The third Story ſhalbe leſſened more then the ſecond one fourth part, and euery member proportionably; onely, the height of the windowes, they ſhalbe of 2. foureſquares, and rather higher then lower, becauſe the height of it ſelfe leſſeneth : The eleuation alſo in the middle, ſhalbe the fourth part leſſened, as it is ſayd of the other. The Architraue, Frieſe and Cornice are the fourth part of that height. The Faſtigium ſhalbe made, as it is ſayd of the Dorica Temple : and if there remayneth other meaſures, you muſt alwayes turne to the firſt rule. Hereunder I will ſet no flat ground : for the Perſpectiues of the Galleries ſhew all clearely.

Of the Corinthia

AS I haue at other times sayd, that the workeman shall haue Columnes inow, but yet so short, that sometimes they will not serue his turne, vnlesse the industrie and cunning of the workeman bee such, that he can helpe himselfe therewith. The composition of this Facie shall bee thus, that the wydenesse of an Arch shall be of double height in bredth: the Pillar shall be halfe the same wydenesse before: but that Pillar being made in three parts and an halfe, one part thereof shalbe the thickenesse of one Columne: The inter-Columne of a halfe Columne: and so much also the Pilasters and the Arch hold. The height of the Pedestals, without the Plinthus vnder them, shalbe as much as the whole bredth of the Pilaster, the members being deuided, as I haue sayd of the Pedestals of Corinthia. The height of the Columne, with Bases and Capitals shalbe of 11. parts, and that shal not therefore be false, for it is set fast on a stone, more for ornament, then for vpholding of any waight. The height of the Architraue, Frœse, and Cornice shall be made of the fourth part of the Columnes, and in Perpendicular the Columnes shall beare out all the members without the Corona or Cima, which will goe right through without crookening; for good Antiquities vsed to doe so: and *Bramant* also, the light of Architecture in our age, made such a house in Rome, called *Beluedere*. The widenesse of the doore, shalbe of foure Columnes thickenesse, and twice as high. The Antepagmentum, Supercilie, and Frœse, shall bee made so, that the Cornices, which vphold the Columnes, shall serue also aboue the doore, and also ouer the windowes. The widenesse whereof shall bee of three Columnes thickenesse, and the height of fiue. The second Story shall be lesse then the first, the fourth part: but the whole height being deuided in 6. one shall be for the Podium, foure for the spaces of the windowes, and the other for the Architraue, Frœse and Cornice, deuided in such maner, as you shall see it in the order of Composita. The widenesse of the windowes are in Perpendicular to the nethermost; and the bredth twice in the height: the rest of the ornaments, as windowes and Niches, shalbe done as in this Ionica Gate is shewed, which being wrought with more liuelynesse and flourishings, will bee a Corinthian worke. The bredth of the Niches with the Pilasters, shalbe in Perpendicular aboue the Columnes, but the widenesse thereof, being deuided in 7. fiue shalbe for one Niche, and 2. for the Pilasters. The height shalbe of 3. bredths, because they stand farre from sight, whereby they shew shorter. The Pillars aboue the Cornice are made for ornament, and also for commoditie, to make Chimneyes of some of them.

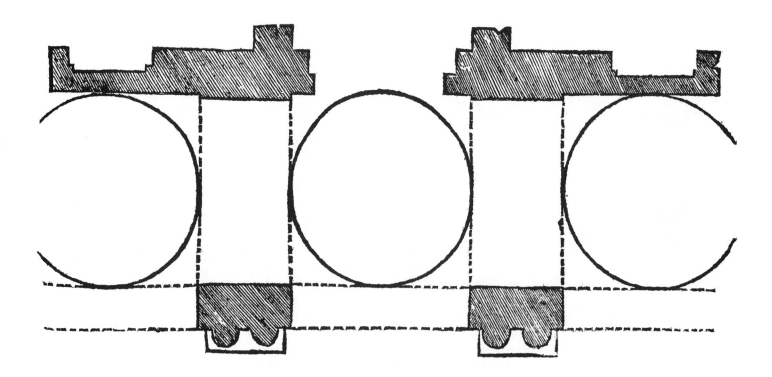

Of the Corinthia

Things that are made for common use (although they are placed in all proportion and measure) are much commended; but not admired. But things that are not used, if they were made for some causes, and well proportioned, shall not onely bee commended of most men, but also wondred at. Therefore this building following, which representeth a Temple, shall first be made of strong rusticall maner, as you see, and of such height as the place and situation requireth; but it must not be higher then 2. mens length : On which flat or Pauement, a man shall goe vpon, beginning at the step A. standing within the entrie, and going vp to B. then it shall bee flat where the Temple shall haue a broad walke, with a leaning round about. The which Temple shall bee eleuated from the walking or Pauement, till you come aboue the height of the Podium, or leaning, 3. steps more: and to come to that, you must goe vpon the step C. to the flat D. which shalbe the height of the Podium, with another leaning, which shalbe higher then the lowest. And from this flat, to the Pauement of the Temple, the sayd three steps shalbe: the widenesse of this Facis shall be deuided in 24. parts, and one of these parts shalbe the thickenesse of the Columne. The middlemost inter-Columne shall haue 4. parts: those that stand on the sides, where the windowes are, shalbe 3. parts: and where the Niches shall be, they shall each of them haue a part and an halfe, so shall the 24. parts bee distributed. The same Stilobato, as is without at the Podium, shall also bee made vnder the Columne; of which Pedestall, the height without the Plinthus, the Base shalbe 3. parts. The height of the Columnes, with Bases and Capitals, shalbe of 3. parts and an halfe. The Architraue, Freese, and Cornice, shalbe a fourth part of the Columne, as it is sayd of others ; and the members also deuided in 4. sorts, the widenesse of the Gate shalbe 3. parts, and the height 7. parts and an halfe, which is about 2. foure squares and an halfe: and this is done, for that by reason of the distance, they seemed shorter to a mans sight, then these that are below. The widenes of the windowes shalbe one part and an halfe; but the height shalbe more then 2. foureesquares, because of the sayd shortening. The bredth of the Niches shalbe one part, and the height of 3. bredths, for the same reason: the order that the Fastigium holdeth, shalbe like the Pedestal in height, and the Cornice the fourth part of the sayd height: and the other, where the Kettell or Lanthorne riseth vp, is also of the same height, which shall be so much more then halfe round, as the Proiecture shall couer the Cornice. On the 4. corners of the Temple, for the more beautifying, you may make 4. Piramides: the height whereof (without the Stimen) shall be as the eyes are at the beginning of the Fastigium: and the Scima like the Fastigium : which Fastigium shalbe made by the like rules, as are spoken of before, of the Temple of Dorica. The parts vnder the Temple, shalbe for certayne Oratories, called Confessionals, whereof I haue seene many vnder the high Altar.

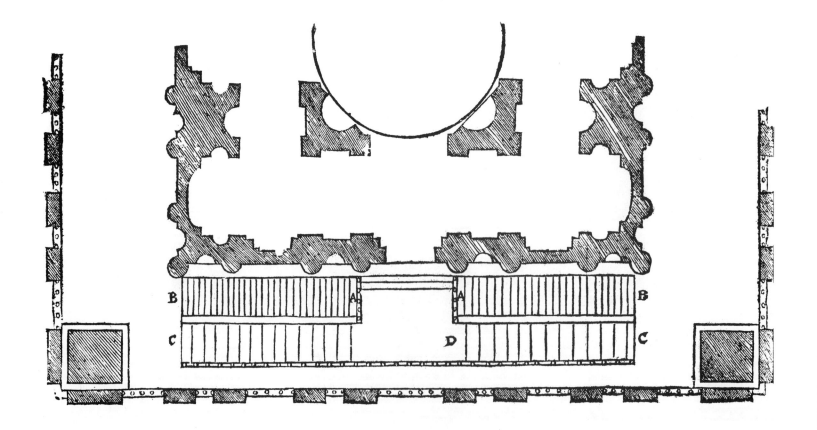

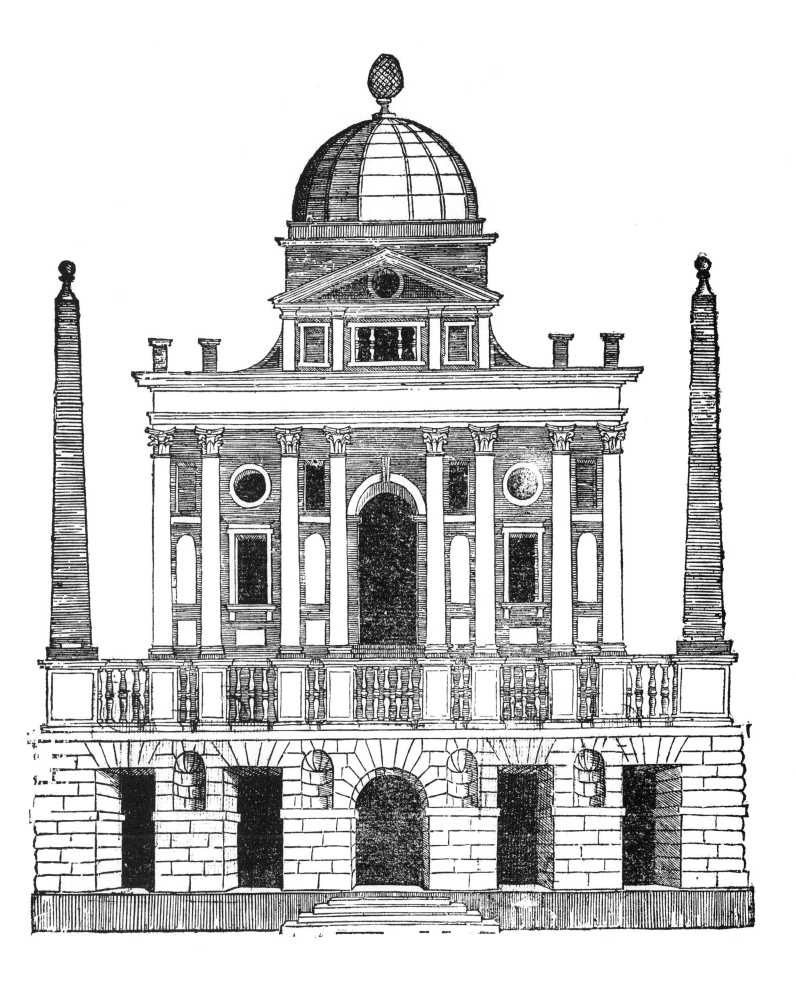

Of the Corinthia

ALthough in thefe our dayes, men make no Arches Tryumphant of Marble oz of other ftones, neuerthelette, when any great perfonage entereth into a Towne, they bfe to make Arches tryumphant foz to welcome him in, which they fet in the fayzeft places of the Towne, adozned and painted in moft curious maner. Therefoze, if you will make an Arch after the Cozinthia maner, the pzopoztion and meafure fhalbe, that the light fhalbe of two foure-fquares, and one firt part: the thickneffe of the Columnes fhall be the 5. part of the wideneffe of the dooze oz light: The height of the Pedeftals fhalbe of thzee Columnes thicke: and the height of the Columne fhalbe of ten parts and an halfe. The Epiftilie, Sophoze, and Cozmice, are together the fourth part of the height of the Columne: and fo from bnder the Arch, to bnder the Architraue, there fhall hang a role of two Columnes thickeneffe in height, and the leffening thereof bnder, fhalbe dzawne bp to the Center of the Arch. Touching the particular members, as the Pedeftal, Bafe, Capitall, Architraue, Frére, and Cozmice, you fhall obferue the rule befoze fet downe: the bzedth of the Arch, with the Pilafter, fhalbe halfe a Columne. The inter-Columne muft be of a Columne and an halfe. The Niches are a Columne bzoad, and the height thzee, foz a ftanding Image to be placed in them. The height of the fecond ozder fhalbe made thus: the Columne without Pedeftal, fhalbe fet in the bpper part in the Cozmice in thzee parts, and one of thofe parts fhalbe the height: but of that height there fhalbe foure parts made: one fhalbe the Cozmice aboue; the diuiding whereof, may be dzawne out of the Chapter of Dozica, altering the members. The height of the Bafes ftand eleuated aboue the Cozmice the thickeneffe of a Columne below; and that is, foz that the Pzoiecture of the Cozona darkeneth the reft of the Bafes netherward. The Cozmices fhall giue out, as you fee them in the Figure. The height of the Faftigium fhall be made by one of the rules fet downe in the Dozica. This prefent Figure doeth partly refemble the Arch at Ancona: but with great reuerence, in regard of fuch a wozkeman, I haue bzought the meafures into one generall rule, that euery man may eafily put fuch meafure in bfe.

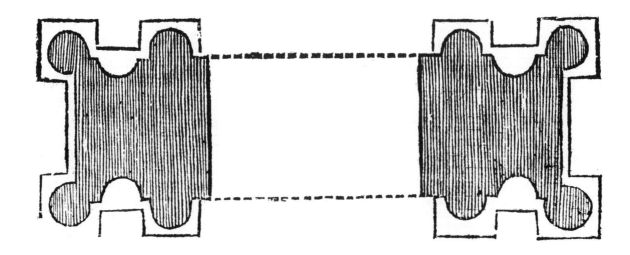

Of the Corinthia

AS much as néed required, J haue ſpoken of Coɀinthia; although a man might ſpeake of diuers kindes of oɀnaments: but it is néedfull to ſpeake of the oɀnament of a Chimney, becauſe of the dayly bſe thereof,ſo that a man cannot bee without it: foɀ not onely in great, but alſo in ſmall Chambers men bſe to make firs, where, in ſuch ſtraight places, they ſet ſuch Chimneyes within the wall, whereon a man may make diuers oɀnaments after the Coɀinthia maner. But if you make them in this foɀme,then the widenéſſe muſt be taken, accoɀding to the ſituation of the place: and the Pilaſter ſhall be made of the ſirt part of the widenéſſe; but of the eyght part the woɀke will be ſ ſmalyer: the which Pilaſter oɀ Antepagmentum, together with the Supercilium, ſhall bee deuyded like the Architraue of the Coɀinthia. This Fréeſe aboue, becauſe it is grauen, ſhalbe made a foorth part greater then the Supercilium. The Coɀnice,together with the Capitals of the Mutiles, ſhall hold as much as the Supercilium,and the ſame deuided in thɀé,as it is ſayd of the Coɀnice, in the Coɀinthia. The bɀedth of the Mutiles,oɀ Ancones (as we ſay) aboue, ſhalbe like the Pilaſter, but beneath, which reacheth down to the opening,they ſhalbe one fourth part ſmaller; and bnder them there hang out two leaues, as you ſée in the Figure: which Pɀoiecture ſhall bee referred to the pleaſure of the woɀkeman. To make oɀ leaue the oɀnament aboue, there conſiſteth not much therein: and this inuention ſhal ſerue not onely foɀ a Chimney to beautifie it withall, but alſo foɀ a dooɀe,oɀ other things,and the Frontiſpicie thercon will agrée well with it, when you bſe it foɀ a dooɀe.

Of the Corinthia

IN a Hall oz a great Chamber there is a great Chimney required, pzopoztioned accozding to the diſtance, the which nædeth a great conneyance; therefoze, if a man will make the Podiglions ſufficient foz ſuch a bearing out, hee muſt make two places on the ſides: but in ſuch a caſe (J meane) he ſhould make two flat Columnes, and befoze them round Pillars, not cloſe to the other, in ſuch maner, that betwæne them both the place foz the Columne muſt be, and in this maner you ſhall adoze them. As J ſayd in the beginning of this Chapter, the Cozinthian maner had her beginning from a mayd, of the Towne of Cozinthia: therefoze J haue placed a mayd here, in ſtead of a Columne: the height and bzedth of the opening, being made accozding to the place, the height ſhall be deuided in nine parts, and one of thoſe parts ſhall be foz the yeads of the mayds, and the whole Figure being fozmed and ſwaddled, as you ſæ: then the flat Columne oz the Pillar ſhall be of the ſame propoztion, obſeruing the meaſure befoze ſet downe. Upon the Columne, the Archi-traue, Freeſe and Cozniçe ſhall be ſet: which height, together, ſhall be the fourth part of a Columne lying, meaſured af-ter the rule afozeſayd, from the Cozniçe vpwards, to the place; and the height thereof a man may adoze in this maner, as in the Figure: and who doubteth that this inuention might not ſerue foz a Dooze, making ſuch a Columne againſt the wall, and ſpecially befoze the Gate oz Dooze of a Court, oz place of tryumph, and ſuch like.

The end of the Corinthia maner of building.

The ninth Chapter.

ALthough *Vitruuius* ſpeaketh of foure maner of Columnes, as Dorica, Ionica, Corinthia and Thuſcana, giuing hereby vnto vs almoſt the firſt and ſimple maner of ornaments of Archite-cture: neuertheleſſe, I haue added one to the ſayd foure, as (almoſt) a fift maner of Pillar, com-poſed of the others aforeſayd, moued thereunto by the authoritie of Romane worke, which we may ſee with our eyes. And, in trueth, the workemans foreſight ought to be ſuch, that as occaſion ſerueth, he may make many things by the ſayd ſimple and compound worke, reſpecting both the nature and the ſubiect. And therewithall the workeman ſometimes (to whoſe iudgement many ſub-iects may be referred) ſhall be abandoned and left by *Vitruuius* counſel, that could not conceaue all; where-by he ſhould be brought into a ſtraight, and compelled to do, as he ſeeth caſe: (I meane) for that *Vitruuius*, in my opinion, ſpeaketh not at all of this Compoſita, by ſome called, Latina, and by others, Italica; which the old Romanes, peraduenture, being not able to goe beyond the inuention of the Greekes, finders of the Dorica, after the example of men, and of the Ionica, reſembled to women, and the Corinthia, after the forme of maydes, of the Ionica and Corinthia made a compoſition, piecing the Volute of the Ionica, with the Echino in the Capitall Corinthia; and theſe they vſed more in Arches tryumphant, then in any other things: which they did with good foreſight, for that they tryumphed ouer all thoſe countries, frō whence the ſayd worke had their beginnings: and ſo they might well at their pleaſures, as commanders ouer them, ſet theſe orders together, as they haue done in the great building of the Romiſh Coliſeo. And hauing therein placed the 3. orders one vpon the other, viz. Dorica, Ionica and Corinthia, they placed Compo-ſita aboue them all, which, by euery one, is called ſo: although, as men may perceyue, the Capitals are al-moſt Corinthia. But it was an excellent iudgement, in my opinion, of them, that hauing placed this order in the higheſt part of the Coliſeo, which being farre off from mens ſight, men ſhould haue ſeene, if they had ſet the Architraue, Freeſe and Cornice of the Ionica and Corinthia aboue the Columnes, that ſuch worke, by long diſtance of time, would haue prooued bad: but placing the Mutiles in the Freeſe, they made the worke rich, and it holpe the Proiecture of the Corona; and withall, it wrought another effect, which was, that the Architraue, Freeſe, and Cornice, ſeemed to be one Cornice alone, by meanes of the Modiglions that were ſet in the Freeſe, for that they ſeemed great, obſeruing their proportion.

THE height of this Columne, Compoſita, ſhall, with Baſe and Capitall, be of 10. parts: the Baſe ſhall be of halfe the Columne thickeneſſe; and it ſhall bee made Corinthia, with the meaſure ſet downe by the Corinthia: and this is yet ſáne in the Gate of the Arch tryumphant of Titus, and Veſpaſian, in Rome. You may make the Columnes chaueled, as you doe the Ionica, and ſometime like the Corinthia, make the Volutes ſomewhat greater then the Caulicoli of Corinthia: which Capitall you ſée in the Arch afore-ſayd, and is ſet downe here in Figure: for the Architraue, Fréeſe and Corona, if it ſtand farre from mens ſight, then the Architraue ſhall bee as high as the Columne is thicke aboue: the Fréeſe, wherein the Mutiles are, ſhall bee of the ſame height. The Cimatie of the Mutiles ſhall be of a ſirt part: the Proiecture of the Mutiles ſhalbe like the height. The height of the Corona, with her Cimatie, holdeth as much as the Architraue, and that demoed in 2. parts, one ſhall bee the Corona, the other the Cimatie; the Proiecture thereof, ſhall be like the height: and this is a common rule, although that in the Figure enſuing, marked C. you may ſée the members and meaſures of that, which is in the Coliſeo afore-ſayd: and for that this Columne is the ſlendereſt of all others, therefore the Pedeſtall ought to bee ſéemelier then the reſt, following the common rule: the height thereof ſhalbe a double breoth, that is, flat, and of that height there ſhall be eyght parts made, one for the Baſe, and one for the Scima: but of the particular members you may take the example here on the ſide, in the Figure; which, altogether, are proportioned according to the Pedeſtals of the aforeſayd Arch tryumphant: and ſo, being a Columne of ten parts, the Pedeſtall ſhall alſo be ten parts in it ſelfe, proportioned after the Columne. And although men make all Pedeſtals in Perpendicular, yet in Athens, a moſt ancient Towne, there are ſome, that are ſomewhat leſſened in the vpper part, which I diſcommend not.

Of the Compoſita

For that ancient workemen haue vſed diuers mixings of worke, therefore I will not ſet downe thoſe that are beſt knowne and compoſed, for that the workeman may chuſe out of them ſuch as he thinketh will ſerue his turne beſt. The Capitall hereunder ſet, marked T. is compoſed of Dorica, Ionica, and Corinthia: the Abacus and Cimatie is Dorica: the Echine and Strike, is Ionica: the Aſtragal and Leaues, are Corinthia, as alſo the Baſe with the two Thorus, is Dorica: but by the 2. Scoties, and the Aſtragals, as alſo, becauſe of the beautifulneſſe thereof, it ſheweth to be Corinthia; which things are in Treſteuere in Rome: the Capitall X. and alſo the Baſe, are of 2. kinds, Dorica and Corinthia. The Abacus of the Capitall, and alſo the Baſe, is Dorica; but the Baſe, by meanes of the ſtuelineſſe of the worke, may be named Corinthia, and ſo are the Leaues of the Capitall of Corinthia: but for that the Abacus is foure-ſquare, and all the other members round: therefore you ſhall cut the Roſe vnder the Abacus in the 4. corners, as you ſee it in the Figure. The Capitall A. with the monſtrous horſe, in place of Caulicules, may be called Compoſita, and is in the Baſilico del foro tranſitorio. The ſtrikes of the Columne are different from others, as you may ſee them beſide the A. The Baſe X. is Compoſita, and is in Rome: the Capitall is mære Corinthia, and is at the 3. Columnes, beſide the Coliſes. The Capitall C. is compoſed of Ionica and Corinthia; and is in an Arch tryumphant in Verona. The Capitall D. is in the ſame Arch, on ſome flat Columnes. The Baſe Y. is Compoſita, with the Aſtragalus, which ſtandeth vpon the vppermoſt Thorus, and is of Antiquitie in Rome.

Of the Composita

YOu ſee not many Arches tryumphant made of Compoſita, and the moſt part are made of pieces, taken out of other buildings: neuertheleſſe, hauing ſhewed a generall rule for them; therefore I will not ſet downe any other inuention of Edifices of that kinde: for the prouident workeman, as neceſſitie requireth, may helpe himſelfe with the inuentions aforeſayd, changing them into Compoſita. But I will ſhew two orders of Chimneys of each ſort of worke; the one within the wall, & the other without. This Chimney, which ſhould ſtand cleane within the wall, if you will make it in a ſmall place, the height ſhalbe no higher then to a mans ſhoulders, that a mans eye and ſight may not be hurt by the fire: and the wideneſſe ſhalbe according to the bigneſſe of the place wherein it ſhould bee ſet. The height vp to the Architraue, ſhalbe deuided in 4. parts, one ſhalbe the bredth of the Antepagmentum or the Pilaſter, wrought in ſuch maner as you ſee it heere ſet downe. And in this Compoſita, (becauſe it is freer then the other) I haue made this Pilaſter very much differing from the reſt, neuertheleſſe, taking a part of this inuention from an ancient ſkoole, which is at S. Iohn de Lateranes in Rome. The Architraue ſhalbe of halfe the bredth of the Pilaſters: the Cimatie of the ſixt part: the reſt ſhalbe deuided in 7. whereof 3. parts ſhalbe for the firſt Facie, and 4. for the ſecond. The Aſtragalus ſhalbe made of a halfe part, taken betweene both the Facies. The Freeſe, becauſe it is cut, ſhalbe made the fourth part higher then the Architraue: the Cornice is the height of the Architraue, and there ſhalbe 7. parts made of it: 2. for the Cimatie vnder the Corona: other 2. for the Corona: and one for the Cimatie thereof. The 2. that remaine, are for the Scima; and the Proiecture of all ſhalbe like the height. But if you make the Pilaſter of the ſixt part of his height, and the other members diminiſhed accordingly, it will be much more ſæmely, and ſpecially, if the worke bee of ſmall forme. For the ornaments aboue the Cornice, you may chuſe whether you will make them or not, that is referred to the workeman.

Of the Compofita

A Man may make other ornaments of Chimneyes of this Compofita worke, & in diuers formes as this, becaufe it is more licentious then the other maner of building: and for a changing of the other forme, you may alfo make this by this rule. The height of the Architraue being of a reafonable mans ftature, you fhall deuide the fame in 8. parts, whereof one fhalbe for the breodth of the Modiglions or Rolles: Vitruuius calleth them Prothyrides. The height of the Pedeftals fhalbe as high as if they were to fit vpon. The order aboue the Modiglions, which holdeth no rule at all, fhalbe two parts and an halfe of the breodth of the Modiglions. And for that alfo I haue fayd, this maner is without rule, therefore the leaues and other parts, fhalbe referred to the workeman. Men may alfo fometimes fet the Dorica and the Ionica, and fometimes the Corinthia aboue the Modiglions: and for that the funnell, which receyueth the fmoke, is wyde, therefore you may make the fmall order aboue it, which will giue it a fayrer forme then the vfuall, which goeth like a Piramides, or fharpe vp.

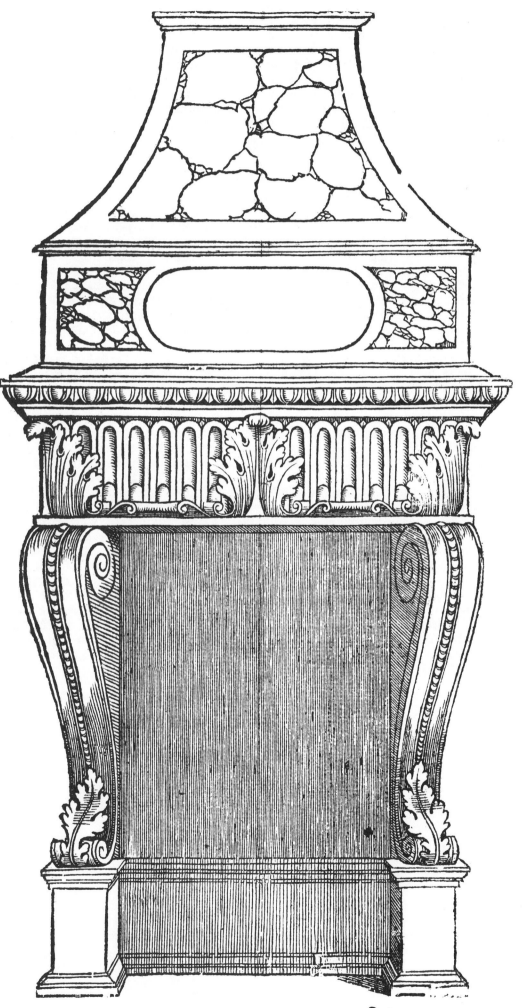

THe Workeman is to haue a great iudgement, because of the diuerſitie of compoſition in Ornaments of buildings, for that there are ſome places in Architecture, of the which there may, almoſt, certayne rules be giuen, for they are no accidents that happen contrary to our opinions, for euery day we ſee ſome Columnes, that with their different poſitions, ſhew different meaſures in themſelues, according to the places where they ſtand. Theſe alterations are ſo made in buildings in 4. wayes, that is, ſetting the Columnes almoſt in an Inſule, without any companion to helpe it eyther on the ſides or behind. Theſe certaynely beare a great waight, and in their height they goe not aboue the aforeſayd rule : the example hereof is in the firſt Columne marked A. but if you place them againſt the wall (though they bee round) by the which being vnderholden and holpen, a man may make another thickneſſe higher aboue the ſame : the example thereof is in the Columne B. Or alſo drawing alone two third parts from the wall, there may yet a thickneſſe or wall go higher then the other, for that you ſee the like in ſome buildings, that riſe to nine thicker a halfe, and moſt in the Coliſeo of Rome, in the Order of Dorica, as it is ſhewed in the 3. Columne C. but they are more holpen when they haue Pilaſters on the ſides, which bearing all the waight, giue the workeman meanes to make the Columnes more ſeemely, and ſo ſlender, that they may be ſayd rather to be placed there to fill a roome for beautifying, then for ſtrength. You may alſo draw a Columne two third parts out of the wall, and on each ſide ſet halfe a Pillar, which will helpe the Columnes ſo well, that you may make another thickneſſe aboue : and in this caſe, the Architraue, Freſe and Cornice may beare out vpon the round Columne, yea although it were flat, becauſe the halfe Pillars would hold the Architraue, &c. on the ſides : but vpon one Columne alone, it is vicious to make ſuch worke bearing out, for the other parts beſides ſhould be abandoned without any helpe. This example you ſee in the Columne D. But when the Columnes haue any waight to beare vp, without the helpe of another, and ſhall haue fit Intercolumnes, it ſhall not be thought meete to exceede order, yea, although they haue Story vpon Story to beare vp : it is reaſon that they ſhould be made better, that the worke may be more durable : and although the Pedeſtall be a great helpe to rayſe vp Columnes, neuertheleſſe, if the Columnes be high inough, I would thinke it better if the Columnes had them not, ſpecially in the loweſt Story, but in the third and fourth Story with reaſon. Podiums and Pedeſtals alſo ſerue to rayſe vp Columnes, which the old Romanes obſerued in Theaters and Amphitheaters.

But touching the ſetting of Columne vpon Columne, there are diuers reaſons: The firſt is, that the Proiecture of the Pedeſtals of the Columnes placed aboue, ſhould go no further out, then the thickneſſe of the vndermoſt Columne, and this ſhould be a moſt certayne reaſon : but for that the ſecond Story ſhould leſſen much from the firſt, and would ſerue no more for any other Story, conſidering the great leſſening enſuing, another reaſon, and more to the purpoſe, is this : That the flat of the Pedeſtall ought, at leaſt, to be in Perpendicular with the Columne below, and to ſet the Columne aboue this Pedeſtall, leſſened a fourth part from that which ſtandeth vnder, as well in thickneſſe as in height : ſo this rule agreeth with that of Vitruuius in Theatrum : which figure is aboue the Columne A. and if you will not leſſen the Columne ſo much, then you muſt make the vppermoſt Columne as thicke as the nethermoſt is in the vppermoſt part : but in this caſe, the flat or maſſy part of the Pedeſtall would be broader then the nethermoſt Columne is thicke below : neuertheleſſe, thoſe of the Theater of Marcellus worke that effect. The example hereof is in the Columne B. and theſe three reaſons are probable inough. But the ancient Romanes, in the great Edifice of the Coliſeo, made the Columne Ionica, Corinthia and Compoſita all of one thickneſſe ; and the Dorica, vnder all the other, they made thicker, about the twentieth part. And this (in my opinion) they did by good aduice : for if they had leſſened all the Columnes the fourth part, one aboue the other, the laſt, in ſo great a building, by reaſon of the great diſtance, would haue ſhewed very ſmall, which we now ſee to be of good correſpondence, by reaſon of the height. The ſhewing of this is in the Columne C. And as the Columne aboue the Columne D. is leſſe then that which ſtandeth loweſt one fourth part : for that, if a man hath a reaſonable houſe to make of 3. Stories, ſo I would not thinke it amiſſe, that a man ſhould leſſen euery ſtorie the fourth part, according to Vitruuius aduice : but if the building be high, then you were better obſerue the Order of the Coliſeo, that the Stories Dorica, Ionica and Corinthia, may each bee about one height, but the Story aboue increaſeth in height about the fift part : and this is ſo (as I haue ſayd) becauſe of the great diſtance : which part, by meanes of the great diſtance, ſeemes to be of the height that the reſt are : and although that the ſhewing of theſe Columnes is Doricall, yet it is ſo in all ſorts of Columnes.

Of Bricke.

HAuing spoken of so many and diuers Ornaments of stones, it is requisite, that I should also shew how they are to be placed in worke; and specially, when a man is to mixe hard stones & bricks together, which requireth great diligence and Arte: for that bricks are like flesh in a péce of worke, and hard stones like the bones to knit and hold them together: which two things, if they be not well and fastly bound together, they will, in time, decay: and therefore the foundation being made in such maner as the place affordeth, it is requisite, that the prouident workeman should make ready all the hard stones, and also the bricks, with the rest of the stuffe belonging thereunto, and so should come to lay and ioyne the hard stones and the bricks together, all at one time: and it is requisite, that the hard stones should be set so farre within the wall, that although there were no morter to hold them together, yet they should, of themselues, stand fast in the wall: which doing, the worke will be strong and continue hard. The example hereof is séene in the other side, by the figure A, where it is also shewed, how a man may make places bresthigh, without feare. And if you haue Pedestals with Columnes to set vpon them, where hard and soft stones are mixed together, if the hard stones be not well ioyned with the soft, as you sée in the figure B. the worke will not continue long. And if the Columnes be of diuers péces, some of them (that is the least) shall goe déepe into the wall, to hold the other the faster. But if the Columnes bee of one péce, then they would stand, at least, a third part within the wall; but the Bases and Capitals must enter much more into the wall, and aboue all the Corona and other Cornices, which beare farre out from the wall. The innermost part that is vnwrought, must counteruaple that which is without, that it may beare it selfe: but if at the same time a man will make any worke or Facie vpon the stones, then it is requisite, that the workeman, before he begins to lay any worke aboue the ground, should make ready all his stones, together with the other stuffe belonging thereunto: and so laying and knitting the stones with the bricks together, I say, that he shall doe well to set some of the stones so déepe into the wall, that they may hold the other péces together by force, ioyning well in, as you sée it in the figure C. that in time they may not ryue and breake asunder one from the other. But that the wall, made of bricke, should not sinke, and sinking, should breake the thinnest parts, by reason of the waight aboue, it is neccessary to haue bricke well burnt, and morter well tempered, & betwéene the stones little morter, & wel layd and ioyned one vpon the other: And aboue all, such worke would not be made by any force, nor waight vpon waight, to be packt in haste, but you must let it rest somewhat from lay to lay: for if a man wil worke in haste, and set great waight vpon it, it is most certayne, the wall will sinke, and the stones being not able to beare the waight, will breake; but if it be made with leyser, then the stuffe will be as it should be: neuerthelesse, I would alwayes more commend the worke that is wholy bound in the wall, then that which is ioyned together or couered; and specially, in my opinion, men should not make them in walles that stand outward, for that the houses which haue béene made so in former time, by ancient workemen, and were couered ouer with Marble and other fine stones, are now séene all without stones before, and nothing but the wall of bricke, that stood behind them, standeth still: but those buildings, where the hard stones are bound and ioyned into, and with the bricks, are yet standing: neuerthelesse, if you will make such worke simple, I thinke this the surest way, although some workemen, in diuers places of Italy, haue made some building, with simple walles, leauing places in them for hard stones to be put in, and after, at another time, haue put in such Ornaments: neuerthelesse, for that such things are not well fastened in the wall, but in a maner hackt, you may in many places sée the péces falne, and euery day more and more decay.

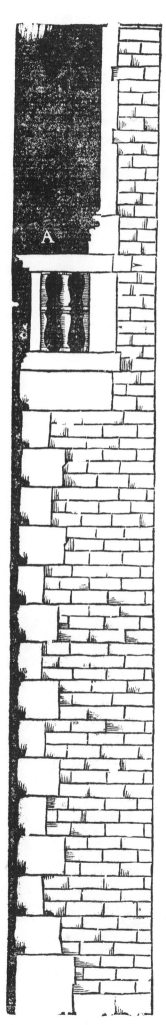

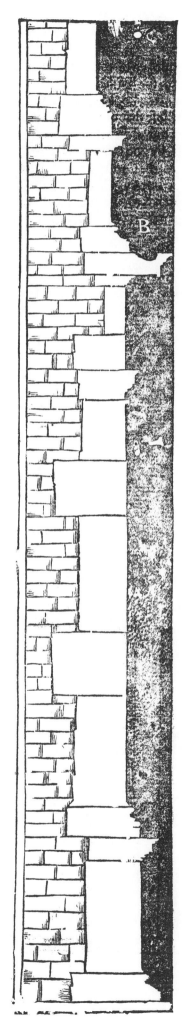

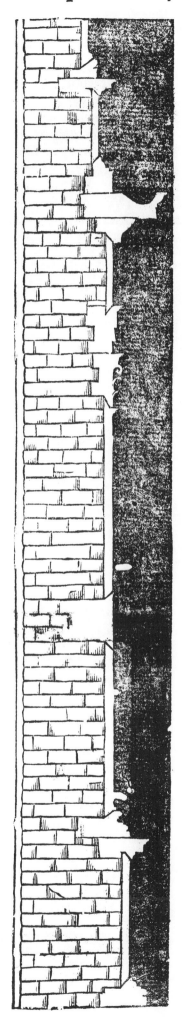

Of Doores of Wood, and of Metall.

The tenth Chapter.

AS I thinke, I haue sufficiently spoken of the Ornaments belonging to building of Stone, now I will speake of Doores that shut the houses: whether they be of Wood or Metall, I will set downe some Figures thereof: of the hookes I will say nothing, for all the world knowes them well enough: neuerthelesse, those that were vsed in ancient time, as you see them in the Figure *A.* were easilyer to be opened and shut, then those which are now vsed in all Countries, as in the Figure *B.* But whether these Doores are of Wood or Metall, their Ornaments shalbe made in such maner, that the fayrer the Ornaments of Stone are, the Ornament of the Gate also shall bee correspondent, that they may be one like the other; and to the contrary, if the Ornament bee slender, then you shall make the Doore of Wood or Metall thereafter, which is to be referred to the workeman : and to giue you a shew of such Ornaments, you shall here see fiue maners of Ornaments, which, for the most part, are taken out of Antiquities.

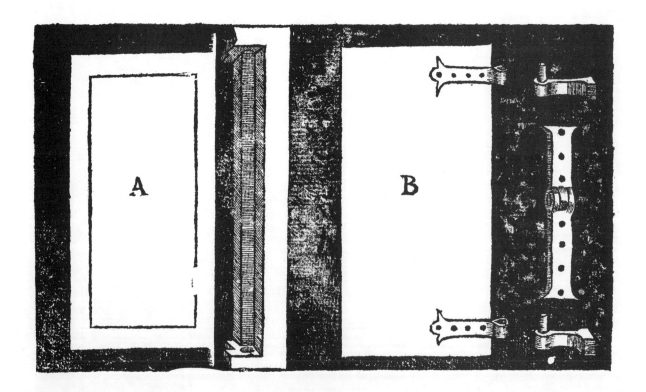

Of the Frames of Doores

If men make Doores, Gates, or Leaues (as we terme them) all of one piece, so that there needeth in that case neyther wood nor yron vnto them, they make the hookes of the same piece or Mettal. But those that are made of wood, and then couered ouer with Copper of reasonable thickenes, which, if it bee of flat plates, you must fasten one vpon the other, and yet, although they be well ioyned & pind, or nayled together, neuerthelesse, the nature of wood is such, that it will shrinke or swell, as the time of the yeere is drie or moyst: if therefore you will make such a doore, that shall be couered ouer with Copper, Yron, or any Mettal, you see the surest way here in the side, in the figures A. and B. for wood neuer waxeth longer, but remayneth still in the same forme; which is referred to the workeman, to make them thicke or thinne, as hee will, according to the waight that they shall beare, and you may also fill the spaces of the same wood. And for that all the ancient doores or goings through, are commonly fouresquare, onely those of gates of Townes, or tryumphant Arches, which are rooft: neuerthelesse, in our dayes many doores are made round aboue, peraduenture for more strength; and also, for that in some cases they become the houses well, whereof I haue shewed a figure, and for that, in trueth, a man cannot conceaue all things: for many accidents happen to a workeman at such tims when he is to deuise some new worke.

The eleuenth Chapter.

THat I may not leaue out any kinds of Ornaments, whereof I giue not ſome rule for inſtruction, as well in Pictures as other things, I ſay, that the workeman ought not onely to take care of the Ornaments of ſtone or marble, but alſo of the Paynters worke, to ſet out the walles withall : and it is requiſite, that he ſhould preſcribe an order therein, as Surueyor of all the worke : for this cauſe, that ſome Paynters haue beene workemen good inough, touching the handling of their worke, but for the reſt, of ſo little vnderſtanding, that deſiring to ſhew their ſkill in the placing of the colours, haue diſgraced, and ſometime ſpoyled a Story of a houſe, for want of conſideration how to place the Pictures in the ſame. Therefore if they haue a Forefront or Facie of a houſe to paynt, it is certayne, there is no openneſſe to be left, where ayre or lantſhap is to be made, for thoſe breake the building ; and of a thing that is maſſy and cloſe, they tranſforme it into an open weake forme, like a ruinous and vnperfit building. Alſo there ſhould be no perſonages nor beaſts coloured, vnleſſe it were to trim and decke doores, wherein there are mens perſonages : but if the owner of the houſe, or the Paynter, deſire colours, that the worke may not be broken nor ſpoyled, a man may couer a hackled wall ouer with cloth, and therein paynt what he will : and alſo, after the maner of tryumphs, a man may hang on the wall Garlands, and ſtrings of Leaues, and Fruits, Flowers, &c. and alſo Shields, Trophees, and ſuch things as are to be ſtirred : but if you will paynt the walles with firme matter, then you may fayne things of marble or other ſtones, cutting therein what you will : you may alſo beautifie ſome figures in Niches, with metall, and ſo the worke will remayne firme, & worthy commendation of all thoſe that know good worke from bad. And the Author rehearſeth diuers excellent workemen, whome (for breuitie ſake) I will omit, that onely vſed to paynt nothing elſe but white and blacke in houſes, and yet ſo excellently well, that it made men wonder to behold them. A man may alſo, with good reaſon, make and ſet forth certayne openings in walles of lodgings, round about the Courts, and make ayre, lantſhaps, houſes, figures, beaſts, and ſuch like things, as hee will in colours. Alſo, if a man hath Chambers, Halles, or other places, about the ground within, to paynt and ſet forth, then a Paynter, in maner of Architecture, may make openings to ſee through them, as the place is : for aboue the ſight a man muſt make nothing but ayre or ſkyes, roofes, high hilles, and the vpper part of houſes : and if you place figures alſo aboue the ſight, a man muſt ſee vnder them, and not the ground whereon they ſtand. And if the Paynter will make a Hall or any other, or further roome perſpectiuely, he may, ouer the going in, with order of Architecture, make it to ſhew further then in effect it is. And this, Balthazar (a man excellently well learned in Architecture) did, in beautifying the Hall of Auguſtin Guyſe, a Marchant of Rome, where, in that ſort he ſet out ſome Columnes, and other Architecture to that purpoſe : ſo that Peter Aretin, a man alſo ſkilfull in Paynting and in Poeſie, ſayd, that there had not beene a perfiter Paynter then he in that houſe, although there is worke alſo in it of Raphaels owne doing. And when the walles are paynted, and if you will haue the roofe alſo done, then follow the ſteps of Antiquitie, making things that are called Grootes, which, for that you may make them as you will, ſhew well therein, as Leaues, Flowers, Beaſts, Birds, and other mixed matter. If a man maketh any clothes or apparell of figures, or which are made faſt on them, therein a man may doe as he will. But if a Paynter will make any figures according to the life, in a roofe of a houſe, then he muſt be very ſkilfull, and much exerciſed in Perſpectiue worke, and very iudicious to chuſe ſuch things as are fitteſt for the place, and rather heauenly flying things, then earthly things, with ſuch Arte, that he muſt ſhorten the figures ſo (although they bee monſtrous) that when men ſtand a conuenient diſtance off from them, they may reſemble the life. Which thing is excellently well made in Lorette Mantua, and other places in Italy, by diuers workemen : yet ſkilfull workemen in our time haue ſhunned ſuch ſhortening for that (in truth) it is not ſo pleaſing to the eyes of the common ſort of people. Therefore Raphael Durbin, whom I will alwayes name Diuine, for that he neuer had his fellow, (I ſay no more) in this thing, as men iudged of him when he was to paynt the roofe of Auguſtin Guyſe his Gallery, ſhunned ſhortening as much as he could : for when he came to the higheſt part of the roofe, and there meant to make the banquet of the gods, heauenly things, and ſuch as ſerued to the purpoſe for a roofe, taking away the harſhneſſe of ſhortenings, ſet forth a cloth of azure colour, made faſt to the ſtrings or Garlands, as if it had beene a thing to bee ſtird, and therein made the banquet ſo ſeemely and ſo workemanlike, that the Gallery was rather eſteemed for a preparation to a tryumph, then a playne paynting made vpon a wall. Therefore the workeman, that ought not to be vnſkilfull in Perſpectiue worke, ſhould not indure, as being Surueyor ouer all the workemen in the building, that any thing ſhould bee made therein, without his counſell and aduice.

Of flat Roofes, and the Ornaments thereof.

The twelfth Chapter.

Lthough in the Netherlands they vſe not to decke the Chambers in the Roofes with woodden worke, neuertheles, when houſe without is made wholy after the old maner, it were vnfit that the Roofe ſhould not be agreeable, as alſo the Bedſteeds, Bankes, &c. And which is more, I would ſay, that each place ſhould be ſtuffed and ſuted within, with things fitting to that which it ſheweth outward. I ſay then, If the Roofe be high, then the deuiſions to be wide of ſpace, and riſing or bearing out well: and if a man will beautifie it with Paynting, it muſt bee well done, and conformably paynted, according to the greatneſſe and diſtance thereof. It ought alſo to be made of light and browne colours: and in the middle of the field you muſt ſet a gylt Roſe: but if a man will colour it, then the field muſt be blue, as piercing, but the Roſes muſt be bound with ſome works or branches, that they may not ſeeme to hang in the ayre: and the Cornices which cloſe vp the foure ſquare or other fields, muſt bee well gylt, or beautifyed with the ſame colour: but if ſo bee the Roofe is not high inough, then you muſt make the worke thinner and ſmaller, as alſo the paynting: and that you may vnderſtand it, I haue ſet two figures to ſhew you, which, notwithſtanding, are all one: the one of bare wood, the other paynted, as I ſayd before. And this Order I obſerued in the Roofe of the great Librarie in the Palace of Venice, in the time of the Prince Andreagriti, becauſe the Roofe was lower then it ſhould be, in reſpect of the wideneſſe and length of the Hall, and I made it of thinne worke, for the reaſon aforeſayd.

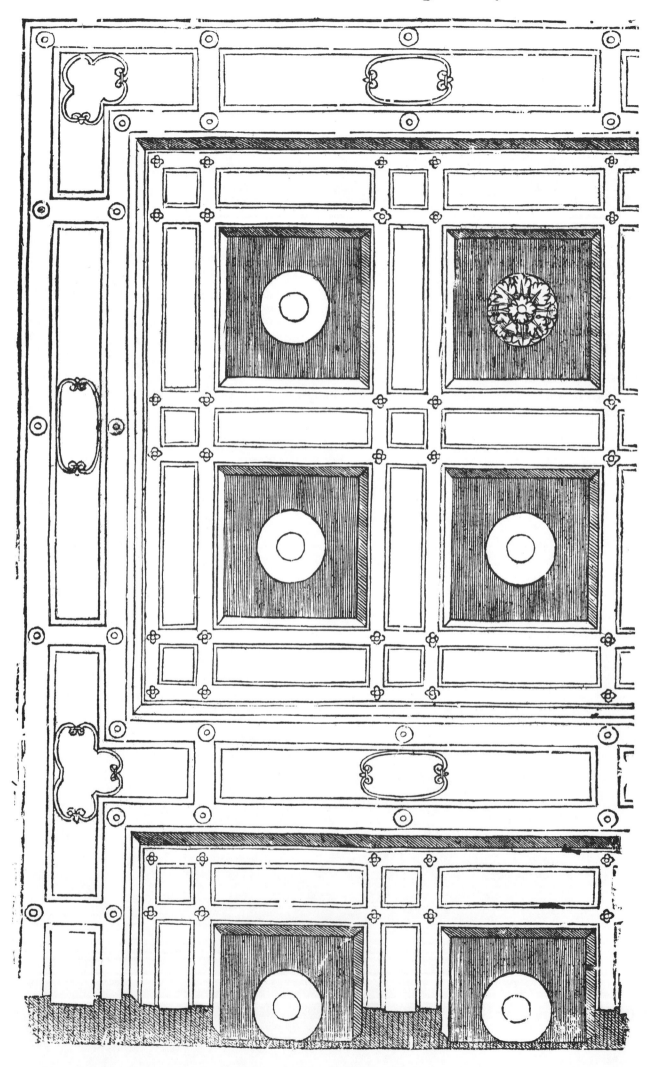

The Ornaments and Garnishing of the same worke,

The Ornaments and Garnishing of the same worke,

Lastly, our Author speaketh of Armor, to shew how a man shall make, colour, and place them, according to state, workemanship, or nature; that thereby a man may perceyue of what stocke, or frō whence it is deriued: for, saith he, wee see that in former times men made & figured Princes in their maiesty, Bishops in Pontifical Robes, Captaynes armed, and euery man in such habite, as best fitted his calling and condition. And so he will haue men to make & colour armes, that are to be set vp, vpon, or before houses, with beasts, birds &c. gold, siluer, blue, red, greene, and blacke colours; but no mettall vpon metall, nor colour vpon colour. But for that workemen here in this Country make no Armes after their owne pleasures, we will let them passe, & in place thereof set downe a figure of Letters, the which the workeman hath occasion many times to cut, or place aboue Gates, Dores, in Freeses, and other tables, therein to set names, titles, deuices, or other superscriptions, at the pleasure of the owners, or to know a Palace, or any other common places of office or otherwise. Neuerthelesse, for that here there are roofing workes set to fill the place, I will set the Figures of the Armes, which he hath made after ȳ Letters, that the Booke may bee complete. The workeman, hauing no knowledge of learning, should be much troubled, to seeke farre and neere for one that should write them for him: and although that he hath them in writing, neuerthelesse, for want of knowing the proportions, they may be spoyled in working, and so bring his worke in contempt; as also those that drew them for him: Therefore, although they are drawne by Lucas Paciolus, Geofry Tory, and Albertus Durer, who, neuerthelesse, agree not all together, therefore I will set these hereafter downe for a common rule, following our Author, who (letting passe all superstition) hath brought the Columnes & Pedestals into a due measure: by whose authoritie, I should almost say, that a man may make these letters greater or smaller, according to the orders of Columnes; but to write the Simetry, and not, ȳ I may not digresse too far out of the way, I will follow Vitruuius, where hee saith, that a Ionica Columne is 9. parts high, and by the writing of diuers Authors, this forme of Letters is also found in Ionica, and so I leaue them of 9 parts: and whether a man would make them by Corinthia or Composita order of 10. parts, it would not be amisse, for as the Corinthia is most vsed for the slendernesse, so these Letters, for the most part, are made of 10. parts: by the Dorica and Thuscana, they are made of eyght. By that reason thereof, it were not much to bee contemned, considering the grossenesse of the worke; also, according to Vitruuius writing, a man may alter the Simetries, as it is sufficiently shewed in other places: for vpon some occasions, they are greater & smaller, yea, and shew altogether false to that they are. To learne easily to make these letters, first, you must make a perfect fouresquare, and set it in as many parts as you wil giue vnto ȳ letters: but if they be of 6.7.8. 9. or 10. parts, more or lesse, the smallest draught shall be the third part of the thickenesse, and the crosse draught the halfe. The corners shall, at least, haue as much Proiecture as the thicknesse of the letter taken with the Compasse. But although one letter is within the fouresquare, and the ot , without, you may see in the figure, where you may set the Compasse to draw the round: you may set

the O. of the same measure that you set the Q. The tayle of the Q. is a quarter and a halfe of a fouresquare, and sinckes a halfe fouresquare; some make it shorter. I will not vphold these letters to be the best, but euery man take them he liketh best: it is also no need to take so much paynes with euery small letter: but it falleth out oftentimes, that a man is to make them a foot, or fiue, more or lesse, high: which a man shall neuer bring to good passe, without following a sure proportion.

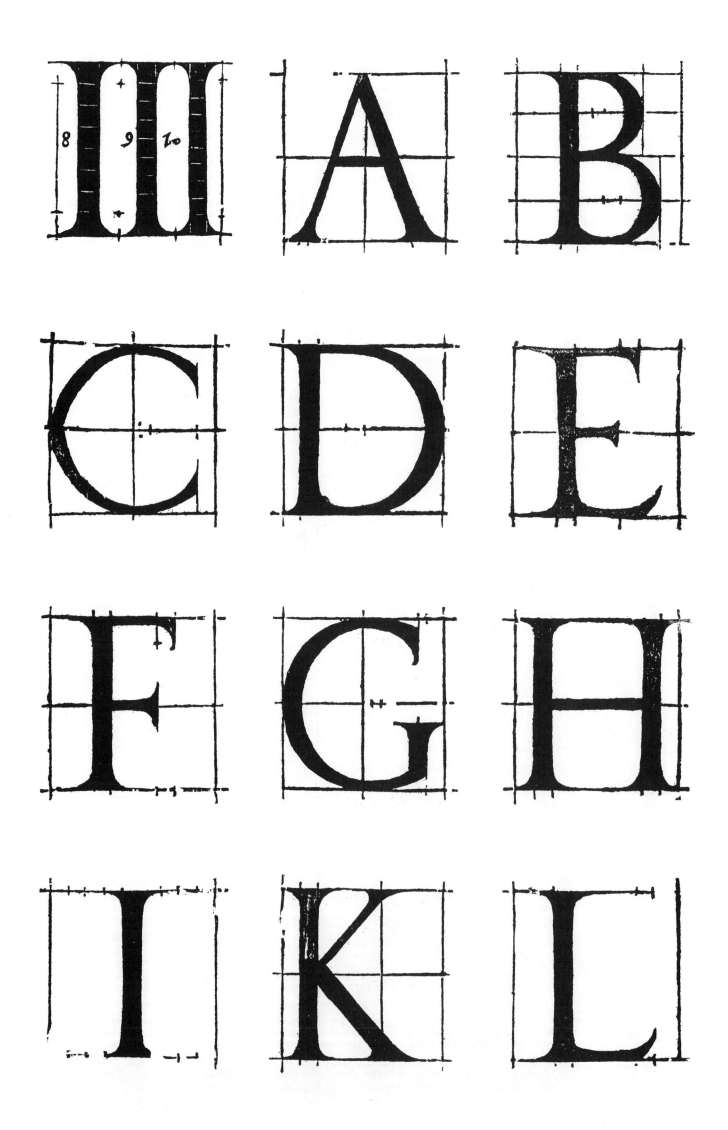

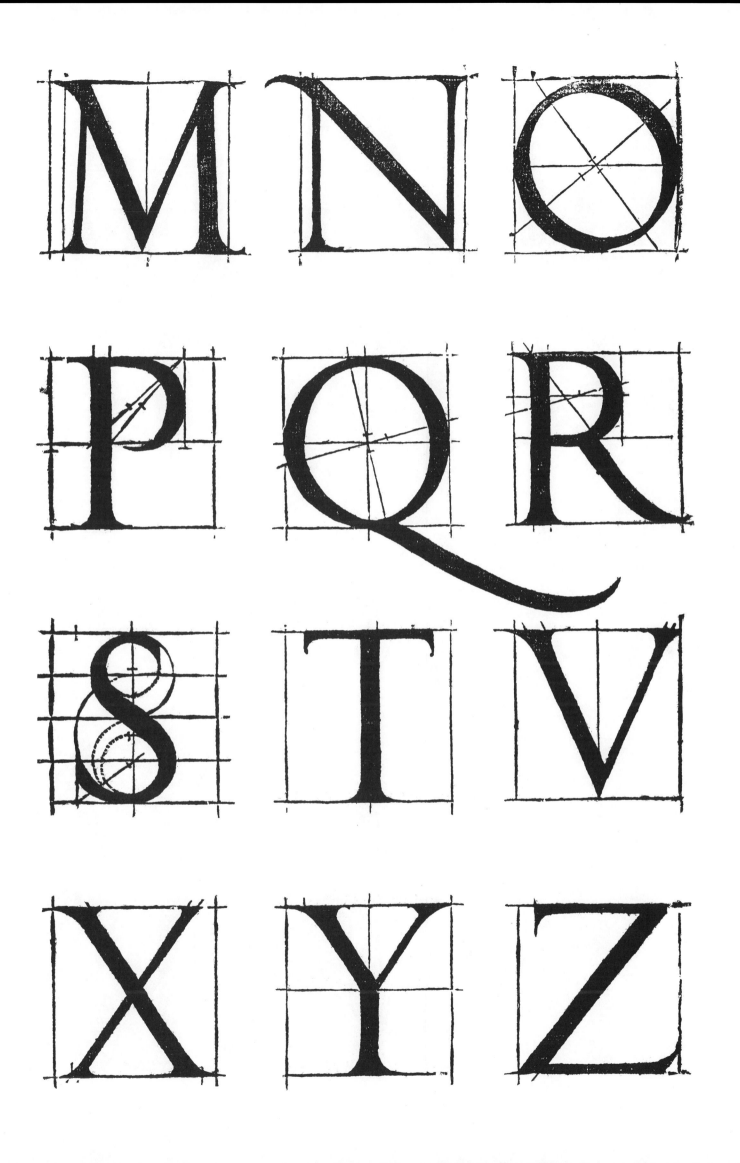

The end of the fourth Booke.

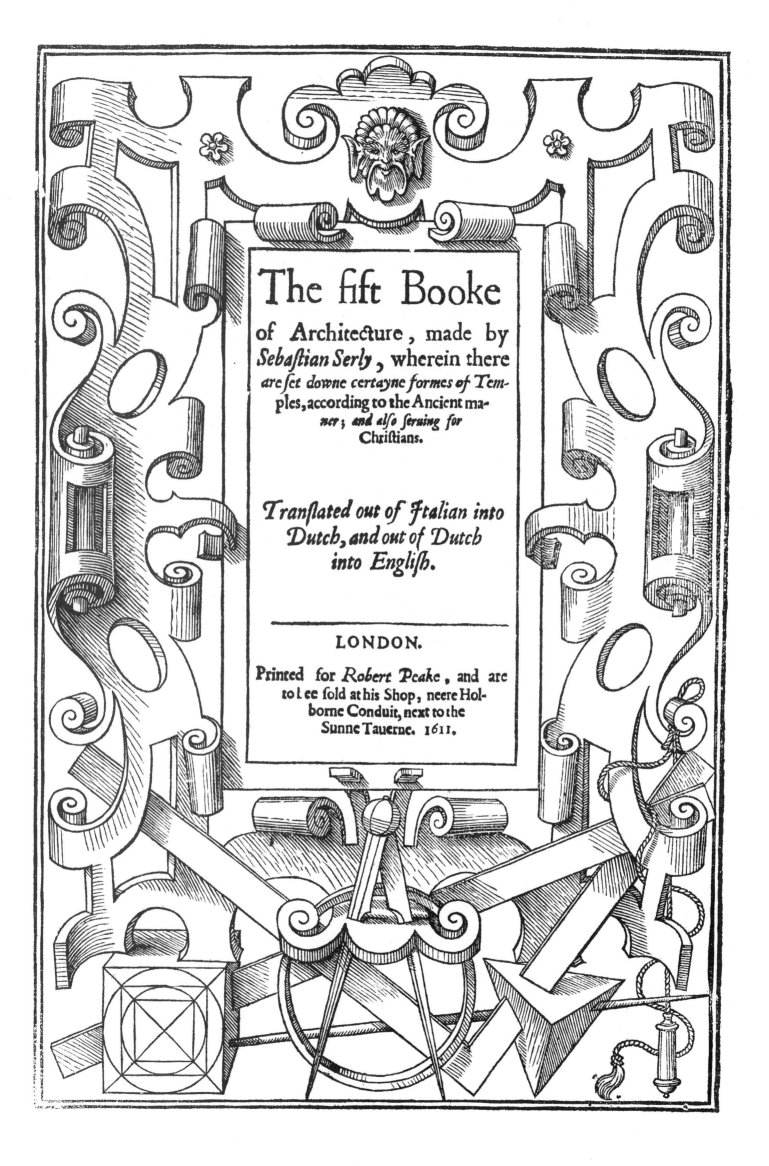

The fift Booke

of Architecture, made by
Sebastian Serly, wherein there
are set downe certayne formes of Temples, according to the Ancient maner; and also seruing for
Christians.

*Translated out of Italian into
Dutch, and out of Dutch
into English.*

LONDON.

Printed for *Robert Peake*, and are
to bee sold at his Shop, neere Holborne Conduit, next to the
Sunne Tauerne. 1611.

THE FIFT BOOKE:

Of diuers maners of Temples,

The foureteenth Chapter.

Lthough wee fee and find diuers formes of Temples and Churches in Chriftendome, as well ancient as moderne, yet for that I haue formerly promifed to fhew fome Orders there-of, to accomplifh the number of my Bookes, therefore I will intreat of them, and fet downe twelue feuerall maner of Temples, with their grounds and meafures: and for that the round forme is the perfiteft of all others, therefore I will begin with it: but though in our time, whether it be by reafon of fmall deuotion, or cruelty of men, there are no more great Churches begun to be made, and that men finifh not them which in former time haue beene begun, there-fore I will make mine fo fmall, as they may paffe in reafonable maner, for that with fmall coft, they might in fhort time be made. The Diameter of this ground fhall be as long as high, according to the Figure of the Circle, that is, of 60. foote. The thickneffe of the wall fhall be the fourth part of the Diameter, that is, 15. foote, that a man may eafily make the Chappels within it: which Chappels fhall be 12. foot broad. The Niches betweene the Pillars fhall bee foure foote broad: the other in the Entrie, and of the three Chappels, fhall be fixe foote and a halfe broad: and to fpare charges of ftone and lime, the great Niches fhall be made without the Chappell: the bredth whereof fhall bee 15. foote. This Chappell is eleuated from the earth at leaft fiue fteps; and if it were higher, it were not amiffe: for the earth in time rifeth, fo that men goe downeward into many old Temples and Churches, whereunto, in former time they afcended vpwards: but this Stayre would alwayes be vneuen, according to *Vitruuius* writing, fpeaking of Temples, where he fayth: that as a man with his right foote begins to clyme vp, he may, with the fayd right foote, ftep vpon the pauement of the Temple. Touching the foundation, a man cannot fayle, if hee maketh it deepe and broad inough: but the leaft bredth that a man can lay, is this: that a man fhould from the Di-ameter of the thickeneffe of the wall, make a perfit fourefquare, and the Diagonus of this fourefquare fhall be the bredth of the foundation vnder the wall. And fo, I thinke, *Vitruuius* writeth, where he fpeak-eth of foundations. But touching the Stofes of foundations, in faft or hard ground, and alfo in watry ground, I neede not fhew it here, becaufe euery man knowes it.

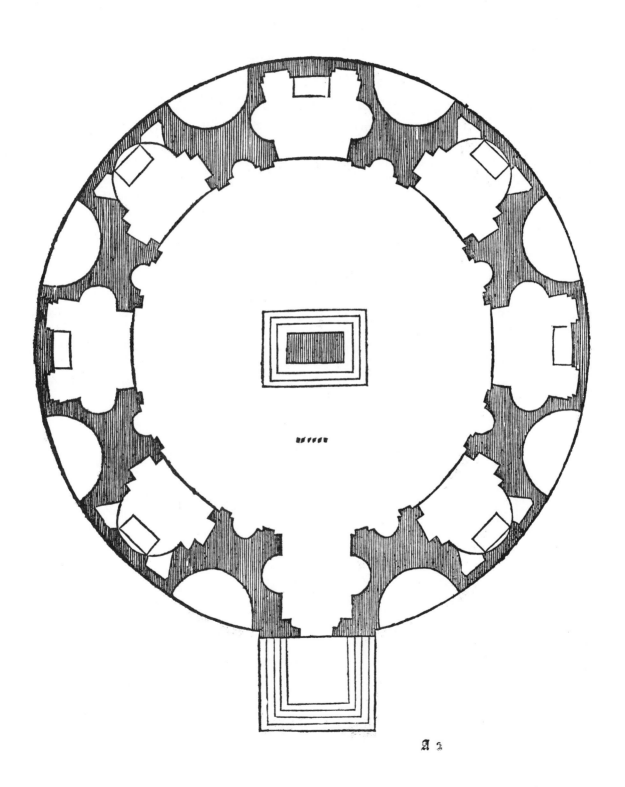

A 2

Of diuers formes of Temples

Hauing shewed the ground of this round Temple, this Figure sheweth the body of the Temple, both without and within, for that it is purposely made broken, to see both. The inner part of the Temple is made after the maner of Corinthia. The whole height from the Pauement below, to the Roofe aboue, is 60. foot; whereof 30. foote are for the Kettle or round roofe: the rest netherwards, shall be deuided in 5. parts and an halfe; whereof one part shalbe for Cornice, Freese and Architraue. The foure parts and an halfe resting, shalbe the height of the Columnes, with Bases and Capitals, whereof altogether, you shall finde the particular measures in my fourth Booke, in the Corinthia. The Niches betweene the flat Pillars, shalbe 10. foot high: the other shalbe of 15. foot high. The hole aboue the Roofe, shalbe the seuenth part of the wideness of the Diameter of the Temple: aboue, vpon that hole, there may bee a Lanthorne made, stopt with glasse, or it may be left open, whereat there will come in light inough to the middle of the Temple, for that the Chappels haue light inough at their windowes: the top of this Temple will best bee couered with Lead: the Cornice without shall stand like that within, but much greater of members, because it standeth in the weather. Touching the Doores, you find them sufficiently set downe in my fourth Booke.

ALthough the ground of this Temple following is round also, yet it hath an alteration by the foure bearings out, which are three Chappels, and also the going in of the same fashion. The Diameter of this Temple is 48. fote: the thickenesse of the wall is a seuenth part of the Diameter. The Chappels are 14. fote in fouresquare, without the Niches. The other 4. Niches or small Chappels shalbe 9. fote broad: the fouresquare Chappels haue their light on the sides; but the light of the Temple aboue in the Roofe, shall be wide the fift part of the Diameter, with a Lanthorne vpon it, as it is sayd of the other: you shall goe vp to this Temple also with fiue stayres, and for that the corners without the Temple lye alwayes foule, I thinke it were not amisse to make a fouresquare wall about it, as high as the going vp, that people may not so easily come to it.

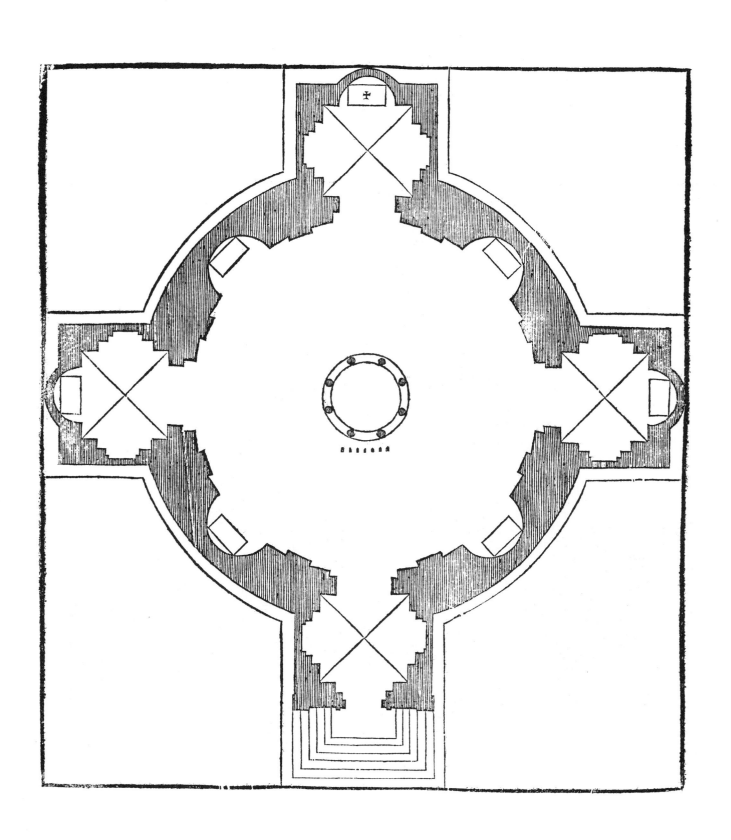

Of diuers formes of Temples

HEre you see the Chappel standing vpright (whereof the ground is on the other side) which sheweth as well within as without, because it seemeth as if it were broken. The height within, is like the Diameter, that is, 48. foot. The halfe shall be for the halfe round roofe, and the hole aboue for the light, as I layd before, shalbe wide the fift part of the Diameter; whereon there shall be a Lanthorne, made with glasse, as the Figure sheweth, and the Roofe without, couered with Lead, or other stuffe. From the Roofe netherwards, the Cornicement shall bee made of two foot and an halfe high, formed like Impost of the Arch of the Theater of Marcellus, in the fourth Booke and the seuenth Chapter, Folio 37. and shall serue for Capitals, vnlesse it be the Plinthus with the Cimatie, which shall serue for Corona. The Pilasters are broad 4. foot can halfe. The great Chappels are 21. foot high. The smalest Chappels shalbe 13. foot and an halfe high, halfe round aboue. Aboue those 3. fouresquare Chappels, and ouer the going in, there may be flat couers, somewhat falling downe, to voyd the water : a man may also make steps within the thicknesse of the wall, to goe vp, and an yron or stone raple, to rest or leane vpon. The Temple may bee couered with such stuffe, as may best be prouided : but Lead would be the surest.

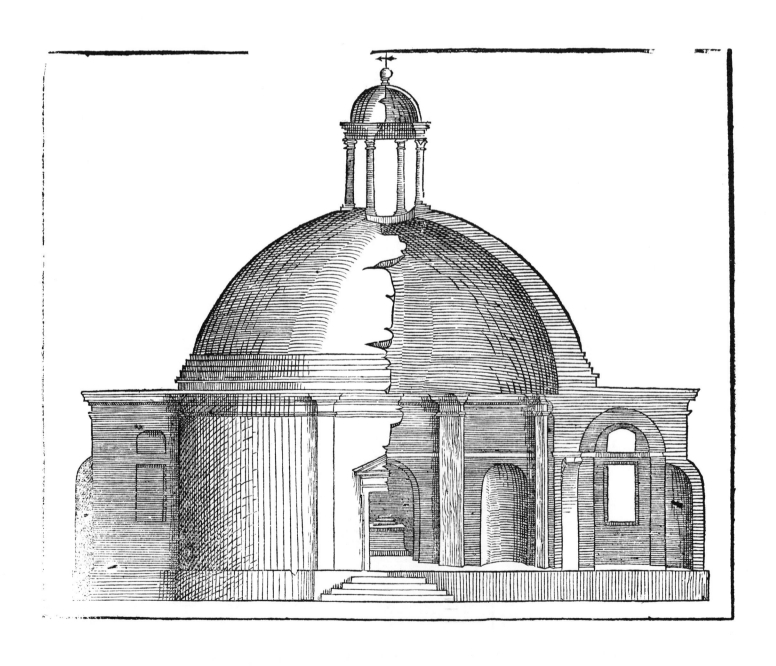

A Fter the round Figure, which is the perfecteſt, the beſt are the Ouale, that is, like an Egge; therefore I haue made a
Temple of that faſhion: which Temple ſhalbe 46. foot bꝛoad, and 66. foot long. The thickeneſſe of the wail ſhail
be 8. foot, ꝙ within it the Chappels ſhall ſtand: and although they be not tꝏ large, yet a man needs not cut them off. The
widenes of the 2. greateſt Chappels, holds 20. foot and an halfe; within the which are two Ꞩiches, each 4. foot bꝛoad.
The Columnes ſhall bee a foote and an halfe thicke, and the halfe Columnes accoꝛdingly. The ſpaces betwæne the
middlemoſt Columnes ſhallbe 7. foot and an halfe: the other ſhall contayne 4. foot and one fourth part. Theſe two
Chappels ſhall each of them haue 3. windowes: the middlemoſt ſhalbe 6. foot wyde, and the other on the ſides each thꝛæ
foot. The Chappell with the high Altar, ſhalbe 10. foot bꝛoad, and 6. foot farre in the wall, with Ꞩiches, like the great,
and a windowe aboue the Altar, of 6. foot wide. The 4. other Chappels ſhalbe a halfe Circle, 10. foot wyde, hauing
the like Ꞩiches alſo, and a windo w of 4. foot wyde, aboue the Altar. And foꝛ that this Chappell hath light inough of
it ſelfe, it might ſuffice foꝛ the whole Temple: but to make it lighter, there may be windowes made aboue the Chappels.
This Temple ſhall alſo go vp fiue ſteps: the dooꝛe ſhalbe ſixe foot wyde, and ſhalbe beautified with 4. Pillars, after the
Coꝛinthia maner: the going in ſhalbe like the Chappell with the high Altar.

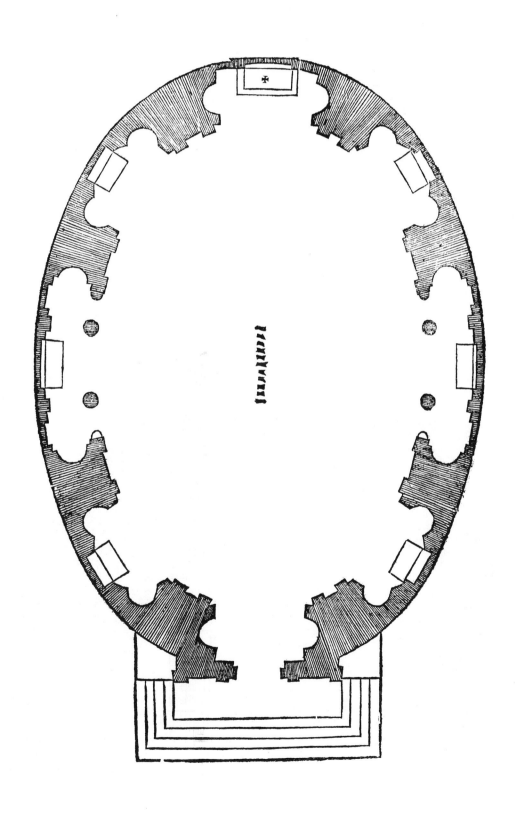

Of diuers formes of Temples.

This Figure enſuing, ſheweth the Ouale Temple within, which from the Pauement to the Roofe, ſhall be as high as broad, that is, of 36. foot: from the Pauement, till you come aboue the Cornice, it ſhalbe 23. foot: which height deuided in fiue, one part ſhalbe for Architraue, Frééſe and Cornice: the other 4. parts ſhall bee for the height of the Pillars, which ſeparate the Chappels. The particular meaſures hereof you finde in my fourth Booke, in the order of Corinthia; for that this Temple is made of ſuch worke. The height of the round Columnes ſhalbe 12. foot. The Architraue, that holdeth vp the Arch, is 2. foot. The Gate (as it is ſayd in the ground) ſhalbe beautified with foure flat Pillars, of ſuch forme and meaſure, as thoſe that ſtand within the Temple; and alſo with ſuch Cornicements: the Gate or Dooze ſhall haue an Arch ſtanding vpon two Pillars, betwéene the flat Pillars: the Roofe of this Temple may be beautified, as you ſée it in the Figure; and richlyer alſo, making the Windowes aboue the Cornice, hanging downewards, as you ſée, and couer the Temple with Lead, which is beſt: and ſo the windowes ſhall bee preſerued well ynough.

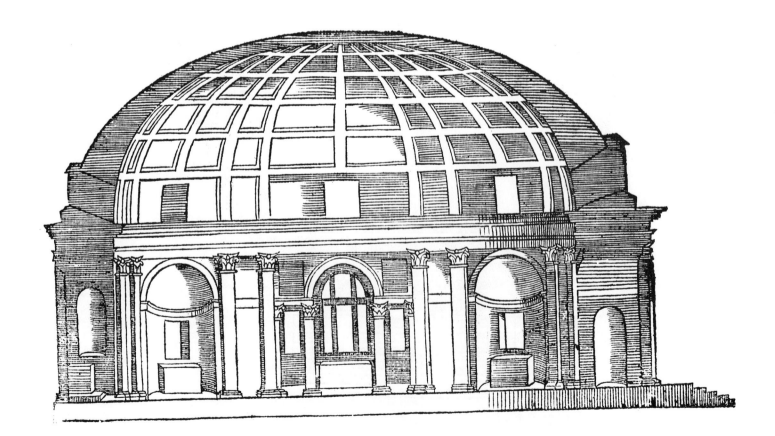

Lthough this forme is fiue corners, which in Building is not so handsome, therefore within I haue made it of ten corners. The Diameter of this Temple is 62. foot long: the Diameter of the Lanthorne is 12. fot: the fiue great Chappels are 15. foot in fouresquare, without the thré Niches, which are ten foote wide. The small Chappels are 15. foot broad, and goe 4. foot into the wall, to the halfe Circle, which is, 13. foot wide. The great Chappels shall haue two windowes, also the small one: the widenesse of the doores is 7. fot and an halfe. The Gallery without, shalbe 10. foot broad, and 24. foot long. The 4. Pillars thereof, shalbe 2. fot fouresquare. The middlemost space betwéene the Pillars, shall be 10. foot, and the other 2. spaces shalbe 4. foot. The sides of the Gallery shall haue a leaning place made with Balusters: In the sides of the Gates, there shall stand 2. payre of winding stayres, to goe vp vpon the Portall, and also round about the Temple. This Temple is 9. foot eleuated from the ground, and it may be made hollow vnderneath.

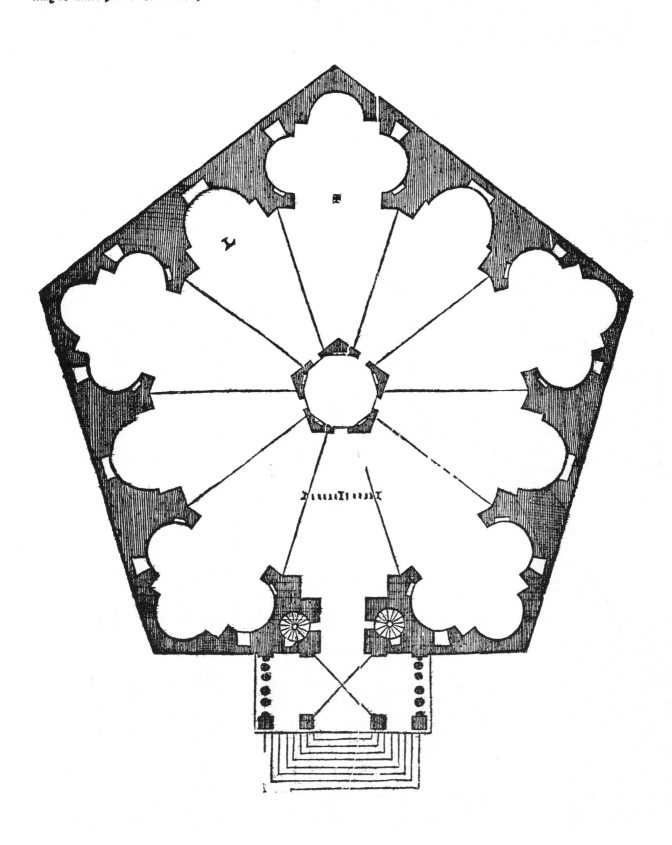

Of diuers formes of Temples

Although this Temple is shut, yet I will shew the measure within; it is as high as broad within, that is, 62. foot. The Lanthorne is also as high as broad to the Cornice: the Roofe is of halfe a Circle. The roofe of the Temple is also halfe a Circle, high 31. foot, the rest netherwards. The Cornice shall haue two foot and an halfe, formed like the Impost of the Theater of Marcellus, in the fourth Booke, in the order of Ionica, marked T. Folio 37. This Cornice shall be set without, like the innermost, but greater. The fouresquare Pillars of the Portall, are 14. foot high, with Bases and Capitall, Dorica. The Architraue is halfe the thicknesse of the height of the Pillar: aboue the Arch, the Cornice is the fourth part lesse then the great, but of the same forme, and shall serue for Capitall vpon the Pillars. Aboue this Cornice, there shalbe a place brest-high, made with Iron Balusters. The two pieces aboue this Temple, shew the Chappels within: and that with the crosse, sheweth the greatest Chappell, whereof the light is 25. foot. The other piece marked L. sheweth the lesse Chappell, which is also 25. foot high: the Pilasters that separate the Chappels, are three foot broad: the height is 19. foot: and there shall be a Cornice made, which shall goe round about the Temple, seruing for Capitals vpon the sayd Pilasters; which forme shalbe made after the Dorica Temple, but a little altered: the Cornicement, vpon the Lanthorne, may be made with Architraue, Freese and Cornice.

The ground of the Temple following shalbe sixe cornerd, being in Diameter 25. foote: and the wall 5. foote thicke. The widenesse of the Chappels are 10. foote, and stand 4. foote within the wall. The widenesse of the Riches is 2. foote. The Doore of the Temple is 5. foote wide, adorned with double Pillars, which are a foote and a quarter thicke. The going vp is 5. steps, or more if you will; yet vneuen. Each Chappell hath a Window, of foure foote and a halfe broad, which will bring in light inough, although there be no Lanthorne. On the 6. corners without the Temple, there shalbe flat Pillars made, of 2. foote and a quarter broad, comming out a little. And if you would make the Temple greater, and for want of stones you could make it no thicker Columnes: then you might make it Corinthia, or Ionica, or Dorica, if you will: and then you may helpe your selfe with Pedestals.

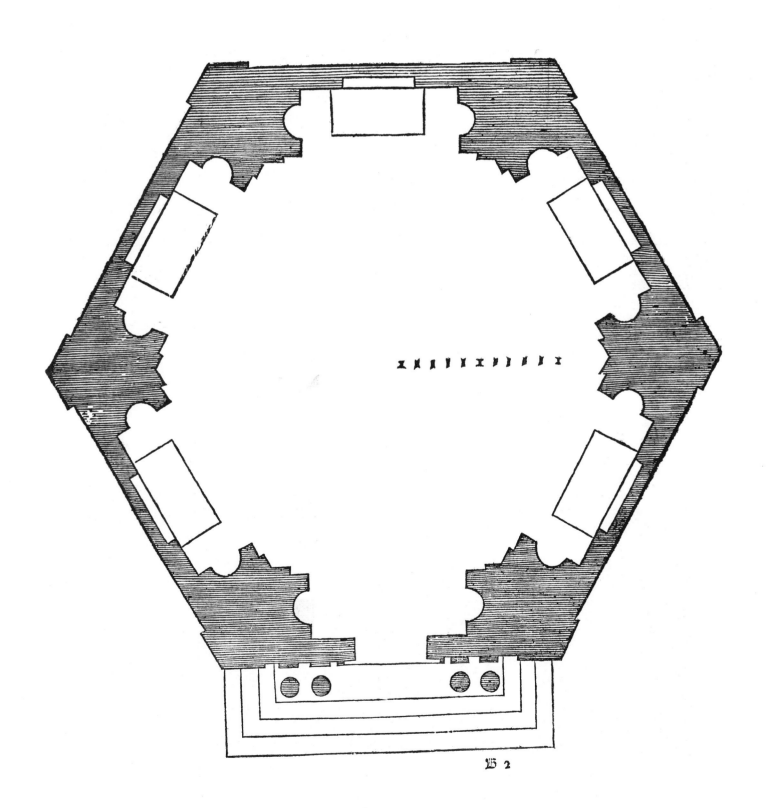

Of diuers formes of Temples

NOw I haue shewed the ground of the 6. cornerd Temple, I must shew it standing vpright, and also describe it, as well within as without: for although the Temple be wholy closed vp, yet I haue set a Chappell aboue ouer it, to see it within, for that they are all fiue of one forme; and the going in also is of the same forme. But touching the outermost part, I say, that the height from the pauement below, till you come aboue the Cornice, shalbe 18. foote. The Cornice round about the Temple, shall be made of a foote and a halfe: but the members of the sayd Cornice shalbe made according to the Chapter of Dorica, for that it shall also serue for Capitall vpon the Pilasters, at the 6. corners. Touching the Plinthus with the Cimatie, for that it shall serue for a Corona, it shall go but right through aboue the Pilasters, as you may see in the Figure. The Portall before shall bee beautifyed with round Columnes, & with flat Counterpillars: whereof the middlemost Intercolumnes (or spaces betweene the Columnes) shalbe 7. foote and a halfe. The Columnes shall bee a foote and a halfe thicke: but the space betweene each 2. Columnes, and Pillars, shall be halfe a foote: these sayd Columnes shalbe 8. foot and three fourth parts high. The Capitals shalbe Dorica: but the Bases, because they stand below at the foote, in the rayne and

the wind, and also for that they should bee the Bases for the flat Pillars, and the great Pilasters, going about the Temple on all sides, therefore they shalbe made Tuscana. The height of the Architraue shall bee a foote, whereon the Arch shall stand: and the Doore shalbe adorned as you see it in the Figure. The going in shalbe 5. steps at the least. The Roofe shall be couered with a thing, which in those Countreyes lasteth long, and is easy to bee had, otherwise it were best to be of Lead: and this is touching the worke without. To speake of the inward part, it is sayd, that I. Chappell serueth for all: the breadth of these Chappels hold each of them 10. foot: and in height 13. foot and a halfe, and enter 4. foot into the wall: on each side they haue a Niche, which is 2. foot broad: aboue the Altar there is a window, which is 4. foot and a halfe broad: and 7. foote high. The Cornice within the Temple shall stand of the same height that the outermost doth, and shall also bee of the same figures: for the Plinthus with the Cimatie, shal also go right through, round about the Temple, without bearing out aboue the Pilasters: otherwise a man may make them much slenderer then they that stand in the rayne and the wind. You may also make the Bases after Dorica: and although all the other Temples shewed before, haue their heights within, like the breadth or the Diameter, so shall this, neuertheleße, though it be so small, be halfe a Diameter more higher, that is a Diameter and a halfe, wheih is seuen and thirty foote and a halfe.

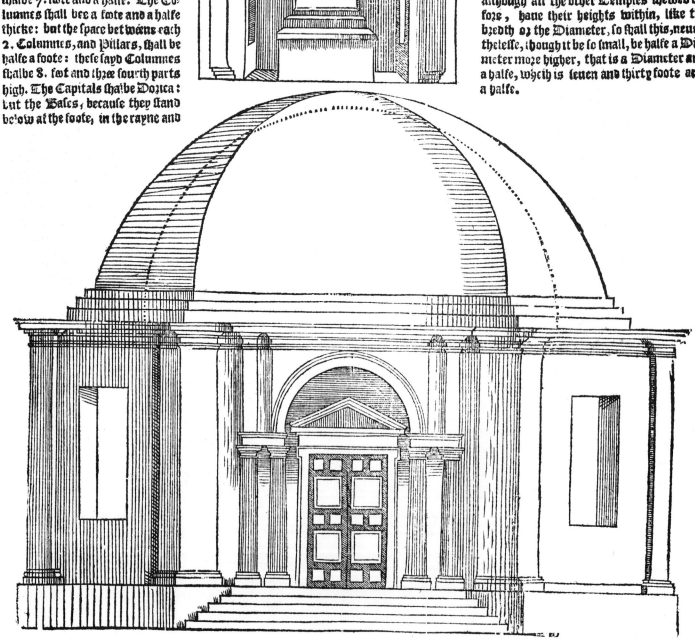

Although thofe aforefayd, and fome Temples following, haue no Stéeple for Bels to hang in, as the Chriftians vfe to haue; nor any Veftries, nor other places for men to withdraw themfelues in: yet they muft, neuertheles, be handfomely made without, but fo, that men may go through the Temple into them: all which fubiects and inuentions fhall not want in my other Booke. The ground of this Temple is 8. fquare: whereof the Diameter within fhalbe 43. foote: and the wall 8. foote. The Chappels are 12. foote wide, and ftand 6. foote within the wall. Thrée Chappels are of halfe a Circle, and the other 3. with the going in are 4. fquare. Each Chappell hath 2. Niches, which are 4. foote broad. The 3. windowes in the halfe Circles are 4. foote broad: the other 3. with the Columnes are 11. foote wide. The Doore is 5. foote wide. In the middle of the Temple a man may fet an Altar, couered with a Tribune, vpon 8. Pilafters. The Diameter hereof fhalbe 12. foote long: and if you will make this Temple greater, you may make it more féete.

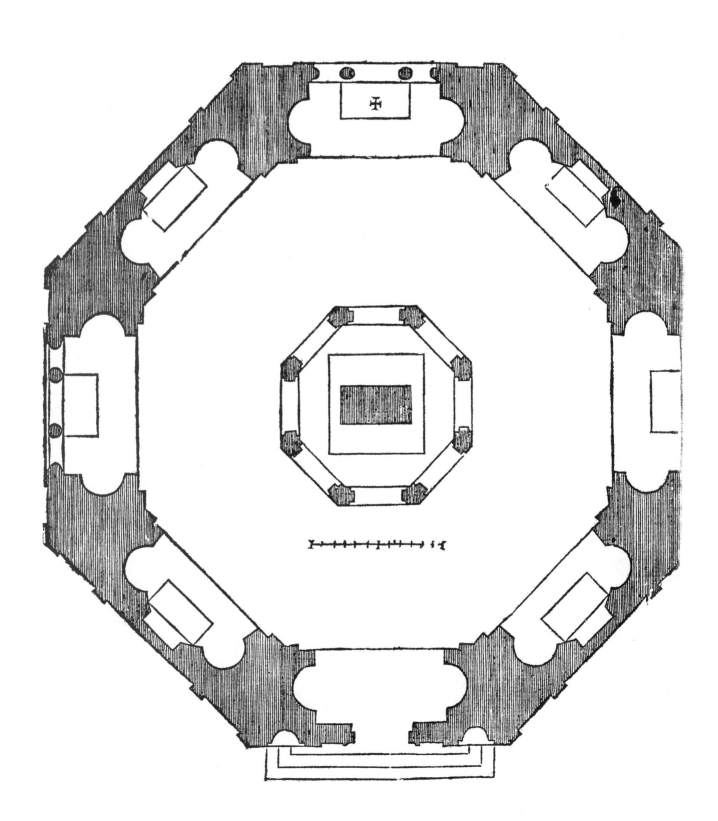

Of diuers formes of Temples.

The Figure hereunder ſerueth for the 8. ſquare ground, afore ſet dotne, and is the ſayd Temple as it is without. From the higheſt ſtep to the vppermoſt part of the Cornice, it is 21. foote and a halfe, which is the halfe of the innermoſt height. The Cornice ſhall contayne 2. foote, deuided as in the Chapter Dorica; and ſhall alſo beare out ouer the Pilaſters, without the Plinthus, as in the Figure. You ſhall alſo ſet a ſimple Baſe vnderneath three fourth parts of a foote high. The breadth of the Pilaſters at the corners, ſhalbe of 3. foote : and thoſe that ſtand inwards ſhalbe but 2. foote broad. The Doore is 5. foote wide, and ſhalbe 13. foote and a halfe high. The Ornaments of this Doore you find in the fourth Booke, by the Ionica, Folio 38. The maner of the wideneſſe is ſufficiently ſeene in the Figure : if you will haue more light in the Temple, then you may make a hole aboue, and that to bee couered with glaſſe, poynt-wiſe, agaynſt the rayne.

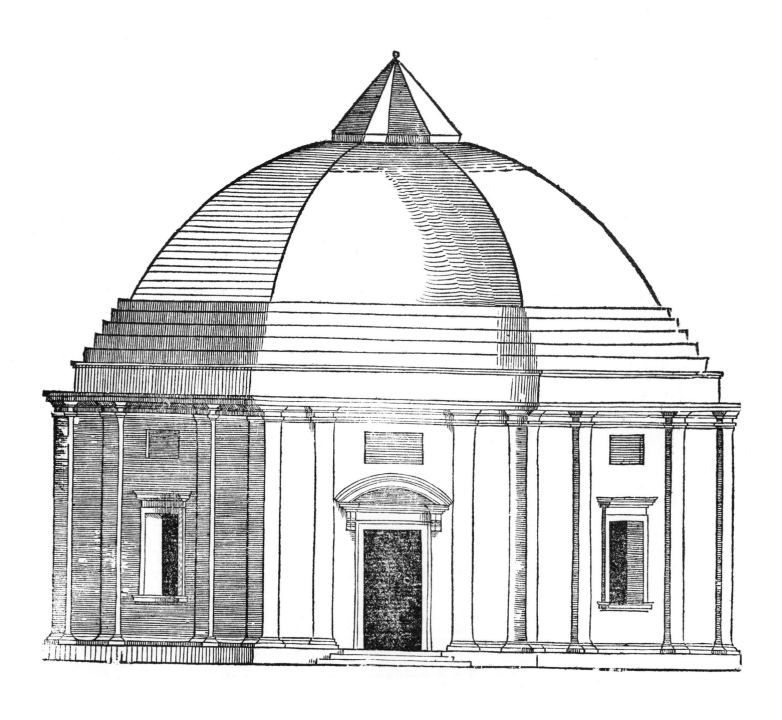

ACcording to this innermoſt Oꝛthographie, the Coꝛnices and Pillars are of ſoꝛme & height like the innermoſt: from the Coꝛnices vpwards, the roofe is a halfe Circle: the 3. greateſt Chappels are rooſt with Arches, and are 18. foot high. The round Columnes ſhalbe thꝛee quarters of a foot thick, and the halfe accoꝛdingly, and ſhall be fiue foot and an halfe high: the Architraue, whereon the Arch comes, ſhall alſo be thꝛee quarters of a foot: the inter-Columnes in the middle, ſhall be foure foot and an halfe, and on eyther ſide two

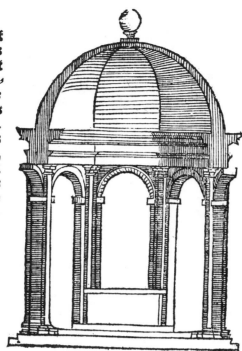

foot and an halfe. The Chappels of halfe a Circle, ſhall alſo be 18. foot high: the Niches of all the Chappels ſhalbe ten foot high: the Tribune that ſhould ſtand in the middle with the Altar, is figured aboue: and from the ground to aboue the Coꝛnice, it is 18. foote high: the Coꝛnicement thereof is thꝛee foot: the reſt is foꝛ the Pillars, where, on the ſides, you may make Pilaſters with Arches, and all Doꝛica woꝛke, as well within as without. The Tribune is of a halfe Circle.

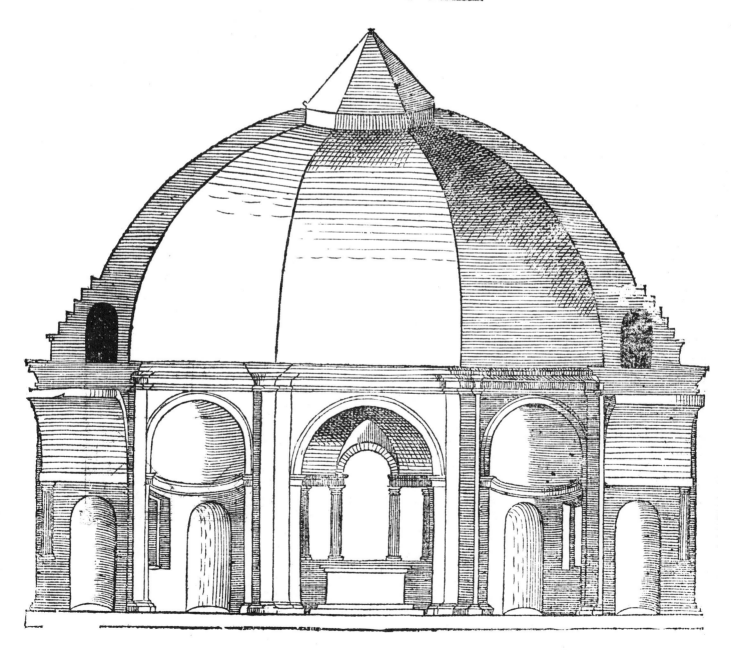

Of diuers formes of Temples.

AL though this ground without is fouresquare, yet within it is 8. cornerd, whereof the Diameter within is 65. fæt, and the wall 16. fæt. The going in of all the Chappels, is 12. fæt, and the wall there, is 3. foot and an halfe thicke. The corner Chappels shalbe 16. foot fouresquare within: the Niches with Altars, shalbe 12. foot broad: the 4. open, and two blind windowes, shalbe 3. foot and an halfe: the two lesser Chappels shalbe 22. foot long within, without the Niches. The Niches shalbe 10. foot broad: the windowes shalbe 6. foot wide: the Portall without, is 27. foot long, and fiue foot wide: right ouer against the flat Pillars stand round Columnes, which are one foot and 3. quarters thicke. The doore is 6. foot wide: the Portall within, is almost like one of the small Chappels. You may also set a high Altar in the middle, with a Tribune, whereof the Diameter is 20. foot: the Pilasters are thre foot and an halfe thicke: the flat Pillars at the corners are thre foot broad.

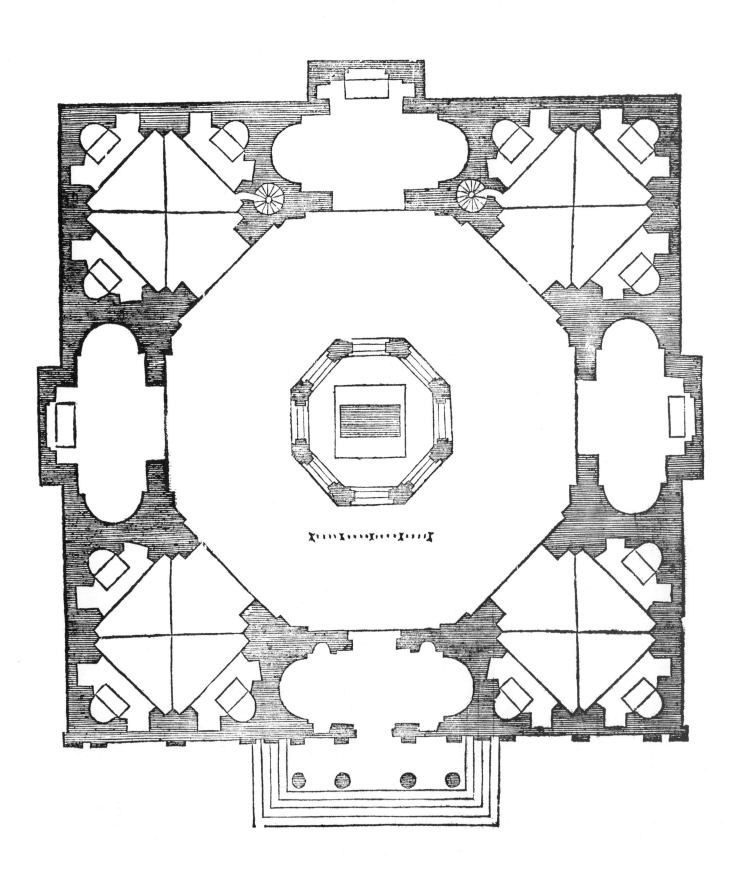

This is the Orthographie of the aforesayd ground, of the eyght corner'd and fouresquare Temple, which is the Figure as it is without, whereof I will describe the height: and first, from the Pauement, to the highest part of the Cornice, it is 22. foot and an halfe: the height thereof deuided in fiue parts, one shall be for the Architraue, Freese and Cornice, the other fiue parts are for the Pillars, which being two foot and an halfe broad, yet they are not to long, because they stand two together, and little rayled vp. The measure of all together, you may find in the order of Ionica, in the fourth Booke. Aboue this Cornice standeth the Tribune, whereon there shall stand a Lanthorne, to giue light into the middle of the Temple, whereof you may easily finde the measure, with the small foot, that standeth in the ground. The round Columnes before the Portall, shalbe 13. foot high: the Architraue is a foot: aboue the Arch, the Cornice shalbe the thickensse of a Columne below, deuided as in the Capitall of Dorica. The Frontispicie riseth to the Architraue of the Temple: the going vp is of fiue steps: the small figure marked with A. is one of the Chappels without, which comes three foot out of the wall: the windowe whereof is 10. foot high, beside the light aboue the Cornice, and aboue it is halfe round, couered as you see.

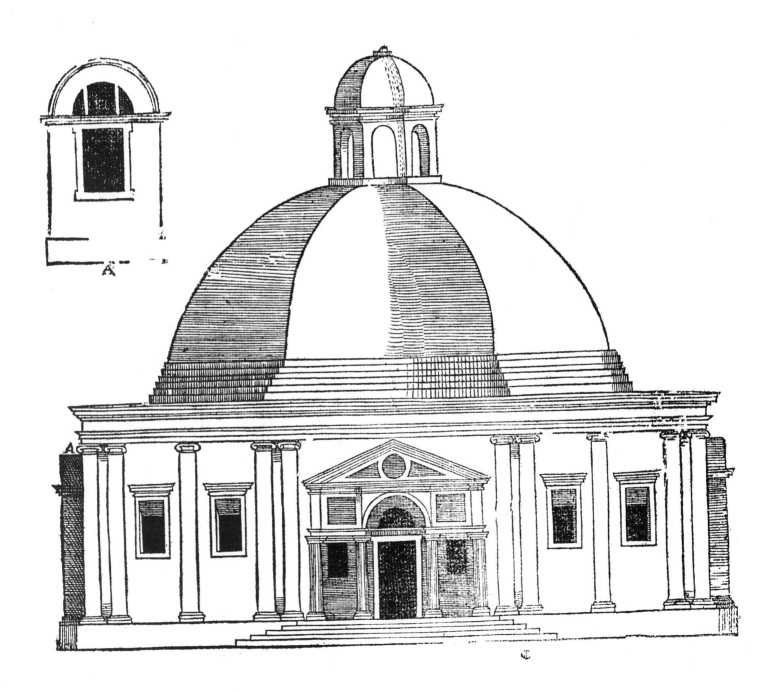

Of diuers formes of Temples.

NOw I haue shewed the ground and Orthography without of the Temple in fouresquare, I will also describe the 8. cornerd Temple within, & set it here beneath in Figure. And here you see how men going vp the Stayres which are figured in the entry of the ground, go vp to the fayre walke. The height of this Temple within is almost like all the Temples before set downe, and also which are found in Antiquities, that is, as high as broad, which forme is taken out of the Circle. The round Roofe, as for the halfe Circle, occupieth the one halfe, and of the other halfe downewards there shalbe 6. parts made, whereof one part shall be for the Architraue, Frese and Cornice, which shalbe made after the Dorica: the other 5. parts are for the wall with the Pillars, which also are 2. foote and a halfe broad, like the outermost, but for Capitall and Base, like the Dorica. The measures both of Capitals, Bases, Architraue, Frese and Cornice, you shall also find in the aforesayd fourth Booke, in the Order of Dorica. The bredth of the going in of all the Chappels is 12. foote: but the height of the sayd Chappels is 24. foote. The 4. greatest Chappels which stand in the corners are 14. foote within, fouresquare, with their Pilasters, with Arches vpon them. The height of all the Niches, as well of those that are 10. foote broad, as those of 12. foote, shall all be 15. foote high. The Lanthorne shall hold 13. foote in Diameter: and the rest the Architector shall easily find with the small foote.

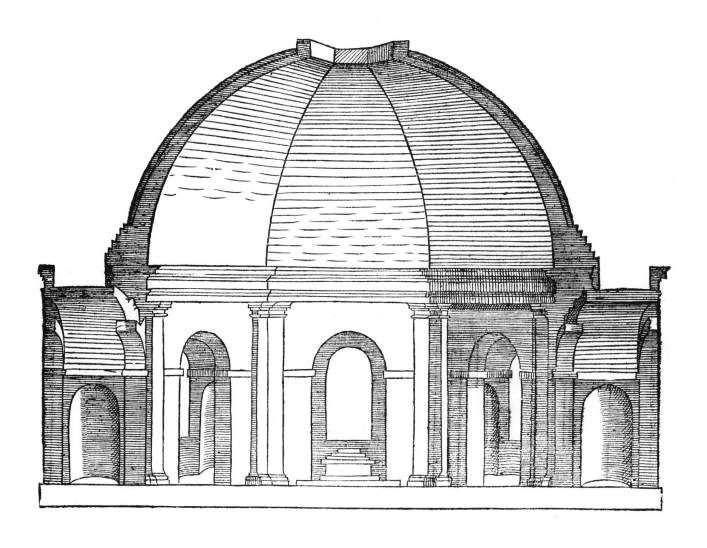

This ground ftanding hereunder may be named croffe-wife, whereof the principall place in the middle contayneth 48. foot in Diameter. The 4. Niches, with the 4. goings through, are each 10. foot broad; but the goings through are 15. foote long. The foure fmall Temples hold in Diameter 36. foote, and their Niches, and Windowes, (wherein you may place Altars) and the Doores are each fiue foot wyde. The 4. places within the 4. corners, may bee Dwellings for Priefts, & other Church Officers, and are 16. foot fourefquare : aboue them, you may place foure Towers, and go vp into them through the ftayres. The foure round formes may be Veftries, and other places for men to withoraw themfelues. This whole fourefquare, without inclofing the innermoft round Temple, contayneth on all fides 88. foot. The principall going in fhall haue 9. fteps, and the Doore may alfo bee greater then the other two in the fides.

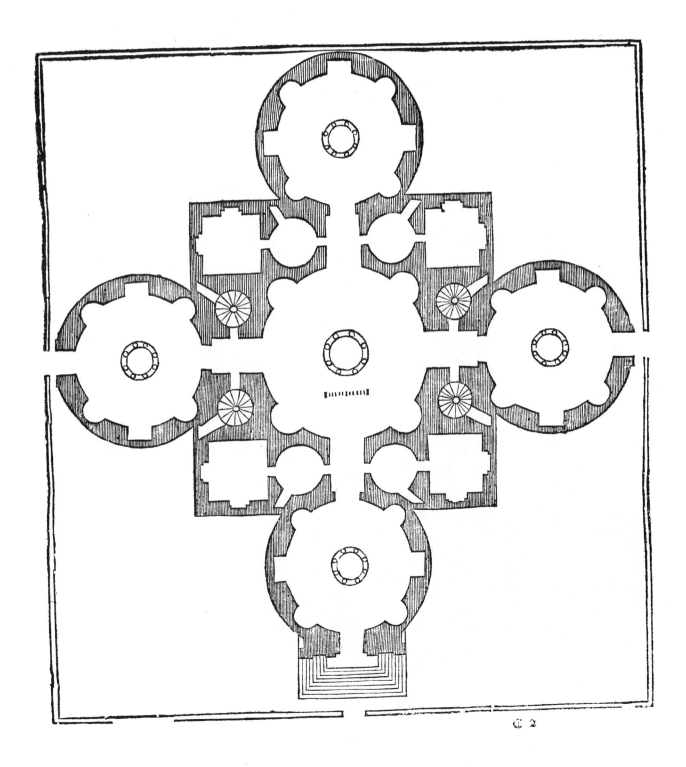

Of diuers formes of Temples

FRom the ground before shewed, here standeth the Orthography of the sayd Temple with one of the sides that is before, although a man should set them out all foure, at least three, in this maner. The height of the first Story, beginning at the highest step of the going vp to the vppermost part of the Cornice, shalbe 38. foote; which height, deuided in 6. parts, one shalbe for the Architraue, Freese and Cornice, and this shall inclose the whole Temple round about. From this first Cornice, to the second of the middle Temple, it shalbe 13. foote: of this height you shall make 5. parts: whereof one shall be for the Freese, Cornice, and Architraue. The same great part of the Cornices shall also serue for the Lanthornes of the 4. last Chappels: which Lanthornes within shall contayne 8. foote in Diameter. The 3. Order agaynst the 4. Towers shall haue but a flat Facie, right like the foote of the greatest Lanthorne which standeth vpon the round roofe. The sayd Lanthorne within shall hold 10. foote in Diameter; and the height without the Kettle stone shalbe 16. foote: this height deuided in 5. the one part shalbe for the Cornicement of this Lanthorne, and the other shalbe Corinthian Pillars. The fourth Order of the Towers shall also be of the same height, and beautifyed with the same Cornicement: and although that from this Cornicement netherwards, the Order of the Towers stands not very handsomely, because they are forced to yeld to the Cornicement of the Temple; yet according to Antiquity, it is a fault to be borne withall. The vppermost parts, which in no sort are tyed to any thing, shalbe as high as the thickenesse of the sayd Towers. The 5. part of that height shalbe for the Cornicement, and the rest, for the Columnes, made after the Ionica. Aboue the Cornice the leaning place shalbe made, with the round roofes, as you see.

HEereunder followeth the Orthographie of the aforesayd Temple within, that is, the halfe of the 3. Temples. And for that the middlemost Temple should receiue more light then from the Lanthorne, as the other also doe by the windowes below, it is requisite to make the Cornice without higher then the innermost, that a man may, almost, receiue the light perpendicular-wise, as you may consider it in the Figure.   From the Pauement, to the highest part of the Cornice, it shalbe 44. foot. The Cornice (because there are neyther Columnes nor Pillars about) a man may make bastard, and at his pleasure, so it haue not much bearing out, that it may not take away the sight of the roofe. The Cornice shalbe a foote and a halfe high, and may bee made according to the Capitall of Dorica.   The height of all the Niches are all 15. foote: aboue the Niches, there shall a Facie goe round about the whole part of the Temple, as well the small Temples as the great.   Aboue the Facie the halfe round roofes of the 4. Chappels shall stand.   Aboue these 4. Chappels there shalbe a playne, made a little hanging, to cut off the water, with a place brest high round about, where, by the Stayres, a man may go through to the Towers : and if that this Temple standeth in any open place, then there will be a faire walke aboue it; you must be carefull that you let no snow lye vpon it, for it soketh in and hurteth the roofe.   The Doores on the sides haue also 9. steps, although they stand not marked in the ground : and as these and the like houses stand so high, or not so high, from the earth, a man may well make them places of deuotion, or otherwise. We see commonly, that round about the Churches all corners lye full, which is vnciuill for sanctified places : therefore I would thinke good, that it should be walled round about as high as the steps, that it might not be so ready for people to goe in, and that it were hallowed for a Church-yard.   The Towers that should stand behind in this halfe, because they stand not vpon this Diameter, and also for lesse cumber, for that men may conceiue how they are placed : therefore they are not set downe in this Figure: and what there wanteth more, it is referred to the discretion of the workeman, who, in building thereof, shall find many accidents which a man cannot write nor remember allat once.

Of diuers formes of Temples.

Lthough the aforesayd Temple is shewed to bee crosse-wise, neuerthelesse, this that is heere set downe is much liker: and first, I will speake of the first going in, which shall serue for all the rest, for that they are all of one forme. The widenesse is 30. foot, and the length 37. foot. The wall is seuen foot thicke: in the middle, on eyther side, there are two Niches, which shall each of them be tenne foot broad. The Doore is eyght foot wyde: the going through, to goe into the Circle, is 22. foot wyde. The Pilasters there, are seuen foot thicke: the Niches, foure foote. Within the Pilasters the stayres shall stand to goe vp, and that the Pilasters should bee the faster to beare the Tribune, in the foure corners, behind against the Pilasters, you shall make these eyght cornerd Chappels, of 18. foot in Diameter, and the wall is foure foot thicke. The Niches, Doores, Windowes and blind windowes, shall be fiue foot wide. The corners of the Temple without, haue their flat Pillars of three foot broad: the going vp is of fiue steps.

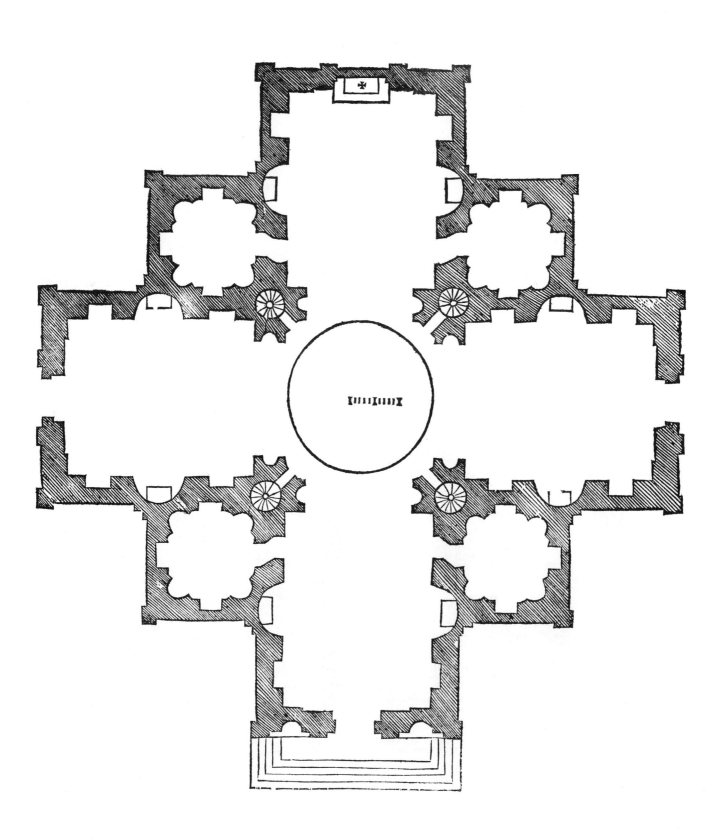

The Orthographie without of the foure cornerd crosse Temple, is hereunder set downe, and is 44. foot broad at the going in; and the height from the ground to the Cornice is 30. foot: the Cornicement is fiue foot: the rest resteth for the Pillars, which should be Ionica. The second story is 22. foot high : which height shall bee deuided in sire parts, one shalbe for the Cornicement, and the other fiue for the Corinthia Columnes.   These two Stories the Temple shall haue, whereof you shall haue the measure in the fourth Booke.   The roofe shalbe 10. foot high, but here in the Land where it bloweth, rayneth, and snoweth much, it may stand much higher.   Aboue the vpper part of this Frontispicie or Roofe, there shall be a Cornice of two foot, whereon the Kettle or the round Roofe shall stand, hauing a Lanthorne vpon it, which is 10. foot high, without his couer.   The part marked C. sheweth the couer or roofe within, and the other marked L. sheweth one of the 4. cornerd Chappels: and although these 5. steps, for a going vp, stand onely to this Doore, they should also be made to the other two doores on the sides : and the ornament of the doores, you shall find in the aforesayd Booke, in the order of Ionica.

Of diuers formes of Temples

Hauing shewed this fouresquare crosse Temple without, now here followeth the part within, as if it were Diameter like, cut euen in 2. parts. And first, speaking of the middle whereon the Tribune standeth, there is from one of the Corners of the Pilasters, to the other, 30. foot. From the pauement below, to the highest part of the Cornice, it is also 30. foote. The height of this Frese, Architraue, and Cornice, is 5. foote, and this shall goe round about the Temple within. Upon this Cornice the Arches rest which beare vp the Tribune. Aboue the Arches there is a great Facie; and from thence vpwards it is 15. foote high. The Cornice shalbe 2. foote: but shall not beare much ouer or out, not to let the roofe. From this Cornice netherwards, to the Facie, there shalbe 8. drawing windowes made, of 7. foote, fouresquare, as you see it in the Figure. The Lanthorne shalbe 5. foote wide. From the pauement, to the hole of the Lanthorne, it shalbe 77. foote high. The place where the high Altar standeth, is right ouer agaynst the principall going in. In the great fouresquare there may be an Altar Table set: and aboue it there shall bee a great round window; as also aboue all the 4. Doores. I nede not write any thing of the second side: for by the ground and this Figure you may easily conceaue it. And although I say nothing here of Towers, yet there may 2. at the least, bee set aboue the Chappels in the corners: also, as in many other places it is shewed, the workeman, vpon good occasion, may alter some things: for although that in Italy, and here in these Countryes (where the sunne shineth much) men desire small windowes for coldnesse: neuerthelesse, those that dwell Northward, where it is rumatike, and many times close weather, may, according to the situation, make the windowes great, and giue more light to the Temples, without breaking Order, as it is sayd in the fourth Booke of the Venetian houses.

AS I promised in my fourth Booke, so I haue shewed diuers fashions of Temples, viz. round, Ouale, or Egge
wise, fouresquare, fiue cornerd sixe cornerd, eyght cornerd, and crosse-wise, not onely after the maner of the Ancients, but also seruing for Christians, in such formes as are at this day made in Italy, and else where, whereby I
thought I had sufficently performed my promise: but for that Temples or Churches are made here in these countries crosse-wise also, like Raphaels ground (of S. Peters Church in Rome) in my third Booke , therefore I will set
two or three more of that forme here, therein following the maner of the Ancients. The greatest going through, or walke
in the middle of the Church, is 30. foot wide: the three Chappels of halfe Circles, besides the 2. smallest walkes, are 25.
foot wide, and shall stand somewhat without the wall.   The Diameter of the Tribune is 36. fot: the foure small Tribunes, or round Roofes, are in Diameter 21. fot, but they shall not come out of the roose.   The crosse-worke hath a
doore on eyther side, and the 3. halfe Circles are each of them 25. fot wide. The hindermost halfe Circle, where the high
Altar standeth, is 31. fot wyde.   Besides the Lauer, there are two eyght-cornerd Uestries, being 21. foot in Diameter.   Before, at the greatest going into the Temple, is the middlemost doore, 12. foote wyde, and the 2. small doores 6.
fot.   On the sides, the Towers are 27. fot wyde : within the stayres, there stands a wyde gate to draw vp the Bels.
And although this Temple hath many steps or stayres, you may make lesse.

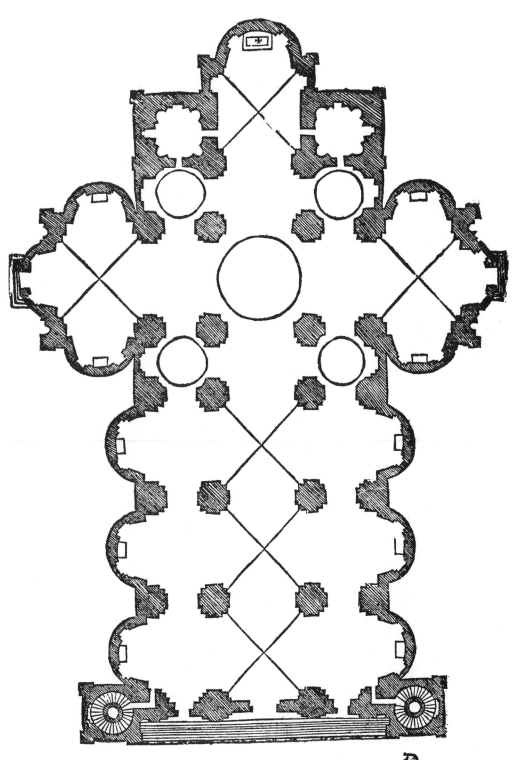

D

Of diuers formes of Temples

This is the Orthographie of the ground aforesayd, whereof the first Cornice standeth 62 foot high: which height deuided in sixe parts, one part shalbe for Cornice, Freese, and Architraue, and the rest shall bee for the flat Pillers, which shalbe fiue foot broad, and of Dorica worke. The middlemost doore is 24 foot high: the two smaller on the sides shalbe 12 foot high. The great and the small doores also shalbe beautified with some workes, as you see in this Figure, taking the particular measures out of the Dorica order, in my fourth Booke. The elevation or rysing vp in the middle, shall to the vpper part of the Cornice be 25 foot; and the Cornice thereof shall be the fourth part lesse then the other Cornice vnder it, made after the forme of the Dorica Chapter. The Frontispicie is fifteene foot high, aboue it stands the couer or the Kettle, with this Lanthorne vpon it, the measure whereof, a man may take out of that before. Below, vpon the first Cornice, besides the middlemost bearing vp, you shall make a Basement of fiue foot high; aboue that Basement, you must place the two Towers, which are 42 foot and an halfe high, making the Cornice the fourth part lesse then the other, formed after the Dorica Chapter. The third order shall be the fourth part lesse then the second, and the Cornice thereafter: the fourth order shall also be a fourth part lesse then the third, and the Cornice thereafter. The places brest-high, aboue these Cornices shalbe foure foot high: and from the List, to the point of the Piramides, there are 36 foot. You may double the windowes out of my fourth Booke.

The Figure following sheweth the aforesayd Temple within, whereof the length and breoth is set downe in the ground: but here I will speake of the height. The Cornice shall stand high, & be as great as the vttermost, that is, the sirt part of 52. foot, but shalbe made after the Ionica maner. The flat Pillars shal also be Ionica: the Impost which beareth the Arches, shal also be Ionica; whose forme, touching the measures, you shal find them all together orderly in my fourth Booke: all the Chappels shall haue their light of themselues, as you see. Aboue the Chappels, the Roofe shalbe broken like a Moone, therein to make an onall round hole, that it may yeeld more light: and that the Tribune may haue more light then from the Lanthorne, you shall, from the couer vpwards, make a Freese with a List, and therein also make round holes for light. This small closed figure, standing alone, aboue the Temple, sheweth one of the side doores of the Temple, in the crosse-worke, whereof the doore is 10. foot wyde, and 20. high. The Architraue, Freese and Cornice, vnder the couer or Roofe, although the Pillars are broken after another maner, with the List of the Portall, shall neuerthelesse agree with the Cornicement that goeth round about the Temple. And although it is not here shewed how the wydest space of the walke betweene the Pilasters and the roofe is, and how that the smallest walke is not so high roofed, nor the forme of the small Kettles and Vestries are not shewed, yet the workeman may vpright it by the ground: for he that vndertaketh such a piece of worke, must not be vnskilfull.

D 2

Of diuers formes of Temples.

This Temple following is 30. foote wide in the middle. The croſſe worke, and alſo the Tribune, together with the high Quier, ſhall each of them contayne 30. foot. The Arches which beare the Tribune, ſhalbe 24. foote wide. The Pillars on the ſides, where the Niches ſtand, ſhalbe 5. foote broad. Each ſide of the Croſſe worke is 38. foot long, and ſhall each of them haue a Doore. The part before the high Quier, towards the Altar, is 4. ſquare. The Pilaſters with the Niches, before the halfe Circle of the high Altar, are 5. foote broad, and ſtand from other 24. foot. The Niche or halfe Circle is 23. foote wide. In the 2. corners on the ſides of the high Quier, there are 2. Veſtries, which ſhalbe 17. foote wide in 4. ſquare. From the Tribune to the principall going in, there ſhall ſtand 5. Chappels on eyther ſide, which ſhalbe 15. foote within 4. ſquare. The walles betwæne both ſhall bee 4. foote thicke. The windowes ſhalbe 6. foote wide, and there Altars ſhall ſtand. The wall at the Doores ſhall bee 4. foote thicke, and on the ſides where the Niches ſtand, 5. foot. Here before there ſhall come a Gallery of 14. foote broad, and of 68. foote long. The Niches ſhalbe 8. foote broad. On the ſides of this Portall the Towers ſhall ſtand, and ſhall ſtand as broad out at the ſides, as the croſſe worke. The Diameter within the Towers is 18. foote : and although they be 8. ſquare, they may alſo be made 4. ſquare. The winding Stayres ſtand in the thickeneſſe of the wall.

Touching the rayſing vpright of the ſayd Temple, firſt I will ſpeake of the Portall, which with the helpe of the fourth Booke, and through the ground, you may find the particular meaſure of this Order. The Portall aboue ſhalbe flat without roofe, to take no light away in the Temple. From the Pauement, to the top of the Cornice which goeth round about the Temple, it ſhalbe 47. foote high. The Architraue, Fræſe and Cornice, are 5. foote. The 2. Order contayneth 37. foote: and their Cornicements ſhall bee a fourth part leſſe then the other: the ſame heights and Cornices ſhall alſo ſerue for the ſecond Order of the Towers, and ſhalbe a fourth part leſſe then the ſecond Order; and the Cornice ſhall alſo leſſen the fourth part: aboue there ſhall ſtand a ſmall riſing or eleuation, whereon the Kettle ſhall reſt.

The Figure aboue the cloſed Temple, marked with A. ſheweth the inner part of the 5. Chappels. The height from the pauement to the vpper part of the Cornice is 27. foote : the Cornice ſhalbe 4. foote thereof, made like a Capitall Dorica. The other vppermoſt Cornices ſhalbe as high as the outtermoſt; and betwæne this firſt and the ſecond Cornices, there ſhall Ionica flat Pillars ſtand; betwæne them the windowes ſhall bee made. The other figure aboue that aforeſayd, marked B. ſheweth the Tribune, the Quier and the ſides of the croſſe worke, with the open and the blynd Doores. Through the one ſide (which was purpoſely broken) you may ſee the Veſtryes within. The Cornice vnder the Arches, which beare the Kettle, is like the other Cornice which goeth round about the Temple. The Cornice which is aboue the Arch, and comes vnder the Kettle, ſhalbe baſtard. The Lanthorne muſt bee made according to the other Lanthornes afore ſhewed. The other part marked C. is one of the Doores on the ſides, and is in that maner couered round. The Doore is 9. foote wide, and 18. foote high.

Of diuers formes of Temples

ALthough that in the Netherlands there are very fayre Temples made, as the maner in these dayes is, not onely with three Iles or walkes in the body, but also fiue: my meaning is not to write of such great Temples, for that each Towne hath her chiefe Church: but these are onely to make such Churches in places, where, by chance, the Churches are decayed, because in these dayes, men could hardly make them vp againe in great forme; and to this end I set this last figure here, which is playner then the other. It shalbe 36. foot wyde, and 54. foot long. At each end before and behind, there shall stand halfe a Circle of 24. foot in Diameter. This halfe Circle where the high Altar standeth, hath two windowes, each 6. foot wyde. The doore to enter into the Temple, shalbe 8. foot wyde. In the crosse of the Temple there shall stand two Chappels, being 18. foot long, and 12. foot broad. The windowes behind the Altar shall be sixe foot wyde: all the great Niches are also sixe foot wyde, and the small three foot. The Columnes are two foot thicke: the inter-Columnes in the middle, are 6. foot, and the other on the sides are 3. foot. The 4. Niches within the body, are beautified with round Columnes standing in the wall. Without the Temple there is a Portall of 10. foot broad, and 52. foot long. The high Pilasters shalbe 6. foot broad, as counterforts; and the other shalbe three foot broad. Within the thickenesse of the wall there shall stand two payre of winding stayres: and although this Church hath no Towers, yet you may make them on it, as the other were.

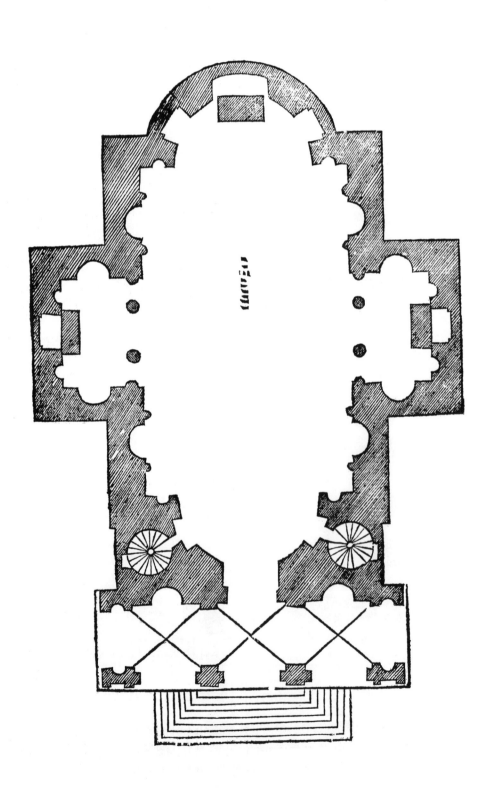

This Figure within is good to vnderstand, and from the Pauement to the firſt Cornice, it is 21. foot high, whereof the Cornicement is a ſixt part : the other is for the Ionica Columnes. The Pedeſtall of the Niches ſhalbe the fift part, whereon there ſtand Columnes of Corinthia. The Frontiſpicies are three foot aboue the Cornice: the blind windowes aboue may alſo be opened. The walkes, with the place breſt-high aboue the Portall, muſt be made leaning forward for the water. The Chappels of the high Altar, marked A. haue ſmall Niches of 7. foot and an halfe high. The foureſquare aboue the Altar, is for a table, broad 10. foot, and high 12. foot. The Temple without hath a Doricall Cornice, as high as the innermoſt. The part of the ſecond order hath Pillars, and Cornices vpon them of two foot, which Cornices ſhal be made according to the Impoſt of the Theater of Marcellus, in the fourth Booke: and for that aboue on the ſide, in the roofe or corner, there is 3. foot of roome to ſpare, there may be a leaning place made, both for an ornament, and alſo for eaſe: the couer may be couered ouer with Lead.

Here endeth the fift Booke: And this alſo is the end of the whole worke of Sebaſtian Serlius; Tranſlated out of Italian into Dutch, and out of Dutch into Engliſh, at the charges of Robert Peake.

Printed at LONDON, by Simon Stafford. 1611.

B. W.